JOURNAL FOR THE STUDY OF THE NEW TESTAMENT SUPPLEMENT SERIES
119

Executive Editor
Stanley E. Porter

Editorial Board
Richard Bauckham, David Catchpole, R. Alan Culpepper,
Margaret Davies, James D.G. Dunn, Craig A. Evans, Stephen Fowl,
Robert Fowler, Robert Jewett, Elizabeth Struthers Malbon

Sheffield Academic Press
Sheffield

Luke and the Restoration of Israel

David Ravens

Journal for the Study of the New Testament
Supplement Series 119

In gratitude to
Tom Baker,
whose lectures on the Gospels (1961–62)
stimulated my study of the New Testament.

Copyright © 1995 Sheffield Academic Press

Published by Sheffield Academic Press Ltd
Mansion House
19 Kingfield Road
Sheffield, S11 9AS
England

Printed on acid-free paper in Great Britain
by Bookcraft Ltd
Midsomer Norton, Bath

British Library Cataloguing in Publication Data

A catalogue record for this book is available
from the British Library

ISBN 1-85075-565-5

CONTENTS

Preface	7
Abbreviations	8
Introduction	11

Part I

Chapter 1
ISRAEL IN THE INFANCY NARRATIVES 24

Chapter 2
STEPHEN'S SPEECH AND ISRAEL'S PAST 50

Chapter 3
THE ROLE OF THE SAMARITANS AND THE UNITY OF ISRAEL 72

Part II

Introduction 108

Chapter 4
LUKE'S VIEW OF JESUS 110

Chapter 5
REPENTANCE AND ATONEMENT 139

Part III

Introduction 172

Chapter 6
LUKE, PAUL AND ISRAEL 173

Chapter 7
LUKE, MATTHEW AND ISRAEL   212

Chapter 8
SUMMARY AND CONCLUSIONS   247

Added Note   256

Bibliography   258
Index of References   270
Index of Authors   284

PREFACE

The present work began to take shape during 1989–90 when I was a part-time postgraduate student in the Biblical Studies Department of Sheffield University. An early draft of Chapter 5 was presented to a seminar at Sheffield and a draft of Chapter 3 was read to the Luke–Acts Group of the British New Testament Conference at Oxford in 1990. I wish to thank Dr Loveday Alexander, my supervisor at Sheffield, for her many constructive comments on the work that I produced during that year. Some of the material in Chapter 4 has appeared in two papers in *NTS* (1988, 1990).

However, much of the work has been done outside an academic environment and I felt the lack of opportunities for frequent professional discussion and comment. For this reason I have appreciated a number of meetings with Colin Hickling who also read parts of earlier drafts. But my greatest thanks must go to John Fenton and Benedict Green, CR. Over some nine years my periodic visits to John Fenton have been occasions when I have received unfailing wisdom and his enthusiastic encouragement. More recently that support has been generously supplemented on visits to Fr Benedict at Mirfield and both have read later drafts, making many valuable comments. Each of these four scholars has saved me from blunders of ignorance and obscurity; those that remain are all my own work. Finally, my thanks must go to my wife, Doreen, for her patience, her support and, not least, for helping to check my amateurish typing.

44 Arthursdale Grange
Scholes
West Yorkshire
LS15 4AW

ABBREVIATIONS

This lists only journals, collections of essays and standard works. The shortened forms of articles and books will, I am sure, be clear from the Bibliography.

AB	Anchor Bible
ASNU	Acta seminarii neotestamentici upsaliensis
AnBib	Analecta biblica
BA	*Biblical Archaeologist*
BAGD	W. Bauer, W.F. Arndt, F.W. Gingrich and F.W. Danker, *Greek–English Lexicon of the New Testament*
BETL	Bibliotheca ephemeridum theologicarum lovaniensium
BJRL	*Bulletin of the John Rylands Library*
CBQ	*Catholic Biblical Quarterly*
ExpTim	*Expository Times*
FRLANT	Forschungen zur Religion und Literatur des Alten und Neuen Testaments
HTR	*Harvard Theological Review*
ICC	International Critical Commentary
IDB	*Interpreter's Dictionary of the Bible*
JAOS	*Journal of the American Oriental Society*
JBL	*Journal of Biblical Literature*
JSNT	*Journal for the Study of the New Testament*
JSNTSup	*Journal for the Study of the New Testament, Supplements*
JTS	*Journal of Theological Studies*
KNT	Kommentar zum Neuen Testament
LCL	Loeb Classical Library
MeyerK	H.A.W. Meyer (ed.), Kritisch-exegetischer Kommentar über das Neue Testament
MNTC	Moffatt New Testament Commentary
NCB	New Century Bible Commentary
NovT	*Novum Testamentum*
NRT	*La nouvelle revue théologique*
NTD	Das Neue Testament Deutsch
NTS	*New Testament Studies*
OTP	J.H. Charlesworth (ed.), *Old Testament Pseudepigrapha* (2 vols.; New York: Doubleday, 1983, 1985).
RTR	*Reformed Theological Review*
SBLMS	Society of Biblical Literature Monograph Series

SBLSP	Society of Biblical Literature Seminar Papers
SBT	Studies in Biblical Theology
SNTSMS	Society for New Testament Studies Monograph Series
SE	*Studia Evangelica*, I, II, III (= TU)
TDNT	G. Kittel, G. Friederich and G.W. Bromiley (eds.), *Theological Dictionary of the New Testament*
TS	*Theological Studies*
TU	Texte und Untersuchungen
WBC	Word Biblical Commentary
WMANT	Wissenschaftliche Monographien zum Alten und Neuen Testament
WTJ	*Westminster Theological Journal*
ZNW	*Zeitschrift für die neutestamentliche Wissenschaft*

INTRODUCTION

Luke's attitude towards the Jews is an issue that continues to fascinate and divide a significant number of Lukan scholars. All agree that there are occasions when Luke is highly critical of Jews yet, on the other hand, all of Luke's heroes and the many thousands of the first believers were Jews. It is not surprising, therefore, that the varied answers to the question depend upon where scholars place their emphasis. But is Luke's attitude to the Jews the fundamental question that it is sometimes taken to be? Put another way, is the question of Luke and the Jews identical to that of Luke's attitude to Israel? Have the hopes and promises for Israel's restoration that feature so strongly in the infancy stories finally been denied at the end of Acts? Here too there is no critical consensus.[1] But if we ask if it was possible for someone to be highly critical of the people of Israel and yet see their own work as being part of God's plan for the salvation of Israel, then we need look no further than the Old Testament prophets for a clear, affirmative answer. Finally, in this group of interrelated questions, when Luke speaks of Israel does he regard it as being composed solely of Jews? The aim of the present study is to examine these and other related issues in the hope that some of the conflicting critical positions may be at least partially resolved.

Luke's Readership

One factor behind the present critical diversity is what is believed about the ethnic and religious composition of Luke's intended readership. In very broad terms, those who think that Luke wrote for Gentiles will be more inclined to hold that he took an unfavourable view of the Jews, while those who think that his readership contained a significant proportion of Jewish believers will see him as taking a more conciliatory attitude to Judaism.

---

1. The following list is a sample of the major contributions to the debate: Brawley, *Luke–Acts and the Jews*; Conzelmann, *Luke, Acts*; Franklin, *Christ the Lord*; Haenchen, *Acts*; Jervell, *The People of God*; Sanders, *The Jews in Luke–Acts*.

Still the most widely held opinion about Luke is that he was himself a Gentile[2] and that he wrote for a predominantly Gentile readership.[3] His two-volume work is often said to describe the extension of the Christian message from its Jewish origins to Rome, the capital of the empire and 'the end of the earth'. Parallel to this expansion of the church among the Gentiles there is an increasing unwillingness on the part of the Jews to accept the Christian gospel. These two characteristics of Acts reflect, so it is held, the predominantly Gentile membership of the church in Luke's day which was somewhere near the end of the first century.[4] Since each of these areas is relevant to an examination of Luke's concern for the restoration of Israel some preliminary remarks must be made about them although comment on Luke's own background is left until the Summary and Conclusions.

Knowing that Luke addressed his two books to Theophilus does not provide us with unambiguous information about his intended readers. 'Theophilus', in spite of its Greek form, was also used by Jews[5] so that there is no sure way of telling whether the addressee was a Jew, a Christian or a pagan.[6] Attempts to solve the readership question from considerations of Luke's own background or from possible places of writing have not produced a consensus and thus only serve to increase the area of speculation. There are three possibilities for the readership: 1. someone or some class outside the church, 2. a mainly Gentile church and 3. a church composed of Jews and Gentiles with each group present in significant numbers.

C.F. Evans is among more recent commentators who argue that Luke–Acts was addressed to those outside the church. He believes that Luke had two aims, to rebut current charges made against Christians in the Graeco-Roman world, and to claim that Christianity, the 'residuary

---

2. Kümmel, *Introduction*, p. 149: 'The only thing that can be said with certainty about the author, on the basis of Luke, is that he was a Gentile Christian'. Fitzmyer, *Luke*, pp. 42-47, suggests that Luke was a non-Jewish Semite because of Luke's supposed connection with Antioch.

3. Fitzmyer, *Luke*, pp. 57-59, discusses the question and concludes that the readers were Gentile Christians. The evidence offered suggests a Greek-speaking readership but this could include diaspora Jews.

4. Evans, *Saint Luke*, pp. 13-15: 'Here we can only guess'. Evans puts the date between 75 and 130 CE; a rough average of other 'guesses' is around 90 CE.

5. Moulton and Milligan, *Vocabulary*, p. 288.

6. Fitzmyer, *Luke*, pp. 299-300, discusses the uncertainties and concludes that Theophilus was a Christian who stands for the Christian readers of Luke's day.

legatee' of Judaism, is the religion for all humankind.[7] Evans concludes that it is more probable that Luke wrote 'an apologia, in the fullest sense of the word, for a non-Christian readership'.[8] Evans does not regard Luke's assumption that his readers would be familiar with the OT and Judaism as an obstacle to those outside the church since there was an interest in things Jewish in the Graeco-Roman world.[9] As far as the OT is concerned, A.D. Nock contested such a view some sixty years ago, claiming that only those who attended synagogues would have been familiar with the LXX because it was both expensive and generally inaccessible.[10] And an even bigger difficulty is raised by Luke's allusive use of the LXX because it is this, rather than direct citation, which would defeat many pagan readers.[11] How many pagans, for example, would recognize the allusions to Elijah in the story of the raising at Nain (Lk. 7.11-17), to Elijah and Elisha in the call to the would-be disciple to follow Jesus (Lk. 9.59-62) or the interweaving of references to the LXX in the infancy stories? Allusion places considerable demands on readers but its use tells us a great deal about the author's intended readers as well as about his own literary background. There is always a danger that allusion may become illusion and that the reader will make connections not intended by the author or may miss carefully laid clues to the author's meaning. There is no need to assume that each reader would recognize all the allusions, particularly where they are as densely packed as they are in the infancy stories, but the corporate nature of some of the readings at church gatherings would help to overcome this problem.

Since this study presupposes that Luke–Acts was written for a Christian readership which contained a significant proportion of Jewish

7. Evans, *Saint Luke*, pp. 108-109.
8. Evans, *Saint Luke*, p. 111. Two recent monographs that strongly imply a cultured Gentile readership are Squires, *The Plan of God*, and Lentz, *Luke's Portrait of Paul*.
9. Evans, *Saint Luke*, pp. 109-10.
10. Nock, *Conversion*, p. 79. It is of course true that Paul, writing to (largely) Gentile congregations, quotes the OT. But it is noticeable that the frequency of his quotations is much higher when he is concerned with Israel or with Jewish influences e.g. Rom. 3 and 9–11; Gal. 3. In these and other cases Paul cites passages from the OT as authoritative support for his theology but there was no need for his readers to have a deep knowledge of the Scriptures. His use of words and ideas that reflect the OT in an identifiable way would not have caused Gentile readers problems in understanding his line of thought.
11. Maddox, *Purpose*, pp. 14-15.

Christians, we must briefly review the evidence for that assumption. First, however, we need to look at the reasons for thinking that the readers were predominantly Gentile Christians and these have been conveniently summarized by Fitzmyer.[12]

1. Luke omits Jewish preoccupations from his Gospel such as Mt. 5.21-48 (assumed to be from 'Q') as well as the controversies about ritual purity and piety such as those in Mk 7.1-23.
2. Hebrew and Aramaic terms are missing from Luke–Acts and are translated into Greek. Luke also uses the LXX when he quotes from the OT.
3. Jervell has shown that when Luke speaks of Israel he means the Jewish people and not a mixture of Jews and Gentile Christians.[13]

Fitzmyer's first point can be explained by Luke's acceptance of Jewish law so that he saw no need to intensify or reinterpret it, a possibility we shall discuss more fully later. Details of Jewish ritual and piety would not require comment for a partly Jewish readership and Luke deals with the distinction between clean and unclean food after the resurrection when the issue is settled on God's authority (Acts 10). Luke is certainly not shy about describing Jewish ritual and piety, as the infancy stories show. If Jews were among the readers Luke would hardly include the condemnations of Jewish purity practices that Mark attributes to Jesus, and Luke's conception of the Gentile mission as a post-resurrection event could explain his omission of the Gentile material in Mk 6.45–8.26.

Fitzmyer's second point ceases to be a problem if the Jewish readers were Greek-speaking and the Gentiles were unfamiliar with Hebrew and Aramaic terms. Luke may even have thought that such terms gave a rather artificial air of authenticity that was unnecessary. On the third point, even if Jervell is correct, it provides little in the way of evidence for a totally Gentile readership against which Jervell himself argues.

In general, arguments for a predominantly Gentile readership seem to be based on the assumption that Luke's overriding concern was the Gentile mission and the parallel exclusion of the Jews. Once this

---

12. Fitzmyer, *Luke*, pp. 57-59.
13. Jervell, *The People of God*, p. 49, is correct in that Luke uses 'Israel' either historically or in speaking of Jewish contemporaries of the apostles. Certainly Luke does not see the church as usurping Israel.

Introduction

assumption is rejected, as it is in this and other studies,[14] then the character of Luke's readership and his motives for writing need to be reassessed. Maddox, for example, has pointed out that the space allotted in Acts to Paul's mission is slightly less than that devoted to his imprisonment and trials[15] and, in any case, this mission is by no means directed solely to Gentiles.

The evidence for the view that a significant number of Luke's readers were Jewish Christians has been convincingly demonstrated by P.F. Esler[16] as well as by Jervell. Jervell's point is that there would have been no need for a lengthy explanation of the circumcision-free Gentile mission (Acts 10–15) to a readership that did not contain an influential Jewish element.[17] Moreover, many of the Gentile converts in Acts are God-fearers and Esler believes that members of this class were among Luke's readers.[18] God-fearers were Gentiles who had attached themselves to synagogues because they were attracted to the ideals of Judaism but who had not undertaken the final step of conversion by being circumcised.[19] Luke uses the term φοβούμενος τὸν θεὸν twice in the story of Cornelius (Acts 10.2, 22) and twice in Paul's address in the Antioch synagogue (13.16, 26). The related term, σεβόμενος, is used to describe devout people attached to Judaism in Acts 13.43 (here they are proselytes), 13.50; 16.14; 17.4, 17; 18.7.

The existence of God-fearers as a recognized historical class has been challenged by Kraabel using archaeological evidence from the synagogue at Sardis and the absence of such a term from inscriptions.[20] However,

---

14. For example, David Tiede, '"Glory to thy People Israel"', opens his essay with 'Luke–Acts is a Jewish–Christian story that fell into Gentile hands'.

15. Maddox, *Purpose*, pp. 66-67.

16. Esler, *Community and Gospel*, pp. 24-26, 30-45.

17. Jervell, *The People of God*, pp. 175-77. His view is challenged by Brown, *Birth*, p. 236, and Fitzmyer, *Luke*, pp. 42-47.

18. Esler, *Community and Gospel*, pp. 36-45. Jervell, 'The Church of Jews and God Fearers', pp. 11-20, presses the evidence too far in claiming that Luke describes no mission to pagan Gentiles. J.T. Sanders, 'Who is a Jew and who is a Gentile', rightly argues against the translation of ἔθνη in Acts as 'God-fearers' although almost all the converts were, according to Luke.

19. Lake and Cadbury, *Beginnings*, V, pp. 84-96, describes God-fearers as a class but not a clearly defined group. See also Moore, *Judaism*, I, pp. 323-27.

20. Kraabel, 'The Disappearance of the "God-Fearers"'. More recently, in 'Greeks, Jews and Lutherans', Kraabel has criticized Esler's defence of the existence of God-fearers.

Esler has drawn attention to the use of σεβόμενοι τὸν θεὸν by Josephus when he describes Gentile sympathizers who contributed to the wealth of the temple (*Ant.* 14.110).[21] Josephus also mentions that many Gentiles were inclined to follow Jewish customs (*War* 7.45; *Apion* 2.282). Gager has also rejected Kraabel's view as no longer tenable, doubting the soundness of Kraabel's interpretation of the Sardis inscriptions and noting also that one of the donors to that synagogue was a pagan priestess, Julia Severa.[22] But perhaps the most telling evidence cited by Gager is from inscriptions from Aphrodisias in Caria which is not far from Sardis. In these, θεοσεβής appears to be used as a technical category for sympathizers who were neither Jews nor proselytes.

God-fearers, in the range of terms used by Luke, may not be a clearly defined class and this may explain Luke's different terms—but neither do they seem to be a theological invention of his.[23] Such people would, by attending synagogues, be more familiar with the LXX than pagans, and their presence in the church would further encourage Luke in his freedom to use the LXX. Gager concludes his article by questioning whether there was an immediate conversion of God-fearers abandoning Judaism in favour of Christianity.[24] But this may assume a too rigid distinction between Christianity and Judaism in the early period. Later we shall discuss the possibility that, in Luke's view, by being baptized in the name of Jesus, God-fearers became full members of Israel without having to undergo the previous obstacle of circumcision.

We shall therefore assume that Luke wrote for a Christian readership of Greek-speaking former Jews, God-fearers and Gentiles who had a good knowledge of the LXX and the cultural sensitivity to follow Luke's own allusive literary style.

Luke, the Jews and Israel

There are a number of other reasons for the lack of agreement about Luke's attitude to the Jews. The first is that there is no unified response by an entity, 'the Jews'. Luke describes a wide range of Jewish reactions to Christian preaching, from joyful acceptance at one end of the

---

21. Esler, *Community and Gospel*, p. 36.
22. Gager, 'Jews, Gentiles, and Synagogues', pp. 91-99.
23. Cohen, 'Crossing the Boundary and Becoming a Jew', examines the various degrees of Gentile attachment to Judaism.
24. Gager, 'Jews, Gentiles, and Synagogues', pp. 98-99.

spectrum to murderous hostility at the other. And a further fact, which is not always given its full weight in the discussion, is that Gentiles show the same range of responses.[25] After Paul's address in the Antioch synagogue the Gentiles are glad and glorify God (13.48) but, at Philippi, Gentiles attack Paul and Silas for healing the girl with powers of divination and have the missionaries thrown into prison where they are beaten with rods (16.16-24). Unravelling Luke's disposition towards Jews is further complicated by the need to take account of his clearly expressed concern for the salvation and restoration of Israel. Certainly Luke describes a developing hostility on the part of some Jews but this need not imply that *he* is hostile to all Jews or that he advocates such a stance to his readers.

From among the numerous contributions to the debate we begin with Haenchen who regards Paul's final words to the Jews at Antioch (13.46) as the 'moment of divorce between the gospel and Judaism',[26] holding also that Luke renounces Israel in Acts 18.6 and 28.28, 'who by her own fault has forfeited salvation'.[27] Similarly, Conzelmann regards Acts 13.46 as 'a reference to the cutting off of the Jews from redemptive history', although he qualifies this by adding that Jews now have a chance to make good their claim to be Israel and that the way of salvation is open to individual Jews.[28]

Contrastingly, in an essay entitled 'The Divided People of God', Jacob Jervell challenged the then widely accepted opinion that Luke described the gospel being offered first to the Jews and, when they rejected it, being preached to the Gentiles. Jervell turned this theory upside down; it was not Jewish rejection of the gospel but Jewish acceptance that was necessary before the Gentile mission could begin.[29] It is those Jews who accept the gospel, most notably the many thousands in Jerusalem, that represent the purified and true Israel which has been restored. According to Jervell, the church does not separate itself from Israel but 'rather, the unrepentant portion of the people has forfeited its membership of the people of God'. The missionary preaching of the church therefore divides Israel into two groups, the repentant who become

---

25. Jervell, *The People of God*, p. 49.
26. Haenchen, *Acts*, p. 417.
27. Haenchen, *Acts*, p. 535. In his essay 'The Book of Acts as Source Material', p. 278, Haenchen says that in Acts 28.28 'Luke has written off the Jews'.
28. Conzelmann, *Luke*, p. 145.
29. Jervell, *The People of God*, pp. 41-74.

Christians and the unrepentant who are excluded from the empirical Israel of believing Jews.[30] In Jervell's opinion, a sufficient number of Jerusalem Jews had become believers and, by the time of Cornelius's conversion, the restoration of Israel had taken place. Jervell cites as evidence for this Acts 15.16-18 with its quotation of Amos 9.11.[31] Jervell's conclusion is that, since Israel has been restored, Paul's quotation of Isaiah to the Roman Jews shows that the mission to the Jews has now come to an end because the gospel has reached the end of the earth.[32]

There is no need to stress the undoubted importance of Jervell's essay which has compelled the attention of all who have subsequently concerned themselves with Luke's understanding of Israel. Jervell's understanding of Israel is that 'In Acts, Israel continues to refer to the Jewish people, characterized as a people of repentant (i.e. Christian) and obdurate Jews'.[33] This definition of Israel raises two difficulties. The first is that it groups together Jews and Jewish Christians in a way that excludes Gentile Christians, for it is hard to accept that Luke envisaged some Christians being within Israel while others were outside. Such a concept would have caused grave pastoral problems for the unity of Christians. Furthermore, it would make little sense of Luke's emphasis on the conversion of God-fearers who, having come so close to Israel, would still be excluded because they were Gentiles. The barrier of circumcision would still exist.

The second difficulty with Jervell's definition is that it fails to take account of Luke's obvious interest in the Samaritans, an interest shared only by John's gospel in the NT. Samaritans were clearly distinguished from Jews, both as historical fact and as Luke depicts them, yet Jervell describes the mission in Samaria (Acts 8) as a Jewish mission[34] and Samaritans as Jews who are within the people of God by the fact of their circumcision.[35] The role of the Samaritans in Luke–Acts and their relation to Luke's understanding of Israel is discussed in detail in Chapter 3.

---

30. Jervell, *The People of God*, pp. 42-43, 55. Conzelmann, *Luke*, p. 146, makes a similar point about the Baptist's divisive preaching.
31. Jervell, *The People of God*, pp. 51-52.
32. Jervell, *The People of God*, p. 63.
33. Jervell, *The People of God*, pp. 42-43.
34. Jervell, *The People of God*, pp. 113-32, esp. pp. 123-24.
35. Jervell, *The People of God*, p. 119.

If Haenchen's understanding of Luke's attitude towards the Jews has been challenged by Jervell, it has been forcefully restated and extended to the whole of Luke–Acts by J.T. Sanders.[36] Sanders accepts that the Jews have become a divided people but he also argues that there is a strand of blanket condemnation of the Jews in Luke's writing.[37] He suggests that this tension can be resolved by separating speech and narrative material about the Jews. The speeches treat the Jews as uniformly bad and obdurate—'by nature...opposed to the will and purposes of God...and [the Jews] have been as a group and a nation, excluded from God's salvation'[38]—whereas the narrative material presents the Jews as divided in their response to the gospel. Nonetheless, argues Sanders, by the end of Acts the difference in attitude between speech and narrative has ceased to exist and the Jews, now excluded from further attempts to convert them, 'have *become* what they from the first *were*'.[39] And since, according to Sanders, Israel always means the Jews and refers only to Jews,[40] we would have to conclude that, on this definition, Israel stands condemned by Luke. Sanders's understanding of the Samaritans further underlines his view of Israel. He rightly dismisses Jervell's false alternative that they must be either Jews or Gentiles but he concludes that 'they belong with the Jewish outcasts and Gentile proselytes and God-fearers, on the periphery of Judaism'.[41] Sanders believes that, for Luke, converting the Samaritans is a transitional stage in the movement from the Jews to the Gentile mission. But to classify Samaritans with those who wish to enter Judaism or who are attracted to it is seriously to misunderstand Samaritan intentions both as historical fact and as Luke describes them.

The debate about Luke's view of the Jews does not lack for those who see his evaluation in much more positive terms than do Haenchen, Conzelmann and Sanders. Franklin takes Luke's picture of Jewish opposition seriously yet he holds that Luke is favourably disposed towards Jews and that Luke was deeply influenced by OT ideas of a

---

36. Sanders, *The Jews in Luke–Acts*.
37. Sanders, *The Jews in Luke–Acts*, p. 49.
38. Sanders, *The Jews in Luke–Acts*, pp. 49-50.
39. Sanders, *The Jews in Luke–Acts*, p. 81.
40. Sanders, *The Jews in Luke–Acts*, pp. 48-49.
41. Sanders, *The Jews in Luke–Acts*, pp. 148-51. Also Cullmann, *The Early Church*, pp. 185-86.

faithful remnant.[42] Brawley argues that Luke attempts to overcome differences between Christians and Jews as well as those between Jewish and Gentile Christians. In this Brawley's expressed intention is to develop and modify the insights of F.C. Baur.[43] Tiede is another scholar who regards Luke as pro-Jewish, emphasizing that the coming of Jesus as Messiah means that the inclusion of the Gentiles will be for the glory of Israel.[44]

Aim and Outline of the Study

As long as Luke's understanding of Israel is thought to be restricted to the totality of the Jews there will necessarily be a conflict between his adverse comments on Jews and his positive statements about Israel's salvation and restoration. That Israel means the totality of Jews for Luke is taken for granted by those who believe Luke to be anti-Jewish as well as those who see him as pro-Jewish, and it is an equation that has led to confusion and stalemate in the current debate. However much Luke may criticize the Jews, 'Israel' is never the subject of criticism.

This study is an attempt to break the deadlock by exploring Luke's understanding of Israel, an understanding which is perhaps wider and more positive than that found elsewhere in the NT. Luke firmly believed that God's restoration was an ongoing process and one that will result in Israel having the unity it once possessed under David, prior to the separation into two kingdoms. Furthermore, Israel still has its role to fulfil in bringing God's salvation to all men.[45]

In Part I, I discuss those aspects of the infancy stories that serve as Luke's opening statement of God's plan for Israel's salvation (Chapter 1) and his treatment of Israel's history (Chapter 2). The history shows that Luke has almost no interest in Israel's past after the division into two kingdoms so that, historically, Luke does not restrict himself to the tribe of Judah. Luke's special interest in the Samaritans is discussed in Chapter 3, where it is suggested that this interest springs largely from his acceptance of the Samaritan claim to be the descendants of the Northern Kingdom, Israel.

---

42. Franklin, *Christ the Lord*, pp. 92-93, 103-104, 175-78.
43. Brawley, 'Paul in Acts', p. 127.
44. Tiede, *Prophecy and History*. Also 'The Exaltation of Jesus and the Restoration of Israel in Acts 1'.
45. Danker, *Jesus and the New Age*, p. 9.

Much of the debate about Luke and the Jews has naturally concentrated on his descriptions of Jewish reaction to Jesus and the Christian mission, together with what his speakers say about the Jews. This evidence is obviously vital but there are other indications of Luke's concern for Jews and Israel. In Part II, the scope of the evidence is extended to his presentations of Christology (Chapter 4) and atonement (Chapter 5). The Lukan forms of these doctrines have long been recognized as primitive, reflecting as they do the marked influence of Jewish beliefs and expectations, and showing only rare glimpses of the more developed Christian forms current when Luke was writing. This becomes clear when we compare Luke's Christology with that of Matthew, and his understanding of atonement with that of Paul.

Luke's view of Israel as I have sketched it is not what we might expect from a Christian writing at a time when the separation of Jews and Christians was becoming increasingly sharp and acrimonious. Nor would we expect such a view of Israel if we had only read, say, Paul, Matthew and, perhaps, Hebrews. In Part III, therefore, I discuss how Luke understood the implications for Israel in the writings of two of his predecessors, Paul and Matthew. This raises the question of Luke's knowledge of Matthew's Gospel and at least some of Paul's letters.

Luke's knowledge and use of Paul's letters is either generally rejected today or else the possibility is simply ignored. This is partly because of the conflicting nature of the accounts of Paul in Acts with those in the letters and partly because Luke appears to know so little of Paul's theology. But ignorance is not the same as deliberate silence. In Chapter 6, therefore, it is argued that Luke's view of Israel and its continuing role is the powerful reason behind both Luke's portrait of Paul and his silence about Paul's theology, of which he was all too well aware.

It is still a matter of debate whether Luke used Matthew or the sayings source 'Q' for the material which is common to both Gospels. But one of the arguments against Luke's knowledge of Matthew—that of the different ordering of much of the common material—might be circumvented if a sufficiently powerful motive existed for Luke's break-up of Matthew's order. The motive proposed here for the differences has to do with the very different understandings of Israel that the two evangelists held. This is discussed in Chapter 7, together with Luke's final statement on the Jews in Acts 28.

Few today would quibble with the description of Luke as a theologian. But in this he was a skilful and subtle polemicist. The target of his polemic was those Christians whom he saw, rightly or wrongly, as trying to cut off themselves and their fellow believers from the historical Israel and whom he regarded as putting something other in its place. The Pauline concept of the Body of Christ (with its apparent setting aside of the law) and the Matthean idea of Christ's church having the keys to the kingdom of heaven are both rejected by Luke. Luke certainly has harsh criticism of some Jews, particularly the Jerusalem leadership and groups in the diaspora. But to focus attention on these attacks as if they were different in kind from those made by Hebrew prophets—or to elevate his concern for the growth of the Gentile mission to be the major purpose of Acts—is to overlook the importance he attaches to the restoration and unity of Israel. This he saw as a continuing historical process that will be completed when Jesus Messiah comes.

Part I

Chapter 1

ISRAEL IN THE INFANCY NARRATIVES

If any doubt existed about the importance that Luke attaches to God's salvation of Israel, it is amply overcome by the first two chapters of his Gospel. It is therefore a major defect of Hans Conzelmann's influential study of Lukan theology that he virtually ignores the infancy stories. He gives as his reason for the omission that the first two chapters are of doubtful authenticity.[1] He makes this comment in relationship to Luke's eschatology, the discussion of which is central to his thesis that Luke, faced with a delay in the parousia, has moved from a futuristic eschatology to a salvation history composed of three epochs. These are the times of Israel, of Jesus and of the church.[2]

An attempt to repair Conzelmann's omission has been made by H.H. Oliver, who argues that the Lukan birth stories support the theory of the three epochs.[3] But the deeply Jewish character of the stories, which Oliver recognizes, makes it difficult to regard John as belonging to the period of Israel in a way that is not also true of Jesus. Paul Minear, on the other hand, holds that it is only by ignoring the birth stories that 'Conzelmann can appear to establish his thesis'.[4] Minear shows that there are many connections between Luke 1–2 and the rest of Luke–Acts, not least is the relation 'of each of the characters to God's plan for the redemption of Israel'.[5] If this view is correct then it would seriously undermine the theory of the three periods of salvation history.

---

1. Conzelmann, *Luke*, p. 118.
2. Conzelmann, *Luke*, pp. 16-17.
3. Oliver, 'The Lucan Birth Stories', pp. 202-26.
4. Minear, 'Luke's Use of the Birth Stories', pp. 121, 124; Franklin, *Christ the Lord*, p. 87, claims that the birth stories show a more favourable attitude than Conzelmann allows.
5. Minear, 'Luke's Use of the Birth Stories', p. 127; Tiede, '"Glory to Thy People Israel"', pp. 26-29.

1. *Israel in the Infancy Narratives* 25

In this chapter, Conzelmann's view of the authenticity of the material is set aside, not from a belief in the historical reliability of the stories but simply on the grounds that they form the prologue to the text of the Gospel as we now have it. Nor, incidentally, do we have any certain knowledge of the nature and extent of Luke's Christian sources or how much of these chapters is Luke's own composition. The only reasonable certainty we have is that the final editor approved of the present form and content of the whole work, since he would hardly include material contrary to his overall purpose.

The present concern with the infancy stories is a limited one, that of examining how the final editor (who for the purposes of the present study will be referred to by the traditional name 'Luke') introduces his readers to his understanding of the destiny of Israel. That is to say, I want to ask and if possible find an answer to the question: what would the reader learn about God's purpose for Israel after reading the first two chapters as they stand before us? In a major study of Luke 1–2, R.E. Brown concludes that these chapters were written after the completion of Acts.[6] We should therefore expect the infancy stories to put forward, at least in embryo, ideas that the author uses in the main body of his work and to provide clues to his purpose in writing. But these two chapters also function in another and more obvious way. They are the beginning of a work that reads as a biographical and historical narrative and this is so whatever reservations we may have about the historical accuracy of Luke's account of events. As we shall see, this dual character of being both narrative and theological prologue causes certain tensions in the birth stories which need to be resolved.

So far as I am aware writers on Luke–Acts, with the possible exception of Jervell,[7] use the word 'Israel' as if it were synonymous with 'Jews'. In this discussion of Luke 1–2 I shall use 'Israel' without regard to its composition. At no time does Luke explicitly say who the members of Israel are but, as we shall see later, there may be faint hints of a wider membership than Jews. This does not mean that people other than pious Jews are involved in the birth stories but it does enable Luke, when using the term 'Israel', to leave open the question of its membership. It should be noted that 'the Jews' do not appear in the Gospel until 7.3 where the term is necessary to distinguish the messengers from the

---

6. Brown, *Birth*, p. 243; Fitzmyer, *Luke*, p. 310.
7. Jervell, *The People of God*, pp. 113-17. Jervell's views are discussed further in Chapter 3.

Gentile centurion and to make it clear that Jesus does not come into direct contact with a Gentile. 'The Jews' only reappear at the trial and death of Jesus in Luke 23.[8]

Before we take a detailed look at certain parts of the birth stories there are some general observations that need to be made about them. The first of these is about the activity of the Holy Spirit. Both Elizabeth (1.41) and Zechariah (1.67) are filled with the Spirit and the angel promises that John too will be gifted in the same way (1.15). Mary is to receive the Spirit and will be overshadowed by the power of the Most High, terms which Conzelmann suggests may be practically identical.[9] Of particular importance for the present discussion is the effect of the Spirit on Simeon. First, it reveals that he will not see death until he has seen the Lord's Anointed (2.26), thus confirming the Christological message to the shepherds (2.11). The second effect is that Simeon is inspired to utter two prophecies about Israel (2.32, 34). Had Luke begun his Gospel at 3.1 then the sequence of the gift of the Spirit would be that it descended first on Jesus (3.21-22) and that he continues under its guidance (4.1, 14, 18; 10.21). Luke is quite consistent on this point because Jesus is one of the two people in the birth stories who do not receive the Spirit directly. Later, both the Baptist (3.16) and Jesus promise that the Spirit will be given to others (11.13; 12.12; Acts 1.5, 8) but, prior to Pentecost, nobody outside the birth stories is said to be empowered by the Spirit. It is only after Pentecost that the Spirit fills and guides the apostles and disciples and becomes freely available to converts, whether Jews, Samaritans or Gentiles (Acts 4.31; 8.17; 10.44-47). References to the Spirit are some six times more frequent in Acts than they are in Luke 3–24 but, in frequency per page, the references in the birth stories have a similar value to that in Acts. There are a number of instances in the OT of people who are given God's Spirit, for example: Joshua (Num. 27.18), Samson (Judg. 13.25) and David (1 Sam. 16.13), but there is nothing like the concentration of Spirit-filled people

8. At 23.51, Arimathea is described as a city 'of the Jews'. The other instances occur in Gentile descriptions of Jesus as king of the Jews (23.3, 37, 38), a title which Luke rejects. According to *BAGD*, p. 381, 'Israel' is the main self-designation of the Jews, yet Josephus often uses 'Jews' to refer to his contemporary kinsmen. In Acts, 'Jews' is used by Gentiles (16.20; 18.14) and by Jews (10.28; 20.19; 21.11, 20, 21, 39). 'Israel' and 'Israelite' are used in direct speech in Luke–Acts with only three exceptions that are editorial (Lk. 1.80; 2.25; Acts 5.21). The usage is therefore what might be expected.

9. Conzelmann, *Luke*, p. 183 n. 2.

that we find in the birth stories. Clearly Luke intends to describe a new intensity of the Spirit's activity, yet within the pre-Pentecost Israel.

The almost pentecostal intensity in the birth stories is also apparent in some rather loose connections between these stories and Peter's use of Joel 2 to explain the significance of Pentecost to the Jerusalem crowds. Although the verbal coincidences are not sufficient to be sure that Luke intended to make the connection, they do suggest that the people in the birth stories show what the Spirit-filled church would, or should, be like.

Luke 1–2	Acts 2/Joel 2
1.67 Zechariah is filled with the Spirit and prophesies (ἐπροφήτευσεν).	2.17 'I will pour out my Spirit on all flesh and your sons and your daughters shall prophesy'. (προφητεύσουσιν).
2.36 Anna is a prophetess.	
1.22 The people in the temple realize that Zechariah has seen a vision (ὀπτασίαν ἑώρακεν).	2.17 'Your young men shall see visions (ὁράσεις ὄψονται) and your old men (πρεσβύτεροι) shall dream dreams'.
1.18 Zechariah is old (πρεσβύτης).	
1.35, 38 The Spirit will come upon Mary the δούλη κυρίου.	2.18 '…on my menservants (δούλους) and on my maidservants (δούλας) in those days I shall pour out my Spirit [and they shall prophesy (προφητεύσουσιν)].
2.25, 29 The Spirit comes upon Simeon who asks that τὸν δοῦλόν σου may depart in peace.	
2.34-35 Simeon prophesies the effects of Jesus' coming.	[ ] is a Lukan addition to the LXX.

A further feature of the birth stories is that each of the people is impeccable. Zechariah and Elizabeth are both righteous before God and keep all the commandments and ordinances without blame (1.6).[10] Zechariah's dumbness is only a narrative device which should not be regarded as a punishment for asking a question (1.18) and which Luke may have based on Abraham's question to God about his childlessness (Gen. 15.1-2). Mary has found favour with the Lord (1.28, 30) and her response to Gabriel is immediate in her acceptance of God's purpose (1.38) and it leads to the announcement of her blessedness (1.45). Simeon is righteous and devout (2.25) and Anna remains in the temple day and night because of her intense piety (2.37). Only the silent Joseph is without any approving epithet, in spite of doing all that is required of

---

10. Zechariah's loss of speech can hardly be a punishment for asking his question, which is very similar to Mary's in 1.34.

him. Like Jesus, Joseph is not described as being under the power of the Spirit.

These two characteristics of the stories do not startle us with their strangeness as perhaps they should. Here are Spirit-filled people prior to the gift at Pentecost and none of them is in need of repentance or, indeed, any form of atonement associated with Jesus' death and resurrection that we find elsewhere in the NT. It can be argued that the gift of the Spirit precedes Pentecost because it is for particular purposes such as we find in the OT. But the piety and excellence of all the people suggests something far deeper and, even after Pentecost, Christians receive special gifts of the Spirit (e.g. Acts 4.31). It is clearly part of Luke's purpose to present the prophecies, visions and events as heralding the dawn of the new age of the Spirit which finds its full expression in Acts. He may also have wanted to give the readers his own vision of what the messianic community will be like. But there is a danger of over-stressing the proleptic aspect of the stories so that the narrative strangeness is obscured or even lost. Let us try to imagine how the first readers might have reacted. To take the narrative time sequence seriously entails taking the strangeness seriously; that it was possible for some members of Israel to keep the law blamelessly and to follow a life of pious devotion even before Jesus had been born. And it is important to note that the events come as a surprise to both Zechariah (1.12, 18) and Mary (1.29, 34), neither of whom was expecting to be involved in a birth, let alone such momentous births as those of John and Jesus.

This element of surprise is dramatically and theologically important because the narrative time places the actions firmly in pre-Christian Israel. Luke emphasizes this atmosphere of pre-Christian Israel in two further characteristics of the birth stories, the first of which is his literary style. Over half a century ago Creed drew attention to the fact that the 'literary versatility of the evangelist is shown at the outset'.[11] There is an abrupt change from the 'irreproachable literary Greek' of 1.1-4 to that of the LXX which Knox describes as 'an orgy of Hebraic Greek'.[12] Although Sahlin ascribes the authorship to Proto-Luke he regards the language as designed for the last book of the OT[13] and, in the words of

---

11. Creed, *St Luke*, p. lxxvi.
12. Knox, *Sources*, p. 40, considers the possible attempt to imitate Hebraic Greek but rejects the idea. Sparkes, 'Semitisms', p. 134, sees a 'reverence for, and imitation of, the LXX'.
13. Sahlin, *Studien zur protolukanischen Theologie*, p. 60.

1. Israel in the Infancy Narratives

Benoit, 'I find it more probable...that Luke has written in an intentionally biblical style, full of almost literal reminiscences of the LXX'.[14]

So, is this Hebraic Greek the result of Luke or a predecessor translating Hebrew or Aramaic sources or is it a deliberate attempt by Luke to imitate the style of the LXX? Stephen Farris surveys these and other less probable options for the origin of the canticles and, in the light of his own and previous studies, concludes that the hymns in the birth stories depend upon Semitic originals from an early Jewish-Christian environment.[15] The septuagintal style is particularly obvious in the canticles but it is used throughout the infancy stories up to and including the start of the Baptist's ministry (3.2).

Farris may well be correct about the origin of the hymns but, for the examination of Luke's purpose, he has not given sufficient weight to Creed's observation. For, if Luke was the stylist that he is generally taken to be, why did he leave the stories and the canticles in their original style? Whether or not they are deliberate imitations or translations, the fact remains that Luke was well able to 'improve' the style—had he so wished.[16] The contrast between the style of 1.1-4 and what follows demonstrates this very clearly and, perhaps, intentionally so. And not only is the style reminiscent of the LXX, but so also is the *content* of the Magnificat and Benedictus in which Creed has noted some forty allusions to a wide range of passages in the LXX.[17] The result is that, even if those who differ on the origins of Luke's style have 'fought themselves to a draw',[18] we are still left with a style which must have seemed to some of Luke's readers a powerful reminder of Israel's Scriptures. To begin a Christian Gospel as though it were a part of Israel's Scriptures is surely of major importance in assessing Luke's overall purpose and it is difficult to escape the conclusion that the septuagintal style and ethos are deliberate on Luke's part.

The second backward-looking feature of the infancy stories is the use of aorists in two of the canticles, notably in the Magnificat. The aorists seem at first sight to be past tenses that point the readers' attention to God's merciful acts towards Israel in the past. But this is a complex issue and we shall return to it later in this chapter.

14. Benoit, 'L'enfance de Jean-Baptiste', p. 175.
15. Farris, *Hymns*, p. 62.
16. Farris, *Hymns*, p. 61.
17. Creed, *St Luke*, pp. 303-307.
18. Brown, *Birth*, p. 246.

Israel in the Birth Stories

We can now move on to Luke's explicit references to Israel, the first two of which come in Gabriel's prophecies to Zechariah about John (1.16) and to Mary about Jesus (1.32-33). The appearances of Gabriel trouble both Zechariah and Mary (ἐταράχθη 1.12; διεταράχθη 1.29) and both receive the same answer: 'Do not be afraid' (μὴ φοβοῦ 1.13, 30). These are the only references to Gabriel in the NT and, even in the LXX, he is mentioned only in Dan. 8.16 and 9.21. A comparison of the accounts in Luke and Daniel shows some similarities that suggest that Luke may have used Daniel as a model for his own descriptions. One possible explanation is that it made a further link between his own narrative and the LXX, and another is that Gabriel's appearance to Daniel is to interpret the vision of the end-time to 'son of man' (Dan. 8.16-17). A further point which may have influenced Luke is that Gabriel interprets Daniel's vision of the destruction of Jerusalem and the sanctuary together with the Anointed One (μετὰ τοῦ χριστοῦ, Dan. 9.26). The destruction of the city (ἐρήμωσις, 9.27) also lies behind the prophecy in Lk. 21.20 (cf. Mt. 24.15).

Gabriel's Appearances

Daniel	Luke
8.17 Daniel is frightened.	1.12 Zechariah is troubled and frightened.
	1.29-30 Mary is troubled.
9.23 Gabriel appears at the start of Daniel's prayers (δεήσεώς) at the time of evening sacrifice (ἐν ὥρᾳ θυσίας ἑσπερινῆς, 9.21). He tells Daniel that he is greatly loved.	1.13 Zechariah's prayer (δέησίς) is heard.
	1.10 Gabriel appears at the hour of incense (ὥρᾳ τοῦ θυμιάματος).
	1.28 Mary is told that she is the favoured one.
8.17 Gabriel interprets Daniel's vision for the time of the end.	
	1.22 The appearance to Zechariah is a vision (ὀπτασίαν).[19]

Gabriel's prophecy to Zechariah outlines John's future role which includes drinking no wine or strong drink (1.15). This Nazirite type of prohibition has led some commentators to see parallels with Samson and

---

19. Brown, *Birth*, pp. 270-71, includes similarities from the vision of Daniel in which Gabriel is not mentioned. He also notes similarities between Luke and the LXX of Theodotion.

Samuel. Of the two, Samson seems to be the more probable candidate since Luke uses the birth of Samuel and Hannah's song (1 Sam. 2.1-10) in the Magnificat.[20] In the LXX only Samson's mother is forbidden wine and strong drink (σίκερα, Judg. 13.4, 7, 14; Lk. 1.15) but in Pseudo-Philo, *LAB* 42.3, which probably dates from the first century CE,[21] Samson himself is to abstain from wine and unclean food. In *LAB* 42.5 (but not in Judg. 13) Samson's father does not believe his wife because he is unworthy to hear such signs and wonders. Further similarities between John and Samson are: both births are foretold by angels (Judg. 13.3; Lk. 1.13), both mothers are barren (στεῖρα, Judg. 13.2, 3; Lk. 1.7, 36), God's Spirit comes upon each (Judg. 13.25; Lk. 1.15) and both are imprisoned by their enemies (Judg. 16.21; Lk. 3.20). But perhaps the most interesting resemblance between the two is that Samson had a preparatory role to that of David, just as John has for the work of Jesus. Samson is to begin to save (σῴζειν, Judg. 13.5) Israel, a task completed by David.

John's role is to go before the Lord in the spirit and power of Elijah (1.17), a statement usually taken to be based on Mal. 3.23-24 (LXX). R.E. Brown sees this as a specific identification of John with the expected Elijah[22] but this view has been challenged by I.H. Marshall who takes it to mean that John will be inspired by the same power as Elijah was.[23] The question of the extent to which Lk. 1.16-17 has been influenced by Malachi is an important factor in understanding John's role in the overall plan. Fitzmyer has noted that, prior to Christian interpretations, there was no expectation that Elijah *redivivus* would precede the coming of the Messiah.[24] The reason is, as A.E. Harvey points out, that prior to 70 CE, Jewish writings make no mention of an Anointed without some further qualification such as 'The Anointed of Aaron'.[25] That is to say, there is no mention of 'The Messiah' as Christians came to use the term in the NT. We shall discuss this further in Chapter 4 because of its relevance for Luke's Christology.

---

20. This assumes that the Magnificat should be attributed to Mary. A few Latin variants of Lk. 1.46 attribute the hymn to Elizabeth. The description of being humiliated (ταπείνωσιν, 1.48, cf. ταπεινοί, 1 Sam. 2.7) fits better with the barren state of Elizabeth (στεῖρα, 1.7; 1 Sam. 2.5). See Danker, *Jesus and the New Age*, pp. 41-42.

21. Harrington, 'Pseudo-Philo', *OTP*, II, p. 299, suggests that a date 'around the time of Jesus is the most likely' for *Liber Antiquitatem Biblicarum*.

22. Brown, *Birth*, p. 276.
23. Marshall, *Luke*, p. 59.
24. Fitzmyer, *Luke*, p. 672.
25. Harvey, *Constraints*, pp. 77-80.

Comparing Lk. 1.17 with Mal. 3.23 shows that there is little verbal agreement although the MT shows some similarity of thought. For a Greek source which refers to the coming of Elijah, Sir. 48.10 seems more appropriate.

Lk. 1.17	ἐπιστρέψαι καρδίας πατέρων ἐπὶ τέκνα
Mal. 3.23	ὃς ἀποκαταστήσει καρδίαν πατρὸς πρὸς υἱὸν καὶ καρδίαν ἀνθρώπου πρὸς τὸν πλησίον αὐτοῦ
Mal. 3.23 (MT)	He will turn the hearts of the fathers to the sons.
Sir. 48.10	ἐπιστρέψαι καρδίαν πατρὸς πρὸς υἱὸν καὶ καταστῆσαι φυλὰς Ιακωβ.

Some commentators also see a reference to Mal. 3.1[26] but, again, there is little if any verbal agreement. There is, however, one link between Luke's account and Mal. 3.2: 'Who can stand when [the ἄγγελος of the covenant] appears (ἐν τῇ ὀπτασίᾳ αὐτοῦ)?' The word ὀπτασία is as rare in the LXX as it is in the NT, occuring some four times in each, and in Lk. 1.22 the ὀπτασία occurs in the temple as it is predicted to do in Mal. 3.1-2. Perhaps Luke has used ideas in Malachi 3, possibly mediated through the account in Sirach 48 where, as in Luke, the idea is applied to the restoration of Jacob-Israel.

Possible interpretations of the second part of Luke's couplet ('...and the disobedient to the thinking of the just ones' [δικαίων]) are discussed by Marshall.[27] Among the suggestions is that John will bring the older generation to share the outlook of the younger. Perhaps so; but another approach is to look at those people in Luke–Acts who are described as righteous or just. They are Elizabeth and Zechariah (1.6), Simeon (2.25), Joseph of Arimathea (23.50) and Cornelius (Acts 10.22). Even without Jesus (Lk. 23.47; Acts 3.14; 7.52; 22.14) it would be difficult to find a better collection of models for the disobedient to contemplate.

Gabriel's prophecy also describes John's task as making ready 'for the Lord a people having been prepared (κατεσκευασμένον, 1.17)'. κατασκευάζω can mean 'to form' or 'to fashion' (Isa. 43.7; 45.7) or 'to furnish' (Num. 21.27). In Luke, the sense appears to be that John is to make the final preparation of a people already equipped for the Lord's use by turning many of the children of Israel to the Lord. In order to stress the eschatological nature of this work Luke has pressed into service the figure of Elijah both by name and by allusion but he avoids the explicit identification of John with Elijah that is found in

26. Brown, *Birth*, p. 277. Marshall, *Luke*, pp. 58-59.
27. Marshall, *Luke*, pp. 59-60.

Mt. 11.14 and 17.11-13. The identification is less clear in Mk 9.12-13 but by doing this Luke avoids the fundamental flaw in Mk 9.12 and Mt. 17.11, where John-Elijah is described as coming to restore all things (ἀποκαθιστάνει πάντα).²⁸ This is manifestly untrue of John and may have originally been applied to Jesus. Luke later attributes this function to the Messiah who is still to come (ἀποκαταστάσεως πάντων, Acts 3.21). The allusions to Malachi and Sirach make clear that John has a preparatory role to play in the restoration but that it is subsidiary to that of Luke's true Elijah figure, Jesus. Nevertheless, Luke describes Gabriel's message about John as good news (εὐαγγελίσασθαί, 1.19) and this is the first use of a verb that is of paramount importance for Luke. The character of John's birth is confirmed by the description of his preaching as good news for the people (3.18). Since these descriptions are found only in Luke they should warn us of making too rigid a distinction between the roles and periods of Jesus and the Baptist.

Jesus' Kingship of Israel

Gabriel's second prophecy concerns Jesus (1.26, 32-33, 35-37) and it is widely supposed to derive from God's promise of a son for David whose kingdom and throne will be established for ever. This son, who will also be God's son, 'will build a house for my name' (2 Sam. 7.12-16). Whether or not Gabriel's words are to be understood to point to a parousia event²⁹ the message is clear enough: the house of Jacob, the people of Israel (e.g. Exod. 19.3) will be established for ever under David's heir who will be called 'Son of the Most High' and 'Son of God' (1.32, 35). Both titles of sonship are anarthrous. Jesus later restates the promise to the apostles who will sit on thrones, judging the twelve tribes of Israel (22.29-30). C.F. Evans has drawn attention to the unique

---

28. Nineham, *St Mark*, pp. 240-41, notes the oddity of 'restore all things' (Mk 9.12) and that it hardly applies to the Baptist. Mt. 17.11 uses the future tense (Mal. 3.23, cf. Sir. 48.10). Nineham's comment that John was prevented from doing so exposes the weakness of the identification by Mark and Matthew since, in both Gospels, John is already dead (Mk 6.14-29; 9.13; Mt. 14.1-12). But neither were all things restored by the earthly Jesus and this is why Luke, a realist, attributes the work of restoration to the future Messiah (Acts 3.20-21). Only Luke uses ἀποκαθίστημι, ἀποκατάστασις of Jesus or the Messiah.

29. Lohse, 'υἱὸς Δαυίδ', p. 484 n. 47, takes it to be a parousia event, but Marshall, *Luke*, p. 68, thinks not. Although Jesus acted with 'kingly power' it still fell short of total restoration.

nature of Jesus' table and kingdom which is peculiar to Luke.[30]

The theme of Jesus' kingship extends throughout the Gospel where it is always as the Davidic king of Israel. Unlike Mark (15.32) and John (1.49; 12.13), Luke does not need to use the full title because descent from David makes it unnecessary and neither Mark nor John have genealogies. To Luke, Jesus is not king of the Jews any more than was David, so when Jesus is questioned at his trial (23.3) 'King of the Jews' is rejected and at the crucifixion the title is a term of derision (23.37, 38). At the entry to Jerusalem, the disciples alone proclaim Jesus to be 'the king who comes in the name of the Lord' (19.37-38), which is a more personal form than Mark's 'Blessed be the kingdom of our father David' (Mk 11.10). For Luke, the kingdom derives from God (also 22.29): this is consistent with Jesus' preaching the kingdom of God throughout his ministry. Luke's account of the entry is preceded by the parable that is told because the people suppose that the kingdom of God is to appear immediately (19.11). In the parable, a nobleman goes to a far country to receive kingly power and is to return (19.12, 15). The implication is that the kingdom will come when the man returns as king (Acts 1.6-7, 11) and that the kingdom will be that of Israel. Although Luke does not quote Zech. 9.9 in his account of the entry (cf. Mt. 21.5; Jn 12.15), it does contain some allusions to Zech. 9.9[31] in which the king is described as δίκαιος and σῴζων. At the risk of further speculation, Zech. 9.10 speaks of disarming Jerusalem and Ephraim, the northern and southern kingdoms, and of the king who 'commands peace to the nations'. Was Luke aware that these verses of Zechariah spoke of a king who would bring peace between the two kingdoms? Certainly Luke continues with the lament over Jerusalem because it did not know the things that made for peace (19.41-44). But Luke's understanding of Jesus' kingship is restrained and cautious and its fulness lies in the eschatological future when he will reign over the twelve tribes of the house of Jacob.

The Magnificat

The next mention of Israel is in the Magnificat, which proclaims that God 'has helped his servant Israel' (1.54). The first part of the canticle

30. Evans, *Saint Luke*, p. 800.
31. Evans, *Saint Luke*, pp. 677-79, but he is not correct in saying that ἐμβιβάζειν is used in Lk. 19.35 and Zech. 9.9. Zech. uses ἐπιβαίνω (cf. Mt. 21.5) and Luke uses ἐπιβιβάζω. Fitzmyer, *Luke*, pp. 1248-49, is more doubtful about an allusion to Zechariah.

(1.46-50) portrays the reaction of Mary[32] to the announcement of her forthcoming motherhood, but it is the presence of verbs as aorists in vv. 51-55 which causes an interpretative problem to which a solution must now be attempted.

The conclusion that the hymns in the birth stories were probably composed in early Jewish-Christian circles[33] suggests a context in which the aorists would make good sense within the hymns. They could well represent the response of Christians who were looking back on the death and resurrection of Jesus and the results which, they believed, flowed from those events. But, if that is the case, it must be said that the content of the hymns is far too general and lacks specific Christian references. Nor does a Christian origin of the hymns explain why Luke has retained the aorists in their present context; he could have changed the tense and thus avoided the conflict which now exists between the past tenses and the narrative time. However, the need for such changes presupposes that Luke intended the hymns only to point forward to the saving work of Jesus.

One possible solution to the problem would be that the aorists do not act as the past tense. For example, Gunkel thinks that they correspond to the Hebrew prophetic perfect and that this would give this section of the hymn an eschatological dimension.[34] Farris accepts much of Gunkel's thesis but he sees the decisive event of God's help for Israel to be the coming of Jesus Christ.[35] This is the event, so Farris believes, that is sufficiently close in time that the results can be spoken about as if they were already present in the narrative time. But this still leaves unanswered the question of why, if Mary was speaking about present effects, she did not use present tenses in vv. 50-55? The only aorist in the personal section of the hymn is translated as 'rejoices' (ἠγαλλίασεν, 1.47) by the RSV, yet even here the past tense could mean that Mary has always rejoiced that God was her saviour.

While there can be little doubt that Luke intended to point forward to the coming of Jesus (the Magnificat is concerned with his imminent birth), the fact remains that vv. 51-55 contain no clear reference to the

---

32. Even if Elizabeth were the speaker, the problem with the aorists remains but perhaps somewhat less so since the hymn would be less obviously concerned with Jesus.
33. Farris, *Hymns*, pp. 97-98.
34. Gunkel, 'Die Lieder', p. 53.
35. Farris, *Hymns*, pp. 115-16.

effects of his coming. As they stand, the verses could apply to events in Israel's history. That some scholars have proposed that the hymn, either whole or in part, could have come from non-Christian circles, even from the Maccabean wars,[36] only emphasizes the hymn's lack of Christian specificity. On the other hand, Luke's Christian readers (and he probably envisaged no others) knew how the story ended and therefore read into the hymn what is not explicitly stated.

Not only is there a lack of anything distinctively Christian in these verses, they also contain a rich mosaic of allusions to Israel's Scriptures. Creed[37] and others[38] have produced lists of such allusions and of these Isa. 41.8-9 is probably the most important in the present discussion.

> Israel my servant (παῖς μου), Jacob, whom I have chosen, offspring of Abraham (σπέρμα Αβρααμ), my friend; you whom I took (ἀντελαβόμην) from the ends of the earth (Isa. 41.8-9).
>
> He has helped his servant Israel (ἀντελάβετο Ἰσραὴλ παιδὸς αὐτοῦ)...as he spoke to Abraham and his posterity (τῷ Ἀβραὰμ καὶ τῷ σπέρματι αὐτοῦ) for ever (Lk. 1.54-55).

Hannah's song (1 Sam. 2.1-10) is thought by many commentators to be a model for the Magnificat and vv. 7-8 describe God's acts in very similar terms to Lk. 1.51-53, although in 1 Samuel the verbs are in the present tense. This is further evidence that Luke's aorists are intentionally chosen to look back to Israel's past, in this case to the birth of Samuel, the prophet and judge of Israel.

The Magnificat is an excellent example of Luke's deliberate use of ambivalence to make two related points. The aorists direct the readers to God's past help for Israel and the form of the hymn alludes to Samuel. But it is the context of the hymn, rather than the content, that tells us that Israel's new prophet and judge is about to be born, one who will fulfil the promises to Abraham and hence show God's constancy towards his people.

The Benedictus

Whatever problems there might be with the Benedictus, one thing is quite clear, that the overriding concern of the hymn is the salvation of

---

36. Winter, 'Magnificat and Benedictus—Maccabean Psalms?'
37. Creed, *St Luke*, pp. 303-304.
38. Brown, *Birth*, pp. 358-60.

1. *Israel in the Infancy Narratives* 37

Israel. This salvation is spoken about in both past and future tenses, a device that again underlines the continuity of God's actions in Luke's eyes. The agents of God's work are Jesus, who is the horn of salvation in the house of David (1.69), and John, a prophet of the Most High who will give knowledge of salvation to the people (1.76-77). Neither child is mentioned by name and, once again, the benefits are described in general terms. Like the Magnificat, the Benedictus is a mosaic of ideas and reminiscences of the LXX as a glance at the margin of N–A[26] will show. Creed's table of OT echoes[39] shows not only the range of quotations but also how deeply Luke has assimilated ideas from different contexts. The strength of Luke's concern for Israel's salvation is also shown in the range of synonyms for salvation and Israel, all in a comparatively short space.

1.68	λύτρωσιν	1.68	Ἰσραήλ
1.68, 78	ἐπισκέπτομαι	1.69	ἐν οἴκῳ Δαυίδ
1.69, 77	σωτηρίας	1.73	πατέρα ἡμῶν [Ἀβραάμ]
1.74	ῥυσθέντας	1.77	τῷ λαῷ αὐτοῦ

Luke's commentators correctly take the house of David (1.69) to be the people of God (cf. Isa. 7.2, 13; Jer. 21.12; Zech. 12.7-12) but the term can also refer to the temple as in Neh. 12.37.

There are a number of LXX texts which, between them, connect the horn (κέρας) with salvation, God's anointed, the house of Israel and with David.[40] Luke is the only NT writer who uses κέρας in a way which seems to be an amalgam of these ideas yet without appearing to fix upon one particular text. That the horn continued to be a symbol of salvation in Jewish expectations during the first century is shown by no. 15 of the Eighteen Benedictions, 'Cause the shoot of David to shoot forth quickly, and raise up his horn by thy salvation'.[41] One further aspect of the horn of salvation is that a man could cling to the horns of the altar and claim sanctuary (1 Kgs 1.49-53). In view of the importance of the temple in Luke 1–2 and the ambiguity of the phrase 'house of

---

39. Creed, *St Luke*, pp. 305-306. Ringgren, 'Luke's Use of the Old Testament', pp. 230-32.
40. κέρας χριστοῦ αὐτοῦ (1 Sam. 2.10).
  κέρας σωτηρίας μου (2 Sam. 22.3 = Ps. 17.3).
  κέρας τῷ Δαυιδ (Ps. 131.17).
  κέρας παντὶ τῷ οἴκῳ Ισραηλ (Ezek. 29.21).
41. Marshall, *Luke*, p. 91. For the text of *Shemoneh 'Esreh* 15, see Schürer–Vermes, *History*, II, p. 458; Vermes, *Jesus the Jew*, pp. 131-32.

David' this aspect should not be ignored in the thinking behind 1.69.

The opening line of the Benedictus is almost identical to 1 Kgs 1.48 and the second line is closely related to Ps. 110.9 (LXX), and there may be a further reference to the psalm in 1.72.

Lk. 1.68   ὅτι ἐπεσκέψατο καὶ ἐποίησεν λύτρωσιν τῷ λαῷ αὐτοῦ
Ps. 110.9 λύτρωσιν ἀπέστειλεν τῷ λαῷ αὐτοῦ
Lk. 1.72   μνησθῆναι διαθήκης ἁγίας αὐτοῦ
Ps. 110.5 μνησθήσεται εἰς τὸν αἰῶνα διαθήκης αὐτοῦ

The allusions to 1 Kgs 1.48 (a son to sit on David's throne) and to Psalm 110 are not in the class of 'prophecy–fulfilment' citations but reminders of past examples of God's salvation of Israel. Once more we detect Luke taking a backward glance to Israel's past while speaking of the present.

For Luke, redemption (λύτρωσις, 1.68; 2.38) has special characteristics that bring out his concern for Israel. λύτρωσις and its cognates are part of the LXX vocabulary of God's redemption, the verb λυτρόομαι principally translates *g'l* and *pdh* and it occurs about a hundred times. In addition to Psalm 110 (above) there are instances in Ps. 129.7, 'O Israel, hope in the Lord...with him is plenteous redemption', and in Isa. 63.4, '...a year of redemption has come'. The only two occurrences of λυτρωτής (Acts 7.35) in the LXX are in Pss. 18.15 and 77.35; in both cases God is the redeemer. What is particularly significant is that on the four occasions when Luke uses these words they always refer to 'Israel', never to Christians or Gentiles (Lk. 1.68; 2.38; 24.21; Acts 7.35).

Similarly, ἐπισκέπτομαι is a part of Israel's salvation vocabulary and it is used several times in the LXX to describe God's visitation of Israel with his care and watchfulness, notably Gen. 50.24; Exod. 4.31; Ruth 1.6 and Sir. 46.14. Luke uses the verb at the beginning and the end of the Benedictus and, in the second instance, the subject of the verb is ἀνατολὴ ἐξ ὕψους. In 1.78 there are two problems about which opinions remained divided. The first problem is whether the tense of the verb is aorist (ℵ² A C D) or future (𝔓⁴ ℵ* B and some versions). Brown,[42] Farris[43] and Evans, with reservations,[44] take the aorist on the grounds that it is the more difficult reading, but Fitzmyer[45] and Creed[46]

---

42. Brown, *Birth*, p. 373.
43. Farris, *Hymns*, p. 128 and references given there.
44. Evans, *Saint Luke*, p. 187, describes the problem as insoluble.
45. Fitzmyer, *Luke*, p. 388.
46. Creed, *St Luke*, p. 27.

prefer the future tense because there is a shift to an eschatological emphasis at the conclusion of the hymn. The future reading is also preferred by N–A[26] and the UBS text. However, part of the evidence for assessing the tense depends upon the solution to the second problem, the meaning of ἀνατολή. There are two main possibilities for the meaning: the first is 'rising star' or 'dawn' and the second is 'shoot' or 'branch'. Farris rightly regards the ἀνατολή as a person from God (ἐξ ὕψους) but his opinion that it may translate ṣmḥ (shoot) needs the caveat that of some 160 instances of ἀνατολή in the LXX only five translate ṣmḥ.[47] Three of these cases are, however, certainly important since they refer to the Davidic heir (Jer. 23.5; Zech. 3.8; 6.12). Of these, Fitzmyer favours a messianic interpretation based on the Davidic son in Zechariah and which is also found in the Qumran literature.[48] 4Q174, which Vermes dates in the first century BCE, has

> He is the Branch of David who shall arise with the Interpreter of the Law [to rule] in Zion [at the end] of time. As it is written, I will raise up the tent of David that is fallen (Amos ix.xi). That is to say, the fallen tent of David is he who shall arise to save Israel.[49]

Apart from the improbability that Luke was familiar with the Qumran style of interpretation which has two 'anointeds' (the Branch of David and the Interpreter of the Law), Luke has a very different understanding of Amos 9.11. Whereas Qumran gives the verse a messianic meaning, Luke takes it to refer to the incoming Gentiles (Acts 15.16-17). Neither in 4Q174, nor in the messianic anthology 4Q175, is there a citation of Zech. 3.8, 6.12 or Jer. 23.5. In 4Q161, Isa. 11.1-3 is taken to refer to the Branch of David who will arise at the end-time but ἀνατολή is absent from the LXX version of the Isaiah verses.

The second possibility, that of 'light' imagery suggested by dawn or the rising star, has much to commend it since he (or it ?) is to appear to those in darkness and the shadow of death (1.79). Support for this interpretation also comes from the frequent use of ἀνατολή in the LXX to mean 'sunrise', and Isaiah has a theme in which the verb ἀνατέλλω describes God's restoration and the newness of his activity.[50] A good example of this use, and one which is appropriate to Luke's way of thinking, is Isa. 60.1:

47. Farris, *Hymns*, p. 140.
48. Fitzmyer, *Luke*, p. 387.
49. Vermes, *The Dead Sea Scrolls in English*, pp. 293-94.
50. Isa. 42.9; 43.19; 44.4, 26; 45.8; 58.8, 10, 11; 60.1; 61.11; 66.14.

Arise, shine; for your light has come, and the glory of the Lord has risen (ἀνατέταλκεν) upon you.

Elsewhere in the NT the clearest connection between Christ and the dawning (ἀνατείλῃ) of the morning star is in 2 Pet. 1.19. The evidence therefore seems to favour the meaning of 'morning star' for ἀνατολή and to indicate that it refers to Jesus. Although Davidic descent is obviously important to Luke, it may be that we have here another example of his deliberate ambivalence. In view of this meaning, the future tense ἐπισκέψεται seems the better reading. Before leaving this question, however, we should note that a similar conflation of the images of light and branch may also exist in Matthew's Gospel. In Mt. 2.23, Jesus is described as the fulfilment of the prophets' saying, 'he shall be called a Nazarene'. Benedict Green notes[51] that Nazarene is a play on the Hebrew *neṣer* (branch) and that the reference is to Isa. 11.1; Jer. 23.5; 33.15 (MT) and Zech. 3.8; 6.12. He further suggests that Mt. 2.23 points toward 4.15-16 where there is a quotation from Isa. 9.1:

> for those who sat in the region and shadow of death light has dawned.

This verse also lies behind Lk. 1.79 and, what is particularly noteworthy for the present discussion, Matthew changes λάμψει in Isa. 9.1 to ἀνέτειλεν.

In the Benedictus, salvation (σωτηρία, 1.69, 71) is 'for us' and 'from our enemies', which in this context can only mean salvation for Israel. A comparison of Lk. 1.71 and 74 with Ps. 17.18 suggests that this verse may have been in Luke's mind, in spite of σωτηρία not occurring in the psalm.

Ps. 17.18   ῥύσεταί με ἐξ ἐχθρῶν μου δυνατῶν
            καὶ ἐκ τῶν μισούντων με
Lk. 1.71   σωτηρίαν ἐξ ἐχθρῶν ἡμῶν καὶ ἐκ χειρὸς
            πάντων τῶν μισούντων ἡμᾶς
Lk. 1.74   ἐκ χειρὸς ἐχθρῶν ῥυσθέντας

In Luke–Acts, σωτηρία and its cognates are used in a similar way to that which we have noticed with λύτρωσις in that they occur predominantly where members of Israel are concerned. σωτηρία[52] appears

---

51. Green, *Matthew*, pp. 60-61.
52. Throckmorton, 'Σώζειν, σωτηρία in Luke–Acts', pp. 515-26, provides a valuable analysis of salvation in Luke–Acts but he does not note that it is directed predominantly to Israel. σωτηρία occurs in Lk. 1.69, 71, 77; 19.9; Acts 4.12; 7.25; 13.26, 47; 16.17; 27.34.

nine times and, apart from Acts 27.34, where the emphasis is on physical survival, it is applied to Gentiles at Acts 16.17 only. Of the three instances of σωτήριον,[53] only one refers to Gentiles, and that is in a speech to a Jewish audience (Acts 28.28). As to σωτήρ,[54] be he God or Jesus, the beneficiaries are Mary (1.47), the shepherds (2.11) and Israel (Acts 5.31; 13.23).

At 1.76 the focus of the Benedictus moves to John, a prophet of the Most High, who will go before the Lord to prepare his ways. Most commentators regard the contrast between John as prophet and Jesus as son of the Most High as showing John's subsidiary role. It is also thought to show that John belongs to the period of Israel[55] but the contrast needs to be accepted with some caution. Not only does Luke present Jesus as a prophet (Chapter 4 below) but, alone among the evangelists, he also describes John as preaching good news (3.18).

The identity of the Lord (1.76) continues to be a matter of debate. Marshall leaves the question open[56] but Fitzmyer[57] and Farris[58] identify the Lord as Jesus. This is partly because Christians regarded John as the precursor of Jesus and partly because, in 1.43, Elizabeth describes Mary as 'the mother of my Lord'. Schneider[59] and Evans[60] take the Lord to be God. While it is clear that Matthew and, very probably, Mark saw John as the forerunner of Jesus, there is some doubt as to whether Luke regarded John in quite the same way. J.A.T. Robinson has argued that there was a primitive Christology in which Jesus was the expected prophet who was 'indeed to be Christ. *But he was Elijah first.*'[61] Robinson points to the role of Elijah as pictured in Mal. 3.23 and Sir. 48.10 and shows that this is how Jesus is sometimes portrayed by Luke

---

53. Σωτήριον, Lk. 2.30; 3.6; Acts 28.28.
54. Σωτήρ, Lk. 1.47; 2.11; Acts 5.31; 13.23. Danker, *Jesus and the New Age*, p. 58, notes the widespread use of the term in Hellenistic circles and this makes Luke's use of the word in a Jewish context all the more surprising. Although σώζειν does not occur in the birth stories, the large majority of cases in Luke–Acts show the same Israel-directed use. Of thirty instances only six involve Gentiles: Acts 11.14; 14.9; 16.30, 31; 27.20, 31.
55. Oliver, 'Luke's Use of the Birth Stories', p. 217.
56. Marshall, *Luke*, p. 93.
57. Fitzmyer, *Luke*, pp. 385-86.
58. Farris, *Hymns*, p. 139.
59. Schneider, *Lukas*, p. 62.
60. Evans, *Saint Luke*, p. 186, points to the parallel with John in Lk. 1.16-17.
61. Robinson, 'Elijah, John and Jesus', pp. 46-47.

as, for example, in Acts 3. We have already discussed the evidence in the birth stories for this view.

There is no doubt that John's role as a prophet prepares the way for the ministry of Jesus, but both prophet and son of the Most High work within God's plan for the salvation of Israel. That John is to prepare the way for God (the Lord) is suggested by the similarity between Lk. 1.76 and Isa. 40.3, a verse that Luke quotes more extensively at 3.4-6 in describing John's work.

> Lk. 1.76 προπορεύσῃ γὰρ ἐνώπιον κυρίου ἑτοιμάσαι ὁδοὺς αὐτοῦ
> Isa. 40.3 ἑτοιμάσατε τὴν ὁδὸν κυρίου

This work is to give knowledge of salvation to God's people. Further evidence that Luke sees John as God's prophet rather than simply the forerunner of Jesus is shown by the introduction to John's ministry in the style of an OT prophet, '...the word of God came to John the son of Zechariah' (Lk. 3.2, cf. Ezek. 1.3; Hos. 1.1; Joel 1.1). This style is absent from Mk 1.4 and Mt. 3.1. Furthermore, John preaches to God's people Israel (1.77) and not just to the people of Judaea and Jerusalem, a point made clear by Luke's omission of Mk 1.5.[62]

Luke 2

In Luke 2 the attention is concentrated on Jesus and, to a lesser extent, on his family. The reader is twice reminded of the Davidic descent of Joseph (2.4) and of Christ the Lord (2.11). There is also a double reference to Bethlehem, the city of David (2.4, 15), and these, together with the story of the shepherds, all point to the Davidic role of Jesus. Bethlehem was the town of David's youth (1 Sam. 16.1-13) and the place where he was anointed king of Israel. The presence of the shepherds also calls to mind Mic. 5.1-3 (LXX).

> But you, O Bethlehem...from among the thousands of Judah, from you shall come forth for me one who is to be ruler of Israel...Therefore he shall give them up until she who is in travail has brought forth (τικτούσης τέξεται, cf. Lk. 2.6; 7.11); then the rest of his brothers shall return to the sons of Israel. And he shall stand and feed his flock (ποιμανεῖ τὸ ποίμνιον) in the strength of the Lord, in the majesty (δόξῃ) of the name of the Lord their God. And they shall dwell secure, for now he shall be great to the ends of the earth.

---

62. Conzelmann, *Luke*, p. 19, suggests that Judaea is too narrow a concept for Luke.

1. Israel in the Infancy Narratives 43

As with other possible allusions that we have noted, the verbal agreement between Lk. 2.8-20 and Mic. 5.1-3 is not strong enough to prove dependence, although Luke does use ποιμαίνω elsewhere in his writings and, in the NT, ποίμνιον is found only in Luke–Acts and 1 Peter. Similarly, μεγαλύνω (Mic. 5.3) is used of Mary (1.46, 58) and Jesus (Acts 19.17). Fitzmyer's judgment is that Luke undoubtedly knew the Micah passage and that 'it may well have figured in his thinking in depicting Jesus as a ruler born in shepherd country'.[63] Matthew also quotes the opening lines of Micah 5 as a proof-text for the birth of Jesus in Bethlehem and as a sign that he is to be ruler of Israel (Mt. 2.6). But Luke goes much further and uses hints of David's anointing; for example, David is shepherding his flock when Samuel arrives (τοιμαίνει ἐν τῷ ποιμνίῳ, 1 Sam. 16.11 cf. Mic. 5.3). Luke's story of the shepherds and their visit to Bethlehem thus draws together David's anointing and Micah's prophecy. This reinforces the idea that Jesus is the anointed king who will restore the nation. This restoration will be accomplished when 'she who is in travail has brought forth'. The return of the rest of the brethren to the sons of Israel (Mic. 5.3) becomes significant for Luke, as we shall see later, because Micah's oracles concern both Samaria and Jerusalem (Mic. 1.1)[64] and they look forward to the restoration of the unity that once existed under David. The one who will perform this restoration is the child born in the city of David, 'a saviour who is χριστὸς κύριος' (2.11). This term is unique in the NT, although in Acts 2.36, there is a similar anarthrous form, καὶ κύριον αὐτὸν καὶ χριστόν. Critics have been puzzled by the expression and a number of solutions have been offered. If we disregard those which involve amending the text,[65] then one possible meaning is 'who is an anointed Lord'. This would be similar in style to χριστὸν βασιλέα, an anointed king (23.2).[66] Luke's Gospel contains several editorial ascriptions of lordship to Jesus but in each case κύριος is accompanied by the article,[67] a usage that is a reading back to the earthly Jesus of a

63. Fitzmyer, *Luke*, pp. 395-96.
64. Winton Thomas, 'Micah', *Peake's Commentary*, p. 632.
65. Winter, 'Lukanische Miszellen', pp. 68, 75.
66. Evans, *Saint Luke*, pp. 205-206, suggests that 'Christ' could here be used as a personal name. See also, although not dealing specifically with Lk. 2.11, Harvey, *Constraints*, p. 81.
67. The uses of κύριος which do not occur in direct speech are assumed to be editorial in the Third Gospel, 7.13, 19; 10.1, 39; 12.42; 13.15; 17.5, 6; 18.6; 19.8; 22.61.

post-resurrection title (Acts 2.36). In the case of χριστός, however, the rest of the third Gospel contains a much more cautious approach than that taken in 2.11 and 2.26. The reason for Luke's reticence elsewhere in the Gospel is discussed in detail in Chapter 4; for the present we shall deal only with the use of χριστός in Luke 2.

The unusual phrase χριστὸς κύριος also occurs in pre-Christian Jewish literature, notably in *Pss. Sol.* 17.32 where most critics amend the text but, as R.B. Wright points out,[68] there is no manuscript evidence to support the change to χριστὸς κυρίου. There is, moreover, a similar state of affairs in *Pss. Sol.* 18.7 (anarthrous χριστοῦ κυρίου) as well as in the psalm's title (τοῦ χριστοῦ κυρίου). *Pss. Sol.* 17.21-43 describes the benefits of the coming king, the son of David who is 'to rule over your servant Israel in the time known to you' (17.21). In vv. 30-32 it is said that he will cleanse Jerusalem, that the nations will come up from the end of the earth to see his glory and that of the Lord, and that their king shall be χριστὸς κύριος. In 17.40 it is said that he will shepherd the Lord's flock (ποιμαίνων τὸ ποίμνιον κυρίου, cf. Mic. 5.3) in faith and righteousness.

There is certainly a great deal in *Pss. Sol.* 17–18 that would have appealed to Luke and which is in tune with his thinking at this stage of his narrative. Direct dependence is incapable of proof but there is enough evidence to suggest that Luke's use of χριστός in 2.11 is much more slanted towards the birth of an anointed king in David's city than to the more customary future Messiah that we find in Acts after the resurrection. What we can say with a fair measure of confidence is that there was a strong theme to be found in 1 Samuel, Micah and the *Psalms of Solomon* of an anointed shepherd king of Davidic character who was expected to rule over a restored Israel. This would have provided a fund of ideas on which Luke would have been able to draw without quoting chapter and verse but which would have been recognized by at least some of the Jewish Christians among his readers.

The kingly role is also implied by the outburst of praise by the host of heaven, 'Glory to God in the highest and on earth peace...' (2.14). This is taken up at the entry to Jerusalem in the shout of the disciples, 'Peace

---

68. Wright, 'The Psalms of Solomon', *OTP*, II, pp. 667-70. But in 17.32 and 18.7, Wright adds the definite article which is not present in the Greek text. This is translated as 'The Lord Messiah'. Vermes, *Jesus the Jew*, pp. 130-31, believes that the Psalms of Solomon are an important guide to Jewish messianic thinking. Also see Jones, 'Christos', pp. 75-76, and Drury, *Tradition*, p. 55.

in heaven and glory in the highest', which is preceded by 'Blessed be the king who comes in the name of the Lord' (19.38). Yet the city did not know what makes for peace because it did not know the time of its visitation (ἐπισκοπῆς, 19.44; cf. 1.68). Luke also connects the birth of Jesus with the story of his entry to Jerusalem when he relates that, after each incident, Jesus enters the temple (2.27; 19.45).

It is, in fact, the temple that provides the setting for almost all of the remainder of the chapter with two scenes twelve years apart. In the first of these, Simeon's oracles show that Jesus is the fulfilment of his hopes for Israel (2.29-32). He has been looking for the consolation of Israel and has been promised that he would see the Lord's anointed before he dies. By seeing Jesus, Simeon now knows that God's promise to him has been confirmed and this means that the readers should also expect that the promise to Abraham (1.72-75) will be secure. There is, possibly, a further hint of Luke's purpose in his description of Simeon. Consolation (παράκλησιν, 2.25) is not common in the LXX but in Jer. 38(31).9 it is used of God's bringing back Ephraim, one of the northern tribes which the Samaritans claimed as their forebears.

> With weeping they shall come, and with
> consolations I will lead them back,
> ...for I am a father to Israel,
> and Ephraim is my first born.

If Luke knew of this passage and had it in mind then it would provide the first indication that the restoration would not be restricted to the tribe of Judah but would entail an Israel in its Davidic unity.

Until this point in the narrative there have been no restrictions or qualifications placed upon God's salvation of Israel. It is Simeon who now breaks that pattern in two ways. In 2.32 he speaks of a light of revelation to the Gentiles for the glory of Israel and this is the first clear indication by Luke that people other than Israel will be involved in God's plan. Evans expresses some surprise that, in 2.33, Mary and Joseph marvel at what Simeon has said because it contains nothing that they did not already know.[69] But the fact that their son should be a revelation to those outside Israel is as new to them as it is to the reader, because until this point in the narrative salvation has been spoken about as if it were for members of Israel alone.

Simeon's second qualification is that not all Israel will accept Jesus as

---

69. Evans, *Saint Luke*, p. 211.

the Lord's anointed so that he will cause falling as well as rising. This is another turning point, that the Anointed will have a divisive effect on Israel and that he will be a sign that will be opposed. Evans has drawn attention to the use of πτῶσις and πίπτω in the LXX where they are widely used to describe the judgment of the wicked.[70]

The final cameo of the infant Jesus in the temple is of Anna the prophetess who speaks to all who are looking for the redemption of Jerusalem. This reinforces the oracles of Simeon and, indeed, the theme of Israel's salvation. The Anna episode may contain reminiscences preserved among the Jerusalem Christian community and her character as a devout widow reflects the description of real widows in 1 Tim. 5.3-16 as those who have set their 'hope on God and continue[s] in supplications night and day' (1 Tim. 5.5, cf. Lk. 2.37-38). There may also be allusions to heroines of faith in the OT; Hannah (Αννα, LXX) the mother of Samuel,[71] and Judith, who like Anna lived to a great age (Judt. 16.23).[72] Recently Max Wilcox has suggested that Serah, the daughter of Joseph's brother Asher, might be another possible model for Anna.[73] Serah is described in a rabbinic midrash as being responsible for identifying Moses as the liberator of Israel. Wilcox suggests that Anna similarly identifies Jesus as the second Moses who will redeem Israel[74] although he does not claim to have proved such a connection. He does, however, think that Luke preserves 'a precious link in the chain of Jewish interpretation of Serah'[75] and that 'early Christian Bible exegesis was part and parcel of contemporary Jewish Bible exegesis'.[76] 'Exegesis' may overstate the present case about someone who is mentioned only as the daughter of Asher (Gen. 46.17; Num. 26.46; 1 Chron. 7.30) and the gap of seven centuries between Luke and the rabbinic account[77] further

---

70. Evans, *Saint Luke*, p. 218.
71. Marshall, *Luke*, p. 123.
72. Brown, *Birth*, pp. 467-68; Marshall, *Luke*, p. 124; Danker, *Jesus and the New Age*, p. 71. A number of commentators note the Jewish nature of the phrase 'night and day' in the description of Anna's practice of worship, i.e. the Jewish day beginning at sunset. Brown (p. 442) is uncertain of this interpretation and persists in quoting 'day and night' (p. 467).
73. Wilcox, 'Luke 2.36-38', pp. 1571-79.
74. Wilcox, 'Luke 2.36-38, pp. 1575-77.
75. Wilcox, 'Luke 2.36-38', p. 1577.
76. Wilcox, 'Luke 2.36-38', p. 1579.
77. *Pirqe de R. Eliezer* 48.82-84. Schürer–Vermes, *History*, I, p. 98, dates the composition as the eighth century CE at the earliest.

1. *Israel in the Infancy Narratives*   47

stretches the credibility of contemporary exegesis. Nevertheless, each of these suggestions for possible models alerts the reader to aspects of Anna that Luke may develop later.

Anna was a member of the tribe of Asher, one of the northern tribes, and Jeremias notes that claims to belong to one of the ten or nine-and-a-half lost tribes are very rare.[78] Luke's pointer to the northern tribes is further hinted by the name of Anna's father, Phanuel.[79] Two men of that name are mentioned in the OT but they come from the southern tribes of Judah (1 Chron. 4.4) and Benjamin (1 Chron. 8.25). But, as a place-name, Penuel/Phanuel is a northern town mentioned in conjunction with Shechem (1 Kgs 12.25), later to become the Samaritan centre. There is one further possible northern allusion; the A-text of Exod. 6.24 has Ασηρ as a variant reading and this corresponds to the Samaritan Pentateuch.[80] As we shall see in Chapter 3, the inclusion of the Samaritans as the descendants of the northern tribes is, for Luke, an indispensable element in the restoration of Israel. Anna's acknowledgment of Jesus as the redeemer of Jerusalem, the city of David (1 Chron. 11.5, 7), is a further indication that Luke himself hopes for the Davidic unity of Israel. In this sense Luke's stress on the fundamental importance of Jerusalem is not to be taken as in conflict with his Samaritan concern.

The final part of Luke's prologue is the account of the twelve-year-old Jesus in the temple and this completes the cycle that began with Zechariah in the temple. We shall leave aside questions of genre and possible sources and focus on the purpose of the story in Luke's overall scheme. The incident is framed by two sayings about the wisdom of Jesus (σοφία, 2.40, 52) and it is Jesus' understanding (συνέσει, 2.47) that amazes his hearers. This is sharp contrast with his parents' lack of understanding (οὐ συνῆκαν, 2.50). Although Luke uses the corresponding verb συνίημι on a number of occasions, this is his only use of σύνεσις. We have already noted that parts of *Pss. Sol.* 17 may have been influential in the story of the announcement to the shepherds and, in *Pss. Sol.* 17.37, the anointed Lord will be powerful in the Holy Spirit and wise in the counsel of understanding (σοφὸν ἐν βουλῇ συνέσεως). Furthermore, in Isa. 11.2, σοφία and σύνεσις are two of the spiritual

---

78. Jeremias, *Jerusalem in the Time of Jesus*, p. 278.

79. In view of Luke's emphasis on the importance of repentance it should be noted that, in *1 Enoch* 40.9, Phanuel is the angel set over all acts of repentance in hope of eternal life.

80. Hatch and Redpath, *Concordance*, II, Suppl. p. 24.

gifts that will characterize the Branch from the root of Jesse, the ideal Davidic king. It may be that Luke is not only telling a story about Jesus' wisdom but is also reinforcing the Christological point in 2.11. The incident also looks ahead to his last Passover when Jesus teaches in the temple, is 'lost', is found on the third day, and then goes to his Father (24.51).

Conclusion

I have discussed the infancy stories with the limited objective of examining how Luke introduces his readers to his view of the destiny of Israel. In the narrative it is Israel, above all, that is the recipient of God's salvation even although Luke recognizes that the coming of Jesus will have a divisive effect. In his essay 'The Divided People of God', Jervell, rather curiously, does not mention Simeon's prophecy. Through this Luke prepares his readers for the division which begins in Jesus' ministry and continues in Acts. In this, Jesus is like all the major Hebrew prophets; not one of them failed to arouse opposition to God's message. But Jesus is not only a prophet, he is the Lord's Anointed, the shepherd king of David's line who will rule over the restored Israel. In the birth stories it is John who is designated the prophet and, as Luke will later show, his fate will be the forerunner of that of the prophetic son (9.9; 13.33).

Luke's stress on the continuity between what is now taking place and what God has done for Israel in the past is central to his message. He brings out the continuity in a number of ways: by the use of a septuagintal style of writing, by his ambiguous use of aorists in the canticles and by portraying members of Israel as impeccable and filled with the Holy Spirit. In addition to these devices there is the multitude of allusions to the LXX and the importance of the temple. It is the temple that is the place of revelation to Zechariah and to Jesus' parents and it is the place where Jesus' wisdom is revealed. Temple sacrifices are mentioned in the first two incidents and they are implied in the third incident at Passover. There is only a slight possible hint of any criticism of the temple in the opening chapters.[81]

It could be argued that Luke is simply retelling events that once happened but the narrative is far too rich in allusion and its implications

---

81. The distinction between ἱερόν and ναός in Luke's writing is discussed in Chapter 2.

1. *Israel in the Infancy Narratives* 49

for the remainder of his work for this to be so. He has written a prologue in which God's coming salvation of Israel is emphatically established and, given the forcefulness of this introduction, it would be extremely surprising if that message were directed to a readership that was largely Gentile.

Such a view of Israel's destiny, even when we take into account the incoming Gentiles, casts severe doubt on a three-fold division of salvation history. Moreover, it would be almost beyond belief if the theme of Israel's salvation ceased to be a dominant concern for Luke or that the promises and prophecies in the birth stories should end in failure.[82]

---

82. A number of recent opinions agree that Luke's infancy stories show his genuine concern for Israel's salvation but they make different assessments as to whether this concern and hope are maintained to the end of Acts. Tannehill, 'Tragic Story', acknowledges that Simeon's statements about the Gentiles and division are brief compared with those which refer to the salvation of Israel (pp. 71-72). Although the promise is made on the highest authority of Gabriel and the OT, Tannehill argues that the rest of Luke–Acts, culminating in the end of Acts, is a tragic story. He rejects J.T. Sanders's charge that Luke was anti-Semitic although the final speech to the Roman Jews 'cannot represent a satisfying end for the author of Luke–Acts' (p. 82). The fulfilment of Isa. 6.9-10 'means that the "hope of Israel" is not being fulfilled'.

While agreeing that there is a tragic theme in Jewish rejection of the gospel I shall try to show that the final restoration of Israel is not within the time-span of Luke–Acts, any more than the ingathering of the Gentiles. Both will be completed when the Messiah comes at a time known only to the Father. I also reach a different, and more hopeful, conclusion about the end of Acts (Chapter 7 below).

Tiede, '"Glory to Thy People Israel"', concludes that the process of Israel's restoration 'has only begun to be inaugurated in the present time of Luke's story' (p. 34). See also Moessner, 'Ironic Fulfillment'.

Chapter 2

STEPHEN'S SPEECH AND ISRAEL'S PAST

We have seen that Luke 1–2 demonstrates beyond doubt the author's concern with God's redemption and salvation of Israel and that the life work of both John and Jesus will be directed towards this objective. These ideas can conveniently be brought together in that of restoration, a term that suggests a return to some past state from which there has been a falling away. The verb that Luke uses for restoration in the context of Israel is ἀποκαθίστημι (Acts 1.6, cf. 3.19-21) and, in the LXX, this predominantly translates *šûb*. In Jeremiah, for example, the verbs are used of the restoration of Israel, either in the sense of returning to God (15.19) or of returning from captivity (16.15; 27[50].19). Just how Luke saw this earlier condition of Israel to which it would be restored is a question of the nation's history and, about this, Luke does not disappoint his readers. Luke's presentation of Israel's past is therefore a major component in helping his readers to understand what the coming restoration will entail. By far the most extensive review of Israel's history in the NT is contained in Stephen's speech (Acts 7) which is the longest speech in Luke's writings, amounting to some six per cent of Acts. In his selection of events and personalities, Luke tells us a great deal about his understanding of Israel. But although the speech itself deals with Israel's history, the incidents that precede and give rise to it are important for the light they throw on Luke's view of the law and the temple. Since these were the pillars of Judaism in the time of the narrative we must examine the implications of the incidents before turning to the history within the speech.

It is not only the more casual reader who has found the historical section of the speech (7.2-50) to be something of a curiosity; scholars too have come to widely differing views of its importance. Foakes-Jackson regards this section as an intrusion into the account of Stephen's martyrdom and, in his commentary, follows Acts 6.15 with 7.51.[1] What

---

1. Foakes-Jackson, *Acts of the Apostles*, pp. 56-69, and 'Stephen's Speech

Foakes-Jackson fails to see is that it is *because* it interrupts the narrative flow that we have to take the historical section as a vital part of Luke's purpose. For Dibelius, the most striking feature of the speech is the irrelevance of the main section 'as a defence against the charges facing Stephen'.[2] Instead, Dibelius sees the speech as inaugurating the section Acts 6–12 which portrays the progress of the gospel to the Gentiles. In Haenchen's opinion 7.2-46 'is simply sacred history told for its own sake and with no other theme'.[3] But it is very doubtful whether anyone tells sacred history just for its own sake, least of all Luke, whose two-volume work is a form of sacred history in its own right. There are, of course, many scholars who take a much more positive view of the speech and we shall examine these in due course. However, by way of preamble, it may help if we draw attention to Stephen's character because the qualities of the speaker give us a valuable insight into the importance that Luke attaches to the speech.

Stephen is a man full of the Holy Spirit (6.5), full of grace and power (6.8) and was one of those chosen because they were full of the Spirit and wisdom (6.3). In addition to these qualities he was able to perform great signs and wonders (6.8) and, at his trial, he had the face of an angel (6.15). All of these descriptions prepare the reader for the speech of a quite exceptional man who spoke with such spirit and wisdom that his opponents were unable to withstand him (6.10). Not only is Stephen more richly endowed with gifts than anyone else in Luke–Acts with the exception of Jesus, but the story also ends with a vision which is granted to no other person in the NT, that of Jesus as the heavenly Son of Man standing at the right hand of God. These facts alone should convince us of the tremendous importance that Luke attaches to the speech and that it is not just a selection of events from Israel's past which are recited for no other purpose.

Sources and Historicity of the Speech

In an extensive study of Stephen and the speech attributed to him, Scharlemann has surveyed the range of views about the possible sources of the speech and its reliability as historical reporting.[4] At one extreme

in Acts'; Trocmé, *Actes et l'histoire*, pp. 212-13.
2. Dibelius, *Studies*, p. 169. There is a similar view in Conzelmann, *Acts*, pp. 57-58.
3. Haenchen, *Acts*, p. 288.
4. Scharlemann, *Stephen*, chs. II–IV.

stands the opinion of Zahn: that Saul was present at Stephen's trial and that he provided a verbatim report of what Stephen said.[5] At the other end of the spectrum stands Cadbury's opinion that the speech is a free composition of the author,[6] a view shared by Stählin.[7] This view has been rejected by Wilkens in the third edition of his *Missionsreden der Apostelgeschichte*, suggesting a pre-Lukan source.[8] This has provoked Sabbe's comment, 'do we really need this unknown authorship and this hardly identifiable Stephen tradition? Could not this unknown Christian be Luke himself, the author of Acts?'[9] Lukan authorship has also been supported by Kilgallen on the evidence of vocabulary and style.[10]

Scharlemann's own position in this debate is on the conservative side and his discussion exposes some of the weaknesses of that position. He adapts an idea which Gerhardsson applied to the synoptic Gospels, that of the 'holy word' of Jesus which would have acted as a powerful force in the continuing oral tradition of the church.[11] It is Scharlemann's belief that the holy word which lies behind Stephen's speech is the saying in Jn 2.19, 'Destroy this temple, and in three days I will raise it up'.[12] The difficulty with this suggestion is that not only are Stephen's accusers described as false witnesses but also any condemnation of the temple which might be present occupies a very small part of the speech (7.47-50, cf. 6.13). Moreover, in Jn 2.19 it is the Jews themselves who are challenged to destroy the temple which is the body of Jesus (Jn 2.21).

Since the bulk of the speech is a selective outline of Israel's history it is difficult to see why Luke, with his deep knowledge of the OT, should have needed any other source, whether written or oral. The obvious importance of the events he relates is such that most well instructed Christians, particularly those of Jewish origin, would have been familiar with them. The important question is that of the basis on which Luke made his selection for, even if he used a source which contained the selection, Luke clearly approved of it. In view of the necessarily

5. Zahn, *Apostelgeschichte*, p. 246.
6. Cadbury, 'The Speeches in Acts', *Beginnings*, V, pp. 409-10, 'the voice is the voice of Luke'.
7. Stählin, *Apostelgeschichte*, p. 112.
8. Wilkens, *Die Missionsrede*, pp. 208-209, 219.
9. Sabbe, 'The Son of Man Saying in Acts 7.56', p. 247.
10. Kilgallen, *The Stephen Speech*.
11. Gerhardsson, *Memory and Manuscript*, pp. 214-24, 229-306, but he does not deal with Stephen's speech.
12. Scharlemann, *Stephen*, pp. 30-31.

speculative nature of the possible sources, we shall be on firmer ground if we take the speech as it stands and leave the question of sources until such time as more secure evidence is available. I have assumed for this discussion that the speech undoubtedly expresses a key element in Luke's overall purpose. Some of the views contained in the speech, notably those which appear to attack the temple, have been taken to conflict with opinions that Luke expresses elsewhere[13] but, as I shall try to show, this conflict is more apparent than real.

The Occasion of the Speech

The outline of Israel's history is preceded by accounts of two disputes, both of which involve Stephen. The first of these is between Hebrew and Hellenist Christians (6.1-6) and this is followed by the conflict between Stephen himself and some Jews (6.8-14). The first incident is relevant to the present discussion because it not only introduces Stephen to the reader but also because it shows that divisions between Christians can be overcome. This would have been particularly important for Luke's readers if, as will become clear, unity among Christians as well as the unity of Israel was a major Lukan concern.

The dispute between Hebrews and Hellenists over the daily distribution (ἐν τῇ διακονίᾳ, 6.1) to the Hellenist widows is the immediate cause of the appointment of the seven. This had been the responsibility of the twelve (6.2) but they saw their function as the ministry of the word (τῇ διακονίᾳ τοῦ λόγου, 6.4). Until this point in the narrative Luke has stressed the unity and common welfare of the Jerusalem church (2.45-46; 4.32, 34-37) so that the dispute comes as a surprise to the reader.[14] Yet there is a further surprise in the brevity of Luke's account and the proposed remedy, that seven exemplary men should be appointed to serve at tables, is hardly a solution since the only two who are mentioned again act as evangelists (6.10; 8.4-10, 26-40; cf. 21.8).

It is because Luke says tantalizingly little about the dispute that a great deal of scholarly effort has been spent in trying to supplement the sparseness of his account.[15] Who were the Hebrews and Hellenists and, more importantly, did Stephen belong to either group? The NT provides

---

13. E.g. Maddox, *Purpose*, pp. 52-54.
14. Esler, *Community and Gospel*, p. 136.
15. Mann, 'Hellenists and Hebrews in Acts VI', pp. 301-304; Wilson, *Gentile Mission*, pp. 138-42.

us with little help in our attempt to answer these questions. Luke does not use Ἑβραῖος again, and when he refers to the language spoken by Jews he uses Ἑβραΐδι διαλέκτῳ (Acts 21.40; 22.2; 26.14). Elsewhere in the NT Ἑβραῖος is used by Paul to describe his own ethnic and religious background (2 Cor. 11.22; Phil. 3.5). Ἑλληνιστής occurs twice more in the NT, one nstance being a variant reading (Acts 11.20). In the other case (Acts 9.29) the Hellenists are almost certainly Jews since they wish to kill Paul, although it is possible that the term refers to pagans.[16] Lake and Cadbury consider that the Hellenists in 6.1 may mean Greek-speaking Jews but that this interpretation has to be derived from the context because the parent verb ἑλληνίζω means 'to Graecize' by speech or custom. They also note that Ἑβραῖος elsewhere appears to refer to race and not to speech since Philo, like Paul, also refers to himself as Ἑβραῖος although both were Greek speakers. This leads Lake and Cadbury to suggest that the difference between the two groups in Acts 6 is between Graecizing and more conservative Jews. They also add the important caveat, which others have not always observed, that although the meaning must be derived from the context, 'the context [Acts 6] is not clear enough to serve'.[17]

In a recent re-examination of the first dispute, Esler comes to the conclusion that the traditional explanation is correct: that the Hellenists were Greek-speaking Jews and that the Hebrews were Aramaic-speaking.[18] In this he agrees with, and partly depends upon, the view of Hengel.[19] As far as language difference is concerned we may well agree with Esler that the identities of the two groups have been established. But this does not take us far enough because the groups were divided on points of doctrine and we have no way of discovering what the differences were.

Because Stephen was involved in both disputes there has been a tendency to carry over understandings of Hebrew and Hellenist when

16. Lake and Cadbury, *Beginnings*, IV, p. 106, commenting on Acts 9.29.
17. Lake and Cadbury, *Beginnings*, IV, p. 64. Moule, 'Once More, Who were the Hellenists?', suggests that the Hellenists were Jews who spoke only Greek and that the Hebrews were able to speak Greek and a Semitic language.
18. Esler, *Community and Gospel*, pp. 136-39, notes that ἑλληνίζειν means 'to speak Greek (perfectly)' (p. 138). Esler also questions Simon's view that diaspora Jews were more lax than Palestinian Jews in their attitudes towards the law and the temple.
19. Hengel, 'Between Jesus and Paul', p. 6.

2. Stephen's Speech and Israel's Past

trying to discover the historical facts about his accusers.[20] Simon concludes that the Hellenists were not only Greek-speaking but also that they were regarded by more orthodox Jews as paganizing.[21] This view, that the Greek-speaking Jews of the diaspora were less orthodox or more lax in their attitude towards the law and the temple, has been challenged by Esler.[22] Stephen's accusers were from the synagogue of Freedmen as well as from the diaspora (6.9) and the latter would almost certainly be Greek speakers. If Esler is correct then there would be no reason to doubt their orthodoxy,[23] and the charges against Stephen support this view (6.13-14).

Hengel has suggested that the Christian Hellenists who were expelled from Jerusalem had put forward the offensive claim that Jesus, as Messiah, had superseded Moses and that the gospel had taken the place of the Exodus and Sinai.[24] But there is little, if any, evidence of this in Acts and, if the speeches of Peter are a fair representation of the preaching of Hebrew Christians (2.22-24; 3.12-15), then it is clear that they too angered the Jewish leaders (4.1-12; 5.27-32). There is also some degree of uncertainty as to whether only Hellenists were scattered (8.1). Luke's statement that only the apostles remained might refer to Aramaic-speaking Christians,[25] and Acts 21.20 would seem to suggest that this was the case, but that only the church leaders were allowed to stay while the ordinary members were expelled is politically very improbable.[26]

As far as the first dispute is concerned, it is possible that Luke's readers had enough additional information to enable them to understand his account. The salient facts are that the dispute was about table fellowship and that it was quickly resolved by the whole church acting in unity (6.5). Esler has demonstrated that table fellowship among groups from different backgrounds was a major issue for Luke's readership,[27] but his

---

20. Simon, *St Stephen*, pp. 84-86, thinks that Stephen goes further than the OT prophets in condemning the temple and that he is influenced by diaspora Judaism.
21. Simon, *St Stephen*, pp. 12-19.
22. Esler, *Community and Gospel*, pp. 138, 145-48.
23. Simon, *St Stephen*, p. 13, acknowledges the orthodoxy of Stephen's opponents.
24. Hengel, *Earliest Christianity*, pp. 72-73.
25. Hengel, *Earliest Christianity*, pp. 74-75.
26. Simon, *St Stephen*, p. 27; also Esler, *Community and Gospel*, p. 139.
27. Esler, *Community and Gospel*, pp. 71-109.

opinion that Luke's church adhered to Hellenist traditions[28] cannot be supported because we do not know what those traditions were.

The Charges against Stephen

The accusations brought against Stephen are the direct result of his preaching, about which Luke provides no details. The charges are:

1. he spoke 'blasphemous words against Moses and God' (6.11),
2. that he 'never ceases to speak words against this holy place and the law; for we have heard him say that this Jesus of Nazareth will destroy this place, and will change the customs which Moses delivered to us' (6.13-14).

If Loisy is correct in regarding 'Moses' and 'God' as synonyms for the law and the temple[29] then the second group of charges can be treated as a sharper restatement of the first group. The law (νόμος) is specifically mentioned in 6.13 and 7.53 but otherwise Luke uses synonyms such as 'Moses' (6.11) and 'the customs that Moses delivered to us' (6.14), although the latter phrase might refer to pharisaic customs.[30] In a similar fashion, Luke refrains from using either of his customary words for the temple, ἱερόν and ναός. Instead he speaks of 'God' (6.11), 'this [holy] place (6.13, 14), 'house' (7.47, 48, 49) and 'habitation' (σκήνωμα 7.46). This reticence is noteworthy because elsewhere Luke has quite specific connotations for ἱερόν and ναός (*pace* Baltzer[31]). Of the 24 instances of ἱερόν in Luke–Acts only one refers to a temple other than that in Jerusalem (Acts 19.27) and this exception may be because of the earlier use of ναός in the same story to denote a pagan shrine. ναός, on the other hand, is used of the Jerusalem temple prior to the birth of Jesus (1.9, 21, 22) and as Jesus is about to die (23.45; cf. Mk 15.29, 38). Both uses of ναός in Acts (17.24; 19.24) refer to pagan shrines but, during the earthly life of Jesus and for his followers after the resurrection, ἱερόν is Luke's usual term. Thus while Jesus is alive, on earth or in heaven, the temple is fully acceptable; prior to Jesus and while he is on the cross, the temple has the taint of paganism. We have, therefore, a very strange situation. Stephen is put on trial for attacking the two principal

28. Esler, *Community and Gospel*, p. 145.
29. Loisy, *Les Actes*, p. 309. Wilson, *Luke and the Law*, pp. 1-2.
30. Maddox, *Purpose*, p. 52, describes it as 'rabbinic halakah'.
31. Baltzer, 'The Meaning of the Temple', p. 273.

institutions of the law and the temple, yet his speech contains neither of the words for temple and the only use of νόμος is when Stephen accuses his judges of not keeping it (7.53). Had Luke wished to make a serious attack on the temple we might have expected him to have used ναός.

The charge that Stephen opposed the temple is based upon his alleged statement that 'Jesus of Nazareth will destroy this place'. This is reminiscent of the false charge in Mk 14.58, that Jesus would destroy 'this temple made with hands' (τὸν ναὸν τοῦτον τὸν χειροποίητον) and that he would rebuild it in three days. Both Mk 14.58 and Acts 6.14 have the future tense of καταλύω but the sense is different in each case. In Mark, the future tense concerns the historical Jesus and it implies that if he is not killed he will destroy the temple, that is, 'I will if I am not stopped' and, in Mk 13.1-4, 14-23, Jesus speaks of the temple's destruction as an eschatological event. The Markan revelation is made to the disciples outside the temple and hence the accusers at the trial do not share the eschatological secret. It is this that accounts for their misunderstanding the words attributed to Jesus. In Acts the situation is different because everyone knows that Jesus has died and therefore the future tense, 'will destroy', can only refer to an eschatological event.

Because the charges are made by false witnesses there are a number of non-exclusive possible understandings.

1. That Stephen never said that Jesus would destroy the temple.
2. That Jesus never said he would destroy the temple. Mk 14.57 makes this point by the use of the false witnesses but Luke omits the Markan saying. It is important to note that Stephen's accusers do not say, 'Jesus said...'
3. Luke knew that the Romans had destroyed the temple and that the event had no connection with Jesus or his work. Luke does, however, attribute Jerusalem's destruction to its 'not knowing the things that make for peace' (Lk. 19.42-44).
4. That the destruction suggested an eschatological expectation with which Luke did not agree (cf. Lk. 19.11-27).

Of these possibilities, the third was the historical determinant and would have led Luke to see that the destruction of the temple could have no part to play in an eschatological scheme in which Jesus was still to return as Messiah. The destruction of Jerusalem and the temple might be *a* judgment but it was not part of the final judgment. But why did Luke omit the false charge from the passion narrative? Simon suggests that the reason is that it would make the charge against Stephen even less plausible.[32] For if Jesus himself had never been accused of threatening the temple then it would be impossible for someone with Stephen's virtues to have put a lie into Jesus' mouth. Simon's further comment, that the temple was acceptable to Luke only as long as it existed, is correct but his attempt to recover Stephen's attitude as utterly hostile to the temple, together with the supposition that Luke tried to minimize that hostility, goes well beyond the evidence.

Scharlemann makes no attempt to account for Luke's omission of Mk 14.58, although he thinks that Jesus did say that he would destroy the temple because of his conviction that God was gathering a new Israel.[33] There is little direct evidence for this in Luke–Acts but E.P. Sanders has concluded, from the sayings in the Gospels and Acts, that Jesus either threatened or prophesied the destruction and that he would have a role to play in this eschatological event.[34]

S.G. Wilson believes that Luke's omission of the Markan accusation from the trial arose from hindsight because he knew that the temple had been destroyed[35] but this cannot be the whole story since Matthew, who also wrote after the event, includes the saying (Mt. 26.61). Nor does hindsight explain what is, in effect, the transfer of the accusation to Stephen, although the Stephen story, with its mention of false witnesses and the use of χειροποίητος (7.47), suggests that Luke made use of Mark's account.

One possible reason for Luke's treatment of the threat of destruction is that the sayings in Mark, Matthew and Jn 2.19, 21 each include the promise that the temple will be rebuilt in three days and this is restated in the crowds' taunts at the crucifixion (Mk 15.29; Mt. 27.40) which Luke also omits. Luke's concern about this point is further emphasized by the absence of a reference to rebuilding in the accusation against Stephen. Whatever the origin of the saying about rebuilding the temple in three days,[36] by the time of John it had become a prefigurement of the resurrection. This was unnecessary for Luke who, by writing Acts,

32. Simon, *St Stephen*, pp. 23-25.
33. Scharlemann, *Stephen*, pp. 105-106.
34. Sanders, *Jesus and Judaism*, pp. 71-76.
35. Wilson, *Gentile Mission*, pp. 131-32.
36. Sanders, *Jesus and Judaism*, p. 73. Also, pp. 77-90 on the coming new temple in Jewish thinking.

was able to deal with the resurrection and its effects as an historical event without recourse to temple imagery. Nor was he faced with the embarrassment of a prophecy that was unfulfilled or a rebuilding which was politically so improbable. By transferring the accusation to Stephen, Luke is able to show that neither Jesus nor his followers were against the temple.

The Speech

Stephen's speech to the Sanhedrin is delivered by one whose face is like an angel's (6.15), a description given to no other person in Luke–Acts. The angel theme recurs in the description of the revelation of God's name at Sinai (7.30, 35, 38) and in Stephen's final comment that angels delivered the law which his opponents do not keep (7.53). We should therefore expect the speech to be a reaffirmation of the nature of the God of Israel and of the vital importance of the law (living oracles, 7.38). The uniqueness of Stephen's appearance and its implications for understanding the speech seems to have been overlooked by commentators.[37] Haenchen regards the angelic appearance as a transfiguration by which God testifies that Stephen is filled with the Holy Spirit.[38] But Luke has already made this abundantly clear (6.5, 10), and other leaders such as Peter (Acts 4.8), Paul (9.17) and Barnabas (11.24) need no such extra testimony. What they say and do is evidence enough, as we would expect from Jesus' promise (Lk. 12.11-12). With Stephen, something more is indicated and the angelic face forms a link between the charges and the speech itself as a defence against the false charges, however indirect that defence may seem to be. It is the vindication of Stephen as an orthodox Israelite who follows the God of Abraham and the law of Moses.

Further evidence that Stephen stands firmly in the Abraham tradition comes in his opening statement that the God of glory appeared to Abraham (ὁ θεὸς τῆς δόξης ὤφθη, 7.2) and, at the conclusion of the speech, his vision includes the glory of God (εἶδεν δόξαν θεοῦ, 7.55). The connection between the two appearances is almost certainly intentional since δόξα and its cognates do not occur in the Abraham

---

37. That an angel reveals the name of God at the burning bush and gives the law on Sinai (Acts 7.38) definitely puts Stephen on the side of the angels.
38. Haenchen, *Acts*, p. 272.

stories.[39] Acts 7.2 also has reminiscences of the account of the first appearance of God to Abraham at Shechem by the oaks of Moreh (ὤφθη κύριος τῷ Ἀβραμ, Gen. 12.7), as well as with accounts of later appearances (Gen. 17.1; 18.1). A third characteristic, already noted, is that he is full of grace and wisdom (6.3, 8, 10), qualities also possessed by Joseph to whom God gave grace and wisdom (7.10). The way in which Luke has presented Stephen's qualities, anticipating those of Abraham, Joseph and Moses (doing signs and wonders, 6.8; 7.36), shows the subtle care in the construction of the speech. This is no mere intrusion into the account of the martyrdom. Luke's particular interest in these three OT figures is further borne out by the space allotted to them compared with the cursory treatment of Joshua, David and, in particular, Solomon. Given the typological potential of Joshua–Jesus and David this may seem surprising. Stephen says almost nothing about the nine centuries from Solomon to Jesus apart from the accusation that the prophets were resisted and persecuted (7.51-52). The speech is, therefore, a highly selective account that shows clearly Luke's view of Israel's past. This view is found elsewhere in Luke–Acts as we shall see later when we come to examine a possible explanation for Luke's historical selectivity.

Although much of the speech seems to be a straightforward chronological account, there is a complex interweaving of themes within the historical format. In this chapter we examine two of these themes which are:

1. that God is not confined to the land of Israel for his revelation, salvation and worship, and
2. that division and separation have always existed in Israel, from the time of the patriarchs to the present.

There is a third theme which involves discussing possible Samaritan implications and this is examined together with further discussion of part of the Moses story (7.23-29) in the next chapter.

The theme of God acting outside the land of Israel is announced at the outset of the speech with the statement that God appeared to Abraham in Mesopotamia (7.2-3) and it is continued in the story of Joseph (7.9-

---

39. Dahl, 'The Story of Abraham', pp. 142-43, notes several septuagintal phrases in the speech which are not in the Genesis account. Dahl believes that these are part of a conscious attempt to give the speech a biblical flavour. He also regards the survey of Abraham's history as a confirmation of Luke's affinity with Hellenistic Judaism.

14). God rescued Joseph in Egypt and this enabled Joseph later to feed his brothers and Jacob his father. Rackham saw this as an antetype of Jesus saving Israel[40] and certainly the mention of Jacob and the twelve patriarchs (7.8) calls to mind the question about the restoration of Israel (Acts 1.6-7) and the promise of judging the twelve tribes (Lk. 22.30).

The story of Moses (7.30-34) describes the appearance of the angel at Sinai and God's self-revelation in the burning bush with his promise to deliver (ἐξελέσθαι 7.34) Israel, an account based upon Exod. 3.1-10. The verb ἐξαίρεω is also used for the rescue of Joseph (7.10), thus reinforcing the idea of God's saving work outside the land of Israel. Wendt has commented that 'the main idea of the speech is that God revealed himself in a strange land and made the place holy', which Haenchen regards as a bold assertion.[41] It may not be the *main* idea but it is surely an important one, otherwise Luke would not have implied it with each of the principal characters. Instead, Haenchen places the emphasis on the promise of deliverance (7.34). When Stephen speaks of Moses leading Israel out of Egypt he describes him as 'ruler and λυτρωτήν (7.35) and, in the birth stories, it is Jesus who is to be the agent of λύτρωσις for God's people and Jerusalem (1.68-69; 2.38), so that Luke may here be adding one more element to his presentation of Jesus as the prophet like Moses. Deliverance is undoubtedly one facet of Luke's account yet, given the overriding importance of the Exodus for Israel's self-understanding, it is surprising that this fundamental act of deliverance is compressed by Luke into one verse (7.36). It is not so much the act of salvation that stands out in the speech as the rejection of God's agent of deliverance.

> Who made you ruler and judge [over us]?' (7.27, 35).
> 'this Moses whom they refused' (7.35).
> …our fathers refused to obey him, but thrust him aside (7.39, cf. 7.27).

Israel's rejection of its future deliverers which began with the treatment of Joseph is now hammered home to the Sanhedrin, with obvious implications for the death of Jesus (7.52). But it must again be stressed that behind each of Israel's deliverers stands the God of Israel (Lk. 1.68) who continues to save even when his agents have been rejected.

Leaving the first theme for a time, we now turn to the theme of separation to see how it too becomes increasingly important from Abraham

---

40. Rackham, *The Acts of the Apostles*, p. 103.
41. Wendt, *Die Aposgtelgeschichte*, p. 144; Haenchen, *Acts*, p. 282.

to Moses. According to Stephen, God removed Abraham into Canaan but he was given no inheritance in 'the land in which you are now living' (7.4). This provides the first hint of a division between Stephen and the council that goes beyond the fact that Stephen is on trial. The council are still 'brethren and fathers' and Abraham is still 'our father', but it is not 'our' land. The implied division is more than a question of geography, as if, as was most probably the case, Stephen was a diaspora Jew. The division also has an historical dimension which becomes clear towards the end of the speech. Until then Stephen always speaks of 'our' fathers, but after the time of David and Solomon they become 'your' fathers who resist the Holy Spirit and persecute the prophets (7.51-52). The distinction between 'our' and 'your' fathers is understood by Klijn to show that Stephen's interpretation of history differs from that found in the rest of Luke–Acts.[42] But, as we shall see, there is no such inconsistency.

Donaldson has correctly suggested that the change from 'our' to 'your' is because Stephen's audience has followed a stream of Jewish history that opposes God's purposes and that Stephen wholeheartedly accepts the institutions of the covenant with Abraham, including circumcision (7.8).[43] And, since Luke has at least edited, if not composed, the speech, we can say that these are also Luke's convictions. We have seen that the historical turning point in the speech is after the reign of Solomon. The time from Abraham to David was not without its division as the speech acknowledges, but after Solomon Israel's history becomes almost unmentionable. Under David the nation had reached a unity under one king but, with Solomon, the rot set in. After Solomon, God's people became the two kingdoms of Israel and Judah and this split still existed.

The theme of division among God's people makes its first appearance in the speech with the story of Joseph. The patriarchs were jealous of Joseph but he was rescued by God and became a leader in a Gentile nation. The Moses story develops the theme; in 7.23-29, the division is emphatically between sons of Israel (7.23, cf. 'brothers', 7.26) and this leads to the physical separation of Moses' exile. The theme returns in the story of the golden calf which leads on to the breakdown between Israel and God (7.39-43). The rejection of Moses is also brought to bear on Stephen's judges with the comment that Moses 'received living oracles

42. Klijn, 'Stephen's Speech', p. 27.
43. Donaldson, 'Acts 7', pp. 31-32.

to give you' (7.38), if we read 'you' ($\mathfrak{P}^{74}$ ℵ B) with Haenchen as against 'us' in the N-A²⁶. Which ever reading is correct, it does not invalidate Stephen's later charge: 'You who received the law but did not keep it' (7.53). But there seems no need to extend the division that would be implied by 'you' to 'Your fathers refused to obey him...' (7.39) as Klijn (n. 42, above) suggests, since Stephen could hardly deny that 'our' fathers, which was the whole of Israel, had participated in the worship of the calf. He could, however, imply at the end of his speech that he and the group to which he belonged still kept the law whereas the Sanhedrin did not.

In addition to the two themes that we have discussed there is a Christological aspect to the speech with the quotation of Moses' words, 'God will raise up for you a prophet from your brethren as he raised me up' (7.37, cf. 3.22; Deut. 18.15). Scharlemann has also noted the parallel between the description of Moses as mighty in words and deeds (7.22) and that of Jesus (Lk. 24.19).[44] There is a further connection between God's work through Moses and through Jesus in the use of ἐπισκέπτομαι[45] (Acts 7.23, cf. Lk. 1.68-69; 7.16), each instance of which also speaks of God raising up a prophet or the Horn of Salvation (ἤγειρεν, Lk. 1.69; ἠγέρθη, 7.16).

M. Simon sees little room in the speech of the earthly Jesus[46] and, in a sense, he is correct because there is no mention of his name, his message or his resurrection, and only a lightly veiled reference to his death (7.52). Even his death is mentioned in the context of the persecution and killing of earlier prophets. Nor could Jesus easily appear in a speech almost entirely devoted to Israel's past. Simon, who regards the speech as pre-Lukan, believes that the absence of any mention of Jesus is evidence that it is almost exclusively an attack on Jewish institutions by a member of a sect of 'advanced', reform Jews.[47] Such a sect might be a good description of early Christians, but the speech can hardly be an attack on Jewish institutions if there is no direct criticism of the law, the temple and circumcision.

---

44. Scharlemann, *Stephen*, p. 86.
45. Sabbe, 'The Son of Man Saying in Acts 7,56', pp. 248-49. This is one of a number of words and phrases which Sabbe believes links Stephen's speech with other missionary speeches in Acts and with Luke's Gospel.
46. Simon, *St Stephen*, p. 74. The speech contains no new Christological ideas either.
47. Simon, *St Stephen*, p. 75.

Concern to discover the historical situation in which the speech may have been delivered may have the adverse effect of obscuring Luke's purpose in editing or composing it. Its purpose is not to preach the Christian gospel to the High Priest because, as far as Luke is concerned, that had already been done by Peter (4.5-12; 5.27-32). In Luke's plan the speech has a number of functions of which the Christological one is to place the rejection of Jesus, the prophet like Moses, within the total history of Israel's practice of rejecting its saviours.

The final part of the speech, beginning with the story of the golden calf, is principally concerned with the Jewish cult. This is interwoven with the themes we have already noted, God's actions outside the land of Israel and division within the house of Israel. The story of the calf is followed by a quotation from Amos and then, mention of the tent of meeting and Solomon's building of the temple. The section concludes with a quotation from Isaiah. Those commentators who regard Stephen's speech as a Christian attack on the Jewish cult often overlook the point that is central to Luke's strategy: that whatever criticism Stephen wants to make about the cult is made through the words of an accepted prophet of Israel. Stephen's own words add little of substance to what has already been said by Amos and Isaiah so that any criticism contained in the speech is neither new nor specifically Christian. The only overt Christian comment that the speech contains is directed at the present Jewish leaders for their betrayal and murder of the Righteous One (7.51-53).

The story of the calf acts as an introduction to comments about the cult, and the description of the idol as the work 'of their hands' (7.41) is taken up in 'the Most High does not dwell in houses made with hands' (ἐν χειροποιήτοις, 7.48). This phrase also occurs in Paul's speech to the Areopagus in his description of pagan worship (17.24). Even so, doubt remains as to whether Stephen is attacking the temple for its paganism, since the Isaiah citation which follows is against any localization of God's presence. The story of the calf also brings out Aaron's responsibility for making the idol (7.40), a point which would not have been lost on the High Priest. It is possible that Stephen objected to the sacrificial aspect of the cult but this seems improbable in the light of Luke's favourable instance of temple sacrifices in the birth stories. Nor does Luke have the condemnations of sacrifice found in Mk 12.33, Mt. 9.13 and 12.7 with their quotations of 1 Sam. 15.22, Hos. 6.6 and Mic. 6.6-8. Luke's view of the temple is that it was a house of prayer[48]

---

48. Brawley, *Luke–Acts and the Jews*, p. 120.

2. Stephen's Speech and Israel's Past

(Lk. 19.46; cf. Acts 2.46; 3.1), and Jewish Christians continued to use the temple long after the death of Stephen (21.20-29).

Simon's opinion, that the speech shows Stephen's unrestricted opposition to the temple[49] is true neither of Stephen nor of Luke and it leaves the problem that, if that were the case, it would play into the hands of the *false* witnesses. It is possible that the speech intends to differentiate between the priestly and prophetic strands in Israel's history, with Moses and Jesus on the side of the prophets, but the absence of any reference to passages such as Hos. 6.6 suggests some other motive. Simon also regards the calf incident as the key to deciding between what is divine and what is human in the Torah: what the law ordained prior to the golden calf is divine and whatever came after is to be rejected.[50] But there is no evidence that Luke accepted the distinction or that he was unaware of what happened after the worship of the calf, that when Moses interceded for Israel God turned away his anger (Exod. 32.7-14). In spite of the calf incident God still renews the covenant and the law (Exod. 34), he still meets Moses in the tent of meeting and promises to drive out the people of the land so that Israel may enter (Acts 7.45). Although both God and Stephen describe the Israelites as stiffnecked (σκληροτράχηλος, Exod. 33.3, 5; 34.9; Acts 7.51), Israel's episode with the calf does not mark the point of God's withdrawal, nor does it mean that all that followed is to be rejected. The tent of Moloch (7.43) is in contrast to the tent of witness that Moses had built and which Joshua ('Ἰησοῦς) brought into the land (7.44-45). This was a sure sign to Stephen and Luke that God had not withdrawn from Israel, not least because David subsequently found favour with God (7.45-46).

Acts 7.45b-47 describes the events leading to the building of Solomon's house but, before we examine their significance, there is the textual problem in 7.46: '[David] asked leave to find a habitation for the God/house of Jacob'. 'House' ($\mathfrak{P}^{74}$ ℵ* B D) is the reading accepted by Nestle but 'God' is preferred by Haenchen,[51] Simon[52] and

---

49. Simon, *St Stephen*, pp. 25, 43, and Maddox, *Purpose*, p. 53, ascribe the attack on the temple to Luke's sources which run counter to Luke's own views. This explanation is unsatisfactory; Luke was well able to edit his sources. Edvin Larsson, 'Temple-Criticism', is perhaps the most recent scholar who sees no fundamental criticism of the temple in the speech, or that the temple is contrasted with the mobile tabernacle.

50. Simon, *St Stephen*, pp. 48-49.

51. Haenchen, *Acts*, pp. 276, 278.

52. Simon, *St Stephen*, p. 51.

Brawley.⁵³ 'House' is the better attested reading as well as being the more difficult (Simon thinks that it makes no sense at all), but Lake and Cadbury take it to mean that David wished to build a habitation of God for the house of Jacob.⁵⁴ They point out that the temple, like the tent, was to be used by the house of Jacob as well as by the Almighty and that the author almost certainly had in mind Psalm 131(LXX). However, comparison of Ps. 131.5 with Acts 7.46 suggests that 'God' is to be preferred.

    Ps. 131.5 εὕρω τόπον τῷ κυρίῳ σκήνωμα τῷ θεῷ Ιακωβ.
    Acts 7.46 εὑρεῖν   σκήνωμα τῷ θεῷ 'Ιακώβ.

In order to understand Stephen's (and Luke's) attitude to the temple we need to go back to David's wish to build a house for the ark like his own (2 Sam. 7.1-2). God rejected the request in terms similar to those in Isa. 66.1-2, which is quoted by Stephen, because God has always had a moveable tent (ἐν σκηνῇ) for his dwelling (2 Sam. 7.6-7). Instead, God promised that David's house will be the continuation of his kingdom through his son and that the throne of that kingdom will be established for ever (2 Sam. 7.12-16, cf. 7.24-29). According to Luke this promise will be fulfilled through Jesus (Lk. 1.32-33). Stephen's criticism of the temple is not against its cult but that it was built because of Solomon's fundamental misunderstanding of the house of David as a building. This had the effect of localizing God and thus failed to acknowledge that all the earth is God's footstool (Acts 7.49). This view could only be sustained by avoiding any mention of God's promise to Solomon that was made during the building of the temple (1 Kgs 6.11-13) and turning instead to Isa. 66.1-2. By doing this Luke is able to set the seal on the theme of God's presence outside the land of Israel, a theme present in the stories of Abraham, Joseph and Moses.

The speech has, therefore, an interweaving of themes and a subtlety of allusion which points very clearly to a deeply pondered literary construction. It is not a defence speech in the style which Paul uses (Acts 22.3-21; 24.10-21; 26.2-23) which sets out to rebut the charges in an obviously 'legal' way. Yet it shows that all the charges are false as Luke has made clear at the outset.⁵⁵ The charges of speaking against God and Moses are overturned while that of speaking against the law is turned

    53. Brawley, *Luke–Acts and the Jews*, pp. 121-22.
    54. Lake and Cadbury, *Beginnings*, IV, p. 81.
    55. On the legal discussion see Esler, *Community and Gospel*, pp. 122-25.

2. Stephen's Speech and Israel's Past 67

into an accusation against the Sanhedrin. On the remaining charge of speaking against 'this holy place', the verdict is at least 'not proven'. Stephen says nothing about the temple that Isaiah would not have said, and there is nothing in the speech that conflicts with Luke's attitude to the temple elsewhere. What has often been taken to be an attack on the temple and hence on Judaism is really an attack on Solomon because he did not grasp the true meaning of the house of David.

Within the narrative of Acts the trial of Stephen stands as the third of a series of trials that show a growing animosity on the part of the Jewish leaders towards Christians. The first trial followed the arrest of Peter and John because the High Priest and the Sadducees were annoyed by the apostles' preaching that Jesus had been raised from the dead (4.1-2). The result of the trial was that the apostles were let off with a warning and the threat of future punishment if they continued to preach. In the second trial the High Priest and the Sadducees were filled with jealousy and arrested the apostles because they had not obeyed the earlier ruling and because 'you intend to bring this man's blood upon us' (5.28). Peter's short speech confirms that this is true (5.30) and, as a result, the leaders wish to kill the apostles who are only saved by Gamaliel's intervention (5.33-40). The result of Stephen's trial is therefore a foregone conclusion in terms of the dramatic scheme: it is the final part of the sequence from which even Gamaliel could not have saved him. In this respect it is irrelevant whether Stephen is stoned judicially or the victim of mob violence.[56] All that matters is that he should die and that in so doing he should confirm that Jesus is the heavenly son of Man.

The Gentile Mission and Rejection of the Jews?

We saw earlier that Dibelius is among those who regard Stephen's speech as beginning the progress of the gospel to the Gentiles. It is not uncommon among those who share this view to see turning to the Gentiles as a corollary of the rejection of the Jews, so we must therefore ask whether the speech implies such a rejection. Kilgallen notes that there is no account of further preaching in Jerusalem,[57] but this falls well short of being convincing evidence for his conclusion that Acts 7 is 'a formal repudiation of the Jews'. J.T. Sanders, in his rather abrasive study of Luke's attitude to the Jews, goes so far as to claim that 'Stephen and,

---

56. Haenchen, *Acts*, pp. 292-93, 294 n. 2, discusses the issue.
57. Kilgallen, *Stephen*, p. 111.

indeed, all Christianity à la Luke oppose the Temple and Mosaic custom'.[58] This opinion cannot be supported from the present analysis of the speech or from the earlier chapters of Acts. Such repudiation of the Jews as the speech contains is limited to the members of the Sanhedrin and even this depends more upon Jewish Scripture than on Christian preaching. Nor can rejection include those Jews who have become believers among whom are a great many priests (6.7), a verse designed to illustrate Luke's division theme by showing the growing isolation of the High Priest. We shall discuss later other reasons for thinking that the small group attacked by Stephen does not represent the whole of Israel. Luke's silence about further preaching in Jerusalem may be no more than the result of his need to cover an enormous area before his story reaches Rome, but it is historically improbable that the apostles gave up devoting themselves to the ministry of the word in Jerusalem.

The relationship of the speech to the Gentile mission is slender indeed. Wilson correctly notes that the speech contains no hint of turning to the Gentiles and yet, because of its position in Acts, he agrees with Dibelius.[59] If the speech is related to the mission it can only be because of the persecution and scattering of believers which followed Stephen's death. And even then the Gentile mission is at several removes and it is given its initial impulse by God himself.

Conclusions

Stephen's speech presents Luke's view of Israel's history as one which, in effect, stops with Solomon who was the last king of the undivided kingdom. Thereafter, the only people who are important to Luke are Elijah and Elisha and we shall discuss their importance in Chapter 4. Luke's view was not dictated primarily by restrictions of space but by his theological standpoint, and it is a view that is completely consistent with his other accounts of Israel's history. In Acts 13.16-25, Paul outlines Israel's past to an audience of Jews and God-fearers. Since this is a group least in need of such instruction we can only conclude that Luke wished to emphasize his historical perspective. Paul begins with the stay in Egypt, briefly mentions the Exodus and then moves briskly on to David. He skips over the nine centuries from David to his true successor, Jesus, concluding with a more extended account of the Baptist and his

58. Sanders, *The Jews in Luke–Acts*, p. 248.
59. Wilson, *Gentile Mission*, pp. 135-36.

2. Stephen's Speech and Israel's Past

preaching of repentance. Paul characterizes the present Jewish rulers as those who killed Jesus because they did not understand the prophets. This speech encapsulates in its small space the same historical perspective as that of Stephen.

There is one other occasion where Luke reveals his view of Israel's history and that is in his genealogy (Lk. 3.23-38). In the section between Abraham and David, Luke's list is very close to that in Mt. 1.2-6a but, where Matthew takes the line of descent through Solomon and the kings of Judah, Luke follows a line through David's son, Nathan. Thereafter, Luke's list coincides twice only with Matthew, with Shealtiel and Zerubbabel (3.27). Here Luke draws attention to Zerubbabel the son of Shealtiel who had returned from the captivity in Babylon and who played a leading role in the rebuilding of the temple. We must also note that one of Zerubbabel's co-builders was Jeshua (Ἰησοῦς) the son of Jozadek (2 Esd. 3.2, 8; 4.3; 5.2). This sudden outcrop of historical people in Luke's post-exilic genealogy shows that Jesus is descended from one of the pillars of orthodox Judaism and it is another reminder of Luke's approval of the temple. The rest of Luke's list is composed of historical nonentities; such is Luke's view of the nation's history after David until Jesus. In order to avoid tracing Jesus' descent through the kings of Judah, Luke invents a son of Nathan since no son is mentioned in the OT. This demonstrates just how far Luke was prepared to go in order to underline his view.

Luke clearly used history for his own purposes, one of which was the building up and support of his church. Fundamental to this work was the concern for unity. Esler has proposed that an important part of Luke's purpose was to legitimate table fellowship between Jewish and Gentile Christians.[60] Because of the mixture of backgrounds there was the danger, and probably the reality, of fragmentation along the lines of pre-Christian allegiances that can be seen in the Hebrew–Hellenist dispute. Stephen's historical review is set in the context of church history and both histories describe the formative period of two institutions, neither of which is pictured in idealized perfection. In Stephen's survey divisions feature strongly but they are overcome. Joseph and his brothers eventually live together with their father; Moses is reunited with his fellow Israelites and becomes their leader and saviour. Even Moses and Aaron are finally reunited after the incident of the calf. Above all this, God never forsakes his covenant with Abraham and his descendants.

60. Esler, *Community and Gospel*, pp. 71-72, 93-97, 105-109.

This covenant is still remembered by God (Lk. 1.55, 72-73) and the Jews are still children of Abraham (Lk. 13.16; 19.9; Acts 13.26). Israel's waywardness, either in the review or in Stephen's onslaught on the Sanhedrin, is insufficient to support Lampe's conclusion that there has been a final rejection of Israel which, he says, 'is not and never has been the authentic people of the covenant for they have continually broken it'.[61] In fact, the reverse can be argued: the speech shows that in spite of everything God still keeps his covenant with Israel and Luke knows that repentance and forgiveness continue to be offered, even for the death of Jesus (Acts 3.17-19). It is God's continuing faithfulness, not Israel's lapses of faith, which is Luke's fundamental axiom.

In an attempt to extract the historical nature of what he calls the Stephen–Philip group, Scobie has suggested that it shared the prophetic hope of Jeremiah, Ezekiel and Zechariah for the reunion of the northern and southern kingdoms.[62] Whatever we can learn about Stephen and Philip can only be discovered from what Luke tells us, so if there was such a hope for reunification in the first-century church then it was almost certainly Luke's hope too. If that is the case then we would expect to find further evidence elsewhere in Luke's writing, and in the next chapter we shall examine the evidence to be found in the Samaritan theme in Luke–Acts. In Luke's time, the claimants to the lines of descent from the two kingdoms were Jews and Samaritans, and we need to note the importance of the Samaritan theme at this point in the discussion since it will contribute to our understanding of the purpose of the Stephen episode.

It is not only the content of the speech but also its position in the narrative which tells us about Luke's purpose. It is placed between two healings of division, the first of which is that between Hebrews and Hellenists, and Stephen has a direct role to play in the healing. The second healing comes about as a result of his death and the scattering of the Jerusalem Christians. This is the success of the mission to a city of Samaria by Philip (8.4-8) and it demonstrates that Jews and Samaritans are being brought together into the embryo of a reunited Israel, just as their forebears had been under king David nine centuries earlier. And it is the success of this mission which provides one reason for the Lukan Stephen's reservations about the temple. For the last three or four

61. Lampe, *St Luke and the Church in Jerusalem*, p. 9.
62. Scobie, 'The Origins and Development of Samaritan Christianity', pp. 399-400.

centuries of its history the Jerusalem temple had been a divisive focus for Jews and Samaritans and, in the first century CE, Samaritans and Gentiles were excluded in theory and largely so in practice.[63] For Luke's readers, however, the temple was a thing of the past and his somewhat ambivalent attitude to the temple reflects this fact.[64] As long as the temple existed in the time-span of his narrative, Jesus and his followers used and respected it because they were members of Jewish Israel, a very important point for a significant proportion of Luke's readers. But, at the time of writing, the temple and its divisive power were gone. It no longer presented a barrier to Samaritans and it is worth noting that the only division in the wilderness years that Stephen mentions is a cultic one (7.39-41).

The speech therefore looks back to a time when Israel, like the church of Luke's day, lived without the divisive presence of the temple. It was this, perhaps, that made the wilderness such a potent symbol for Luke and which is emphasized in the speech (7.30, 36, 38, 42, 44).[65] He does not regard it as a time of special virtue but as one of broad tribal unity under Moses. Luke's scarcely veiled dislike of Solomon reflects not only his role as temple builder but also that it was in his reign that the seeds of national division began to grow. Luke is deeply concerned for the restoration of a united Israel under its new Lord, the prophet like Moses and the Davidic king.

---

63. Moulton and Milligan, *Vocabulary*, p. 23. Josephus, *Ant*. 15.417 has 'let no foreigner (ἀλλοεθνῆ, but ἀλλογενῆ [MM]) enter within the screen and enclosure surrounding the sanctuary'.

64. Esler, *Community and Gospel*, pp. 133-35.

65. In view of Luke's concern for the law it should be noted that later rabbinic teaching (*Mekilta*, Exod. 19.2) says that the law was given in the wilderness rather than in the land of Israel so that Israelites could not claim it as their own property. 'It is common property; whoever will accept it, let him come and accept it'. See Montefiore, 'The Spirit of Judaism', *Beginnings*, I, pp. 45-46. Also Sanders, *Palestinian Judaism*, pp. 88-89.

Chapter 3

THE ROLE OF THE SAMARITANS AND THE UNITY OF ISRAEL

The discussion so far has established that the birth stories show clearly Luke's concern for the salvation of Israel under the new Davidic king. It is equally clear from Luke's surveys of Israel's history and his genealogy that Solomon's misunderstanding of the true nature of David's house and the division of the kingdom are two aspects of a catastrophe that God will rectify through Jesus. I have also suggested that Luke believed that the Samaritans had a role to play in the restoration of that unity. We must now examine Luke's treatment of the Samaritans to test whether the suggestion is sustainable.

Luke's interest in the Samaritans is in sharp contrast to that of Mark, who never mentions them, and Matthew who excludes them from Israel and from the mission of the disciples (Mt. 10.5-6), at least until after the resurrection ('all nations', 28.19). Only in the Fourth Gospel are Samaritans present to a comparable extent to that in Luke–Acts, although John limits their appearance to two days (Jn 4.40) whereas Luke develops the theme more slowly. Unlike Jn 4.9, Luke never supplies editorial explanations of Samaritan attitudes[1] which suggests that such comments were unnecessary for his readers. Both evangelists describe successful missions to a city in Samaria (εἰς πόλιν τῆς Σαμαρείας, Jn 4.5; cf. Acts 8.5), either by Jesus (Jn 4.39-42) or by Philip (Acts 8.4-8). What is so striking in both accounts is the willingness with which the Samaritans accept the message compared with the reluctance of many Jews, although both writers are aware that Samaritans could be connected with magical practices (Jn 8.48; Acts 8.9-11). John envisages a time when Jewish and Samaritan differences about the true place of worship will come to an end. This will be when the Messiah comes and the Father will be worshipped in spirit and truth

---

1. Jervell, 'The Lost Sheep of the House of Israel', *The People of God*, pp. 113-32.

(4.20-26). Luke not only shares this view but, as I shall try to show, extends it to epitomize the coming unity of the two kingdoms.

Samaritanism

A brief outline of the Samaritans and their relations with Jews is necessary in order to put Luke's presentation of them into context. Although there has been a growth in Samaritan studies during this century,[2] a number of major problems remain, and will probably continue to remain, for the period in which Luke was writing. The most important of these is that the Samaritan writings date from long after the time with which we are concerned. For example, the *Memar Marqar*, which is the earliest collection of Samaritan theology, dates from the fourth century CE.[3] It is very probable that this contains much older traditions but, as with rabbinic writings, great care is needed in trying to recover ideas of earlier times. Jewish writings about the Samaritans often pre-date the *Memar Marqar* and they are usually polemical in purpose. Even so, there are some that show a grudging acceptance of Samaritan claims. Yet, in spite of all these difficulties, some of the main features of Samaritan history and practice are fairly well established.

According to R.J. Coggins,[4] the first clear indication of a community that can properly be described as Samaritan, which lived at Shechem and had its sanctuary at Mount Gerizim, is the mention of 'the foolish people who dwell at Shechem' (Sir. 50.25-26; cf. 'the city of the senseless', *T. Levi* 7.2). This would mean that such a community was in existence by 180 BCE and that it was an object of scorn among Jews. There may be another hint in Zech. 11.14, if this section of Zechariah comes from the early Greek period,[5] where the prophet symbolizes the annulment of the 'brotherhood between Israel and Judah'. In 128 BCE, John Hyrcanus captured Shechem and destroyed the Gerizim temple which, according to Josephus,[6] had existed for two hundred years. This

---

2. Bowman, *The Samaritan Problem*; Coggins, *Origins of Samaritanism*; MacDonald, *Theology of the Samaritans*; Montgomery, *Samaritans*; Purvis, 'The Samaritans'; Goulder, 'Two Roots'.
3. MacDonald, *Theology*, pp. 42-43.
4. Coggins, *Origins*, p. 82.
5. Ackroyd, 'Zechariah', *Peake's Commentary*, p. 651.
6. Josephus, *Ant.* 13.254-56; *War* 1.63-64. Montgomery, *Samaritans*, pp. 79-80.

dating of the origin of the Gerizim temple to the time of Alexander the Great was long regarded as doubtful but archeological findings from Tell-er-Ras now give strong support to Josephus's dating.[7] What did this community claim for itself? It claimed to be descended from the tribes of Ephraim, Manasseh and Levi and that it worshipped Yahweh at what had always been the true Israelite sanctuary. It observed circumcision on the eighth day, kept the festivals, and its only Scripture was the Pentateuch.[8] Samaritan observance of the Sabbath is acknowledged in *m. Ned.* 3.10. They therefore saw themselves as Israel and they regarded the descendants of the tribe of Judah as heretics. Purvis puts the situation succinctly: 'What the Samaritan community claimed for itself was what the Jewish community claimed for itself'.[9]

The origin of the Jewish–Samaritan schism cannot be traced back to one particular event, rather, it was a developing split with certain growth points. The division of the nation after Solomon into the kingdoms of Israel in the north and Judah in the south was one such point, and this was followed by the Assyrian deportation of the inhabitants of Samaria in 722 BCE. The Jewish view, in 2 Kings 17, speaks of wholesale deportation but the *Annals of Sargon* (11–17) tell of a relatively small number, about 27,000. This event was followed by the repopulation of the land by foreign settlers among whom were the Kutim (2 Kgs 17.24) and it was to these that the Assyrians sent an Israelite priest to teach the people about Yahweh (2 Kgs 17.27-28).[10] The Samaritan view was that the schism went back to the time of the judges, when Eli set up a sanctuary at Shiloh to rival Gerizim. According to Purvis, the final stage of the break was caused by the exclusive attitude of the Jews who had returned from the Babylonian exile over the rebuilding of the Jerusalem temple.[11] Certainly from around 300 BCE, with the existence of rival

7. Purvis, 'Samaritans', pp. 596-99. Bull, 'The Excavation of Tell er-Ras'.
8. Schürer–Vermes, *History*, II, p. 17: 'For, calumnies apart, according to all that is known of the religion of the Samaritans it was pure Jewish monotheism...The only difference between them and the Jews was that their centre of worship was not Jerusalem but Mount Gerizim.'
9. Purvis, 'Samaritans', p. 591.
10. Dexinger, 'Limits of Tolerance', examines the historical traditions of 2 Kings, Ezra 4 and 2 Chronicles as well as those in Josephus's *Antiquities*. He argues that the *Somronim* (2 Kgs 17.29) were northern Israelites and not pagan settlers.
11. Purvis, 'Samaritans', p. 595. According to *4 Bar.* 8, those who built the city of Samaria were Jews who had intermarried during the Babylonian exile. They were refused permission to return to either Jerusalem or Babylon.

3. *The Role of the Samaritans* 75

sanctuaries, the division was sealed. After the Jewish attacks on Samaria in the second century, the Romans brought a period of relative peace when, in 64 BCE, Pompey took Samaria from the Hasmoneans. After this Samaria was largely free from the fear of Jewish aggression.[12] During this time the majority of Samaria's population was pagan but the Samaritan religion was a *religio licita*, with its own recognized territory and a diaspora at home in the Greek world.[13]

How did the Jews regard their northern neighbours? One quite early indication is in the account of Israel's history in Jubilees (second century BCE) where the blessing of Ephraim and Manasseh (Gen. 48.1-20) does not appear.[14] In the older part of the *Martyrdom and Ascension of Isaiah* (2.12-16)[15] Samaritans are condemned for their worship of Baal, and the Samaritan who betrays Isaiah (Belkira, 2.12) is later represented as the devil incarnate (5.4-9). Those writings which dwell on the rape of Dinah by Shechem and the subsequent slaughter of the Shechemites (*Jub.* 30; *Jos. Asen.* 23.14; *T. Levi* 7) would certainly not have encouraged Jewish toleration of Samaritans.

Josephus refers to the northerners as Shechemites or, more disparagingly, as Kutim, a reference to one of the Mesopotamian cities to which Israel had been deported. He calls them two-faced and he thinks that they are not to be trusted. 'When they see the Jews prosper they pretend they are allied to them and call them kinsmen. When they see them falling they say they are not related to them.'[16] 'They are apostates from the Jewish nation...[and] because Alexander had honoured the Jews they decided to call themselves Jews.'[17] Probably popular Jewish opinion agreed with Josephus and, even today, some NT scholars share that view. Jeremias, for example, begins a survey with, 'Descending to the lowest degree of the scale, we come to the Samaritans'.[18] This may be a fair assessment of the common Jewish

---

12. Montgomery, *Samaritans*, p. 82. MacDonald, *Theology*, pp. 25-26. Josephus, *War* 2.232-35, describes an incident at Gema, on the Samaria–Galilee border between 48 and 52 CE.
13. Montgomery, *Samaritans*, p. 88, discusses the boundaries between Samaria and Judaea. Evidence for the Samaritan diaspora is given by Kraabel, 'Synagoga Caeca', pp. 220-24.
14. Wintermute, 'Jubilees', *OTP*, II, p. 35.
15. Knibb, 'Martyrdom and Ascension of Isaiah', *OTP*, II, pp. 158-59.
16. Josephus, *Ant.* 9.288-91.
17. Josephus, *Ant.* 11.340-44.
18. Jeremias, *Jerusalem in the Time of Jesus*, p. 352.

view but it was not that of all Jews. It is important to recognize that there were more sympathetic Jewish opinions because there is a danger that, in emphasizing the undoubted antipathy, we may misread Luke's attitude as that of popular Judaism.

Although rabbinic opinion hardened with time, Montgomery has suggested that in the earlier strata of the Babylonian Talmud there are views which are quite favourable towards Samaritans.[19] To R. Simon b. Gamaliel, who died c. 165 CE, is attributed the saying that 'every command that the Samaritans keep they are more scrupulous in observing than Israel.'[20] A Jew was allowed to say 'amen' to a Samaritan blessing,[21] he could buy kosher meat from a Samaritan[22] and he could discharge his Passover duty with Samaritan unleavened bread.[23] But, it has to be said that in each case there was a qualifying clause—for example, in buying kosher meat the Jew should ask the Samaritan to put some in his own mouth first. The implication is that although there is a lack of trust, the Jews knew that Samaritans also kept the food laws and would not eat non-kosher food. There was, therefore, some Jewish recognition of a Samaritan connection with Jews, even if that recognition was a cautious one. This view is crystallized in the last halaka of *Kutim*, a tract appended to the Babylonian Talmud: 'When shall we take them back? When they renounce Gerizim and confess Jerusalem and the resurrection of the dead. From this time forth he that robs a Samaritan shall be as he that robs an Israelite.'[24]

The Gospel's Central Section, 9.51–18.14

The importance of this much discussed and analyzed section of the Gospel for the present discussion is that it contains all of Luke's direct references and two possible allusions to Samaria and the Samaritans. Although 'Central Section' begs fewer questions than other titles and is

---

19. Montgomery, *Samaritans*, ch. 10 esp. p. 166, gives a list of the relevant rabbinic literature containing references to the Kutim. The Mishnah reflects an ambivalent attitude to Samaritans; *Ber.* 7.1; 8.8; *Dem.* 3.4 show some concessions but Šeq. 1.5; *Roš Haš.* 2.2; *Ket.* 3.1, *Qid.* 4.3 and *Nid.* 4.1-2 all show Jewish antagonism.
20. *Qid.* 76a; *Ber.* 47b.
21. *M. Ber.* 7.1; 8.8; Montgomery, *Samaritans*, p. 172.
22. *Mas Kutim* 17. The quotations are from Montgomery's translation pp. 201-203.
23. *Mas Kutim* 24.
24. *Mas Kutim* 28.

therefore to be preferred,[25] R.H. Lightfoot spoke of the ministry in Samaria and the Samaritan Section without considering it necessary to justify the use of the terms.[26] Half a century later that response is no longer possible. The purpose of our discussion is to see whether Luke's readers, who probably had a similar level of knowledge of Palestinian geography to Luke's, could be excused if they saw the section as particularly concerned with Samaritan interests. Perhaps, knowing that Jesus spoke of the Christian sequence of mission to be Jerusalem, Judaea and Samaria, they saw Jesus, after Galilee, moving in the reverse direction.

Luke's geographical ignorance has not lacked for advocates[27] and, although this section of the Gospel is a travel account in that Jesus states his intention of going to Jerusalem (9.51; 13.22; 17.11), it tells the reader almost nothing about the progress of the journey. Even as late as 17.11, Jesus is 'passing along between Samaria and Galilee' and the expression διὰ μέσον has worried copyists and commentators alike. The use of διά with the accusative to mean 'through' is found on rare occasions in Greek poetry,[28] but the more usual meaning is 'because of' or 'for the sake of'. So, did Luke mean that Jesus went through Samaria and Galilee to Jerusalem (in spite of it being in the wrong direction) or along the border between the two areas? Conzelmann's suggestion that Luke was writing as if from outside the area[29] is almost certainly correct but, if that were the case, why did he not simply accept Mark's indication of a journey through Perea (Mk 10.1) or check his geographical information in the interests of accuracy (Lk. 1.2-3)? Each synoptic author knew that Jesus had moved from Galilee to Judaea and Jerusalem and the two maps show their solutions. Map A represents the journey in Matthew and Mark. Map B is based on Conzelmann's reconstruction of Luke's geography.[30]

---

25. Evans, 'Central Section', pp. 40-41; Fitzmyer, *Luke*, p. 138, the 'Travel Account'.

26. Lightfoot, *Locality and Doctrine*, pp. 137-39.

27. McCown, 'Geography', pp. 62-63, notes Luke's deliberate omission of Mk 10.1 and every allusion to Perea and Decapolis. 'The only legitimate conclusion is that he intended his Gospel to mean just what any reader who did not know Mark or Matthew would understand it to mean: that the central section records a supposed mission in Samaria.' See also Streeter, *The Four Gospels*, pp. 203, 215, 424.

28. Fitzmyer, *Luke*, p. 1153.

29. Conzelmann, *Luke*, pp. 68-73.

30. Conzelmann, *Luke*, p. 69.

According to Luke, the Jordan lay further to the east[31] so that Jesus had no need to cross the river. Luke's omission of 'across the Jordan' (Mk 10.1) may be because he does not wish to show Jesus working in the Baptist's territory, although Jesus does cross to the other side of the lake (8.22, 26). It is also possible that, knowing Israel to have crossed the Jordan to enter the land, he did not want to show Jesus going back again. Yet, whether or not Luke was geographically ill-informed makes no difference to the overall impression that, in this section of the Gospel, Jesus works in Samaria. Luke simply lacks the geographical clarity and knowledge shown by John (4.3-4, 43).

The section contains only two indications of Jesus' location and both mention Samaria (9.52; 17.11).[32] Attempts to discover where Jesus is at any other time rely upon deductions from the text, comparisons with other Gospels or invoking possible sources. The results vary in their credibility and do little to change the conclusion that Samaria was Jesus' area of ministry.[33] That there is a measure of parallelism between the Galilee ministry and 9.51–18.14[34] further suggests a deliberate comparison of the two areas. But, having said that, the real importance of Samaria to Luke is the Samaritans. It was the people rather than the geography that determined Luke's scheme even although the area contained Jews intermingling with Samaritans, just as he tells a parable about a Samaritan travelling in Judaea (10.30-37).

In his discussion of what he terms the 'travel account', Fitzmyer notes three sub-sections, each of which is marked by a statement that Jerusalem is Jesus' objective.[35] He further comments that 'the division at these points is otherwise insignificant',[36] in spite of noting that the first and third subdivisions are associated with Samaritans. I shall argue later that the second point of division is followed by a saying which may well have Samaritan allusions (13.29, see below). There is not the slightest doubt about the importance of the Jerusalem theme but, by the same token of the three divisions, the Samaritan theme must also be important.

---

31. Conzelmann, *Luke*, pp. 19, 20.
32. Conzelmann, *Luke*, p. 65.
33. *Pace* Robinson, 'Context', p. 29.
34. Lightfoot, *Locality and Doctrine*, pp. 137-39.
35. Fitzmyer, *Luke*, pp. 138-40.
36. Fitzmyer, *Luke*, p. 825 and also his note on 9.52 on p. 828.

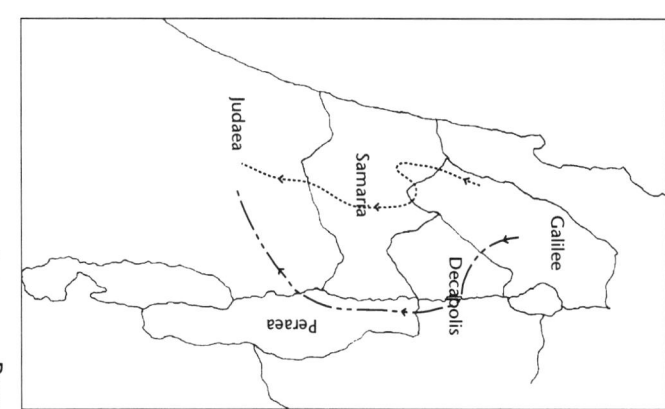

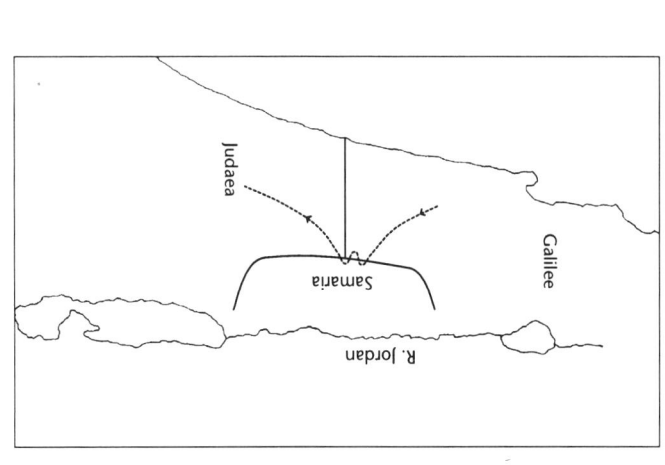

·············▶ Possible Lukan routes to Jerusalem
─·─·─▶─·─ The route according to Mark and Matthew

Maps. *Jesus' journey from Galilee to Judaea and Jerusalem*

The emphasis in the Central Section is on the teaching of Jesus[37] but does the teaching cohere, or at least not strongly conflict, with what we know of Samaritan thinking and expectations?

1. The Samaritans held strictly to the written law and rejected Pharisaic practices of purity and tithing.[38] In this section Luke exhibits a very conservative view of the law (10.25-28; 16.16-17) and criticizes Pharisaic practices of tithing (11.42) and purity (11.39-41; cf. 12.1). The Samaritans also rejected belief in a resurrection because it could not be shown to be in the law. Luke certainly believes in the resurrection but, at the end of the Lazarus story, Abraham says that the resurrection will not convince those who are not already convinced by Moses (the law) and the prophets (16.31).

2. Samaritan future hopes included a prophet like Moses (Deut. 18.15), and by the fourth century he had become the *Taheb*, the One who Returns. They did not expect a Messiah of David's line,[39] and the title 'Christ' is not found in the Central Section. A number of scholars have argued for Deuteronomic patterns in the Central Section,[40] while others believe that the Deuteronomic similarities have been overstated.[41] But more recently, Moessner has presented a case for the journey showing Jesus as the prophet like Moses.[42] Even allowing for some stretching of the evidence, there remains a strong core of Mosaic thinking that is also supported by the portrait of Jesus as the prophet who is to die in Jerusalem (13.33-34). It is uncertain whether the *Taheb* or some returning figure was a part of first-century Samaritan thinking, but it is noticeable that Jesus' sayings about the Son of Man are, with the exception of 17.25, about his future coming, that is, the return of Jesus.[43]

3. Jesus' threefold insistence on Jerusalem as his destination is a refutation of both Samaritan and Jewish attitudes towards the city. The Samaritans initially reject Jesus' messengers because of his destination, and Jesus prophesies that when he reaches the city it will kill him as it has the other prophets (13.34; cf. 11.49-51). This is because all the

---

37. Reicke, 'Instruction and Discussion'; Robinson, 'Context'.
38. Schürer–Vermes, *History*, II, pp. 19-20.
39. Goulder, 'Two Roots', pp. 73-74.
40. Evans, 'Central Section'; Drury, *Tradition*, p. 64.
41. Wenham, 'Synoptic Independence'.
42. Moessner, 'Luke's Preview'; Ravens, 'Luke 9'.
43. Marshall, *Luke, Historian and Theologian*, p. 152.

inhabitants are offenders (13.4), a comment followed by the parable of the fruitless vine (13.6-9). Matthew's version of the lament over the city (23.37-39) takes place after Jesus has entered Jerusalem (21.9) so that the words 'you will not see me henceforth until you say "Blessed is he that comes in the name of the Lord"' would refer to Jesus' coming in glory.[44] Luke, by placing the lament outside the city, provides an audience which is less likely to be restricted to Jews alone and also makes the comment refer to the entry itself. To Jews in the audience the lament would be heard as condemnation of their failure to bear fruit for God, but to Samaritans it would be heard as a fitting end to the city and its temple as well as an invitation to be gathered in by Jesus.

4. There is one further piece of evidence that the audiences in the Central Section were not composed of Jews alone; the absence of λαός to describe the crowds (apart from a textual variant at 11.53). In Luke–Acts, λαός almost always refers to Jews exclusively, whereas ὄχλος can denote either Jews (e.g. 3.7, 10; 4.42; 5.1 etc.) or Gentiles (Acts 14.11; 24.18). If λαός had been used uniformly throughout the Gospel we would expect to find approximately fifteen instances in the Central Section.[45] The absence of λαός therefore suggests a deliberate avoidance of the term in spite of the fact that Luke is well aware of the presence of Jews in the area (e.g. 11.37-44; 14.1; 17.20).

Whatever knowledge of Palestine Luke and his readers possessed, in the absence of other indications of place, the Central Section appears to record a ministry in Samaria. And the teachings of Jesus about the law, his own role and the character of Jerusalem are such as to take account of Samaritan beliefs and hopes.

Samaritans in the Gospel

Luke's first mention of the Samaritans comes, as we have noted, at what is widely recognized as a theological turning point in the Gospel (9.51-55). Some commentators see the rejection of the messengers as

---

44. Fenton, *Saint Matthew*, p. 378.
45. The calculation is based on a total number of verses in the Gospel as 1160, of which 351 are in the Central Section, 9.51–18.14. There are 35 instances of λαός in the remaining 809 verses, which, in a uniform distribution, would lead us to expect 15 instances in the Central Section. A similar calculation for the 41 occurrences of ὄχλος throughout the Gospel predicts 12 or 13 instances in the Central Section, which in fact contains 9. The approximately uniform distribution of ὄχλος makes the absence of λαός look deliberate.

parallel to the rejection of Jesus at Nazareth,[46] even though Jesus does not come into direct contact with the villagers. J.T. Sanders rightly stresses the main difference between the incidents, that in the second Luke gives a reason for the rejection; that Jesus has set his face towards Jerusalem (9.53).[47] Luke's explanation would only make sense, however, if he knew that his readers appreciated that the fundamental conflict between Jews and Samaritans was whether Jerusalem or Gerizim was the true place at which to worship Yahweh. It is therefore an important clue to the knowledge possessed by Luke's readers. When the messengers return, James and John wish to emulate Elijah who had called down fire from heaven on the king of Samaria's emissaries (2 Kgs 1.10-12). The two apostles are rebuked by Jesus (9.55).

The remarkable fact that this turning point involves an intended mission to Samaritans, rather than Jews, has not been sufficiently emphasized by commentators who focus instead on the rejection. Yet the stated reason for the rejection has nothing to do with what Jesus might be expected to say, and it is clear that Jesus accepts the reason and that he refuses to condemn the rejecters. If 9.51 is the theological turning point that most scholars believe it to be, then the incident demonstrates just how important the Samaritans are to Luke's purpose.

That importance is further shown by Luke's use of the same introductory phrase for sending out the seventy (ἀπέστειλεν...πρὸ προσώπου αὐτοῦ, 9.52; 10.1), for, since there is no mention of a change of location, his readers would assume that Jesus was still in Samaria. That the mission is directed to a non-Jewish audience is implied by Jesus twice telling the missionaries to eat what is offered to them (10.7, 8). This instruction was unnecessary for the Galilean mission of the twelve (9.1-6; cf. Mk 6.7-12; Mt. 10.5-15), and Luke does not deal with the issue of table fellowship between Jews and Gentiles until Peter's vision and the visit to Cornelius. The instructions therefore suggest an audience about whom Jews might have doubts about food sharing and for this the Samaritans are obvious candidates (*m. Ber.* 7.1; 8.8; *m. Šeb.* 8.10).

---

46. Conzelmann, *Luke*, pp. 65-66; Enslin, 'Luke and the Samaritans', p. 282; Fitzmyer, *Luke*, p. 189. Tannehill, *Narrative Unity*, p. 230, believes that the Samaritans reject Jesus because they do not understand Jesus' 'divinely determined destiny' in Jerusalem. But neither do his disciples (9.45). A more likely explanation is Luke's knowledge of Samaritan rejection of the city and its temple.

47. Sanders, *The Jews in Luke–Acts*, p. 144.

3. *The Role of the Samaritans*   83

But, as regards a Samaritan location, a possible difficulty arises with Jesus' denunciation of the Galilean towns, Bethsaida, Capernaum and Chorazin, the last of which is otherwise unknown (10.13-15). According to Luke, Jesus has already worked in Capernaum (4.23, 31-36) and Bethsaida (9.10-17), but the only reported response is that of people's amazement at the exorcism in the Capernaum synagogue (4.36). By comparison, the return of the seventy describes their joy at the success of their newly received authority over the demons (10.17; cf. 10.9). This suggests a further contrast between the response of the Galilean towns and the implied Samaritan acceptance of the seventy's message which, incidentally, contains no mention of Jerusalem.

The next appearance of a Samaritan is in the parable in which he serves as a contrast to the priest and the Levite (10.30-37). The behaviour of the two Jews is usually explained by reference to their religious scruples and, according to Jervell, anyone who subscribed to the view that Samaritans were lax about the law would see the point of the parable.[48] The difficulty with this interpretation is that Samaritans, whose only Scripture was the Pentateuch, were no more likely to be lax about the law than Jews. For a layperson, corpse impurity made one unclean for seven days (Num. 19.11-13) but, for a priest, corpse impurity was allowed only in the case of nearest kin (Lev. 21.1-3). If the man at the roadside was assumed to be dead by the travellers (Lk. 10.30), then the Samaritan would be unclean for seven days, having bathed on the third day.[49] Montgomery sees the point of the contrast being that the Samaritan would have the same religious scruples as the priest and the Levite.[50] Thus the Samaritan's neighbourliness comes not from a lack of scruples but in spite of them. How far Luke appreciated the more stringent restrictions for the priest we do not know.

But there is more to the parable than the question of keeping to the law and two further questions bring this out. The first is why there should be a move in describing the neighbour from the one to whom mercy is shown to the one who shows mercy. The answer given by Ellis is almost certainly correct: that being a neighbour requires at least two

---

48.   Jervell, *The People of God*, pp. 116, 128 nn. 11-12.
49.   E.P. Sanders, *Jewish Law*, pp. 41-42, discusses the legal problems as if the story were about an historical event.
50.   Montgomery, *Samaritans*, pp. 161, 170, seems to regard the story as an indication of Jesus' own attitude towards Samaritans. This is open to question in view of the treatment offered by Mark and Matthew.

people, such that it is not a case of 'he is my neighbour', but 'we are neighbours'.[51] The Samaritan who helps and the Jew who is helped are neighbours to each other.

The second question is more complex. Why did Luke use a Samaritan? Answers to this vary: S.G. Wilson suggests that it may be a shock tactic and an indication that belonging to the people of God is no longer the exclusive right of the Jews. This now depends 'on obedience to God and that both Samaritans and Gentiles can achieve this too'.[52] This answer does scant justice to the Samaritan because as far as he was concerned he too was a member of the people of God, unlike the Gentiles. Jews were well aware of this claim even if they did not accept it. It is also probable that Luke and his readers were aware of it, otherwise the point of the parable would be lost since the helper, like the Jews, must know the law. Sellin rightly believes that a Samaritan is used *because* he knows the law but that he forms a bridge between Jews and Gentiles.[53] J.T. Sanders holds a similar view about the Samaritans in Luke–Acts, that they have the same role as God-fearers and proselytes, forming a natural transition group.[54] This solution leaves the Samaritans without a role of their own and it fails to answer the question of why Luke did not use one of the other groups. The answer is obvious: there would be less of a shock to Jewish readers because God-fearers and proselytes were expected to behave like Jews. Samaritans, proselytes and God-fearers are not interchangeable categories for Luke, and we shall get closer to the reason for Luke's choice when we look at the LXX background to 'neighbour' ($\pi\lambda\eta\sigma\iota\text{ov}$) where it usually means a fellow Israelite.[55] It is a major concern of the parable that Jews and Samaritans are seen as fellow Israelites and that just as the Samaritan showed mercy to a Jew, so the Jewish lawyer should do likewise and show mercy to Samaritans.

51. Ellis, *Luke*, p. 160.
52. Wilson, *Luke and the Law*, pp. 15-16.
53. Selling, 'Lukas als Gleichniszähler', pp. 42-43.
54. Sanders, *The Jews in Luke–Acts*, pp. 148-50. The major difference, which Sanders does not mention, is that proselytes and God-fearers *wanted* to be close to Judaism; not so Samaritans.
55. Fichtner, *TDNT*, VI, pp. 312-15. See, for example, Deut. 4.42; 5.20 (5.17 LXX); Isa. 3.5. In Isa. 19.2, $\pi\lambda\eta\sigma\iota\text{ov}$ is used of Egyptians but it refers to people of the same nation. Also Wilson, *Luke and the Law*, p. 15. Ringgren, *Israelite Religion*, p. 134, notes 'that the word *rea'*, "neighbor" refers primarily or even exclusively to one's fellow Israelites. What we have...is not love of one's neighbor in a Christian sense, but more of a kind of national solidarity.'

3. The Role of the Samaritans

Therein lies the shock of the parable for Jewish-Christian readers.

Luke's third Samaritan story is the account of the healing of the ten lepers (17.11-19). The story is related to the earlier healing of a leper (Lk. 5.12-14; Mk 1.40-44) but it has a quite different purpose. In the first story the emphasis is on Jesus' healing power, whereas in the second the emphasis is on the response of the Samaritan who is often regarded as a model of faith and thankfulness when compared with the nine others. Yet the only reason for going to the priests is to be certified as being free from leprosy and to offer the appropriate sacrifice and, since all are healed on the way (17.14), they all show faith in Jesus. This suggests that the story is as much about giving glory to God as about who shows faith, a conclusion reinforced by the omission of 'your faith has saved you' from Vaticanus. Furthermore, if the nine go to the priests and offer the Levitical sacrifices, surely they have given glory to God for their healing?[56] So could the Samaritan be glorifying God for something more than healing (δοξάζων, v. 15, δόξαν, v. 18)? Jesus, being a Jew, describes the Samaritan as a foreigner (ἀλλογενής, v. 18) and in the LXX the foreigner is excluded from the congregation of Israel in worship[57] and marriage.[58] This exclusion also applied to the temple in the first century and foreigners were forbidden to enter beyond the court of the Gentiles on pain of death.[59] According to Josephus, Samaritans entered the temple in the time of Herod the Tetrach but were later excluded because they desecrated the temple at Passover.[60] Luke does not make clear whether the lepers are to go to the Jerusalem temple and the use of the plural 'priests' has led Marshall to propose that the Jews would go to Jerusalem and the Samaritan to Gerizim;[61] however, as Jervell points out, Jesus would hardly direct someone to a cult which was heretical to orthodox Jews.[62] According to Lk. 9.51-53 it is clear that Luke appreciated the point.

There is one notable exception to the general LXX view of foreigners, and that is in Isaiah 56.

---

56. Lev. 14.
57. E.g. Num. 1.51; 3.10; 18.7. The ἀλλογενής shall be put to death.
58. 1 Esd. 9.7-15.
59. Josephus, *War* 5.194.
60. Josephus, *Ant.* 18.30.
61. Marshall, *Luke*, p. 651.
62. Jervell, *The People of God*, p. 121.

[Thus says the Lord,] 'Let not the foreigner who has joined himself to the Lord say, "The Lord will surely separate me from his people"' (56.3).
'And the foreigners who join themselves to the Lord...every one who keeps the Sabbath...and holds fast my covenant—these I will bring to my holy mountain, and make them joyful in my house of prayer; and their burnt offerings and sacrifices will be accepted on my altar' (56.6-7).

The cultic motif in Luke's story springs from the fact that leprosy is the only disease for which the law requires priestly certification of healing (Lev. 14.2-57), and it seems probable that Luke intended his readers to infer that all the lepers set out for Jerusalem. If that is the case, then Luke's use of ἀλλογενής on the lips of Jesus, the only instance of the word in the NT, points to the possibility that Luke was influenced by Isa. 56.3-7. This would imply that the Samaritan glorifies God, not only for his healing, but also because he has been acknowledged as a member of Israel by Jesus the Jew. No real Samaritan would have been impressed by the fulfilment of a prophecy not contained in the law, nor would he have glorified God for being allowed to make an offering in the Jerusalem temple. Luke's readers, however, were intended to see the situation differently, as one of restoration by the prophet like Moses. Luke never extends the possibility of a non-Jew going to the temple, other than this Samaritan. Nowhere does he describe Gentiles going to the temple, nor does he describe it as a house of prayer for all nations (Lk. 19.46; Mk 11.17; Isa. 56.7). He was not prepared to follow Isaiah that far because, in Luke's eyes, the temple had been for Israel alone.

Enslin has drawn attention to a further aspect of the story, that it contains allusions to Elisha's healing of Naaman (2 Kgs 5) and this reminds the reader of the many lepers in Israel at the time of Elisha (Lk. 4.27).[63] Enslin's observation suggests that Luke presents Jesus going further than Elisha by healing lepers in Israel, just as he had surpassed Elijah by raising a widow's son in Israel (7.11-15).

Luke's presentation of the Samaritans in the Gospel has a three-stage development. He begins with the acknowledgment of the cultic division with the Jews and then moves on to the basis on which the division is to be healed: the recognition that they are neighbours, fellow members of Israel. On the assumption that the Jewish and Samaritan lepers go to the same priests, the final stage of the process represents the transcending of the division. In this way Luke prepares his readers for the development

---

63. Enslin, 'Samaritans', pp. 295-96.

3. *The Role of the Samaritans* 87

in Acts where the mission to Samaria is an unqualified success and the Samaritans are unhesitatingly accepted by the Jewish-Christian leaders.

Samaritans in Acts

The mission to a city of Samaria (8.4-8) is preceded by Stephen's speech and martyrdom, and these, together with the persecution that follow, form the dramatic cause of the mission. The speech itself has long been thought to contain Samaritan echoes and, more than a century ago, E.H. Plumtre suggested that the burial of the patriarchs at Shechem (7.16) and the mission to Samaria might reflect a Samaritan tradition behind the speech.[64] Since then much more extensive claims for the use of such traditions have been made by Spiro. He lists fourteen points that, he believes, support the theory that Stephen was a Samaritan and that the speech was not delivered to the Sanhedrin but was a missionary tract to diaspora Jews.[65] Although Spiro's conclusions about Stephen and the speech's missionary character have not gained wide acceptance, a number of scholars hold that the speech does contain some Samaritan influences. Spiro's thesis has been subjected to point-by-point criticism by Mare who concludes that the evidence equally supports its Jewish character.[66] Spiro,[67] Scharlemann[68] and Scobie[69] have each produced lists of what they consider to be Samaritan features in the speech and we shall now examine the more important points from the debate. This is done under two main headings:

A. textual, where references from the OT appear to use a text closer to the Samaritan Pentateuch (SP) than to the MT or LXX.
B. Other possible Samaritan features.

A. *Textual*

1. In Acts 7.4, Stephen says that Abraham left the land of the Chaldeans after the death of his father. According to Gen. 11.32 (MT, LXX), Abraham's father, Terah, lived for 205 years, but in Gen. 11.26 it states that Abraham was born when Terah was 70, and in Gen. 12.4 that

---

64. Plumtre, 'Samaritan Element', pp. 36-39.
65. Spiro, 'Samaritan Background'.
66. Mare, 'Acts 7'.
67. Spiro, 'Samaritan Background', pp. 285-89.
68. Scharlemann, *Stephen*, pp. 50-51.
69. Scobie, 'Samaritan Christianity', pp. 393-96.

Abraham was 75 when he left. This would make Terah 145 when he died and this is the age given in the SP. Richard has disputed dependence on the SP[70] not least because Philo also agrees with Luke[71] and no one suggests that Philo used the SP. On the overall textual issue, Richard argues that a wider study of the evidence favours a common text tradition behind Acts, Philo and SP.[72]

2. Acts 7.5 states that God gave Abraham no inheritance (κληρονομίαν) in the land. The LXX of Deut. 2.5 lacks κληρονομία but Wilcox notes that the SP and Targum contain words that are widely translated by κλῆρος and κληρονομία.[73] Scobie regards this as evidence of dependence on the SP[74] but Richard rejects this, proposing instead Luke's use of a Greek *Vorlage* that had its roots in a Hebrew recension.[75]

3. Acts 7.32 quotes from Exod. 3.6, 'I am the God of your fathers, the God of Abraham and of Isaac and of Jacob'. In the MT and LXX of Exod. 3.6 the singular 'father' is used but the SP has the plural. Again, Scobie sees dependence on the SP,[76] and again Richard argues for a textual solution. He notes the plural in two miniscules of the LXX and similar forms in Justin Martyr.[77] This leads him to posit an original plural form in the LXX and that it was used by Luke.

4. The last example is in Acts 7.37. Thus far Luke has followed the narrative sequence of Genesis and Exodus but he now inserts God's promise of a prophet (Deut. 18.15). The SP contains a similar insertion into Exodus 20. Scobie regards this as another hint of Samaritan influence,[78] an opinion rejected by Richard in the light of evidence from the Qumran scrolls. Richard offers two suggestions: either the use of a Palestinian (proto-Samaritan) text type or, more probably, the direct quotation of Deuteronomy by Luke.[79]

The result of this review of the discussion of the four verses points to

70. Richard, 'Samaritan Evidence', pp. 196-97. Pummer, 'Samaritan Pentateuch', pp. 441-43, also rejects the idea of Samaritan textual influence.
71. Philo, *Migr. Abr.* p. 177.
72. Richard, 'Samaritan Evidence', pp. 196-97.
73. Wilcox, *The Semitisms in Acts*, pp. 27-30.
74. Scobie, 'Samaritan Christianity', p. 393.
75. Richard, 'Samaritan Evidence', pp. 197-99.
76. Scobie, 'Samaritan Christianity', p. 393.
77. Richard, 'Samaritan Evidence', pp. 199-202.
78. Scobie, 'Samaritan Christianity', p. 393.
79. Richard, 'Samaritan Evidence', pp. 202-206.

3. *The Role of the Samaritans* 89

an open verdict rather than clear proof or disproof of Samaritan influence from the SP. Richard's study puts forward alternative explanations about which we can be no more certain than we can about the case he challenges. And, as Coggins points out, the argument based on text types available to Luke raises the question of why Samaritanisms of this sort are not found elsewhere in Acts.[80] Richard also looks at the general question of how the evidence has been evaluated and he is rather scathing about those critics who argue their case on the cumulative effect of the evidence.[81] From the logical viewpoint he is, of course, correct: two weak arguments do not make a strong one. But, in a work where the purpose of the author requires subtlety and allusion, proof and disproof may be the wrong criteria to apply. It would have been sufficient for Luke to have used words and ideas that would strike chords in the readers, just as they still do with commentators today.

B. *Other Features*
Of the suggested Samaritanisms mentioned by Spiro and Scobie we will select three.

1. Acts 7.16 implies that Abraham, Jacob and Jacob's sons were all buried at Shechem. Genesis 23 records Abraham's purchase of the cave at Machpelah and, in Gen. 49.31-32, that Abraham and Isaac were buried there as was Jacob (Gen. 50.12-13). According to Gen. 33.19, Jacob bought a field at Shechem. The burial places of Jacob's sons are not mentioned in the OT, although Josh. 24.32 tells of the burial of Joseph's bones at Shechem and, in later literature, all the brothers except Joseph were buried in the field at Machpelah.[82] There is no question here of Luke using a Samaritan source, since there was no tradition that the patriarchs were buried at Shechem, in spite of it being the Samaritan sanctuary.[83] Did Luke simply confuse the two purchases, or is the double mention of Shechem a deliberate 'mistake' on his part? There is no evidence that later copyists saw it as a mistake and these are the only mentions of Shechem in the NT apart from a variant reading at

80. Coggins, 'Samaritans and Acts', p. 424, regards the absence of 'Samaritanisms' in the rest of Acts as the most noteworthy evidence for Samaritan influence in Stephen's speech.
81. Richard, 'Samaritan Evidence', pp. 193-95.
82. Haenchen, *Acts*, p. 280. *Jub.* 46.8-9. Josephus *Ant.* 2.199 says that Joseph's brothers were buried at Hebron.
83. Scobie, 'Samaritan Christianity', p. 394, regards it as a Samaritan counter-claim against Jews, seeking to place the burial of the Patriarchs in their own country.

Jn 4.5. Luke does not mention that God appeared to Abraham at Shechem (Gen. 12.6-7), presumably because it would detract from the appearance in Mesopotamia (Acts 7.2) which, as we saw in Chapter 2, serves another purpose for Luke. The composition of Luke's church may provide a clue to the puzzle for, as Esler has demonstrated, it contained a significant number of Jews.[84] If this is the case then it is particularly difficult to believe that Luke, with his knowledge of the OT, should have left the blunder uncorrected. Coggins thinks that Luke did not have the geographical knowledge to realize his mistake.[85] Yet, given Luke's interest in Samaritans, it is hard to accept that he did not realize the implications and the probable effect upon his Jewish readers. Perhaps it was an attempt to remind his readers that Abraham and the patriarchs were the fathers of Samaritans as well as of Jews.

2. The two remaining points from Spiro's article can be dealt with briefly. The first is that at Acts 7.44-45 Joshua is described as bringing in the tent of witness and, in Samaritan tradition, Joshua established the cult at Gerizim and was therefore considered next in importance to Moses.

Secondly, Gaster notes that Samaritan belief in the *Taheb* is not the same as Jewish belief in a princely Messiah but closer to the deuteronomic prophet.[86] We have discussed this point above (pp. 80-81).

3. There is one further possible Samaritan feature in the speech that has been overlooked in this area of discussion. At 7.23 Moses visits 'his brethren, the sons of Israel' (cf. Exod. 2.11). When Moses returns the next day after he has killed the Egyptian he finds two Israelites fighting. He tries to reconcile them by saying 'Men, you are brothers, why do you wrong each other?' (7.26) but, in the Exodus account, the men are not described as brothers but Hebrews. At the time of Stephen and Luke the term 'Hebrew' was used by Samaritans as a form of self-designation.[87] It would therefore be inappropriate here because it might be understood as Samaritans fighting among themselves, or it might be misunderstood in view of the different sense of the word in Acts 6.1. Stephen's repetition of 'brethren' (7.23, 25, 26, cf. also vv. 2, 13, 37)

---

84. Esler, *Community and Gospel*, pp. 30-33.
85. Coggins, 'Samaritans and Acts', p. 425.
86. Gaster, *IDB*, IV, pp. 190-97; Maddox, *Purpose*, p. 53. It is important to note that the *Taheb* will restore the tabernacle, not the temple. The Samaritans did not rebuild their own temple after its destruction.
87. Spiro, 'Samaritan Background', p. 292. Josephus, *Ant*. 11.344.

suggests that the fighting brothers may have some added significance, since what Moses says in v. 26 is not strictly necessary as a reason for his subsequent rejection.

A further, if somewhat tenuous, indication lies in the description of the aggressor as 'the man who was wronging his neighbour' (πλησίον, 7.27; Exod. 2.13). 'Neighbour' is not as common among the evangelists as we might expect, given its popularity with Christians today. In Mark and Matthew it occurs only in quotations of, or references to, Lev. 19.18. This is also true for Luke, but Jesus then tells the parable in which the neighbour is a Samaritan. Samaritans regarded themselves as descendants of Jacob-Israel and so, to them even if not to Jews, they were entitled to be called sons of Israel. It is quite possible that Luke is making the point that, just as the brethren are neighbours who should live in peace with each other, so too are Jews and Samaritans. Luke has already given a strong hint of this in the answer to the lawyers question and the parable in Lk. 10.25-37.

The role of Moses in giving salvation (7.25) is not confined to delivering Israel from Egyptian oppression but it also includes the call to brotherhood for all who are members of Israel. This aspect of salvation was not understood by the two men and it led to the rejection of Moses; moreover, it preceded the call to deliver Israel from Egypt by forty years (Acts 7.30). The implication is that Jesus, the prophet like Moses whom God would raise up 'from your brethren' (7.37), would also have the task of healing the divisions in Israel, a role attributed to Jesus (Acts 3.22-23) and hence to his followers.

Stephen's speech contains a number of Samaritan overtones and allusions, and although they may not be compelling when taken singly, they do have a cumulative effect (*pace* Richard). Scobie believes that it would have been impossible for Luke to have written the speech with all its Samaritanisms because the outlook of the speech is not in line with Lukan theology.[88] He accepts that Luke edited the speech, but this only makes the matter more confusing because it would mean that Luke deliberately retained material with which he disagreed. The present study shows that, given Luke's obvious interest in Samaritans, the speech is not merely consistent with his theology but is an essential part of the expression of that theology as well as being the necessary preface to the mission in Samaria.

---

88. Scobie, 'Samaritan Christianity', p. 396.

The Mission in Samaria

Philip's mission to a city in Samaria (8.4-13) is to proclaim the Christ and to preach the good news of 'the kingdom of God and the name of Jesus Christ' (8.5, 12). The combination of the message and the signs leads not only to a widescale acceptance of the gospel but also to the conversion of the influential Simon. Later, this mission is followed by preaching in the Samaritan villages, although Luke makes no comment on the level of success (8.25). He does, however, say that the church throughout Judaea, Galilee and Samaria had peace and was built up (9.31)[89] and for Luke these three areas comprise the land of Israel.

Apart from the dramatic necessity within the narrative for the immediate and uncontroversial conversion of the Samaritans, there is also a contrast between their eager acceptance of the gospel in Acts and the initial rebuff to Jesus' disciples (Lk. 9.52-53).[90] There is a nice sense of balance in the mission: now the message is brought by those fleeing from Jerusalem and who share with the Samaritans—if for different reasons—rejection by the Jewish leadership. On the other side, the Samaritans now accept the Jewish hope of the coming Messiah (cf. 3.20-21).

The admission of the Samaritans caused none of the problems for the church that were raised by the admission of Gentiles because Samaritans were circumcised on the eighth day and observed the law. The apostles could therefore quickly ratify the mission by sending Peter and John so that the converts could receive the Holy Spirit (8.14-17). The gift of the Spirit to the Samaritans is Luke's first account since Pentecost of a group receiving the Spirit; there is no such description of the gift for the five thousand Jewish believers (4.4), although there is little doubt that the gift is implied. The next major outpouring is on the Gentile house of Cornelius (10.44-47).

The Samaria mission is seen by some as the stepping stone to the Gentile mission and, in terms of the narrative development, this is true. But there is one all-important difference between the two missions in

---

89. Massyngbaerde Ford, 'Reconciliation and Forgiveness', pp. 89-90, mentions several disputes between Jews and Samaritans. Is Luke's comment about peace throughout Judaea, Galilee and Samaria (Acts 9.31) intended to show Christianity as the healer of past disputes?

90. Danker, *Jesus and the New Age*, p. 209, notes that the Samaritans receive (δέδεκται, 8.14) the word of God, thus reversing their action in Lk. 9.53 (οὐκ ἐδέξαντο).

3. The Role of the Samaritans

that the one to the Gentiles requires the direct and special intervention of God whereas the one to Samaria does not. This is a clear indication that Luke regards Jews and Samaritans as being within a fundamental group to which even the most devout God-fearer does not belong. The conversion of the Samaritans therefore has no theologically necessary consequence that there should be a Gentile mission and Jervell is correct to say that Samaritans are not Gentiles or half-Gentiles.[91] Unfortunately this has led him to the *non-sequitur* that Samaritans must be Jews, albeit Jews that have gone astray,[92] thus they are part of the people of God and have a special status within Israel.[93] That the Samaritans are part of Israel is confirmed by the apostles' unqualified acceptance of the result of Philip's mission, but this does not mean that the Samaritans are Jews. In fact, their *raison d'être* in Luke–Acts is that they are Israelites and not Jews.

The Restoration of Israel

I must now try to show how the Samaritan theme fits into the wider context of Israel's restoration as Luke presents it. The salvation of Israel that is set out in the birth stories reappears at the end of the Gospel in the disciples' statement that they had hoped that Jesus would be the one to redeem Israel (24.21). The implication is that it was the death of Jesus, rather than a failure in his ministry, that had caused their hope to fade. That ministry had been directed towards Israel and, with the possible exception of the Gerasene demoniac (8.26-39),[94] Gentiles do not meet Jesus. Even the worthy centurion speaks to Jesus through Jewish intermediaries (7.3).

It is the resurrection that rekindles the earlier hope and the apostles' first words in Acts ask whether Jesus will restore (ἀποκαθιστάνεις) the kingdom to Israel at this time (1.6). ἀποκαθίστημι is used on a number of occasions in the LXX in the context of Israel's restoration, for example, 'Thus says the Lord: "If you return (ἐπιστρέψῃς), I will restore you"' (ἀποκαταστήσω, Jer. 15.19) and, in Jer. 16.15 and 27[50].19, restoration involves both the northern and southern kingdoms.

---

91. Jervell, *The People of God*, p. 128 nn. 11, 12.
92. Jervell, *The People of God*, p. 118.
93. Jervell, *The People of God*, pp. 119, 123.
94. Regardless of the variants of place, the fact that the man lived among tombs (8.27) strongly implies that he was a Gentile.

In Mal. 3.22-23 the verb is used for the results of Elijah's return, and in Sir. 48.10 it is promised that Elijah will restore (καταστήσαι) the tribes of Jacob-Israel.

The first question we have to consider is whether Luke envisages the restoration taking place in history or whether it is to be an eschatological event. In Jervell's opinion the event had already taken place by the time of the Jerusalem council (Acts 15) and had resulted in the Jews being divided into two groups: the repentant, who believed in Jesus, and the unrepentant. It had also been necessary for Israel to recognize that its mission to the Gentiles had begun under God's initiative and that the converted Gentiles were a part of the restored Israel.[95] At the end of Acts, the adverse judgment is finally passed on the Jews and 'the Gentile mission is really only beginning'.[96]

Jervell's thesis has been challenged by Wainwright in favour of eschatological restoration. He suggests that the answer to the apostles' question is given in the prophecy of the two men who appear after the ascension: 'This Jesus...will come in the same way as you saw him go into heaven' (1.11). Although the time of his coming is unknown it has been fixed by the Father's authority (1.7).[97] Wainwright is also correct to point to the future character of Acts 3.19-21:[98]

> Repent and turn again (ἐπιστρέψατε) that your sins may be blotted out and that times of refreshment (ἀναψύξεως) may come from the presence of the Lord, and that he may send the Christ appointed for you, Jesus, whom heaven must receive until the time of establishing (ἀποκαταστάσεως) all that God spoke by the mouth of his holy prophets of old.

In view of the use of ἀποκαθιστάνεις in 1.6, it makes better sense to translate ἀποκαταστάσεως in 3.21 as 'restoration'. This is also the sense of the word when Josephus describes the restoration of Jerusalem (*Ant.* 11.63, 98), as it is in Jer. 15.19 (above). For Luke, as for Jeremiah, restoration depends upon (re)turning to God and, by combining

---

95. Jervell, *The People of God*, pp. 51-53, 56, 60. His comment that 'the Gentiles have gained a share in what has been given to Israel' (p. 53) implies membership of Israel for believers.
96. Jervell, *The People of God*, pp. 63-64. This view is discussed further in Chapter 7 (below), and Jervell's view of the end of Acts is rejected.
97. Wainwright, 'Restoration'.
98. Wainwright, 'Restoration', p. 77.

3. *The Role of the Samaritans*

the restoration with the coming of Christ, he reinforces the view of Acts 1.11.[99]

Another piece of evidence that points to an eschatological restoration is the appointment of the apostles as judges of Israel's twelve tribes (Lk. 22.30). This had not taken place by the time that Luke was writing and the fact that the martyred James was not replaced can only mean that his position as one of the judges is preserved in heaven. This point alone argues forcibly against Jervell's opinion that judgment has been passed on Israel by the end of Acts.

One reason for the different critical solutions to the problem of the time of Israel's restoration is that Luke has, in effect, a two-stage eschatology. There is the time of the church, the new age of the Spirit prophesied by Joel (Acts 2.17-21), in which Israel is in the process of being restored. There is also the time when the Messiah comes and finally restores the kingdom to Israel.[100] Yet restoration does not mean that Luke regarded the church as the new Israel, although some critics think that he held such a view. Fitzmyer, for example, has suggested that the apostles' question about restoration and the appointment of Matthias (1.21-26) point in that direction,[101] suggesting also that the early Christians, like the Qumran Essenes, saw themselves as the Israel of the end days.[102] On the other hand E.P. Sanders notes that the Qumran covenanters did not exclude other Israelites[103] and, however much Luke may have regretted that all Israel had not become believers, he neither excluded non-believing Jews nor thought that Christians were a new Israel.

The final words of the risen Jesus promise the apostles that they will receive the gift of the Spirit and be his witnesses 'in Jerusalem, Judaea and Samaria and to the end of the earth' (1.8). The usual identification of 'the end of the earth' with Rome finds some support from *Pss. Sol.* 8.15, where Pompey is described as coming from the end of the earth and, secondly, it is where Luke finishes his narrative. But these facts do not do sufficient justice to the OT background. There are enough instances of ἕως ἐσχάτου τῆς γῆς in Isaiah alone to suggest that

---

99. Franklin, *Christ the Lord*, p. 102. Jervell, *The People of God*, pp. 58-59, does not discuss the eschatological aspect of Peter's speech in Acts 3.11-26.
100. Franklin, *Christ the Lord*, p. 96.
101. Fitzmyer, 'Jewish Christianity', p. 236.
102. Fitzmyer, 'Jewish Christianity', p. 244.
103. Sanders, *Jewish People*, pp. 175-76.

Luke's vision of the gospel's progress did not stop at Rome[104] but that it was to go throughout the world. Furthermore, each of the following citations is in the context of eschatological salvation.

> Be broken, you peoples (ἔθνη), and be dismayed; give ear, *all you far countries* (Isa. 8.9).

> Turn to me and be saved (σωθήσεσθε) all the ends of the earth (οἱ ἀπ' ἐσχάτου τῆς γῆς)!
> For I am God, and there is no other! (Isa. 45.22).

> declare this with a shout of joy, proclaim it, send it forth *to the end of the earth*;
> say, 'The Lord has redeemed his servant Jacob' (Isa. 48.20).

> Behold, the Lord has proclaimed *to the end of the earth*: Say to the daughter of Zion,
> 'Behold, your salvation (LXX ὁ σωτήρ, saviour) comes;
> ...And they shall be called The holy people,
> The redeemed (λελυτρωμένον) of the Lord' (Isa. 62.11-12).

In addition to these examples, each of which contains ideas present in Luke–Acts, there is the citation of Isa. 49.6 which is used as the justification for turning to the Gentiles (Acts 13.47).[105] Also, the fact that Jesus is God's servant (Acts 3.13, 26; 4.27, 30), who is a light to the nations (Lk. 2.30-32) suggests that Luke was aware of the full verse:

> you should be my servant to raise up the tribes of Jacob and to return the scattered of Israel (διασπορὰν τοῦ Ισραηλ ἐπιστρέψαι). I will give you as a light to [the] nations, that my salvation (σωτηρίαν) may reach *the end of the earth* (Isa. 49.6).

If this was the work of Jesus it was also to be the continuing work of the Church, to raise up the tribes of Israel and to restore the diaspora. This puts the Gentile mission into its true context because it is, strictly speaking, the mission of Israel[106] as well as part of Israel's own restoration. There can be no Gentile mission without a mission to Israel at the same time, and this is why Paul's last recorded speech is to members of the diaspora. As early as Lk. 2.30-32 the reader is told that God's salvation

---

104. Ellis, 'End of the Earth', notes that in the geographical use of the phrase it refers not to Rome but to Gades as the westward limit, west of Gibraltar.
105. Haenchen, *Acts*, pp. 143-44.
106. Jervell, *The People of God*, pp. 60, 61. Ringgren, *Israelite Religion*, p. 294. 'Israel is called to a position of leadership among the nations; this consists primarily in making known the will of Yahweh.'

3. *The Role of the Samaritans* 97

is a light of revelation to the Gentiles and for Israel's glory. This calls to mind not only Isa. 49.6 but also 46.13:

> I will bring near my deliverance (LXX δικαιοσύνην: justice, vindication, acquittal)...and my σωτηρίαν will not tarry; I will put σωτηρίαν in Zion for Israel my glory (δόξασμα)!

In Acts, the missionary sequence begins in Zion and follows the plan of 1.8, spreading through Samaria and the diaspora. Although there is an almost parallel Gentile mission to that among the diaspora, it is very significant that no preaching to Gentiles is reported in Rome.[107]

The Israel theme continues after the ascension with the first act of the apostles, the election of Matthias. He completes the twelve who will judge the twelve tribes (1.21-26; cf. Lk. 22.30) but the fact that he is never mentioned again shows that his sole function is to complete the number of judges.[108] The obvious point that the twelve tribes must include the ten northern tribes has not been sufficiently emphasized by commentators. Yet the twelve tribe theme was sufficiently important to Luke for him to have apparently invented a new word, δωδεκάφυλον (Acts 26.7).[109] We have already noted Stephen's contribution to the theme (7.8). Luke's stress on the twelve tribes makes it quite clear that the restoration of Israel cannot be confined to the tribe of Judah alone and it is for this reason that the Samaritans take on the importance that they have for Luke. The Samaritans are a stepping stone to the Gentile mission because there is a theological imperative to show signs of the healing of the old division of Israel. Hence the success attributed to Philip's mission before the Gentile mission can begin.

When Luke speaks of Israel he uses the word in more than one sense. There is the contemporary use as a form of address, 'men of Israel' which is common in Acts and which is directed only to Jews. Secondly, there is the general use where the composition is not defined, a sense we have noted in the birth stories, for example. This is also the sense of Israel as a united nation. The third aspect of the term is found in the Nazareth sermon, where it means the northern kingdom (Lk. 4.25, 27). When Jesus speaks of widows and lepers in Israel he means the ten tribes whose capital was Samaria. Elijah worked in Samaria in the time of Ahab (1 Kgs 17.1, 9; 18.17-40), and Elisha was known as the

---

107. In Chapter 7, I argue that some Jews are converted in Rome.
108. Rengstorf, 'Election of Matthias'.
109. Moulton and Geden, *Concordance*, p. 236.

'Prophet in Samaria' (2 Kgs 5.3). Moreover, according to *Liv. Proph.* 22.3 from the first century CE, he was buried in Samaria. Both Elijah and Elisha had the task of telling the northern kingdom to return to Yahweh in obedience and true worship. Elijah and Elisha are typologically important to Luke in his understanding of Jesus (see Chapter 4, below) and we have already seen that both incidents in which Jesus is involved with Samaritans contain allusions to the two Samarian prophets. We cannot, therefore, separate Luke's Christology from his concern for the Samaritans.

The Samaritan Role in the Restoration

The fact that Luke is nowhere explicit about the Samaritan role in Israel's restoration might seem a powerful argument against the view proposed here. After all, if Samaritan membership was so important in Luke's thinking why has he not made it thoroughly obvious? Whatever the reasons for the lack of an unambiguous statement, we can at least see that such a view of Samaritans is not unique in the NT, as a brief comparison with John's Gospel will show. We have already noted that both Luke and John describe missions to Samaria and that the Samaritan response contrasts sharply with a Jewish reluctance to believe. And there are other important similarities in the thinking of the two evangelists. In spite of John's frequent scathing criticism of the Jews and his belief that Jesus takes away the sin of the world (1.29), he, even more than Luke, keeps Jesus away from Gentiles and his only uses of ἔθνος is to refer to the nation of Israel (11.48, 50, 51, 52; 18.35). The Greeks that he mentions (7.35; 12.20) are not Gentiles but Greek-speaking Jews, as both contexts show,[110] thus the Johannine Jesus does not go beyond the people of Israel, which is composed of Samaritans, whose father is Jacob (4.12), and Jews, who claim Abraham as their father (8.53). As in Luke, 'King of the Jews' is used only by Jesus' accusers but, unlike Luke, John explicitly uses the title 'king of Israel', yet only on the lips of those who know and believe in Jesus' true status (1.49; 12.13). John supports his belief that Jesus is king of the whole nation of Israel with Jesus' self-descriptions in terms that come from Israel's past: the vine (15.1-6), shepherd (10.11-16) and manna (6.31-

---

110. Marsh, *St John*, pp. 339-40, and Lightfoot, *St John*, p. 251, take the Greeks to be Gentiles. Robinson, 'Destination and Purpose', strongly advocates that they were Greek-speaking Jews.

35).[111] How John saw the constitution of Israel after the death and resurrection of Jesus we are not told, and fortunately it is not a question that need be pursued here. But it is clear that for John, the historical Israel to which Jesus' mission is directed contains both Jews and Samaritans. This does not, of course, guarantee that such a view was shared by Luke, but it does show that if we are right about Luke, his views were not unique in NT Christianity.

Of the four evangelists, two take a positive and accepting view of Samaritans while Matthew, probably writing for a Jewish-Christian congregation in Syria, specifically excludes them from Jesus' mission. In this he reflects the hard line Jewish attitude and he confirms this by tracing Jesus' descent through the kings of Judah. Matthew is also the only evangelist who finds no offence in the title 'king of the Jews' (2.2). For Matthew, the historical Israel is Jewish. Mark probably wrote for a Gentile readership in Rome where it might reasonably be expected that Jewish–Samaritan relations in the church were not an issue and he therefore omits any mention of them. For Mark (15.32) and Matthew (27.42), 'king of Israel' is interchangeable with 'king of the Jews' (Mk 15.18; Mt. 27.11) as a term of mockery but, at Lk. 23.35, 'king of Israel' is changed to 'the Christ of God, the Chosen One'.

Luke's view of the Samaritans was very probably conditioned by the Jewish side of the division, but it was also strongly influenced by Samaritan claims to be the true descendants of the northern tribes. We have seen that some rabbinical writings give a grudging acknowledgment of that claim and, for Luke, Samaritans were the only possible candidates for that role, however doubtful it might have seemed to him. It was his concern for Israel's restoration that made the Samaritans vital to his thesis. This restoration did not just entail the conversion of Jews alone but something altogether more grand: nothing less than a return to the unity that had once existed under David. Nothing less could be expected of the one of whom the first prophecy was that he would be given the throne of his father David and that he would reign over the house of Jacob for ever (Lk. 1.32-33).

Hope for the reunification of the two kingdoms was no new hope but went back to the prophets, of which Ezekiel is an excellent example.

> Son of man, take a stick and write on it, 'For Judah and the children of Israel associated with him'; then take another stick and write on it, 'For

111. Robinson, 'Destination and Purpose', p. 114.

Joseph (the stick of Ephraim) and all the house of Israel associated with him'; and join them together into one stick, that they may become one in your hand (Ezek. 37.15-17).

Gaster considers that this passage is evidence that Ezekiel shows no doubts about Ephraim's purity of descent or that they were not the genuine tribes of northern Palestine.[112] Isaiah too has the same hope of return and unity.

In that day the Lord will extend his hand yet a second time to recover the remnant which is left of his people, from Assyria...He will raise up an ensign [the stem of Jesse, 11.10] for the nations, and will assemble the outcasts of Israel, and gather the dispersed (διεσπαρμένους) of Judah from the four corners of the earth (Isa. 11.11-12).

Both oracles describe the Lord working through human agents, the prophet who is addressed as 'son of man' and the Davidic scion, the 'stem of Jesse'. Such ideas, particularly that of a Davidic ruler whom the nations will seek, agree well with Luke's own outlook. Other passages from the prophets will be cited later in this chapter.

Some of the pseudepigraphal writings also express a hope for the return of the northern tribes. *4 Ezra* 13.40-48 looks for their return in the last days as does *2 Baruch* 78. But in each case, and more clearly so in *4 Ezra*, the lost tribes had crossed the Euphrates to a land where no one had ever lived (*4 Ezra* 13.42). This means that they had been preserved free from outside contamination until the eschatological ingathering, a state of affairs that the author could hardly have applied to Samaritans.[113]

Given the existence of this hope, does Luke give further hints that he shared this hope for the two kingdoms? There are four passages which, I suggest, are open to interpretation in this way.

1. *Luke 13.28-29*

There you will weep and gnash your teeth, when you see Abraham and Isaac and Jacob and all the prophets in the kingdom of God and you yourselves thrust out. And people will come from east and west, and from north and south, and sit at table in the kingdom of God.

There are major differences from the parallel passage in Mt. 8.11-12. First, Matthew's version is set within the story of the centurion's servant and hence it implies the presence of Gentiles. The saying that the

112. Gaster, *The Samaritans*, p. 14.
113. Bowman, *The Samaritan Problem*, p. 57.

centurion's faith is greater than that found in Israel is followed by the saying about who will sit with the patriarchs, while 'the sons of the kingdom' will be cast out. This suggests a comparison between unbelieving Jews and faithful Gentile Christians. Luke's setting is on the way to Jerusalem and suggests a non-Gentile audience. Secondly, in Luke's account, it is the audience, those who have not striven to enter by the narrow door (13.24), who will be cast out. Thirdly, Luke includes those from the north and south (ἀπὸ βορρᾶ καὶ νότου, 13.29) who will sit in the kingdom. It is this addition that is at the centre of this discussion. Some commentators suggest that the four points of the compass may be a quotation from Ps. 106.3 (LXX) which describes the gathering of the redeemed of the Lord (v. 2). The difficulty with this suggestion is that both the MT and LXX read 'sea' in place of 'south' and, as Marshall notes, in the OT east and west are sufficient to signify the whole world.[114] In favour of reading 'sea' is the fact that seafarers are among those redeemed from trouble (vv. 23-32).

It has been suggested that the incomers are Gentiles[115] or diaspora Jews,[116] but neither suggestion is wholly satisfactory because each fails to do justice to Luke's addition of north and south which may refer to the two kingdoms. In Isa. 11.12-13 (see above) the prophet looks for the return of God's people from Assyria and peace between Ephraim and Judah as well as for the gathering of the dispersed from the 'four corners of the earth'. The idea of the reunification of God's people to live in peace with each other makes these verses a plausible background to Luke's thinking in 13.28-29.

The use of north and south to refer to the two kingdoms is found in the OT, sometimes coupled with the idea of reunification. For example, Jer. 16.14-15 speaks of the days that are coming when it will be said 'As the Lord lives who brought up the house of Israel out of the north country (γῆς βορρᾶ)'. In Jer. 3.11-12 the prophet is commanded to proclaim to the north, 'to faithless Israel [who] has shown herself less guilty than false Judah', to return because the Lord is merciful and will bring them to Zion. Jer. 13.19 speaks of the cities of the south (νότον) in the context of Judah. It would therefore seem quite possible that Luke

---

114. Marshall, *Luke*, p. 568. Fitzmyer, *Luke*, p. 1026, suggests that *ûmiyyām* should be read *ûmiyyāmîn*.
115. Marshall, *Luke*, p. 568. Wilson, *Gentile Mission*, p. 33. Evans, *Saint Luke*, p. 559.
116. King, 'Universalism', pp. 201-203.

used 'north' and 'south' to refer to the two kingdoms, particularly in view of Jeremiah's restoration theme. The use of the terms in 13.19-20 would thus be a pointer to the reuniting of the descendants of the two kingdoms, to Samaritans as well as Jews. After the mission to Samaria Philip is told to go toward the south (Acts 8.26) although the word used here is μεσημβρίαν. It appears that there is a deliberate ambiguity in the saying about who will enter the kingdom: it can be taken to include Gentiles from the four corners and it can mean the ingathering of the descendants of the two kingdoms, Jews and Samaritans. It is important to note that these verses immediately follow the second mention of Jerusalem as Jesus' destination (n. 35 above) and precede the description of Jerusalem as the place of the prophet's death.

2. *Luke 15.11-32*

The parable of the returning son is also open to a two-kingdom interpretation. In origin it may have been an answer to those Pharisees who protested against Jesus eating with outcasts.[117] But it is also a parable that is particularly susceptible to allegorical treatment, largely because of the merciful generosity of the father. For example, it has been proposed that the two sons represent Israel and the nations who now have to learn to live together in the same house.[118] The suggestion I want to explore in the present context was made by Quell in commenting on Jer. 31.[LXX 38] 18-20.[119]

> I have heard Ephraim bemoaning: 'Thou hast chastened me...like an untrained calf;
> bring me back (ἐπίστρεψόν) that I may be restored (ἐπιστρέψω),
> for thou art the Lord my God.
> For after I had turned away I repented (μετενόησα);
> ...I was ashamed, and confounded, because I bore the disgrace of my youth'.
> Is Ephraim my dear son (υἱὸς ἀγαπητός)?
> Is he my darling child?
> For as often as I speak against him,
> I do remember him still.
> Therefore my heart yearns for him;
> I will surely have mercy upon him, says the Lord.

---

117. Linnemann, *Parables*, p. 73. Jeremias, *Parables*, p. 131, describes the parable as 'a vindication of the Good News in reply to its critics'.

118. Van Goudoever, 'The Place of Israel', p. 121.

119. Quell, *TDNT*, V, p. 973.

Quell's comment, which he does not develop, is that 'one may clearly perceive the original of the parable of the prodigal'. C.F. Evans says of Quell's comment that it becomes blurred when God is mentioned directly in the parable alongside the father.[120] True as Evans's comment is, it is not necessary to construct an allegory with a one-to-one correspondence for Quell's suggestion to be helpful, moreover, to see the parable's father as disclosing the character of God is a view almost as old as the parable itself. In the parable the younger son goes to a far-off Gentile country and wastes his inheritance on harlots, and 'playing the harlot' was a prophetic accusation of Israel-Ephraim's apostasy (Jer. 3.6; Hos. 4.15; 5.3). The fact that the son goes willingly is clearly required by the story so that the son may still receive his inheritance in spite of his conduct. When he returns, to the joy of his father, the elder brother refuses to enter the same house; he does not use the word 'brother', unlike his father (vv. 27, 32), and only reluctantly admits that the brother is his father's son (v. 30). The elder son's attitude mirrors those rabbinic opinions about Samaritans, recognising the common descent with Jews but little more. That it is the younger son who returns may reflect the fact that Joseph, the father of Ephraim and Manasseh, was younger than Judah. There is much in the parable of the returning son that could well have suggested to Luke's readers that the coming of Jesus entailed the return of the Samaritans to the one Father and, perhaps, to recall Jeremiah's oracle about Ephraim. In this sense the parable is fulfilled in Acts 8.4-17, at least in part. This interpretation of the parable does not rule out the other uses to which it has been put but, as we have seen elsewhere, Luke was quite capable of working with more than one layer of meaning.

3. *Luke 18.1-8*

Luke alone records the parable of the widow and the judge with its promise of God's willingness to answer the prayers of his elect and to vindicate them speedily. Fitzmyer notes the OT background in which 'elect' refers to Israel, although he takes the elect to be Christian disciples[121] to whom the parable is addressed (17.22). One of the passages noted is Sir. 47.22 but this suggests an alternative interpretation of the parable. The verse is in a section describing the strengths and failures of Solomon whose actions brought wrath upon his children and led to

---

120. Evans, *Saint Luke*, p. 589.
121. Fitzmyer, *Luke*, p. 1180.

the formation of the disobedient kingdom of Ephraim (47.20-21). But, in spite of this:

> The Lord will never give up his mercy,
> nor cause any of his works to perish;
> he will never blot out the descendants
> of his *chosen one*, nor destroy the posterity of him who loved him;
> so he gave a remnant to Jacob,
> and to David a root of his stock (47.22).

The use of the singular, 'chosen one', in Sirach and the plural form by Luke, makes at most a tenuous connection between the two[122] but there are others: God's mercy is also directed towards Ephraim; a descendant of David will be part of that mercy; and the blame for the break-up into two kingdoms lies principally with Solomon. These are ideas that appear in Luke's writings.

In the OT, the widow (χήρα, Lk. 18.3, 5) is often the recipient of oppression but, in Isa. 49.21 and Bar. 4.12, 16, she is a symbol of bereaved Zion whom, in Isaiah, God promises to restore and to bring back her sons and daughters (49.18-22). And again, in Sir. 35.12-15,[123] the Lord listens to the one who is wronged and to the widow when she pours out her story. In Sir. 35.17, the prayer of the humble (ταπεινοῦ) reaches the clouds and 'he [the humble] will not be consoled until the Most High visits him (ἐπισκέψηται) and does justice for the righteous' (κρινεῖ δικαίοις, 35.18; cf. ἐκδίκησόν, ἐκδικήσω, ἐκδίκησιν: Lk. 18.3, 5, 7). The connection of widow–humble in Sirach may have also contributed to Luke's juxtaposition of the parable of the widow and the account of the tax-collector with its point that 'he who humbles himself (ὁ δὲ ταπεινῶν) will be exalted' (18.14). Given that the purpose of the parable is to encourage the disciples always to pray and not to lose heart (18.1), we must ask what was their principal hope. According to Luke, it was the restoration of Israel (Lk. 24.21; Acts 1.6). It therefore seems that the parable is at one level concerned with the speedy vindication of God's chosen Israel and that this includes the kingdom of Ephraim.

4. *Luke 23.30*

There is one more allusion to be considered. In Jesus' speech to the daughters of Jerusalem he includes a quotation from Hos. 10.8: 'Then

---

122. The plural form, meaning the descendants of Jacob, is found elsewhere in the OT, e.g. Isa. 65.9, 15, 23; Ps. 105.6, 43. See Fitzmyer, *Luke*, p. 1180.

123. Evans, *Saint Luke*, p. 636; Danker, *Jesus and the New Age*, p. 295.

shall they begin to say to the mountains "Fall on us"; and to the hills "Cover us"'. Hosea's mission had been to the northern kingdom (N.B. Hos. 1.10-11) in an attempt to turn the nation from its debased worship of Yahweh. (Did Luke exclude Hos. 6.6 because it was not directed to the Jerusalem cult alone but to that of Ephraim also?) Luke's quotation comes immediately before the death of Jesus, and the preceding verse in Hosea reads,

> Samaria's king shall perish,
> like a chip on the face of the waters.
> The high places of Aven, the sin of
> Israel shall be destroyed (Hos. 10.7-8).

If Luke had this verse in mind then Jesus' speech would not only warn of the destruction of Jerusalem but also the end of the 'kingdom' of Samaria and hence the purification of its worship of Yahweh (cf. Jn 4.21-24). Clearly Luke would have to tread with very great care; if he shows restraint about Jesus as king of the Jews he would be even more reluctant to speak of Jesus as king of Samaria. Yet it is only by the 'deaths' of the kings of the Jews and Samaria that the way is open for the new Davidic king of the united people of Israel.

None of the four passages that I have discussed would, when taken singly, constitute strong evidence that Luke envisaged a restored Israel in which the Samaritan descendants of the northern kingdom were included. But, when taken together, they add weight to such a view and show it to be more pervasive than the overt Samaritan passages might suggest.

Summary and Conclusions

It is not uncommon to see the Samaritans in Luke–Acts as a thankful, generous, almost 'Christian' foil to the unresponsive Jews. This is a serious underevaluation of both groups. We have seen that whatever Luke's opinion of the Jews (and this varies according to the context), his belief is that God will save Israel. His understanding of the restored Israel is rooted in the idea of one nation under a Davidic king, modelled on the nation before its division into the two kingdoms. That these kingdoms should be reunited he would have found in the oracles of Isaiah, Jeremiah, Hosea, Ezekiel and Zechariah.

The Samaritans in Luke–Acts do not have the same role as God-fearers or proselytes and they were not on the periphery of Judaism, trying to get in. No Samaritan who took religious faith and history seriously would wish to become a member of the heretical tribe of Judah with its sanctuary at Jerusalem. Luke does not describe Samaritan or, for that matter, Jewish aspirations for a united Israel. He was a Christian, expressing what he saw as a Christian theology of the people of God in a way that took both history and the new age of the Spirit with the utmost seriousness. Luke's treatment of Samaritans, like John's, can only be understood if he accepted their claim to be the true descendants of the northern kingdom of Israel and if he was aware of their antagonism to the Jerusalem temple. That he *was* aware goes some way at least towards explaining Luke's oblique comments on the temple in Stephen's speech. The temple was both the house of prayer and the setting for the arrests of Peter (Acts 4.1-3) and Paul (21.30-33). His ambivalence derives, in part, from his undoubted sympathy with Samaritans, yet seen from the Jewish side of the divide. Luke regarded the temple as important in the early development of Christianity but, now that it no longer existed, its divisive role had also been destroyed.

Although Luke makes no direct connection between the Samaritans and the northern kingdom, such a connection brings together a number of his special interests: the twelve tribes, the roles of Elijah and Elisha, Israel's history, the restoration of Israel, and, of course, the Samaritans themselves. When we go on to take account of Luke's emphasis on the resurrection of Jesus then we have a perspective that calls to mind the question in *Kutim*: 'When shall we take them back? When they renounce Gerizim and confess Jerusalem and the resurrection of the dead.' Without the return of the Samaritans there could be no restored Israel and without an Israel in the process of restoration there would be nothing for the Gentiles to enter. For where else could the God of Israel be served and worshipped?

Part II

INTRODUCTION

In Part I of this study we examined the evidence that Luke looked for God's restoration of an Israel modelled on a reunited nation under the new Davidic king. This expectation is, in itself, a clear indication of a significant proportion of Jewish believers among his readership. Yet, however much Luke may have wished to breathe new life into the prophetic hope, he lived and wrote as a Christian, a member of a church that had become, or was in the process of becoming, separated from its Jewish origins. The further that separation developed, the more isolated Jewish believers might feel and tensions between Jews and Gentiles in the church could only increase. To Luke, disunity, whether in the church or in the historical Israel, had to be overcome and shown to be overcome. We have seen the importance of this in his account of the Hebrew–Hellenist dispute as well as in Stephen's speech.

Luke regarded Israel's unity as a theological necessity for its restoration and it is only when there are unmistakable signs of that unity, after the missions in Jerusalem and Samaria, that God initiates the acceptance of Gentiles. But the subsequent influx of Gentiles had, by Luke's time, brought its own pastoral problems. Not only were there questions about table fellowship but also about beliefs, and Jewish believers would have been under pressure from Jews outside the church and Gentiles within (Acts 20.28-30). There were powerful voices in the church that challenged in fundamental ways the value of the historical Israel. There were those who proclaimed that Jesus had lived as the Messiah on earth and that his death had opened up a new way of salvation, not only for Gentiles but also for Jews. Such teachings could only serve to widen the separation of the church from Israel and cause difficulties for Jewish believers. However much Christians might use the Jewish Scriptures to support the truth of their beliefs, there could be no concealing the radical differences between those beliefs and those of Judaism. It should also be noted that the beliefs that Luke ascribes to the first disciples were also those of the Church when it had its greatest success in preaching to Jews.

Introduction

In Part II, therefore, we examine how Luke attempted to express the two cardinal Christian beliefs, Christology and atonement, in ways which would reassure Jewish believers and, at the same time, remain compatible with God's promise to restore Israel. This programme entailed formulating these beliefs in ways that appear to be, and may in fact be, their primitive forms. Luke did this not simply out of historical interest but from a pastoral concern, to set before his readers the fundamental Christian beliefs as being faithful to their Jewish origins and to which the church of his own time should return.

Chapter 4

LUKE'S VIEW OF JESUS

The NT provides us with a rich and varied picture of Christological thinking and, from what we know from the pre-Lukan writings, we might have expected Luke to show a greater degree of Christological development.[1] That he does not do so can be explained away on the assumption that he was primarily concerned with the early history of the church and the first stages in its move towards a fuller understanding of the person of Jesus. This assumption may well be justified, but it can hardly be the whole story because it does not give a convincing explanation of Luke's deliberate stand against the flow of development of which he must have been aware. In the age of the Spirit, antiquarian interest alone, without the motive of bringing the past to bear on the present, seems most improbable. In this chapter we shall examine some of the ways in which Luke made his stand and his reasons for making it.

Luke offers his readers a wide range of titles for Jesus, some of which are peculiar to him.[2] This has naturally led to different assessments about which title was the most important for him. For example, A.R.C. Leany regards 'king' as the dominant title,[3] whereas Franklin believes that 'Lord' is the most characteristic.[4] This view is supported by D.L. Jones, who concludes that the use of the absolute 'the Lord' in the Gospel means that there is 'no distinction between the earthly and the exalted

---

1. Moule, *Origins*, pp. 1-4, discusses the relative merits of evolution as against development in early Christological thinking. He favours development. Dunn, *Christology*, provides a convenient survey of early Christological development. His concern is *'to let the NT writers speak for themselves*, to understand their words as they intended...and thus let their own understanding(s) of Christ emerge' (p. 9).
2. Fitzmyer, *Luke*, pp. 192-219, reviews eight major titles and a further seven less frequently used by Luke.
3. Leaney, *St Luke*, pp. 34-37.
4. Franklin, *Christ the Lord*, pp. 49-55.

Lord'.[5] E.E. Ellis believes that the 'main theme of Luke's Gospel is the nature of Jesus' Messiahship and mission',[6] although Ellis includes titles such as Son of God and Son of David as traditional terms for the Messiah. The approach of Ellis raises the question as to whether it is legitimate to extract Luke's Christology from only one of his books. C.F.D. Moule has given strong reasons for thinking that the Christology of Acts differs from that of the Gospel,[7] and he makes a valuable point in recognizing what he calls 'continuity of person but novelty of interpretation in the post-resurrection period'.[8] Jones, on the other hand, is among those who believe that a successful quest for Luke's Christology must begin with the speeches in Acts.[9] He poses the question of whether the Christology of Luke–Acts was the one current shortly after the death and resurrection of Jesus or whether it belonged to Luke's own time, 'indeed, of Luke himself'.[10] There are two questionable assumptions behind Jones's position. The first is that we may read back from the Christology of Acts into the Gospel portrait of Jesus and this is to ignore Moule's arguments for a difference of interpretation in the two books. The second assumption is that Luke reflected one or the other of the two alternatives, whereas it is much more probable that he put forward a Christology with his own 'novelty of interpretation' which was one that conformed to his own purposes.

The present study makes no attempt to examine or discuss all of the titles used by Luke—that would be a full-length study in itself. Instead, we shall concentrate on the two titles that most closely relate to Jewish hopes and expectations: 'Christ' and 'prophet'.

The Anointed One

From his analysis of both the Gospel and Acts, Conzelmann concludes that *Christos* 'preserves—or regains—to a considerable extent its character as a title'.[11] It ceases to be, in effect, Jesus' second name. This conclusion is justified, but we must add the proviso that it must not be

---

5. Jones, '*Kyrios*', pp. 85-101.
6. Ellis, *Luke*, pp. 10-12, makes the important point that Luke is not concerned to prove Jesus' messiahship but to show the nature of it.
7. Moule, 'Christology of Acts', pp. 159-85.
8. Moule, 'Christology of Acts', p. 166.
9. Jones, '*Christos*', p. 69.
10. Jones, '*Christos*', p. 69.
11. Conzelmann, *Luke*, p. 171.

assumed that *Christos* has exactly the same meaning in Acts that it can have in the Gospel or that it always carries the sense of Messiah in its fully developed form of the expected one.

Jewish beliefs about God's Anointed at the time of Jesus included a figure based upon a Davidic king, a son of David who would redeem Israel and restore it both politically and spiritually and so fulfil the prophetic hopes.[12] But within this broad picture there was a wide variety in matters of detail,[13] and Vermes distinguishes between the messianic *expectations* among Palestinian Jews and the 'peculiar *speculations* characteristic of certain learned and/or esoterical minorities'.[14] Vermes suggests that a reliable account of Israel's messianic hopes is to be found in *Pss. Sol.* 17–18 and in the Eighteen Benedictions.[15] Some verses from *Pss. Sol.* 17[16] show the type of expectations.

> See, Lord, and raise up for them their king, the son of David, to rule over your servant Israel in the time known to you, O God (v. 21).
>
> He will gather a holy people whom he will lead in righteousness; and he will judge the tribes of the people that have been made holy by the Lord their God (v. 26).
>
> And he will have the Gentile nations serving him under his yoke, and he will glorify the Lord in (a place) prominent (above) the whole earth. And he will purge Jerusalem (and make it) holy as it was even from the beginning, (for) nations to come from the end[s] of the earth (ἀπ' ἄκρου τῆς γῆς) to see his glory (vv. 30-31).
>
> ...for all shall be holy, and their king shall be [the] Lord Messiah (βασιλεὺς αὐτῶν χριστὸς κυρίου [χριστος κυριος]) (v. 32).[17]
>
> ...for God shall make him powerful in the Holy Spirit (v. 37).

Hopes for a Davidic king who will be served by the Gentiles, judge the tribes of the people, be powerful in the Spirit and rule Israel in a time known to God—these are messianic features that are present in Luke–Acts.

---

12. De Jonge, 'Anointed', p. 133 and n. 1. Harvey, *Constraints*, p. 79 n. 50. Vermes, *Jesus the Jew*, p. 197.
13. De Jonge, 'Anointed', p. 141.
14. Vermes, *Jesus the Jew*, p. 130.
15. Vermes, *Jesus the Jew*, pp. 130-34.
16. Wright, 'Psalms of Solomon', *OTP*, II, pp. 665-70, 667 n. z.
17. Rahlfs's edition gives κυρίου but the editions of Gebhardt (1895) and Swete (1887) have κυριος.

4. *Luke's View of Jesus*

There is no writer in the NT who does not recognize Jesus as the Christ in the full messianic sense of God's final deliverer. But there are instances in Luke–Acts where a wider concept of χριστός is used as the adjective 'anointed', rather than the specific title of Messiah. The distinction can be seen in the LXX where χριστός describes a wide range of people who have been set aside for God's purposes, people such as kings, priests and prophets, and it is these titles that specify the role. Only much later does the word come to have the more restricted meaning of the eschatological Messiah in which χριστός itself becomes the title. We have already noted the use of χριστὸς κύριος in the announcement to the shepherds (Lk. 2.11) and Simeon's use of τὸν χριστὸν κυρίου (2.26).[18]

Immediately prior to the transfiguration, Peter confesses Jesus to be God's anointed (τὸν χριστὸν τοῦ θεοῦ, Lk. 9.20; cf. Mk 8.29; Mt. 16.16), a title that is also used by the mocking crowd at the crucifixion when Jesus is challenged to save himself (23.35). In Acts 3.18-20 Peter speaks of the sufferings of the earthly Jesus as those of 'his [God's] anointed' and he goes on to speak of the future coming of the Messiah. The Lord's or God's χριστός (3.18) has the OT sense of an anointed one whereas to speak of God's (expected) Messiah would be redundant, for who but God was expected to send the Messiah? The ways in which Luke qualifies χριστός are notably absent from Mark and Matthew. If they wish to add some further clarification to 'Christ' then they use an extra title such as 'son of the living God' (Mt. 16.16), 'son of the Blessed' (Mk 14.61) or 'king of Israel' (Mk 15.32), titles that serve to emphasize Jesus' messianic character. Thus whereas Mark and Matthew reinforce the messianic status, Luke makes the role less well defined and this difference becomes even clearer when similar sayings are compared.

Matthew	Luke
11.2 When John...heard about the deeds of the Christ,	7.18 The disciples of John told him of all these things.
16.20 [Jesus] strictly charged them to tell no one that he was the Christ.	9.21 [Jesus] charged and commanded them to tell this to no one.
24.4-5 'What will be the sign of your coming...?' Jesus answered them, '...many will come in my name, saying "I am the Christ"'.	21.7-8 'Teacher, when will [the destruction of the temple] be?' And he said, '...many will come in my name saying "I am he"'.

---

18. Jones, *'Christos'*, pp. 75-76. Drury, *Tradition*, p. 55.

Similar instances occur at Mt. 26.68 (cf. Lk. 22.64), and Mt. 27.17, 22 (cf. Lk. 23.18-25).

Leaving aside considerations of textual relationships, we can see that Luke is much more restrained in these passages than Matthew. This is all the more surprising when it might be expected that Luke would show a somewhat later stage of Christological development. There is much in the use of χριστός in Luke's Gospel that calls to mind the Septuagintal meaning of an anointed figure rather than the Messiah of Christian teaching.[19]

The evidence presented thus far contradicts Conzelmann's opinion that 'For Luke Jesus is already on earth Christ' and that Luke 'makes no distinction between the historical figure and the Exalted Lord'.[20] On the contrary, the evidence suggests that in the ministry of Jesus Luke is far more restrained and cautious than either Mark or Matthew in presenting Jesus as the Messiah on earth. This may, in part, be because he wished to play down the possible political overtones of the title, but this is very unlikely to be the main reason, as we shall see later.

Although Mark and, particularly, Matthew are stronger than Luke in their assertions of Jesus' messiahship, there is very little in their accounts to show what was expected of the Messiah or what was specifically messianic in the life of Jesus. Both Mark and Matthew use χριστός to describe Jesus' messianic status but neither evangelist describes a uniquely messianic role. All the evangelists tell of Jesus as a miracle worker who announced the forgiveness of sins—in short, that he proclaims the nearness of God's kingdom. Yet these wonderful acts are associated with other titles such as the Holy One of God (Mk 1.24), Son of Man (Mk 2.10) and Son of David (Mt. 20.30-31).

What makes Luke's portrayal of Jesus unique in the Gospels is that he tells us *why* Jesus was anointed; alone among the evangelists, Luke applies the verb χρίω to Jesus (4.18). The importance of this for Luke's understanding of χριστός has not been given sufficient emphasis, in spite of the wide recognition of the programmatic nature of the Nazareth episode (Lk. 4.16-30).[21] In the Nazareth synagogue Jesus reads from Isa. 61.1-2 and 58.6.[22]

---

19. Harvey, *Constraints*, p. 80, thinks that Luke retains the intertestamental idiom.
20. Conzelmann, *Luke*, p. 176.
21. Jones, '*Christos*', pp. 74-75, notes the verb but not its unique significance.
22. Leaney, *St Luke*, p. 53.

4. Luke's View of Jesus

> The Spirit of the Lord is upon me,
> because he has anointed (ἔχρισέν) me to preach good news to the poor.
> He has sent me to proclaim release to the captives
> and recovering of sight to the blind,
> to set at liberty those who are oppressed,
> to proclaim the acceptable year of the Lord (4.18-19).

Jesus concludes the quotation with 'Today this Scripture has been fulfilled in your hearing' (4.21).

Apart from Isaiah, the OT records Elisha as the only other prophet who was anointed (1 Kgs 19.16). Both prophets have roles to play in Luke's presentation of Jesus although Elisha, being Elijah's assistant and successor, has the minor part. At the anointing of David, the spirit of the Lord came upon him mightily (1 Sam. 16.13)[23] yet, perhaps surprisingly, Luke has chosen the anointing of a prophet as the model for the work of Jesus. This has important Christological implications since, until the entry into Jerusalem, Jesus' public ministry is cast in prophetic and not regal-messianic terms. The descriptions of Jesus in the birth stories as the Davidic royal son and as χριστὸς κύριος are made to a very select audience that includes the readers. The readers are therefore let into the full meaning of Jesus while, in the public ministry, the meaning of his role remains hidden or is alluded to under the oblique figure of the Son of Man.

Luke is not the first person to use the idea of an anointed prophet in an eschatological context.[24] A Qumran fragment (11QMelch), dating from the first century BCE, is an eschatological midrash on Isa. 61.1 and it speaks of Melchizedek as a heavenly redeemer and judge. He is identified with the messenger in Isa. 52.7 who is the 'Anointed One of the Spirit'. Vermes conjectures that there was a quotation of Isa. 61.2-3 in the text[25] and, if this were so, then it would bring together the ideas of a royal redeemer and judge (Melchizedek), an Anointed One of the spirit, and the use of Isa. 61.1-3.

Peter's speech to the house of Cornelius (Acts 10.34-43) contains a number of allusions to the Nazareth incident and the anointing.

---

23. Fitzmyer, *Luke*, pp. 529-30, is right to assert that the passage does not refer to Davidic—royal—anointing. Tannehill, *Narrative Unity*, p. 63, disagrees with Fitzmyer and makes too firm a connection between the prophetic anointing and the post-resurrection understanding of royal Messiah.
24. De Jonge, 'Anointed', pp. 141-42.
25. Vermes, *Dead Sea Scrolls*, pp. 300-301.

1. 'In every nation anyone who fears [God] and does what is right is acceptable (δεκτός) to him' (10.35; cf. δεκτόν, Lk. 4.19). Together with δεκτός at Lk. 4.24 these are the only instances of the word in Luke–Acts.
2. 'You know the word which [God] sent to Israel, preaching the good news of peace through Jesus Christ' (εὐαγγελιζόμενος, Acts 10.36; cf. εὐαγγελίσασθαι, Lk. 4.18).
3. '...how God anointed (ἔχρισεν) Jesus of Nazareth with the Holy Spirit (cf. Lk. 4.1, 14, 18) and with power; how he went about doing good and healing all that were oppressed by the devil, for God was with him' (10.38).

Some commentators[26] see an allusion to Isa. 61.1 in Acts 10.38 but this is only true indirectly. Luke points to the incident at Nazareth, which includes the Isaiah citation, by the use of 'Jesus of Nazareth'; he uses the same method at Lk. 4.34; 18.37; Acts 3.6 and 4.10 where healing miracles are performed, and at Lk. 24.19, Jesus of Nazareth is described as a prophet mighty in word and deed. χριστός is added only in the post-resurrection instances.

There are not only verbal coincidences between Peter's address and the Nazareth sermon but the description of Jesus' work in Acts 10.38 broadly corresponds to what is promised in Lk. 4.18-19. Moreover, 'you know' (Acts 10.36) is also intended as a reminder to the reader since there is no hint in the story of what, if anything, Peter's hearers know about Jesus. Cornelius has acted at the direct prompting of God's angel, not as the result of Christian preaching (10.3-6).

There is one further reference to the anointing of Jesus which is in Peter's prayer (Acts 4.27) but there is no allusion to the Nazareth sermon. It is an interpretation of Ps. 2.1-2 (Acts 4.25-26) and the psalm is used as a Davidic prophecy of opposition to Jesus as the Lord's anointed. Yet in spite of the opportunity to use χριστός in a truly messianic sense, Peter chooses to refer to Jesus twice as 'thy holy servant' (4.27, 30). Since Peter is obviously speaking here and in the address to Cornelius of the earthly Jesus, we can see just how consistently restrained Luke is in reading back the title of Messiah, even after the resurrection. The earthly Jesus is still the Lord's anointed so that to translate τοῦ χριστοῦ αὐτοῦ (Acts 4.26) as 'his Messiah' and ἔχρισας

---

26. E.g. Haenchen, *Acts*, p. 352; Brawley, *Luke–Acts and the Jews*, pp. 12-13. Both commentators point to Nazareth in Luke 4.

(4.27) as 'thou didst make Messiah'[27] is to jump the gun. Isa. 61.1 is not a messianic anointing[28] if by messianic is meant the figure whom later Judaism expected at the end of the age. The phrase refers to the earthly Jesus and, as such, to the anointing of a preaching and healing prophet. This is shown in Lk. 4.18, Acts 10.38 and, to a less obvious extent, Acts 4.27. This prophetic role of Jesus is confirmed by the saying that no prophet is acceptable in his own country (4.24), a saying almost immediately fulfilled in 4.28-29.

So far we have discussed Luke's relative reticence in using χριστός in a messianic sense without further qualification. But prior to the resurrection there are a number of occasions where χριστός is used without additional qualifying comment yet, with one exception, the word occurs either in questions or in statements that are untrue (Lk. 3.15; 20.41; 22.47; 23 [2], 39). The exception follows the demons' recognition of Jesus as the son of God, to which Luke adds that Jesus 'would not allow them to speak, because they knew he was the χριστός' (4.41). The parallel accounts in Mk 1.32-34 and Mt. 8.16-17 contain no titles so that Luke's addition may be analogous to his editorial use of 'Lord', giving χριστός its post-resurrection, messianic sense. However, the use of the title is only for the readers' benefit; it is not disclosed to the narrative audience.

Luke takes great care to make clear that Jesus was anointed as a prophet[29] because he is setting out a Christological programme which, almost certainly, does not reflect trends current in the church of his own time. In fact, there is the strong possibility that it was Luke's deliberate intention to challenge current Christological thinking. The other evangelists[30] had written their accounts of Jesus in the belief that he was the Christ-Messiah and they had compressed this faith into the form of Gospels, reading back their post-resurrection belief into the life of Jesus. Luke solved the problem differently by reducing the messianic character of the earthly Jesus so that, in Acts, he was free to deal with the title of Messiah in a way that agreed with early Jewish-Christian understandings.

---

27. Lake and Cadbury, *Beginnings*, IV, p. 47; also Brawley, *Luke–Acts and the Jews*, p. 12.

28. *Pace* Brawley, *Luke–Acts and the Jews*, p. 13.

29. De la Potterie, 'L'onction', pp. 240-46; Brawley, *Luke–Acts and the Jews*, p. 14.

30. I take this to be true of all the Gospels; how many were known to Luke I leave as an open question.

By doing this he was able, to a large extent, to leave post-resurrection beliefs until after his account of the resurrection. Just how he tackled this programme we will now examine.

In the middle of Peter's speech (Acts 2.22-36) he gives scriptural 'proofs' of Jesus' resurrection and he concludes with a proclamation to the house of Israel 'that God has made him both Lord and Christ, this Jesus whom you crucified' (2.36). This is not, in itself, conclusive evidence that the resurrection and ascension constituted the messianic turning point but there is further supporting evidence. It is only after the resurrection that Jesus refers to himself as the χριστός (Lk. 24.26-27, 46) and, at his trial, his answer is less clear-cut than in Mark's account (Lk. 22.67-68; cf. Mk 14.61-62). After the resurrection it is the χριστός who must suffer whereas, before then, suffering is the destiny of the Son of Man (Lk. 9.22; 17.24-25).

The next stage of Luke's programme is also set out in a speech of Peter's to the 'men of Israel' (3.12). Peter describes Jesus as the Holy and Righteous One (3.14) and the Author of Life (3.15) but it is in 3.18-26 that Luke's main Christological statements are made. Throughout this section the emphasis is on the idea that all that has happened, is happening and will happen has been foretold by the prophets.

1. That God's Anointed should suffer (3.18).
2. The coming of the Messiah will be the time of restoration of all that God has promised (3.20-21).
3. God would raise up a prophet like Moses (3.22-3).
4. 'These days' have been foretold by the prophets since the time of Samuel (3.24). We should note that Samuel was the prophet who anointed David.

Luke is the only evangelist who speaks of the suffering χριστός and who has Jesus claim that this was foretold by the prophets and in the Scriptures (Lk. 24.25-26, 46; Acts 3.18; 17.2-3). According to Mowinkel[31] and Fitzmyer,[32] prior to the NT there was no Jewish belief that the Messiah should suffer and although Luke, like the other evangelists, uses citations and allusions to the OT in the passion narrative,[33] they fall well short of 'proving' that the Messiah should suffer. There is a similar problem with the Son of Man whose suffering has been

---

31. Mowinkel, *He That Cometh*, pp. 325-33.
32. Fitzmyer, *Luke*, p. 200.
33. E.g. Lk. 22.37, cf. Isa. 53.12; Lk. 23.34, cf. Ps. 22.18; Lk. 23.36, cf. Ps. 69.21.

foretold by the prophets (Lk. 18.31-32) and who goes 'as it has been determined' (22.22).[34] But, again, there are no Scriptures that speak of a suffering Son of Man. The situation is hardly surprising since there were many in the OT who were anointed and several who were called 'son of man' and although some of them suffered, there were others who did not. Nor was either a term a unique title in the NT sense so that the suffering Son of Man or χριστός was never a Jewish problem. It only became a problem for Christians when they used the terms as titles for the crucified Jesus.

There is a clear pattern in Luke–Acts: statements about the suffering Son of Man are made by the earthly Jesus whereas statements about the suffering χριστός occur only after the resurrection. Only after the resurrection, when Jesus has been appointed Messiah, is he described as the suffering χριστός (Lk. 24.26, 46; Acts 3.18; 17.3; 26.23).[35] According to Vermes, it is probable that Jesus spoke of his future suffering using the circumlocution 'Son of Man'[36] which the Gospel writers then took over as a title, adding to it the idea of a glorious return. Luke makes a further addition to this scheme, the idea of the prophet who must die in Jerusalem (Lk. 13.33).

It is the resurrection that is the turning point from anointed prophet to the expected Messiah of the end-time and therefore the change in the role of the χριστός. All the Gospels speak of the coming of the glorious Son of Man but Luke is the only evangelist to speak unambiguously of the Messiah still to come, yet he does not do this until after his account of the resurrection (Acts 3.20). Luke therefore gives the same role to the Son of Man as he does to the χριστός, each suffers and each will come at the end of the age. But, for the present, Jesus is in heaven at the right hand of God, both as Messiah (Acts 2.31-33) and as Son of Man (Acts 7.55-56), awaiting the final time. Acts 3.20 confirms that Jesus has already been appointed (προκεχειρισμένον) as Israel's Messiah and this means that Luke is the only evangelist who explicitly identifies the

---

34. Cf. Mk 14.21 and Mt. 26.24; 'as it is written'.
35. Fitzmyer, *Luke*, p. 200, and Evans, *Saint Luke*, pp. 75-77, like many commentators, stress the undoubted importance of the suffering Christ in Luke–Acts. But there is a danger of not recognizing Luke's ambivalent use of 'Christ' to mean both 'anointed' and 'Messiah to come'. Jesus is not crucified as the Messiah but his suffering and death are the way to his becoming Messiah. It is in this sense that Evans' remark that '...it is his death as the Christ that is crucial' (p. 75) is accurate.
36. Vermes, *World of Judaism*, pp. 90-95.

Son of Man with the coming Messiah. To repeat: Jesus suffers as God's anointed prophet and Son of Man but he will come as the glorious Son of Man and the (unqualified) Messiah of Jewish expectations.

Now that the Messiah has been appointed and identified the people of Israel are to repent and turn to God so that their sins may be blotted out and the Messiah may be sent. His coming will be the times for establishing (χρόνων ἀποκαταστάσεως) all that has been foretold by the prophets (3.21), a phrase that suggests that it is the answer to the apostles' question about the time of Israel's restoration (τῷ χρόνῳ τούτῳ ἀποκαθιστάνεις, 1.6). In the present, Israel is to remember its descent from the prophets as well as God's covenant in which all the families of the earth shall be blessed (3.25). It is therefore the time of Israel's mission to the Gentiles[37] when the prophecies of Joel (Acts 2.17) and Isaiah (Lk. 3.6) are being fulfilled and God is pouring out his spirit and salvation on all flesh. Failure to listen to the prophet will mean destruction but the fig tree still has time to produce its fruit (Lk. 13.6-9).

This analysis has some similarities to the view taken of Acts 3.19-20 by J.A.T. Robinson.[38] However, he made his own objection: 'that Jesus suffered as *the Christ* is clearly incompatible with the idea that he is still, even after the Resurrection, only the Christ-elect'.[39] Moule's response to the objection is to interpret the passage as 'that Jesus is *already* recognised as the *previously* predestined Christ' who will be 'sent *back again* into the world'.[40] Neither Robinson's objection nor Moule's attempt to answer it are satisfactory since, as Moule himself acknowledges, 'back again' must be read into the text. The source of the difficulty is the assumption that χριστός in Luke–Acts always means Messiah. Luke's restraint in his messianic usage in the earthly life of Jesus is strong evidence against that assumption. The reason for this portrayal is not primarily political caution or historical accuracy but a compelling pastoral purpose. Luke knew something of Jewish expectations of a messianic figure and he knew that his Christian contemporaries spoke and wrote of Jesus as the Messiah yet, in spite of all that Jesus had done, he had not brought all those expectations to fulfilment. *Some* of the poor had

---

37. According to Luke, Paul may have had Gentile helpers in his missionary work (Acts 19.22; 20.4), but we are not told of Gentiles preaching in the way that Apollos the Jew did (18.28).
38. Robinson, 'Primitive Christology', pp. 143-44.
39. Robinson, 'Primitive Christology', p. 145.
40. Moule, 'Christology of Acts', p. 168.

responded to the good news, *some* of the sick had been healed and *some* of the captives of sin had been released. But many more still remained who were in need of the benefits of the messianic age, physically, politically and spiritually. And those Christians who were most vulnerable to this realization of the partial fulfilment of the hopes and promises would be those from a Jewish background. Tannehill recognizes that the expectations of the messianic kingdom and of God's purpose of salvation for Jews and Gentiles that are set out in the birth stories had not been fulfilled, and he attributes this to Jerusalem's rejection of the messianic king.[41] But this explanation can only hold good if Jesus was the Messiah on earth as Mark and Matthew maintain and it is precisely this belief that Luke is at pains to challenge in his two stage Christology. There can be little doubt that Luke reflects the sense of anticlimax that must have been felt by many, that the expected age had not yet fully arrived. This is why Luke looks forward to the time when the Messiah will come. This will not be a coming back as Messiah since, at his first coming, Jesus was the anointed prophet and Holy Servant. Luke had not lost the fundamental eschatological hope that there was more, much more, still to come.

We find further evidence of this two stage scheme in the parable of the pounds (Lk. 19.11-27) in which there are a number of differences from the version in Mt. 25.14-30.[42] According to Luke, the parable was told as Jesus neared Jerusalem and because the people expected God's kingdom immediately (19.11). The nobleman who is hated by his citizens (cf. 4.24, 28-30) goes to a far country to receive kingly power and, on his return, rewards the good servants and punishes his enemies. This is an earthly judgment and not, as in Mt. 25.21-30, seemingly a matter of heavenly inclusion or exclusion. In the context of the delayed parousia, the parable affirms that the man who departs with one noble status will return with the highest rank (19.15).

There is therefore clear evidence of Luke's restraint in his use of χριστός for the earthly Jesus[43] whereas, in Acts, Jesus is preached as the Messiah. Baptisms and healings are performed in the 'name of Jesus Christ', a phrase that is a contraction of 'the [coming] Messiah whose

---

41. Tannehill, *Narrative Unity*, pp. 8-9.
42. Jeremias, *Parables*, pp. 58-60.
43. Some indication of Luke's caution can be gathered from the fact that χριστός occurs approximately the same number of times in Luke–Acts as it does in Ephesians, although Luke–Acts is about six times longer.

name is Jesus'. When Jesus appears in visions it is either as Lord (Acts 9.4-6, 10-16; 22.6-10; 26.13-18) or as Son of Man (7.56) so that, even in his appearances after the resurrection, he is not seen in his messianic glory. Commenting on the order of composition of Mark and Matthew, Bennedict Green notes Matthew's greater reverential tone and 'that we should expect on general grounds a progression in devotional attitudes from the less developed to the more developed'.[44] This is obviously not the case with Luke's treatment of χριστός, and a case might be made for Luke showing Jesus' own political caution. But by Luke's time such caution was unnecessary since he describes Paul using the title in front of Roman officials and these are the very people who might be expected to take offence at the title (24.24; 26.23). More probably Luke feared a misunderstanding of the title in the church, that Jesus had been the Messiah on earth and that the Messianic age had arrived. Even such a crude guide as the frequency of the word per-page shows that Paul's major letters speak of χριστός some six times more frequently than Acts, which was written at least twenty years after the letters.[45]

If it should be thought that I have stretched the evidence for Luke's Christological shyness too far it is worth noting that this is not confined to χριστός but extends to the divine sonship of Jesus. Once again, a comparison with Matthew shows Luke's more restrained approach, as if he were reacting against the more developed view of his contemporaries.

Matthew	Luke
7.21 'Not everyone who says to me, "Lord, Lord", shall enter the kingdom of heaven, but he that does the will of my Father who is in heaven.'	6.46 '…why do you call me "Lord, Lord", and not do what I tell you?'
10.32 'So everyone who acknowledges me before men, I also will acknowledge before my Father who is in heaven.'	12.8 '…the Son of Man also will acknowledge before the angels of God' (cf. also Mt. 10.33; Lk. 12.9).
12.50 'whoever does the will of my Father in heaven is my brother, and sister…'	8.21 'My mother and my brothers are those who hear the word of God and do it' (also Mk 3.35).

There are further instances where there is a form different from 'my Father', for example, see Lk. 22.18 (Mt. 26.29) and 22.42 (Mt. 26.39); there are also six occasions where Jesus speaks of 'my Father' in

---

44. Green, *Matthew*, p. 4.
45. Dunn, *Unity and Diversity*, p. 43.

Matthew that do not occur in any form in Luke.[46] Finally, there is a small group of sayings, less easy to classify, but pointing in the same direction.

Matthew	Luke
5.11 'Blessed are you when men revile you and persecute you…on my account.'	6.22 'Blessed are you when men hate you,…and revile you,…on account of the Son of Man!'
24.3 'When will this be, and what shall be the sign of your coming and of the close of the age?'	21.7 'Teacher, when will this be and what will be the sign when this is about to take place?'
24.5 'For many will come in my name saying, "I am the Christ"'.	21.8 'For many will come in my name, saying "I am he" and "The time is at hand"' (cf. Mk 13.4, 6).

Even if it could be shown with certainty that Luke used earlier forms of the saying (as the Markan parallels would suggest), we are still faced with the question, why is Luke so clearly out of step with contemporary developments?

There are, however, two cases where the change is in the opposite direction. At Caesarea Philippi the Matthaean Jesus asks, 'Who do men say the Son of Man is?', followed by 'But who do you say that I am?' (Mt. 16.13-15). Luke's account has 'I' in both cases (9.18-20) and so avoids the oblique 'Son of Man'. Matthew's version serves to identify Jesus as the Son of Man, an identity that Luke does not make explicit until after the resurrection (Acts 7.55-56). In the second case the disciples are promised judgment-thrones over the twelve tribes when the Son of Man sits on his glorious throne (Mt. 19.28; Lk. 22.29-30). Luke sets the words at the last supper when the cross is only hours away. The public ministry is complete and the need for reticence is over. In the context of table fellowship with his apostles, Jesus is free to speak of 'my Father', 'my table' and 'my kingdom'. This kingdom has been appointed by the Father and will one day be restored to Israel (Acts 1.6). This is the everlasting throne of David which the reader was told about at the outset (Lk. 1.32-33) but which was never openly declared during the public ministry where it was always God's kingdom that was proclaimed.

---

46. Mt. 15.13; 16.17; 18.10, 19, 35; 20.23.

Jesus the Prophet

Luke–Acts displays a much closer connection between the roles of χριστός and prophet than we find anywhere else in the NT. It is generally accepted by modern critics that Luke portrays Jesus in a prophetic role, but whether as *a* prophet or as *the* (eschatological) prophet is still a matter for debate.[47] In his study of prophecy in the NT, David Hill warns against restricting our attention to the occurrences of 'prophet' and associated word groups, advocating instead a functional approach to the investigation.[48] In the present study our interest is in those occasions where Luke uses 'prophet' to describe Jesus, as well as in the words and actions that show Jesus as a prophet, including those cases where Luke involves OT prophets, either directly or by allusion. By combining these approaches it should be possible to see clearly Luke's intentions.

There is broad agreement in the synoptic tradition about the kind of things that Jesus said and did. For example, all three Gospels relate stories of Jesus raising the dead, but in Mk 5.22-24, 35-43 and Mt. 9.18-19, 23-26 there is no explicit Christological comment. This is also true of the Lukan parallel 8.41-42, 49-56. Yet, in the special Lukan story of the widow's son at Nain (7.11-17), there are not only clear allusions to Elijah's miracle in 1 Kgs 17.10, 17-24 but the crowd glorifies God because 'a great prophet has arisen among us'.

When the Lukan Jesus announces that he has been anointed for the prophetic work described by Isaiah the emphasis is on the prophet as preacher, healer and liberator who is to be rejected by his own people. Mark and Matthew also have stories of the rejection in the *patris* but their sayings have a slightly less negative nuance than Luke's. 'A prophet is not without honour except in his own country' (Mk 6.4; Mt. 13.57) might at least imply honour among the Gentiles and this is confirmed in their gospels (e. g. Mk 7.24-30; Mt. 15.21-28). The Lukan form, 'No prophet is acceptable in his own country' (4.24), concentrates

---

47. E.g. Franklin, *Christ the Lord*, pp. 67-69; Fitzmyer, *Luke*, pp. 213-15; Marshall, *Luke, Historian and Theologian*, pp. 125-27; Tiede, *Prophecy and History*. There is a tendency among scholars to grade the titles, regarding 'prophet' as inadequate and 'overtaken and corrected' by terms such as Christ; so Evans, *Saint Luke*, pp. 69-70. This does not do justice to Luke's unique scheme and his awareness of later developments.

48. Hill, *Prophecy*, pp. 2-5.

4. *Luke's View of Jesus*

on the prophet's rejection by his own people without a hint that he will be accepted by others. And so it transpires. The Lukan Jesus has direct contact with only one person who is even possibly a Gentile, the Gerasene demoniac (8.26-39), and even here the local people reject him (8.37). Because the mission of Jesus the prophet is almost exclusively directed to Israel we must be cautious about interpreting the Nazareth incident as an early indication of Luke's concern with the church's Gentile mission.[49]

It is obviously a crucial aspect of the Nazareth incident that Luke intensifies the theme of prophetic rejection. He quotes the examples of Elijah and Elisha, both of whom become Lukan antetypes for Jesus in ways we shall examine shortly. The violence of rejection is confirmed immediately by the crowd's attempt to kill Jesus (4.28-30). Rejection and death are, according to Luke, the marks and the fate of the true prophet and he shows this in Jesus' attack on those who build the tombs of the prophets in which the verb 'to kill' (ἀποκτείνω) occurs three times (11.47-51). The theme reappears at 13.33-34 where it provides the reason for Jesus' journey to Jerusalem. These verses are preceded by the Pharisees' warning that Herod wants to kill Jesus (ἀποκτεῖναι, 13.31) which is itself a reminder of the Baptist's fate. John, a prophet of the Most High, had been killed because he was a prophet (9.9; cf. 3.2) and this is sufficient reason for Luke who does not need elaborate explanations of John's death (cf. Mk 6.17-29; Mt. 14.3-12). Finally in Luke's scheme there is Stephen's accusation that the fathers of the present generation had persecuted the prophets and killed (ἀπέκτειναν, Acts 7.52) the Righteous One. This accusation contributes to his own death.

Jesus' acceptance of his prophetic destiny in Jerusalem is central to Luke's understanding of the death of Jesus. Elsewhere in the Synoptic Gospels, Jesus points to his death under the figure of the suffering of the Son of Man but, in Lk. 13.33, we have the only direct saying of Jesus in

---

49. Siker, 'First to the Gentiles', pp. 73-90, rightly points to the Gentiles healed by Elijah and Elisha. He argues that there is a contrast between the absence of miracles at Nazareth and the healings at Capernaum, which 'anticipates the Jew/ Gentile reversal' (p. 84). But neither Jesus nor the apostles go first to the Gentiles. The Nazareth sermon hints at the Gentile mission but Siker's case is weakened by failure to recognize that Israel in the sermon is the northern kingdom and by his classing of Samaritans as Gentiles (p. 73). Tannehill, *Narrative Unity*, p. 71, similarly believes that Elijah and Elisha going to Gentiles foreshadows the Gentile mission in Acts. But Elijah and Elisha preached in Samaria, not to Jews. Luke is quite clear about the order of the mission: Jews, Samaritans, then to 'the end of the earth'.

Luke's Gospel that gives the human motive for his own death. From what Luke says about the prophetic vocation we must infer that only by his death is the prophetic role of Jesus confirmed. For Luke, the death of Jesus has Christological rather than soteriological significance as the ultimate mark of the true prophet. At this point in the discussion we should note that although both Mark (8.28) and Matthew (16.14; 21.11, 46) record popular opinion that Jesus was a prophet, they nowhere show approval of the title. In fact, the opposite seems to be true: for Mark and Matthew, those who regard Jesus in this way miss the true meaning of his ministry.

The death of Jesus is connected with his role as a prophet after the crucifixion (Lk. 24.19-20), and we have previously noted that 'Jesus of Nazareth' is used to remind the reader of the Isaianic episode in Luke 4 (Acts 10.38). 'Jesus of Nazareth' is the most human and least doctrinal of all the descriptions of Jesus[50] and it is used at the exorcism of the unclean demon (Lk. 4.34), at the restoration of sight to a blind man (18.37) and also in Acts. At 2.22, Jesus of Nazareth is described as 'a man attested by God with mighty works and wonders', and it is in the name of Jesus Christ of Nazareth that lame men are healed (3.6; 4.10). The healing of a blind man (Lk. 18.37) fulfils the prophecy of 4.18 (cf. Isa. 29.18) and, according to Isa. 35.5-6, the healing of the blind and lame are two of the signs of God's salvation.

Nazareth is not only the place where Jesus was brought up, as it is in the other Gospels, but it is also the place of his anointing and where his death as a prophet is prefigured. The description therefore has a far richer meaning for Luke than for Mark and Matthew, who each describe the rejection as taking place 'in his own country' (Mk 6.1; Mt. 13.54). Even as late as one of Paul's accounts of his commissioning

---

50. Luke's normal form of the place name is Ναζαρέθ except in Lk. 4.16, where it is Ναζαρά (which is named as the place where Jesus was brought up). 'Jesus of Nazareth' occurs in three forms: Ναζαρέθ (Acts 10.38), Ναζαρηνός (Lk. 4.34; 24.19) and Ναζωραῖος (Lk. 18.37; Acts 2.22; 3.6; 4.10; 6.14; 22.8; 24.5; 26.9). The latter form raises problems discussed by Fitzmyer, *Luke*, pp. 1215-16, who thinks that it probably means 'a person from Nazara/Nazareth'. It may also have a Hebrew nuance: *nazir*, 'a consecrated one', or *neṣer*, scion (of David). The second sense may possibly be present in 18.37, where it would fit in with Son of David in 18.38. Whether Luke was aware of any Hebrew nuance is open to question; moreover, when Matthew, the more Hebraic of the two, uses Ναζωραῖος he connects it with the town (Mt. 2.23; 26.71). It seems unlikely, therefore, that Luke intended to do more than refer to the home town of Jesus.

4. Luke's View of Jesus

it is 'Jesus of Nazareth' who speaks to him (Acts 22.8; cf. the variant reading at 26.15). Although 'Jesus of Nazareth' is an intentional pointer to the Nazareth episode and to other marks of the Isaianic prophet, it is not the only one. In the answer to John's question, 'Are you the one who is to come?', four of the signs cited by Jesus go back to Nazareth: restoration of sight to the blind, preaching good news to the poor (4.18), healing lepers (4.27) and raising the dead (4.25-26; cf. 1 Kgs 17.17-24).

There is, therefore, ample evidence that Luke shows Jesus as a prophet; we must now see if there is evidence that Luke presents Jesus as *the* eschatological prophet. An example of Jewish expectations of the eschatological prophet is found in *T. Benj.* 9.2, probably composed in the second century BCE.

> The twelve tribes shall be gathered in there [in the latter temple] and all the nations, until such time as the Most High (ὕψιστος) shall send forth his salvation through the ministration of the unique prophet (τὸ σωτήριον αὐτοῦ ἐν ἐπισκοπῇ μονογενοῦς προφήτου).

Not only do we find Luke being concerned with the twelve tribes and the ingathering of the nations, but there are also items of the vocabulary that are notably Lukan.[51]

The first clear piece of evidence for Luke's eschatological understanding is Peter's description of Jesus as the prophet promised by Moses (Acts 3.22-23), a view implied by Stephen's quotation of Deut. 18.15 and 18 (Acts 7.37). This is a view of Jesus that is not explicit elsewhere in the NT, although C.H. Dodd suggests that it may be present in Jn 6.14[52] and, perhaps, in Jn 5.46. Luke's use of the idea of the prophet promised by Moses does not mean that he regards Jesus as a new or returned Moses. For example, Mt. 2.13-16 describes Jesus' escape from the massacre of the children in a way reminiscent of the rescue of Moses (Exod. 1.15–2.10).[53] Luke has no such story and neither does he describe Jesus reinterpreting the law on the mountain (Mt. 5.1–8.1).[54]

---

51. ὕψιστος, Lk. 1.32, 35, 76; 2.14; 6.35; 8.28; 19.38; Acts 7.48; 16.17. σωτήριον, Lk. 2.30; 3.6; Acts 28.28. ἐπισκέπτομαι, Lk. 1.68, 78; 7.16; Acts 6.3; 7.23; 15.14, 36. Luke does not use μονογενής of Jesus but it is used to describe three children healed by Jesus (Lk. 7.12; 8.42; 9.38). For the Greek text of *T. Benj* see de Jonge, *Testamenta XII Patriarchum*.

52. Dodd, *Scriptures*, pp. 55-56. See also Jn 1.21.

53. For a fuller treatment of Jesus–Moses in the birth stories, see Brown, *Birth*, pp. 2-6, 214-18, 228-29.

54. Filson, *St Matthew*, pp. 28-32.

Although Luke uses the expression 'the law and the prophets' (Lk. 16.16; Acts 13.15), more frequently he speaks of 'Moses and the prophets' (Lk. 16.29, 31; 24.27, 44; Acts 26.22; 28.23) which has the double function of suggesting Moses the lawgiver as well as Moses the prophet. This expression is peculiar to Luke in the NT and it is clearly important to Luke's scheme to link Moses with the prophets in order to underpin the idea of the prophet like Moses.

At the transfiguration Moses and Elijah talk with Jesus about his 'departure' (ἔξοδον, 9.31), an event that has been variously interpreted as his death[55] and his ascension.[56] ἔξοδος occurs in two other places only in the NT: in Heb. 11.22 it refers to the historical event under Moses and, in 2 Pet. 1.15, it refers to Peter's martyrdom which is followed by what purports to be Peter's account of the transfiguration (2 Pet. 1.16-18). There can be no doubt that Luke is looking ahead to what happens to Jesus in Jerusalem (it is, after all, 'his exodus'), but there are also powerful hints that he is looking back to the earlier deliverance of Israel under Moses. What Jesus will accomplish through his death and glorification is to be seen in terms of God's earlier salvation of Israel. And, like the first Exodus, it entails release for the captives and setting free those who are oppressed (Lk. 4.18). Luke draws out this meaning by emphasizing the Moses typology in several ways. First and most obvious is the use of ἔξοδος itself which, among a range of meanings in the LXX, is used to describe Israel coming out of Egypt (Exod. 19.1; Num. 33.38; 1 Kgs 6.1; Pss. 104.38; 113.1).[57] The next indication is that Moses is glorified together with Elijah and Jesus (he appears ἐν δόξῃ, 9.31, *contra* Mk 9.4-5; Mt. 17.3). In the account of Moses coming down from the mountain we are told that his face shone (δεδόξασται, Exod. 34.29, 35, δεδοξασμένη, 34.30) and that the sons of Israel, like the three apostles, were afraid (ἐφοβήθησαν, Exod. 34.30; Lk. 9.34). One further clue is in the command by the heavenly voice to hear Jesus (αὐτοῦ ἀκούετε, 9.35; cf. αὐτοῦ ἀκούσεθε, Deut. 18.15) whereas in Mark and Matthew the word order is inverted.

---

55. Conzelmann, *Luke*, pp. 57-59, 59 n. 2. For other examples of exodus meaning death, see Evans, *Saint Luke*, p. 418.

56. Davies, *He Ascended*, pp. 39-41.

57. I find it odd that commentators are reluctant to give serious consideration to the obvious backward-looking character of 'exodus', particularly given Luke's extensive use of Moses typology and his concern for the salvation of Israel. However, see Mánek, 'New Exodus'.

4. Luke's View of Jesus

In view of this evidence, the conclusion of C.F. Evans that 'there are no good grounds for giving *exodos* the further theological meaning of "deliverance (from Egypt)" and so "redemption"'[58] seems over-cautious. In Fitzmyer's opinion, Moses and Elijah are 'foils to Jesus' and disappear because they represent the old Israel.[59] The weakness of this interpretation is that they are not representatives of Israel nor do they disappear because they are in some sense outmoded. In Luke's account they are present as authenticators of Jesus the prophet and this is why Luke describes them in their heavenly glory, just like the glorified Jesus.

Evans proposes that the Central Section of the Gospel is based upon Deuteronomy,[60] and this has been developed by Moessner, who sees Lk. 9.1-50 as a preview of Jesus' journey to Jerusalem as the prophet like Moses.[61] Moessner believes that the deaths of both Moses and Jesus have atoning significance for the sins of Israel[62] but there is no evidence that Luke regards the death of Jesus in this way. Luke's use of Deut. 18.15-18 hinges upon Moses' promise of a prophet whose words will be consistent with his own, that is, with the law. That is why Israel must listen to the prophet. The Lukan Jesus has some Mosaic characteristics but Luke never attempts to portray Jesus as a returned Moses nor does Deuteronomy 18 envisage such a return. There is some evidence of Jewish speculation about Moses being given a crown as a ruler[63] and this may be rooted in imagery from Daniel 7[64] but such speculations have no part in Luke's thinking.

The prophet promised by Moses is the only one with which Jesus is explicitly identified but others, notably Elijah and Elisha,[65] appear as antetypes through Luke's use of unmistakable allusions. Of the two, Elijah is by far the more important with Elisha in a supporting role, as he is in the OT. Apart from Luke, every other writer in the NT ignores Elisha, as does the Judaism of the period with the exception of the *Lives of the Prophets*.[66] To Luke, it is the healing of Naaman which is

58. Evans, *Saint Luke*, p. 418.
59. Fitzmyer, *Luke*, p. 795.
60. Evans, 'Central Section', pp. 37-42.
61. Moessner, 'Luke 9.1-50'.
62. Moessner, 'Luke 9.1-50', pp. 596, 598 n. 2, acknowledges that Deuteronomy does not see Moses' death as atoning; cf. Moessner, 'Wilderness Generation', p. 339.
63. Robertson, 'Ezekiel the Tragedian', *OTP*, II, pp. 803-19, vv. 68-76, 83-86.
64. Robertson, 'Ezekiel the Tragedian', p. 812.
65. Evans, 'Elijah/Elisha', pp. 75-83; Ravens, 'Prophetic Role', pp. 127-29.
66. Hare, 'The Lives of the Prophets', *OTP*, II, p. 397.

important, both in connection with rejection (4.27) and as a possible model for the healing of the ten lepers (17.11-19). But Luke's most consistent use of Elisha and Naaman is in the healing of the centurion's servant.[67] Plummer denied any connection between the two stories[68] but the evidence below argues against Plummer's view, especially when we note that items marked* are absent from the account in Mt. 8.5-13.

2 Kings 5	Luke 7
v. 1 Naaman is a highly respected Gentile officer.	vv. 2, 4 The centurion is a worthy* Gentile officer.
2-3 A Jewish girl has a role to play in the healing.	3 Jewish elders play a role in the healing.*
5 The king acts on behalf of his sick commander.	2-3 The centurion acts on behalf of his sick slave.
10 The use of intermediaries.	3, 6 The use of intermediaries.*
14 The healing takes place at a distance. Elisha does not meet Naaman.	10 Healing at a distance. Jesus does not meet the centurion.*

There are two further points that connect the Naaman story with Luke 7. The first is that Naaman is made clean by dipping (ἐβαπτίσατο) in the Jordan and this leads to his conversion to the God of Israel (2 Kgs 5.14-15). Luke may see this as a contrast to the Pharisees' refusal of John's baptism (7.30). Secondly, Elisha tells Naaman that he has been healed so that he may 'know that there is a prophet in Israel' (2 Kgs 5.8). Luke's story of the centurion is followed by that of the raising of the widow's son at Nain where Jesus is recognized as a great prophet (7.16). The story of the widow's son shows some signs of being related to Elisha's raising of the Shunammite's son (2 Kgs 4.18-37) but this may be because both stories are themselves influenced by Elijah's miracle at Zarephath (1 Kgs 17-24) which we shall discuss below.

There is also an allusion to Elisha in Lk. 9.61-62, when a would-be disciple wishes to say farewell at home before he follows Jesus but he is told that 'No one who puts his hand to the plough and looks back is fit for the kingdom of God'. When Elisha was asked to follow Elijah he made a similar request to that of the would-be disciple (ἀκολουθήσω, Lk. 9.61; 1 Kgs 19.20). Elisha then slayed the oxen with which he was ploughing (ἠροτρία, 1 Kgs 19.19; ἄροτρον, Lk. 9.62, NT hap. leg.) and followed Elijah. There may be a further possible allusion to Elisha in Jesus' command that the seventy should salute no one on the road (10.4).

67. Ravens, 'Anointing', p. 287.
68. Plummer, *St Luke*, p. 197.

This is similar to Elisha's instruction to Gehazi (2 Kgs 4.29) but there are no verbal agreements that would help to confirm Luke's intention.

Luke's treatment of Elijah is not only far more extensive than that of Elisha but it also differs markedly from the views of Elijah in Mark and Matthew. There are four principal differences.

1. Luke has none of the sayings by which Mark and Matthew identify John as Elijah (Mk 9.11-13; Mt. 17.10-12).[69] Matthew makes the identity explicit by adding, 'then the disciples understood that he was speaking to them of John the baptist' (17.13). All the Gospels agree that the Baptist did no miracles (cf. Jn 10.41) whereas both Elijah and Jesus did.
2. Luke, like the Fourth Gospel, has no description of John's appearance which is probably based on that of Elijah in 2 Kgs 1.8 (Mk 1.6; Mt. 3.4).
3. Jesus' cry of dereliction (Mk 15.34-36; Mt. 27.46-49) is absent from Luke's account, hence the crowd do not think that Jesus is calling to Elijah.
4. In Mt. 11.10 and Lk. 7.27 Jesus quotes from the LXX in his estimate of John: 'Behold, I send my messenger before thy face who shall prepare thy way before thee'.

The quotation, but without 'before thy face', also occurs at Mk 1.2 where it is ascribed to Isaiah. Many critics regard the quotation in the three Gospels as coming from Mal. 3.1 but interpreted by the evangelists in the light of the promised Elijah of Mal. 4.5 (3.22-23). Irrespective of its origin, Matthew understood the verse to identify John with the expected Elijah and this is confirmed by the saying 'and if you are willing to accept it, this is Elijah who is to come' (11.14), a saying absent from Luke. The first line is in closer agreement to Exod. 23.20 than it is to Mal. 3.1:[70]

Lk. 7.27   ἰδοὺ ἀποστέλλω τὸν ἄγγελόν μου πρὸ προσώπου σου
Exod. 23.20 ἰδοὺ ἐγὼ ἀποστέλλω τὸν ἄγγελόν μου πρὸ προσώπου σου
Mal. 3.1   ἰδοὺ ἐγὼ ἐξαποστέλλω τὸν ἄγγελόν μου

69. Robinson, 'Elijah, John and Jesus', argues strongly that Jesus was originally regarded as Elijah who is to come. There is further evidence of this in Mk 9.12, where the restoration of all things cannot apply to the Baptist (also Mt. 17.11-12). Both Luke and John had to remove this anomaly (pp. 47-48).

70. Marshall, *Luke*, pp. 295-96; Fitzmyer, *Luke*, pp. 670-72; Ravens, 'Anointing', pp. 288-89.

Comparison of the second line with the two possible sources shows even greater discrepancies.

Lk. 7.27   ὃς κατασκευάσει τὴν ὁδόν σου ἔμπροσθέν σου
Exod. 23.20   ἵνα φυλάξῃ σε ἐν τῇ ὁδῷ
Mal. 3.1   καὶ ἐπιβλέψεται ὁδὸν πρὸ προσώπου μου

A further problem is that all three Gospels use κατασκευάσει for 'prepare', although the verb is never used in the LXX to translate the Hebrew verbs *šmr* (Exod. 23.20) and *pnh* (Mal. 3.1). This suggests that Luke used the verb found in Mark and which he had previously used to describe John's preparative role (Lk. 1.17). In Exod. 23.20 the messenger's task is to guard Israel's way into the promised land[71] whereas, in Malachi, the messenger is to prepare the way of the Lord—which Mark and Matthew take to mean 'Elijah' preparing the way for Jesus. But as M.M. Faierstein has shown, the coming Elijah in Mal. 3.23-24 was not regarded as the Messiah's forerunner by Judaism.[72] Luke does by allusion and omission what the Fourth Evangelist does openly when he has the Baptist say, 'I am not Elijah' (Jn 1.21). In Luke's view it is Jesus who has the role of Elijah: if anyone in the NT is the forerunner of the day of the Lord, that person is surely Jesus.

The positive evidence for believing that Luke sees Jesus as the expected Elijah is contained in three incidents. The first is the raising of the widow's son at Nain (7.11-17) and this has well known parallels with Elijah's miracle at Zarephath (1 Kgs 17.10-24). These are:

1. the dead man is the son of a widow.
2. there is a meeting at the city gate.
3. the son is given back to his mother by the prophet.

It is very important that, in Luke's narrative sequence, this incident is followed immediately by the question of John's disciples about the Coming One and Luke's refusal to identify John as the expected Elijah.

The second incident follows the rejection of Jesus' messengers by a Samaritan village (9.51-55). As early as Marcion it was known that the

71. Danker, *Jesus and the New Age*, p. 166.
72. Faierstein, 'Scribes', pp. 75-86. Vermes, *Jesus the Jew*, pp. 94-95, thinks that there was a very early identification of Jesus with the expected Elijah. However, the role was soon taken from Jesus and given to John and, if Vermes is correct, it further confirms Luke's conservatism. Manson, *Sayings*, p. 69, points to another rabbinic theme, that of Elijah being High Priest of the messianic age: 'He is thus the colleague of the Messiah rather than his forerunner'. Luke agrees.

4. Luke's View of Jesus

request to bring down fire from heaven was 'as Elijah had done'.[73] According to Luke the apostles saw Jesus as the expected Elijah but in this case it was a role that Jesus was not prepared to fulfil. The third group of allusions is based upon the fact that Elijah was the only OT prophet who was taken up into heaven, although, in later traditions, Moses too ascends. It is therefore no surprise to find hints of the Elijah story in the account of Jesus' ascension in Acts.

Acts 1	2 Kings 2
v. 4 The apostles are told not to leave Jerusalem.	vv. 2, 4, 6 Elisha is told to wait at each resting place.
v. 5 Jesus recalls the baptism by John in the Jordan.	v. 8 Elijah parts the Jordan so that he and Elisha can cross on dry land (cf. Moses, Exod. 14.21-23).
v. 5 Jesus promises the Holy Spirit to the apostles. They witness his ascent.	vv. 9-10 Elisha is promised a double portion of Elijah's spirit if he sees him go.
v. 11 Jesus has been taken up into Heaven (ἀναλημφθείς).	v. 11 Elijah went up into heaven (ἀνελήμφθη).

J.G. Davies has also noted some verbal agreements between Acts 1.3, 11, 12 and 1 Kgs 19.8, the account of Elijah's forty-day journey to Horeb, the mountain of God.[74] Davies regards Luke's account of the transfiguration as a prefiguration of the ascension[75] which suggests that Luke completes his Elijah typology in Acts 1.4-11. The presence of allusions to Moses in the ascension are much less clear but Josephus (*Ant.* 4.323-26) mentions that at the end of his life Moses disappeared in a cloud while he was on a high mountain near Jericho.[76]

There is one further level of significance to Luke's presentation of Jesus in terms of Elijah and, to a lesser extent, Elisha. This lies not only in the fact *that* they appear but also *where* they appear in Luke's narrative. Their appearances establish a three-fold pattern in the Gospel[77] which begins with the programmatic event in the Nazareth synagogue.[78] This is followed by a mission culminating in the choice of the twelve and the sermon on the plain. The second element in the pattern begins with

---

73. A C D W add 'as did Elijah'.
74. Davies, *He Ascended*, pp. 189 also 53-54.
75. Davies, *He Ascended*, pp. 39-41.
76. Lake and Cadbury, *Beginnings*, IV, p. 9.
77. Ravens, 'Prophetic Role', pp. 128-29.
78. Creed, *St Luke*, p. 65; Tiede, *Prophecy and History*, pp. 19-20; Brawley, *Luke–Acts and the Jews*, ch. 2.

Lk. 7.2-50 which provides a further typological affirmation of Jesus as the eschatological prophet.[79] Here too are Elijah and Elisha as well as hints of other prophets and this precedes another period of mission. This starts at 8.1 and concludes with the mission of the twelve (9.1-6). The final section starts with 9.7-62 and it gathers together for the third time the various elements that confirm the prophetic role of Jesus. This inaugurates the mission of the seventy and the journey to Jerusalem (10.1–19.45). It is there that the rejection that was prefigured at Nazareth is brought to its conclusion and the prophecy in Lk. 13.33 is fulfilled.

Two OT figures dominate Luke's portrayal of the earthly Jesus, Moses and Elijah. There are, it is true, a number of minor roles but these are always subservient to the two principals. What Luke has done is to identify the prophet promised by Moses as the returning Elijah, the one who is to come (7.19, 20). This term describes the expected prophet, not the Messiah. The origin of this identification may have been Mal. 3.24 which concludes with the promise that Elijah will return and the injunction to remember 'the law of my servant Moses which I commanded him on Horeb for all Israel'.[80]

Conclusion

The evidence that has been discussed suggests that Luke's Christology consists not only of two stages but also two distinct functions, that of prophet and that of coming Messiah. These two stages are bound into a unity by the prophetic anointing at Nazareth as well as by the titles 'Lord' and 'Son of Man', titles that Luke uses for both the earthly and the heavenly Jesus. Luke has brought together two lines of Jewish thinking, the prophetic and the messianic, in a way that is unique in the NT and which is all the more remarkable for the time when Luke was writing.

The Hebrew prophets pictured the day of the Lord in a wide range of images and a diversity of purposes[81] some of which are contradictory. It

79. Ravens, 'Anointing', pp. 290-91.
80. Schmidt, 'Luke's "Innocent" Jesus', p. 119, draws attention to a further possible connection between Jesus, Moses and Elijah. At his trial, Jesus is accused of perverting the nation (διαστρέφοντα τὸ ἔθνος, 23.2). At Exod. 5.4 the king of Egypt accuses Moses and Aaron of turning the people from their work (διαστρέφετε τὸν λαόν), and at 1 Kgs 18.17 King Ahab accuses Elijah of perverting Israel (ὁ διαστρέφων τὸν Ισραηλ).
81. Von Rad, *Old Testament Theology*, pp. 119-29.

can be described as a day of darkness (Amos 5.18-20; 8.9; cf. Lk. 23.44), a day of terror (Isa. 2.19-21) and always as a day of divine judgment. This judgment is sometimes focused on the nations (e.g. Isa. 13; Ezek. 26–32) and sometimes upon Israel, as in Ezekiel 7. But the day was also seen as the time of Israel's restoration (e.g. Zeph. 3.14-20) and the influx of the nations (Mic. 4.1-4). Yet there is one passage in which the day of the Lord will be preceded by the return of Elijah (Mal. 3.19-24) and it will be the time when evildoers will be punished and the righteous rewarded. This is the only occasion in the Hebrew Scriptures where the day of the Lord is preceded by the return of a notable figure from the past.

The Anointed One, as a future deliverer, does not appear in the OT or the Jewish intertestamental literature before the second century CE.[82] In *Pss. Sol.* 17 and 18 and in the *Similitudes of Enoch* (*1 Enoch* 48.10; 52.4), the anointed figure is always further qualified, as for example, 'the anointed of the Lord of the Spirits' (*1 Enoch* 48.10). How *an* anointed deliverer became *the* Anointed Jesus of Christian belief is far from certain[83] but, whatever the route, the ascription was clearly established by the time of Paul. Yet the fact that the Jews do not seem to have formulated a specification for the Messiah does not mean that they did not expect an anointed saviour or that they did not have clear ideas about what deliverance would be like. It was the deliverance, rather than the figure of the deliverer, that was their prime and practical concern.[84]

Within the Christian church Luke was in something of a delicate position. He was well aware that many of his fellow Christians believed that Jesus was the Messiah of Jewish expectations and he would also realize that those expectations had not been fulfilled. In fact, from the standpoint of Judaism, the situation had become far worse than it was when Jesus was alive. Far from being delivered, Jerusalem had been besieged and defeated and, worst of all, the temple had been destroyed. After 70 CE Jewish Christians would have found their faith in Jesus as Messiah under a considerable strain. This would be a potent factor in Luke's Christology and eschatology.[85] His plan was to show that it was

---

82. Harvey, *Constraints*, p. 79.

83. Harvey, *Constraints*, pp. 80-81, suggests that the title may have originated as a nickname to distinguish between Jesus known as anointed from others with the same name, e.g. Jesus called Justus (Col. 4.11).

84. Harvey, *Constraints*, pp. 77-78.

85. For internal evidence of Luke's belief that the parousia was still to come see Hiers, 'Delay of the Parousia'.

possible to present belief about Jesus in ways which take account of political and biblical realities. He used the language of contemporary Christianity yet gave it a different, more primitive sense. Jesus was the χριστός but as the prophet who followed the role described by Isaiah and the prophet promised by Moses. These Luke combined under the figure of the expected Elijah who would precede the day of the Lord. Like Elijah, he had ascended into heaven and from there he would return, now as the Messiah who would restore the kingdom to Israel at the end of the age.[86] Incidentally, we should note Luke's care to tell of the removal of possible pretenders such as Theudas and Judas the Galilean (Acts 5.36-37).[87]

There is one further factor behind Luke's apparently less-developed Christology; that Luke's thinking is, in the words of C.F. Evans, 'profoundly theological in the sense of concentrated upon God'.[88] Among the evidences which Evans cites are the following features:

1. God has supplied Jesus as the only saviour of Israel and that nowhere else in the NT are the Davidic promises and God's salvation brought together as they are by Luke.
2. God stands as the initiator of all the major actions in Acts, either directly or indirectly.
3. What is preached and received in Acts (and sometimes in the Gospel) is the word of God (Lk. 5.1; 8.11, 21;[89] 11.28; Acts 4.31; 6.2, 7; 8.14; 11.1; 13.5, 44, 46, 48; 17.13; 18.11).

In addition, we note that the only use of 'word of God' in the other Synoptics is at Mk 7.13 (par. Mt. 15.6) where it refers to the law in contrast to the traditions of men; the verse is omitted by Luke. That Jesus preaches the word of God further points to Luke's presentation of him in the tradition of the Hebrew prophets (cf. Lk. 3.2).

We can extend Evans's observations one step further. Luke is careful, particularly in Acts, to make clear that he is speaking about the God of

---

86. Davies, *He Ascended*, p. 39, Jesus as Messiah designate; Mowinkel, *He That Cometh*, p. 303, describes Jewish thinking.

87. Haenchen, *Acts*, pp. 252-53, notes Luke's historical blunder, but this is secondary to Luke's main purpose which is to show that since the time of Jesus (the census, ἀπογραφή, Acts 5.37, cf. Lk. 2.2) there have been no other claimants to the messianic role and title.

88. Evans, *Saint Luke*, pp. 53-54.

89. Evans, *Saint Luke*, p. 378 on Luke's revision of Mk 3.35. Also, Evans, p. 496 on Lk. 11.28.

Israel. He is the 'God of our/your fathers' (3.13; 5.30; 7.32; 22.14), 'the Lord God of Israel' (Lk. 1.68), 'God of this people' (Acts 13.17), 'God of Abraham, Isaac and Jacob' (Lk. 20.37; Acts 3.13; 7.32), 'the God of Jacob' (Acts 7.46). In Peter's speech to men of Israel he speaks of 'the Lord our God' (Acts 2.39). Lk. 20.37 has parallels in Mk 12.26 and Mt. 22.32, but otherwise the only similar occasion is in Mt. 15.31. Luke insistently reminds his readers that it is the God of Israel whom they have to recognize and this is the theological reason behind his portrait of Jesus; Luke is theocentric rather than Christocentric. And since it is the God of Israel who offers salvation (Lk. 1.47; 3.4-6; Acts 28.28) there will be radical consequences for Luke's understanding of the way of atonement, as we shall see in the next chapter.

Luke's God-centredness has been the subject of a recent study by J.T. Squires in which he demonstrates the importance of God's plan in Luke's writings.[90] Squires places Luke–Acts in the context of Hellenistic historiography as evinced by Diodorus Siculus, Dionysius of Halicarnasus and Josephus, each of whom saw history as under the guidance of the gods, fate or God. Squires argues that Luke wrote an apologia for Christianity in a way that would appeal to a Hellenistic readership[91] using such descriptive devices as prophetic fulfilment, epiphanies and portents. If Squires's thesis about Luke's style and purpose is correct (but not to the exclusion of other styles and purposes) then it is not difficult to see why Luke should place such emphasis on the God of Israel at work in Jesus and the expansion of Christianity. In an age in which belief in fate, providence and gods was commonplace, it was essential that his Gentile readers should be under no illusion about the God in whom they must believe; it was the God of Israel and no other (e.g. Acts 14.11-17; 17.22-31; 19.23-41, especially v. 34).[92]

Luke insists that behind all that has happened stands the God of Israel and that he is remembering his covenantal promises to Israel and the nations. It is this fundamental conviction that controls Luke's messianism so that, even in the church, God works through the traditional agents,

---

90. Squires, *The Plan of God*.
91. A Hellenistic readership could include Jews as well as Gentiles.
92. It hardly needs stating that every NT author believed that it was the God of Israel whose plan was at work in the Christian movement. It is this that makes Luke's reminders all the more noteworthy. Squires fails to notice Luke's insistence that it is the God of Israel.

his angels and his Holy Spirit.[93] In this way Luke reclaims χριστός as a true title (see n. 11 above) for the one who, in God's time, will come to restore Israel. Luke's Christology is not simply the result of historical curiosity but of theological necessity. As such it would encourage Jewish Christians in the rightness of their decision to join the Way and, at the same time, act as a warning to those believers who seemed to claim too much.

---

93. Evans, *Saint Luke*, pp. 53-54.

Chapter 5

REPENTANCE AND ATONEMENT

In Chapter 4 we saw how Luke set out to reclaim χριστός as a title for Jesus by re-establishing it within the context of Jewish expectations. It had been in this context that the early Jewish believers applied the title to Jesus but, as the influence of Gentile believers grew, there was a growing separation from Jewish ways of thinking. But to re-establish Christology in something approaching its original context would have a knock-on effect for a theology of atonement since the significance of what Jesus did and its effects was bound up with who he was. In this chapter we examine how Luke formulated his understanding of atonement in a form consistent with his Christology and with his overall purpose.

Among the characteristics of Luke's soteriology that have long been recognized are his emphasis on repentance and an atoning role for Jesus in which his death has little, if any, part to play. In both of these respects his theology shows a marked difference from the other Gospels and, indeed, from many of the NT letters. We must therefore ask how these two ideas are related and how they are connected with Luke's purpose.

The Vocabulary of Repentance

The Judaeo-Christian vocabulary of repentance in the first century CE is not without its complexities and a brief outline is necessary. In rabbinic Hebrew, the standard word for repentance is $t^e š û b â$, of which the root, $š û b$, means 'to turn' and, in the present context, 'turn to God'.[1] We cannot overestimate the vital importance of repentance in Judaism because, together with restitution and the sincere resolve not to sin

---

1. Sanders, *Jesus and Judaism*, p. 106, states that there is no word in classical Hebrew that would be translated by 'repentance'. Repentance is one of the themes in Jewish literature that looks forward to restoration.

again, it was the way for the sinner to remain within the covenant.[2] Repentance expressed the sinner's desire to return to God and it was therefore an essential step on the path to forgiveness of sins. It was thus a vital part of the Day of Atonement, both when the temple existed and after its destruction in 70 CE.

The word šûb occurs frequently in the OT and, in the LXX, it is usually translated by ἀποστρέφω or ἐπιστρέφω, there being only one instance where the usual NT verb, μετανοέω, is used (Isa. 46.8). The corollary of this is that we need to be aware that the idea of repentance in Luke–Acts may not be restricted to μετανοέω but might also be conveyed by ἀποστρέφω and ἐπιστρέφω. Of these two verbs ἀποστρέφω occurs only twice in Luke–Acts. In Lk. 23.14 there is no suggestion of repenting but there is at Acts 3.26 where it is said that God has sent his servant to the Jews first 'to bless you in turning (ἐν τῷ ἀποστρέφειν) every one of you from his wickedness'. The verb is not used by Mark and in neither instance in Matthew (5.42; 26.52) is repentance implied. ἐπιστρέφω occurs seven times in the Third Gospel, of which four refer to turning in a religious sense (1.16, 17; 17.4; 22.32). In 17.4 the verb is combined with repenting (μετανοῶ) for sin and being forgiven. In Acts, eight of the eleven instances of ἐπιστρέφω[3] concern turning in a religious sense and of these, two occur with μετανοέω (3.19; 26.20). Although ἐπιστρέφω is more common than ἀποστρέφω in Mark and Matthew, only in Mk 4.12 and the parallel in Mt. 13.15 is turning to God mentioned and this is a quotation from Isa. 6.10.

A strong indication of the importance that each evangelist attaches to μετανοέω and μετάνοια comes from a comparison of the word frequencies in the Gospels. There are three occurrences in Mark, seven in Matthew and none in John. Luke's Gospel has fourteen instances and there are a further eleven in Acts. Of the cases where the words are

---

2. Sanders, *Palestinian Judaism*, pp. 174-80. Neale, *Sinners*, has examined Luke's use of the term (ch. 3) and concludes that it is almost impossible to define sociologically. It represents an ideological contrast for those who see themselves as righteous, 'a symbol for the enemies of God' (pp. 96-97). Certainly Luke never tells his readers the sort of things sinners did so as to acquire the title, and I have made no attempt to speculate about that upon which Luke is silent. But I would add that both Luke and Jesus had in mind something far more serious than despised trades (pp. 72-75).

3. Acts 3.19; 9.35, (40); 11.21; 14.15; 15.19, (36); (16.18); 26.18, 20; 28.27. In 15.3, ἐπιστρέφω is used for the conversion of Gentiles. References ( ) concern nonreligious uses.

5. Repentance and Atonement 141

attributed to Jesus there is one in Mark (1.15) and four in Matthew (4.17; 11.20, 21; 12.41) compared to twelve in Luke. But Luke's emphasis is selective and he omits two sayings from Mark (1.15; 6.12).

One of the main objectives of repentance is to obtain forgiveness of sins and we therefore must see how these two ideas are related in the synoptic tradition. Apart from Luke's use of χαρίζομαι in the story of the woman who anoints Jesus (7.42, 43), ἄφεσις and ἀφίημ are the usual words. Mark uses ἄφεσις twice, of which only one is in connection with repentance and that is in a saying attributed to the Baptist (1.4). Of the eight occurrences of ἀφίημι to mean 'forgive', only one involves turning to God (4.12, cf. Isa. 6.9). In Matthew, supposedly the most Jewish of the Gospels, forgiveness and repentance never occur together. In Luke–Acts, a very different picture emerges, as we shall see.

Jewish Views of Repentance[4]

In cases where the LXX uses μετανοέω-μετάνοια to translate a Hebrew root, then the root is *nḥm* (with the exception of Isa. 46.8 noted above) which can mean turning from wickedness (Jer. 8.6; 31.19 MT) but, more often, it connotes no more than changing one's mind. It is really only in the Greek wisdom literature that μετανοέω and μετάνοια carry the weight of meaning that they do in the NT. In the wisdom writings the words state or imply turning from sin in sorrow for what has been done. Three examples make the point.

> Yet to them who repent (μετανοοῦσιν) he grants a return,...Turn (ἐπίστρεφε) to the Lord and forsake your sins (Sir. 17.24-25).

> For all this the people [in the time of Elijah and Elisha] did not repent (οὐ μετενόησεν), and they did not forsake their sins (Sir. 48.15).

> They will speak to one another in repentance (μετανοοῦντες), and in anguish of spirit they will groan (Wis. 5.3).

Wis. 5.3 is specially notable because it will be the people's response to their rejection of the righteous one (ὁ δίκαιος) who brings unexpected salvation (σωτηρίας) and who is now numbered among the sons of God (5.1-5). The rejection of the Righteous One is mentioned in Acts 7.52, and, in Acts 3.14, denial of the Righteous One is the accusation that precedes Peter's call to repentance (3.19). Sir. 17.24-25 also makes

---

4. This very brief summary is deeply indebted to the detailed studies by G.F. Moore and E.P. Sanders.

a distinction between μετανοέω, which is turning from sin, and ἐπιστρέφω, which is turning to God, as twin aspects of the same reality (cf. Acts 3.19). Other examples of repentance language in the wisdom literature are in Wis. 11.23; 12.10, 19; Sir. 44.16.

In the Greek text of the *Prayer of Manasseh*, which is probably no later than the first century CE,[5] there is a strong connection between repentance, humility and deep sorrow for sins (vv. 7, 8). The passage is remarkable because not only was Manasseh *the* great sinner (2 Kgs 21.1-16) but also because the sinner speaks of himself in the first person. Furthermore, repentance is said to spring from God's great mercy and compassion because he is the God of those who repent (ὁ θεὸς τῶν μετανοούντων, v. 13). Two other examples from the literature of this period further illustrate the importance of repentance. In the *Apocryphon of Ezekiel* (fragment 2 = *1 Clem.* 8.3), the house of Israel is called to repent (μετανοήσατε) and if they turn (ἐπιστραφῆτε) to their Father with their whole heart then he will listen to them as a holy people.[6] In *Joseph and Asenath* 9 and 10.14-17, the repentance of a Gentile from her idolatry leads her to put on sackcloth and ashes and, in 16.4 she is told, 'happy are all those who attach themselves to the Lord God in repentance'.[7] In each case μετάνοια-μετανοεώ is used.

G.F. Moore, in his major study of Judaism, says of the Jewish definition of repentance that to it 'belong[s] the reparation of injustices done to a fellow man in his person, property or good name, the confession of sin, prayer for forgiveness, and the resolve and endeavour not to fall into sin again'.[8] This view of the cardinal importance of repentance has been forcefully endorsed by E.P. Sanders in a recent study.[9] Such repentance is the basis on which God forgives the sinner, it is rooted in the fundamental act of God's election of Israel[10] and it shows the sinner's desire to remain within the covenant. Repentance is therefore 'the sovereign means of atonement'[11] and, together with forgiveness, 'may properly be

---

5. Sandmel, *Judaism*, p. 70. Charlesworth, 'Prayer of Manasseh', *OTP*, II, pp. 625-37.
6. Mueller and Robinson, 'Apocryphon of Ezekiel', *OTP*, I, p. 494.
7. Burchard, 'Joseph and Aseneth', *OTP*, II, pp. 214-16, 228-29.
8. Moore, *Judaism*, I, p. 117.
9. Sanders, *Jesus and Judaism*, pp. 373-74 n. 51 and *Palestinian Judaism*, p. 175.
10. Sanders, *Palestinian Judaism*, p. 177.
11. Sanders, *Palestinian Judaism*, p. 180.

called the Jewish doctrine of salvation'.[12]

In taking account of rabbinic opinions we must bear in mind the obvious danger in reading back to the first century from a written source dating from after 175 CE.[13] Nevertheless, as earlier literature shows, on such a vital issue as repentance the rabbis were not expressing ideas new to their own time.

Jewish confidence in the divine mercy and the efficacy of repentance is expressed in the statement that 'All Israelites have a share in the world to come' (*m. Sanh.* 10.1).[14] After taking account of the rabbinic lists of exceptions Sanders arrives at the conclusion that 'the *universal* view is that every individual Israelite who indicates his intention to remain in the covenant by repenting, observing the Day of Atonement and the like, will be forgiven for all his transgressions'.[15] The importance of the right intention is made quite clear in *m. Yom.* 8.9: 'He who says "I will sin, and repent and sin again and repent", he will be given no chance to repent. [If he said] "I will sin and the Day of Atonement will effect atonement" then the Day of Atonement effects no atonement.' Given the right intention, the Day of Atonement will atone for sins between man and God and for transgressions between a man and his neighbour. The Mishnah quotes in evidence for this view, Lev. 16.30; Ezek. 36.25 and Jer. 17.13. Maccoby says of this passage that it makes clear that repentance and reparation are the primary methods of atonement and that there is no magical efficacy in the rites of the Day of Atonement.[16]

12. Moore, *Judaism*, I, p. 500.
13. Sandmel, *Judaism*, p. 103.
14. Davies, *Jewish and Pauline Studies*, p. 18. Another example that shows the merciful basis of forgiveness is *Sifra* on Lev. 26.41: '"If then their uncircumcised heart is humbled"; These words apply to repentance. For as soon as they humble their hearts in repentance I immediately return and show mercy, as it is said, "If then their uncircumcised heart is humbled and they make amends for their iniquity"' (Sanders's translation).
15. Sanders, *Palestinian Judaism*, p. 182. Eichrodt, *Theology of the Old Testament*, II, p. 446, emphasizes that the sacrifices in the priestly law were regarded as established by God himself. Therefore, 'atonement is to be regarded as the gracious creation of the covenant God who bestows upon his congregation the possibility of expiating all those things that call for expiation, and of assuring themselves, through these visible signs, of his forgiving grace and enduring clemency'. Eichrodt also points out that, although not always mentioned, these sacrifices were accompanied by confession and prayer which 'correspond to the general conviction of the necessity of contrition and repentance'.
16. Maccoby, *Rabbinic Writings*, pp. 89-92; Danby, *Mishnah*, p. 172.

After the destruction of the temple repentance became the substitute for all the sacrifices prescribed in the law.

Repentance in Luke's Gospel

We must first notice how Luke's treatment of repentance compares with those of Mark and Matthew. He agrees with Mark that the Baptist preached a baptism of repentance for the forgiveness of sins (Mk 1.4; Lk. 3.3) and that the people were baptized (Mk 1.5; Lk. 3.21). But according to Matthew, John preaches repentance because the kingdom is near, not for forgiveness of sins (3.2). The reason for this is, no doubt, because, for Matthew, forgiveness depends upon the death of Christ (26.28; 28.19-20);[17] nevertheless, the crowd confess their sins and are baptized (3.6). Luke, by contrast, does not make the forgiveness of sins dependent upon the death of Jesus so that he has no qualms about agreeing with Mk 1.4 on the content of the Baptist's preaching.

In both Mark (1.14-15) and Matthew (4.12, 17), Jesus begins his public ministry by preaching a call to repent because the kingdom is near. Luke omits Mk 1.15 and Conzelmann believes that the reason for this is that Luke wants to distinguish between the preaching of Jesus and the Baptist.[18] Yet the reverse is the case: both John and Jesus preach good news (3.18; 4.18, 43), and neither calls for repentance because the kingdom is near. Certainly the Lukan Jesus preaches both the coming kingdom and repentance for forgiveness but, unlike Mark and Matthew, he never makes repentance dependent on the nearness of the kingdom. For Luke, the motive for repentance appears to be the same as it is in Judaism: the restoration of the sinner. The important distinction to note is not between preaching by Jesus and the Baptist but between Luke and his predecessors about the motive for repentance.

The other Lukan omission is of Mk 6.12, the command to the twelve to call people to repentance. In Luke's Gospel the twelve and the seventy are to preach the kingdom of God (9.2; 10.9, 11; see also 9.60). It is only after the resurrection that Jesus' followers preach both the kingdom and repentance but, as in the Gospel, repentance is not linked directly to the kingdom.

The Lukan Jesus' first mention of repentance is set in the context of a meal at the house of Levi the toll collector (5.27-32), a story that has

17. Green, *Matthew*, p. 62.
18. Conzelmann, *Luke*, p. 99.

5. Repentance and Atonement

similarities to the *Prayer of Manasseh* 8.[19] As in Mk 2.13-17, this is a conflict story in which the Pharisees and their scribes question Jesus about his eating with toll-collectors and sinners.[20] Mark has no reason for the call to sinners other than as an invitation to a meal, presumably in anticipation of the messianic banquet in the kingdom. Luke's addition of calling sinners 'to repentance' does not need the context of a meal in order to make sense and it makes the invitation of sinners into the kingdom without condition 'innocuous since no right minded Jew could take offence at a summons of sinners to repentance'.[21] Exactly so: it is Luke's purpose to show the Pharisees that Jesus is doing just what would be expected of a true prophet and thus he greatly reduces the tension of the conflict. Calling sinners to repent is as much a part of Jesus' ministry as the statement in 4.43, 'I must preach the good news of the kingdom of God'. Luke locates this preaching in the synagogues of Judaea (4.44, the best attested and more difficult reading)[22] and not, as in Mk 1.39, in Galilee. Whatever Luke's knowledge of Palestinian geography, he clearly intends to show Jesus preaching in the heartland of Judaism.

The next mention of repentance is in the woes pronounced on the Galilean towns (10.13-15)[23] and a comparison with the account in Mt. 11.20-24 shows the evangelists' different understandings. Luke's account is set between talk of the possible rejection of the seventy and their joyful return (10.10-12, 17) whereas Matthew's version follows a comment on the rejections of John and Jesus (Mt. 11.16-19) and begins with a comment about the lack of repentance in the cities where Jesus had done his mighty works (11.20). Luke has already told of a miracle at or near Bethsaida (9.10-17) and he has also implied that people from Tyre and Sidon were among those who had come to be healed by Jesus (6.17-18). Tyre and Sidon were notorious Gentile cities (see e.g. Isa. 23) and repentance was not a contemporary Gentile practice,[24] yet even they would have been moved to repent in sackcloth and ashes (cf. Dan. 9.3-19). If Gentile cities would do this how much more should Jews,

---

19. Neale, *Sinners*, p. 133.
20. Bultmann, *Synoptic Tradition*, pp. 92, 327.
21. Evans, *Saint Luke*, p. 309.
22. Fitzmyer, *Luke*, pp. 557-58.
23. According to Marshall, *Luke*, p. 424, Chorazin, although unknown, was probably in Galilee.
24. Evans, *Saint Luke*, p. 236.

with their traditions, repent of their sins (cf. 5.32). Lk. 11.32 takes a somewhat similar view,[25] that Gentiles would be more responsive to Jesus than the present generation of Israel. Here the example is the men of Nineveh who had repented at Jonah's preaching. According to Jon. 3.5, 8, 10, the Ninevites believed in God and turned from their evil ways. In Jon. 3.8, 10 the verb is ἀπέστρεψαν whereas Luke, like Mt. 12.42, uses μετανοέω. In Jon. 3.9, 10, this verb is used of God changing his mind.

The two Lukan stories of Pilate and the Galileans and the tower of Siloam (13.1-5) have not been identified historically but Luke's purpose is clear enough. The Galileans were sinners and the tower victims were offenders (ὀφειλέται), a word that may reflect the Aramaic *hayyab*, a debtor.[26] Both words reinforce the emphasis on the Jewish view of repentance, that 'unless you repent you will likewise perish' (13.3, 5).[27] This emphasis is particularly noteworthy in view of the absence of any overt Christian preaching or interpretation of the stories.

This incident is immediately followed by the parable of the fruitless fig tree in the vineyard (13.6-9) which urges that the time left for bearing fruit (of repentance? 3.8) for the owner is strictly limited. Marshall,[28] Fitzmyer[29] and Evans[30] each caution against taking the vineyard and the fig tree as symbols for Israel, Jerusalem or individual Jews. But, in the light of passages such as Isa. 5.1-7 which describes God's destruction of the vineyard that is the house of Israel, and God's punishment of Judah in Jeremiah 8, the vine without grapes and the fig tree without figs (8.13), such caution seems overstated. Luke omits Mark's cursing of the barren fig tree (11.12-25), a story that D.E. Nineham[31] and J.C. Fenton[32]

---

25. Bultmann, *Synoptic Tradition*, pp. 112-13.
26. Fitzmyer, *Luke*, p. 1008. But on p. 906 (Lk. 11.4) he suggests that Luke changed 'debts' to 'sins' for the sake of Gentile readers. Why, then, did he not make the change at 13.4?
27. Although the rabbis debated whether all Israel would have a share in the world to come, there seems little doubt that only 'unregenerate sinners' would be excluded. Sanders, *Palestinian Judaism*, pp. 147-50.
28. Marshall, *Luke*, p. 555.
29. Fitzmyer, *Luke*, p. 1005.
30. Evans, *Saint Luke*, p. 548.
31. Nineham, *Mark*, pp. 298-99, holds that the fig tree in Lk. 13 'clearly represents the house of Israel'.
32. Fenton, *Saint Matthew*, pp. 335-36, suggests that the story may have originated as a saying of Jesus and cites Lk. 13.6.

5. *Repentance and Atonement*

regard as a sign of God's judgment on Israel. It appears that Luke has replaced it with a parable in which judgment on Israel is withheld for a period during which the offer of repentance remains open. It seems that Lk. 13.1-9 contains two statements of the same message.

The parables of the lost sheep and coin (15.3-10) are bound together by the theme of table fellowship (15.2, 6, 9) and by the mention of sinners (15.2, 7, 10). The emphasis here is on the divine joy when sinners repent and the corresponding mercy of God in seeking the lost through the mission of Jesus (cf. 19.10). The theme of joy is very much to the fore in the parable of the returning son (15.11-32). We have seen that this parable is open to a corporate interpretation (Chapter 3 above), but this should not obscure the obvious individual side to the story. Jeremias is no doubt correct to say that the parable 'describes what God is like, his goodness, his grace, his boundless mercy, his abiding love'.[33] The qualities listed by Jeremias were not, however, previously unknown to Israel; they are just the qualities that motivated all repentant sinners. There is no mention of repentance in the parable but we are probably intended to see it in the words and actions of the younger son in returning to his father.[34] The only motive we are told about is that he will be better off when he returns, but then so is anyone who repents. In this sense I can also agree with Jeremias when he says that the parable (and we can add the earlier pair vv. 3-10) is not primarily a proclamation of the good news but a vindication of it to its critics. The method of vindication is to show that it is consistent with what Israel already knows about God. There is certainly no need to ask the Christological question that Talbert says we are forced to ask, 'Who is this who professes to know the mind of God?'[35] Any reasonably well instructed Jew would have known the mind of God in these matters.

In the context of the present discussion the story of the rich man and Lazarus (16.19-31) is exceptional because it contains the only instance in the Gospel where repentance is mentioned by someone other than John

---

33. Jeremias, *Parables*, p. 131.
34. Sanders, *Palestinian Judaism*, p. 178, notes a parable attributed to R. Meir in *Deut. R.* 2.24 ('Thou wilt return to the Lord thy God') in which a king sends a message to his son who has taken to evil ways. The son is too ashamed to return but his father sends another message, 'My Son, is a son ever ashamed to return to his father? and is it not to your father that you will be returning?'
35. Talbert, *Reading Luke*, p. 152: but Danker, *Jesus and the New Age*, p. 274, correctly comments that 'what Jesus does on behalf of sinners is no different from God's concern with rebellious Israel in the period of the OT'.

or Jesus. Abraham's remark, 'If they do not hear Moses and the prophets, neither will they be convinced if someone should rise from the dead' (16.31), certainly expresses Luke's own view. The belief, stated with all the authority of Abraham, that even rising from the dead will not produce repentance, would surely come as a shock to some of Luke's readers except, of course, those who retained their Jewish view of the law and the prophets. Abraham's reply to the rich man's plea shows how far Luke endorses the Jewish view of the law and the prophets together with repentance as the way of return for sinners. These aspects of the story can be easily overlooked if it is assumed that Luke wrote for a predominantly Gentile readership.

The last mention of repentance prior to the resurrection concerns sins committed against a brother (17.3-4). Rabbinic teaching held that it was more difficult to atone for sins committed against a fellow Israelite than for sins against God. This was because restitution was not always possible in the case of a fellow human being.[36] In Luke's account it is not the sinner who is addressed but the offended brother and it is he who is called to forgive the penitent up to seven times a day.[37] What is new is that although the sinner must repent, there is no injunction, as in later Jewish practice, for the penitent to make restitution. It is also implied that the injured party should neither ask for nor expect it. Matthew's version of the story (18.15) contains no mention of repentance. Since Jesus' saying is addressed to the disciples it suggests that Luke regarded the practice of repentance as a necessary part of church life because 'temptations (σκάνδαλα) are bound to come' (17.1). This casts some doubt on Conzelmann's opinion that repentance in Luke–Acts is a once-only event that is part of conversion.[38] This view is correct as far as ἐπιστρέφω is concerned but not in terms of μετανοέω.

The special Lukan story of the chief toll-collector (19.1-10) must be included in this discussion if only because it is widely supposed that the Jewish crowd is correct in calling Zacchaeus a sinner. But toll-collectors were not necessarily sinners by definition, otherwise there would have been no point in the Baptist specifying how they could behave justly while remaining in their work (3.12-13). Jesus neither calls Zacchaeus to repent nor does he announce forgiveness for there is nothing to forgive. Jesus does, however, vindicate Zacchaeus to the crowd as a 'son of

---

36. Sanders, *Palestinian Judaism*, p. 179 and n. 161.
37. E.g. Sir. 27.30–28.5 on the need to forgive others.
38. Conzelmann, *Luke*, p. 99 n. 3.

5. *Repentance and Atonement*

Abraham' (19.9). The story deals with the problem of restitution which was particularly difficult for toll-collectors. The rabbinic view was that they should make restitution to those whom they knew and, 'for the rest should make public utilities out of them'.[39] In Luke's story the present tenses, 'I give' and 'I restore', describe how Zacchaeus behaves when he has unintentionally ('if I have', 19.8) defrauded anyone. The story shows Jesus bringing salvation to Zacchaeus, not by calling for repentance but by vindicating a man who has been falsely accused by the Jewish crowd. In doing this Jesus seeks and saves the lost (ἀπολωλός, 19.10, cf. 15.4, 6, 24, 32). Saving the lost entails that they are restored not only to God but also to the people of Israel, just as the lost sheep is restored to the shepherd *and* to the flock (15.3-7).[40]

Jesus' post-resurrection commission of the apostles (24.44-49) again reminds them and the readers of the cardinal importance of repentance and forgiveness of sins. These are now to be proclaimed to all nations in the name of Christ. This commission is in contrast with the more ecclesiastical command in Mt. 28.18-20 in which the eleven are told to make disciples, baptize in the threefold name and teach all the commands of Jesus. Luke's account contains no suggestion of new commands other than the extension of the offer of repentance to the Gentiles. This avoidance of newness is also seen in the backward-looking character of the speech. Jesus has fulfilled all that was written about him 'in the law of Moses and the prophets and the psalms' (24.44-46). In preaching repentance the church's understanding of Jesus is to be firmly grounded in the Jewish Scriptures.[41] Here, for the first time, the Lukan Jesus extends the Jewish way of atonement to all nations because of, and in the name of, Christ. Luke does not regard the death and resurrection of Jesus as a new way of salvation but as the turning point that enables the 'old' way of repentance to be offered to all.

Finally in this section of the discussion, we must look at the four instances in the Gospel where forgiveness is offered but without a call to repent. The first case is in the prophecy that John will 'give knowledge of salvation to [God's] people in the forgiveness of their sins' (1.77). However, when John begins his ministry he preaches a baptism of repentance for forgiveness (3.3). The next two announcements of the

---

39. Maccoby, *Rabbinic Writings*, pp. 91, 142, *t. B. Meṣ.* 8.26.
40. A more detailed argument for the vindication of Zacchaeus is given in my article, 'Zacchaeus'. For a different view see Neale, *Sinners*, pp. 179-90.
41. Fitzmyer, *Luke*, pp. 1579-80.

forgiveness of sins are made by Jesus but without calling for repentance. In the story of the healing of a paralytic (5.17-26) the section on forgiveness (vv. 20-24a) appears to be detachable from the miracle and Bultmann thinks that it may reflect the need of later Christians to base their claim to forgive sins on Jesus' authority.[42] But, even if this was Mark's motive it does not appear to be Luke's since nowhere in Acts are Christians described as forgiving sins. The proclamation always makes reference to Jesus.

The second incident is in the story of a sinful woman who anoints Jesus (7.36-50) and here it must be assumed that her actions show her penitence. In both this story and that of the paralytic it is the status of Jesus that is questioned: 'Son of Man' (5.24) and 'prophet' (7.39). Both stories therefore have Christological motives and the authority of Jesus to announce forgiveness without calling for repentance is his alone, because of his status. For a Christian to be forgiven by a brother, repentance is necessary (17.3-4).

The final instance is in the Lord's prayer: 'and forgive us our sins, for we ourselves forgive every one who is indebted to us' (11.4). None of the three ancient versions of the prayer (Mt. 6.9-13; Lk. 11.2-4; *Did.* 8.2) mentions repentance. This is because praying for forgiveness is in itself an essential part of penitence since it acknowledges that sins have been committed. Luke uses both 'sins' and 'debts', the latter term having a religious connotation for Semitic readers[43] (cf. 13.4).

Repentance in Acts

The first mention of repentance in Acts is in Peter's Pentecost speech (2.14-40) the first part of which (vv. 14-36) places the death and resurrection of Jesus in the context of three OT citations, Joel 2.28-33, Pss. 15.8-11 and 109.1(LXX). This use of the OT follows the lead given by Jesus in Luke 24.44-46 by expounding the Christ from the Scriptures. The next section of the speech, vv. 37-40 deals with the Jews' question, 'What shall we do?' and this has echoes of the Baptist's actions in calling Israel to repent (Lk. 3.3-18), as several commentators have noted.[44] The similarities in Table 1 suggest that the reminiscence is deliberate.

42. Bultmann, *Synoptic Tradition*, pp. 14-16.
43. Fitzmyer, *Luke*, pp. 557-58, 897, 906.
44. E.g. Rackham, *Acts*, p. 30.

Acts 2	Luke 3
37 What shall we do? τί ποιήσωμεν;	10, 12, 14 What shall we do? τί (οὖν) ποιήσωμεν;
38 Repent and be baptized…for the remission of sins. μετανοήσατε καὶ βαπτισθήτω…εἰς ἄφεσιν τῶν ἁμαρτιῶν	3 …preaching a baptism for the remission of sins, κηρύσσων βάπτισμα μετανοίας εἰς ἄφεσιν ἁμαρτιῶν
38 You shall receive the gift of the Holy Spirit (3 There appeared to them tongues as of fire).	16 He will baptize you with the Holy Spirit and with fire
40 Peter exhorted them, παρακάλει αὐτούς	18 with other exhortations he preached…ἕτερα παρακαλῶν εὐηγγελίζετο
40 Save yourselves from this crooked (σκολιᾶς) generation	5 …and the crooked (τὰ σκολιά) shall be made straight

Notes: These last items contain the only occurrences of σκολιός in Luke–Acts. It should also be noted that both Peter and John are imprisoned (Lk. 3.20; Acts 12.4). One by Herod the tetrarch and the other by Herod the king.

Table 1. *Parallels between John's Preaching (Luke 3) and Peter's (Acts 2)*

Luke's motive for making the connection has been variously assessed. C.S.C. Williams believes that it shows the superiority of Spirit baptism over John's water baptism,[45] and M.D. Goulder suggests an involved typology that initiates the actions that follow, both in the Gospel and Acts.[46] Certainly the purpose of the parallel is to show that the missions of Jesus and of the church both begin with a call for Israel to repent of its sins but the contrast between the different baptisms is only part of Luke's purpose here since both John and Peter regard repentance baptism as a precursor to the gift of the Spirit (Lk. 3.16; Acts 2.38). The real contrast comes later in 19.1-6 when John's baptism is now performed in the name of the Lord Jesus, although the Spirit is conferred by the laying on of Paul's hands.[47] The contrast should not, however,

---

45. Williams, *Acts*, p. 70.
46. Goulder, *Type and History*, pp. 43, 54-55.
47. Haenchen, *Acts*, p. 554, notes that ὡσεί need not contradict the exact number, yet sees no allegorical significance (n. 2). But there are clear indications in the account—'about twelve', speaking with tongues and the gift of prophecy—of Luke's intention to point back to Pentecost and Joel's prophecy.

detract from the importance that Luke attaches to John's baptism as the continuing reminders show (Acts 1.22; 10.37; 13.24, but see also 18.25 and 19.3-4).

The next reference is also in a speech by Peter which, like the first speech, is addressed to 'Men of Israel' (3.12; cf. 2.22). The particular sin is that the people and not just the leaders have denied the Holy and Righteous One, killing the Author of Life whom God has raised from the dead (3.14-15). There were, however, mitigating circumstances because not only did rulers and people act in ignorance (3.17) but, in doing so, they fulfilled God's plan that his χριστός should suffer (3.18). Here we find both aspects of repentance (μετανοήσατε, ἐπιστρέψατε, 3.19) which, when they occur together, express turning in sorrow from sin and turning to God.[48] As we have seen, the verbs do not need to occur together for these meanings to be apparent but their proximity makes the difference clearer. One further point that the speech makes is that repentance is required before God will send his Messiah 'appointed for you' (3.20) and, with the coming of the Messiah, the restoration of all that God has promised. No other NT writer combines the themes of repentance and national restoration as Luke does here, giving them an eschatological impetus. This whole passage is given an even richer Jewish perspective by the use of key figures from Israel's past: Moses' promise of a future prophet and the promise to Abraham of the blessing of all nations in his posterity are both fulfilled in Jesus (3.22-25). The result is that every Israelite shall be blessed in turning from his wickedness (ἐν τῷ ἀποστρέφειν, 3.26; cf. *m. Sanh.* 10.1).

The appearance of Peter and the apostles before the High Priest and the Sanhedrin (5.27-32) leads Peter to charge his accusers with the killing of Jesus (cf. Stephen, 7.52). But 'the God of our fathers' has raised Jesus and exalted him as Leader and Saviour 'to give repentance to Israel and forgiveness of sins' (5.31). Thus far in the narrative, repentance has been associated with the name of Christ (Lk. 24.47; Acts 2.28) and, rather loosely, with the death of Jesus (3.19) but there has been little to suggest some new power that enables sinners to repent. In 5.30-31, however, the emphasis lies not on the death of Jesus but on his exaltation by God. This is the event that marks the birth of the new age and the reader is again reminded of Luke's God-centredness. Just as the God of Israel determines Luke's Christology, as we saw in Chapter 4, so we

---

48. Haenchen, *Acts*, p. 208. The difference is still preserved in the Anglican order of baptism, where the candidate professes 'I turn to Christ. I repent of my sins'.

5. *Repentance and Atonement*

find 'the God of our fathers' as the source and provider of salvation. It is he who has raised up Jesus as ἀρχηγός (as in Acts 3.13-15) and σωτήρ (cf. Acts 13.23; Lk. 1.47). It is the fact that Jesus has been exalted by the God of Israel and that he will come as Messiah that gives the urgency for Israel to repent.

The Simon Magus incident (8.18-24) provides insufficient and inconclusive evidence towards understanding Luke's theology of repentance. In part this is because Luke does not say whether Simon was a Samaritan;[49] certainly Simon's practices and his claims for himself would be totally opposed to Samaritan monotheism and keeping the law. However, since Luke tells of Gentile and Jewish indulgence in magic (19.13-20), as well as Gentile divination and idolatry (16.16-18; 17.22-25, 29), Simon's practices might even form part of a three-fold pattern. Most probably Luke assumed that because Simon was in Samaria he was a Samaritan. As far as the need for repentance is concerned, his wickedness (κακίας, 8.22) is in offering money for the gift of the Spirit and, if he repents, the intent of his heart will be forgiven (ἀφεθήσεταί, 8.22).

The next major development is the recognition by the Christian advocates of circumcision in their dispute with Peter that God has granted to the Gentiles also 'repentance unto life' (τὴν μετάνοιαν εἰς ζωήν 11.18). There is no mention of forgiveness of sins at this point but, in his address to Cornelius, Peter had said that all who believe in Jesus Christ receive 'forgiveness of sins in his name' (10.43). Cornelius is the ideal Gentile in Luke's eyes: he is a devout God-fearer (εὐσεβὴς καὶ φοβούμενος τὸν θεόν), he prays constantly to God and he gives alms liberally to the people (τῷ λαῷ, 10.1-2); he is not called upon to repent. If λαός here refers to Israel[50] then Cornelius' charity further demonstrates his love for Israel.[51] Cornelius is as near to being a devout Jew as it is possible to be without being circumcised and, with the interpretation of the Cornelius episode in 11.18, we see the beginning of the bringing together of repentance and forgiveness of sins for Gentile believers. Peter's challengers are compelled to accept that Gentile believers, even if

---

49. Casey, 'Simon Magus', *Beginnings*, V, p. 152, notes the suggestion that Simon was a Samaritan has been made on the later evidence of Justin Martyr. Justin's use of Σαμαρεύς is strictly geographical so that he is a resident of Samaria. Haenchen, *Acts*, p. 303, takes Justin to have been a Samaritan and hence Simon also.

50. Dahl, 'A People', p. 324.

51. Haenchen, *Acts*, p. 346.

not circumcised, have become members of Israel by God's direct action (11.17).

Of the four remaining references to repentance, two look back to the ministry of John. The first comes at the end of Paul's brief survey of Israel's history in which John is seen as the forerunner of Jesus (13.24). The second incident (19.4) raises a number of complex historical and doctrinal issues[52] that need not concern us here. We have commented on the status of John's baptism above.

In the first of the two remaining incidents Paul tells the Ephesian elders how he has testified to Jews and Gentiles 'of repentance (μετάνοιαν) to God and faith in our Lord Jesus Christ' (20.21). Here, conversion rather than forgiveness of sins seems to be the primary concern. It is only in the second and final incident, when Paul addresses King Agrippa, that the Lukan Paul at last mentions that the Gentiles will receive forgiveness of sins (ἄφεσιν ἁμαρτιῶν, 26.18) and that he has preached that both Jews and Gentiles should repent and turn to God (μετανοεῖν καὶ ἐπιστρέφειν, 26.20). There can be little doubt that in view of the mention of forgiveness in 26.18, μετανοεῖν represents the moral component and ἐπιστρέφειν the 'turning to God' component of the total act of conversion. This is supported by Paul's injunction to perform 'works worthy of their μετανοίας' (26.20), once again reflecting the importance of the Baptist's ministry (Lk. 3.8). The process of bringing together repentance and forgiveness for Gentiles has now reached its climax and completion; the command of Jesus is, after a slow start, being fulfilled. And the fact that Jews, Samaritans and Gentiles now share the same way to God's forgiveness is also evidence that Israel is on the way to restoration.

Having surveyed the use of repentance in Luke–Acts we can now classify the instances into two broad groups. The first group contains those sayings where the narrative audience or the subject is solely Jewish. Prior to the resurrection, this is the case in Lk. 3.3, 8; 5.32; 13.3, 5; 15.7, 10; 16.30; 17.3, 4. In this group there are only two exceptions to the explicit combination of repentance and sinners. In the first exception (3.8) the Baptist is clearly addressing sinners—'a brood of vipers fleeing from the wrath to come'—who have come to John's baptism for

---

52. Haenchen, *Acts*, pp. 554-57. His comment that John's baptism 'has become merely an expression of repentance' overlooks the fact that Jesus and the church preach repentance. The real issue in 19.1-7 is, as Haenchen points out, the gift of the Spirit.

5. *Repentance and Atonement*

sinners (3.3). The other exception is in the rich man's plea to Abraham (16.30). He has lost his share in the good world to come and he is well aware that his brothers are sinners, in danger of the same fate if they do not repent. Abraham's answer reminds Luke's readers of the primacy of the law and the prophets. The second group of pre-resurrection sayings involve Gentiles of Tyre, Sidon (10.13) and Nineveh (11.32). In neither case is the forgiveness of sins mentioned and the Gentiles are used as a spur to Israel to repent.

After the resurrection, Jesus' commission to preach to all nations includes the offer of repentance for remission of sins to Jews and Gentiles alike (Lk. 24.47) but, in Acts, the pattern established in the Gospel still dominates. In Acts 2.38; 3.19 and 5.31, it is the Jews who are to repent of their sins and, in 11.18, 17.30 and 20.21 where Gentiles are present, forgiveness of sins is not mentioned as the motive. On the two occasions when Paul refers to the work of the Baptist there is no mention of forgiveness but this is very probably because the purpose of the baptism was well known (13.24; 19.4). The only real exception to the pattern is in 26.18-20, which we have already discussed as representing the culmination of Luke's theology of the extension of atonement to the Gentiles.

There remains the command to Simon Magus to repent (8.22). Although Simon is wicked and unrighteous he is not described as a sinner because he is not a Jew. But neither is he a Gentile[53] so he cannot be told to repent without further qualification or told to turn to God. As a Samaritan he was a member of Israel and had already turned to God. His repentance must therefore acknowledge that he is not technically a sinner in Luke's sense nor a Gentile who must turn to the God of Israel.

A clear and distinctively Lukan pattern therefore emerges in his understanding of μετάνοια-type repentance. Where Jews are concerned, those who are sinners must repent of their sins because this is the way back into unencumbered covenantal membership of Israel. Gentiles, on the other hand, are not members of the covenant and cannot, therefore, come within the technical meaning of 'sinners'—that is, Jews who have transgressed the law given to Israel. For Gentiles, whatever their moral condition, repentance means first and foremost turning to the God of Israel and believing in Jesus as the promised Messiah. There are exceptions to this pattern of repentance that we have noted, but the overriding position is clear and it is supported, as we shall see, by Luke's careful

---

53. Casey, 'Simon Magus', *Beginnings*, V, p. 152.

use of the vocabulary of sin: ἁμαρτία, ἁμαρτωλός and ἁμαρτάνω.

In first-century Judaism sinners were 'persons of proven dishonesty and followers of suspected or degrading occupations'.[54] However, just what these occupations were is still a subject of debate and lists of them are very dependent upon later rabbinic collections.[55] The principal Hebrew word for sinners is $r^e\check{s}\bar{a}\,\hat{\imath}m$, a term that Sanders considers to be best translated by 'the wicked' or, more precisely, 'the lost'. In the MT the Hebrew word most often translated by ἁμαρτωλός is $r\check{s}'$, someone who has deliberately renounced the covenant and who will not repent. In the strict sense, therefore, the term could only be applied to Jews, those who had been in the covenant but now, by not repenting, had placed themselves outside it.[56] Luke largely adheres to this covenantal way of thinking, using both 'sinner' (ἁμαρτωλός) and 'lost' (ἀπολωλός) of Jews only. Neither term occurs in Acts and they are both restricted to the ministry of Jesus. In the same way, ἁμαρτάνω is used only of Jews who are considered either to be sinning against God or human beings. For example, in his defence before Festus, Paul claims that he has not offended (ἥμαρτον, 25.8) against the law, the temple or Caesar. Of the 19 occurrences of ἁμαρτία in Luke–Acts, 17 are in solely Jewish situations, although one case is the commission of Christ to preach forgiveness of sins to all nations (Lk. 24.47). The remaining two instances, Peter speaking to Cornelius (Acts 10.43) and Paul before Agrippa (26.18), confirm Christ's commission.

Summarizing the discussion so far we can see that Luke handles the related ideas of repentance, sin and forgiveness in ways that strongly reflect their usages in Judaism and which are thus unique in the NT. We have seen that 'sin' and 'sinner' are used almost exclusively in Jewish settings so that 'sinner' has almost become for Luke a technical term for a Jew who has infringed the law of Israel. Luke never specifies how a particular sinner has broken the law and hence David Neale is partly correct in saying that sinners represent all who are in need of God's mercy.[57] But this neither sufficiently recognizes that sinners are always Jews nor accounts for the absence of the term in Acts to describe those, Jew or Gentile, who need God's mercy. Once Luke has established the

54. Abrahams, *Studies*, p. 55.
55. For a recent discussion see Neale, *Sinners*, pp. 72-75.
56. Sanders, *Jesus and Judaism*, pp. 177-79, notes that the 'lost' in Lk. 15 shows that Luke 'seems to have been on the right track'.
57. Neale, *Sinners*, p. 193.

Jewish understanding of sin, repentance and forgiveness, he slowly unfolds the extension of Christ's commission to the Gentiles. First comes the announcement of forgiveness of sins (10.43), then the recognition that repentance has been offered; finally the two aspects of atonement are brought together (26.18, 20) for the Gentiles. Luke's distinctive and frequent use of repentance shows the great importance which he attached to it. A comparison of the third Gospel with those of Matthew and John, which probably date from about the same time as Luke–Acts, demonstrates Luke's very different understanding. It was a time, so many scholars believe, when the initial influx of Jews into the church had become a mere trickle and when division between Jews and Christians was both clear and acrimonious. It was also a time when the church was beginning to develop its own practice of repentance for sins committed after baptism. Among the writings of the apostolic fathers, the *Shepherd of Hermas* is an extended argument for one further chance of repentance,[58] and exhortations to repent are found in the letters of Ignatius (e.g. *Phil.* 8.1; *Smyrn.* 9.1), Clement (*1 Clem.* 7.4-7; 57.1; cf. *2 Clem.* 8.1-2; 9.7-9) and the *Didache* (15.3). It is possible that Luke was a part of this development which may also be reflected in Revelation, the only other NT book that has a comparable stress on repentance to that in Luke–Acts. The later we date Luke–Acts,[59] the more probable Luke's part in that development becomes.

There is, however, a strain in the writings of these early fathers that is absent from Luke–Acts: the saving consequences of Christ's death. This way of thinking is found in Ignatius (*Rom.* 6.1, cf. *Smyrn.* 7.1; *Eph.* 1.1), but one of the most telling examples for the present discussion is in *1 Clement*, immediately prior to his exhortation to repentance.

> Let us fix our gaze on the blood of Christ,
> and let us know that it is precious to his Father,
> because it was poured out for our salvation,
> and brought the grace of repentance (*1 Clem.* 7.4).

Clement's belief that Christ brought the grace of repentance into the world does not mean that it was new to Israel, since he supports the need to repent by pointing to the OT prophets. Presumably what he had in mind was that repentance was now available to all who believe in

---

58. Lake, *Apostolic Fathers*, II, p. 2.
59. Green, 'Matthew, Clement and Luke', p. 25, suggests that Luke is later than Clement.

Christ, in which case he and Luke are in agreement. But the extent to which they differ in their view of Christ's death as a sin offering can be seen by comparing their respective treatments of Isaiah 53 (Lk. 22.37, Acts 8.32-33; *1 Clem.* 16). The way of relating the death of Jesus to human salvation as found in *1 Clement* and other second-century[60] writers is quite alien to Luke.

Luke and Paul Compared

We have seen how Luke's understanding of atonement differed from the early fathers, in particular from his near-contemporary, Clement. The early fathers' talk of repentance is combined with a soteriology rooted in the death of Christ in ways not found in Luke–Acts. Before we discuss the wider aspects of Luke's view of atonement and its implication for his understanding of Israel, we must consider how and why Luke differed from earlier Christian ideas of atonement. For this purpose Paul is particularly suitable for comparison because he not only provides the earliest written evidence but he is also Luke's hero in the church's mission in the diaspora. For the purpose of the present comparison it is not strictly necessary to examine whether or not Luke knew Paul's letters (or Paul) but in the following chapter, in which there is further discussion of Luke and Paul, the evidence for Luke's knowledge will be considered.

1. *Repentance*

One further reason for examining differences between Lukan and Pauline atonement theologies is that Paul leaves his readers in no doubt as to his own Jewish origins. From Rom. 11.1, 2 Cor. 11.22 and Phil. 3.4-6 we learn that he is an Israelite of the tribe of Benjamin, a Hebrew born of Hebrews and that he had been a Pharisee in his attitude to the law, which he kept without blame. Yet, given such an orthodox background, repentance plays a notably small part in his letters. μετάνοια is mentioned only three times (Rom. 2.4; 2 Cor. 7.9, 10) and μετανοέω is used only once (2 Cor. 12.21). In Rom. 2.4 Paul says that God's kindness is meant to lead to repentance; in 2 Cor. 7.10 he tells his readers that godly grief leads to repentance which in turn leads to salvation (μετάνοιαν εἰς σωτηρίαν) and, in 2 Cor. 12.21, Paul mourns over Christians who have sinned but not repented. There is nothing in

---

60. Lake, *Apostolic Fathers*, II, pp. 348-49.

5. *Repentance and Atonement*

the verses that conflicts with the views of Judaism so why does he ignore the terminology of repentance elsewhere? In agreement with his scant treatment of repentance is the paucity of his references to God's forgiveness of sins, yet he offers an extensive analysis of sin as the fundamental human flaw. In Rom. 4.7-8 he quotes Ps. 31.1-2 (LXX), 'Blessed is he whose iniquities are forgiven (ἀφέθησαν) and whose sins are covered. Blessed is the man against whom the Lord will not reckon his sin.' This is Paul's only use of ἀφίημι in the sense of 'forgive'. In Rom. 11.27 he quotes Isa. 27.9, that a deliverer will take away Israel's sins, and in the third case he says that 'God was in Christ reconciling the world to himself, not counting their trespasses (παραπτώματα) against them' (2 Cor. 5.19). When Paul speaks of forgiving a fellow believer he uses χαρίζομαι (2 Cor. 2.7, 10; 12.13). The verb occurs in Eph. 4.32; Col. 2.13 and 3.13; in each case it is God who forgives. It is worth noting that Luke is the only evangelist to use the verb for 'forgive' (7.42, 43).

E.P. Sanders has argued that the reason why repentance and forgiveness are almost absent from Paul's writings is that they 'do not *respond to the real plight of man*'.[61] This plight has been brought to a head because Christ came to be Lord of all and therefore human beings are under a different lordship. 'Man's transgressions do have to be accounted for: God must overlook them or Christ must die to expiate them but they do not constitute the problem. Man's problem is not being under Christ's Lordship.'[62] For Paul, atonement depends upon Christology, according to Sanders. Because God is God of the Gentiles as well as the Jews (Rom. 3.29) and Jesus is Lord of all, then the way of atonement *must* be the same for both Jew and Gentile. If human beings are to be

---

61. Sanders, *Palestinian Judaism*, p. 449, Sanders's italics.
62. Sanders, *Palestinian Judaism*, pp. 500-501. But it is not only a question of finding an explanation of Paul's omission. Moore, *Judaism*, III, p. 151, sees that the omission 'seems from a Jewish point of view inexplicable' and that Paul had to prove that Judaism is not a way of salvation at all. This is the key to the problem: Luke's audience contained a sufficient number of Jews to whom Paul's omission *was* inexplicable. Paul's atonement theology cannot be explained solely in terms of his emphasis on Spirit possession as the '*sine qua non* of salvation' (Sanders, p. 501), because Luke is just as emphatic about possessing the Spirit, yet he retains repentance and forgiveness. Paul aimed his theology principally at Gentiles and he did not take enough account of the sensitivity of former Jews for whom the way of atonement was clear and well tried. Paul's all-or-nothing approach may have seemed inevitable to him but it was not so for Luke.

justified by faith apart from works of the law then it would follow that repentance, so intimately bound to the practicalities of the law, would receive only marginal consideration.⁶³ But this is not the *necessary* consequence of Jesus' lordship, it just happens to be the conclusion that Paul drew. Luke shows that it is quite possible to assert the lordship of Jesus and to conclude that the way of atonement must be the same for Jew and Gentile, yet still to endorse the terminology of repentance for the forgiveness of sins. We have seen how Luke re-established the Jewish character of Christology and gave back to χριστός its role as a recognized title.⁶⁴ We can see the Israel-directed nature in the emphasis on Jesus' succession to the throne of David (Lk. 1.32-33; 2.11; 3.23-31; 18.38; [19.12, 38]; Acts 2.29-31; 13.22-23). Paul, no doubt for sound pastoral and theological reasons, never refers to Jesus in terms of kingship and only once as descended from David (Rom. 1.3).

2. *Sin*

Closely related to the different treatments of repentance and forgiveness is a difference in the Lukan and Pauline views of sin. Some 84% of the occurrences of ἁμαρτία in Paul's letters take the singular form in which sin is seen as a demonic power over human beings. 'Sins', as acts of misconduct, play a relatively small part in the letters, in spite of the many moral problems encountered by his readers. For Paul, sin is universal, an infection of Jew and Gentile alike; it is the result of Adam's disobedience and the consequence for all is death (Rom. 5.12, 21; 6.23). Not only are all humans mortal but they die as the direct consequence of their disobedience (1 Cor. 10.6-11; 11.29-30; cf. 15.55-56). It was because Paul was more concerned with the treatment of the disease rather than the symptoms that he was led to place repentance and forgiveness on the periphery of his thinking.

By contrast, Luke's understanding of sin is essentially practical and so too is the remedy. Sin lacks the double aspect of transgression and demonic power,⁶⁵ and Luke does not speculate on the origin of sin. As I

---

63. Stendahl, 'The Apostle Paul', pp. 201-202, holds that because of Christ, the old covenant and its provision for the forgiveness of sins is no longer a valid alternative. The only repentance that now counts is the one available in Messiah Jesus.

64. Dunn, *Unity and Diversity*, pp. 43-45, holds that the title retained its importance in '*distinctively Jewish circles*' (his italics).

65. Rom. 2.12; 5.12; 6.20; 7.17. Whiteley, *St Paul*, p. 53; Sanders, *Palestinian Judaism*, pp. 498-99.

have argued, 'sinner' and 'sin' are almost technical terms for acts done by Jews, although Luke is well aware of the wickedness of non-Jews.

3. *The Law*

Paul's treatment of the law is complex and it contains what appear to be major contradictions.[66] As a result, attempts to clarify the picture continue to occupy scholars but without a consensus being reached.[67] There are instances where Paul accepts the law as holy and good (Rom. 7.12), where he claims that 'we' uphold the law (Rom. 3.31; cf. 2.13) and where he delights in the law of God (Rom. 7.22). He was also prepared to use the law to uphold church practices: 'it is written in the law of Moses...' (1 Cor. 9.9; cf. 14.21). Views such as these could only win Luke's approval, but it is those passages in which Paul rejects the law that would offend Luke. For example:

> but now we are discharged from the law,
> dead to that which held us captive, so that
> we serve not under the old written code
> but in the new life of the Spirit (Rom. 7.6).

> For Christ is the end of the law, that everyone
> who has faith may be justified (Rom. 10.4).

In Paul's eyes, the law was powerless to lead people to righteousness and it served only to bring home the fact of human sinfulness (Rom. 7.7; 1 Cor. 15.56).[68]

E.P. Sanders is very probably correct when he makes a distinction between the law as entrance requirement, which Paul sets aside, and the law as moral commands, which Paul upholds. The moral aspect is particularly important for Paul where sexual immorality or idolatry are concerned.[69] J.D.G. Dunn favours a similar solution to Paul's paradox by distinguishing between works of the law as identity markers (e.g. food laws and circumcision) and the law as a whole.[70] However, Paul's

---

66. Whiteley, *St Paul*, pp. 79-83; but 'balance' (p. 79) is no final answer.
67. Sanders, *Jewish People*, pp. 3-4.
68. Thielman, 'Paul's View of the Law', examines Paul's use of the law in 1 Corinthians where the issue is raised for the first time, i.e. prior to Galatians and Romans. He concludes that Paul distinguishes between the 'obsolete and aspects of continuing validity' (pp. 252-53).
69. Sanders, *Jewish People*, pp. 95, 106-113. Cf. Rom. 1.18-32; 1 Cor. 5.10-11; 6.9; 7.1-2; 8.4; cf. also Deut. 6.4; 2 Cor. 12.21; Gal. 5.19-22.
70. Rom. 8.3 and Gal. 3.11 speak of the 'law' while Rom. 3.20, 28 and Gal. 2.16

statements that have been quoted above speak of the law, not works of the law. In Romans 7, Paul indicts the law for its failure to deal with sin and, in Rom. 9.31-32, Israel failed to fulfil the law because it pursued works and not faith. Paul used νόμος both for 'getting in' and 'staying in' and, although his opposition to idolatry and sexual immorality was based on the law, he does not mention the law when faced with these issues at Corinth (1 Cor. 5.1-2, 9-13; 6.9-11, 15-20; 10.14-22).

Paul saw fundamental reasons for rejecting reliance on the law:

> for if righteousness were through the law, then
> Christ died to no purpose (Gal. 2.21).

> for if a law had been given which could make alive, then righteousness would indeed be by the law (Gal. 3.21).

These passages show that it was the death of Christ and its significance, together with the need to include the Gentiles, that so overwhelmed Paul that his previous reliance on the law as the way to righteousness *had* to be rejected.[71] Here we come to the root of the difference between Luke and Paul over the law. Because Luke did not regard the death of Jesus as the determining event for the way of salvation he was not compelled to reject the old way.[72] Hence, for Luke, the law retains to a very large degree its original importance and value so that it has a strong, positive role in Luke's writings. To put the difference again: on Paul's view, because Christ's death had brought about the possibility of salvation for all, then it must necessarily render the Jewish ways of righteousness and atonement not only obsolete but anti-Christian. Luke, on the other hand, saw no new way of salvation in Jesus' death and hence the law and repentance remain valid. In practice, Luke too makes a distinction between 'staying in' and 'getting in' by accepting that Gentiles are free from the need to be circumcised while keeping some food laws. But as far as conduct is concerned, the law and repentance remain. He would have seen no sense in the paradox that the law is holy but has been superseded by faith.

---

speak of 'works of the law'. For part of recent discussion see Cranfield, 'Works of the Law'; Dunn, 'A Response'; also Dunn, *Jesus, Paul and the Law*, ch. 8.

71. Sanders, *Palestinian Judaism*, pp. 442-43. Also, Stendahl, 'The Apostle Paul', pp. 201-202.

72. It is, of course, possible that the reverse was the case, and that it was Luke's prior acceptance of the law and repentance as the way to forgiveness that led him to reject an atoning significance for the death of Jesus.

5. *Repentance and Atonement*

Luke's advocacy of the law is not just for the sake of Jewish believers alone but because he saw that it was needed by Gentile believers. The immorality that Paul had faced at Corinth may have sprung from a belief that 'all things are lawful' (1 Cor. 6.12; 10.23) or from a perversion of Paul's statements that the law was a thing of the past. For Luke the danger and the remedy would have been obvious.

There is one further piece of evidence for the difference between Paul's thinking and Luke's. In 1 Cor. 1.22-23 Paul claims that Christ crucified is a stumbling block to Jews because they demand signs yet, according to Luke, it is signs that are offered to them. In Acts, signs and wonders become almost commonplace in the Christian mission and cause many Jews and Samaritans to believe in Jesus. Parallel to the importance of signs is Luke's marked reluctance to mention the cross. 'The cross' is never mentioned in Acts and 'crucify' occurs twice only (2.36; 4.10). Elsewhere in Acts Luke speaks of Jesus 'hanging from a tree' (κρεμάσαντες ἐπὶ ξύλου, 5.30; 10.39)[73] and, on one occasion, he describes the method of execution as 'affixing' (προσπήξαντες, 2.23). Not only is it true that 'crucifixion play[s] no part in the proclamation',[74] but Luke, it seems, can hardly bring himself to use the word and this near to the time when, for Ignatius, the instrument of execution represented the death itself (*Eph.* 18.1; *Trall.* 11.2; *Phil.* 8.2).

4. *Salvation and Atonement*

For Paul, as indeed for Luke, salvation in all its fulness is a future state for which the present life is, or should be, both a preparation and a foretaste. Sanders has drawn attention to the fact that the tenses of σώζω in Paul's letters are either present or future and that the one

---

73. Haenchen, *Acts*, p. 251. 'Hanging on a tree' (cf. κρεμάσητε αὐτὸν ἐπὶ ξύλον, Deut. 21.22) was the method of killing a criminal deserving of death. This is Luke's confirmation of Jewish responsibility for the death of Jesus as in Acts 3.14-15 and the expression is used again at 10.39. After each occasion Peter asserts that God raised Jesus from the dead so that Jesus' death under the law becomes part of God's plan to make him Messiah. This is a very different use of the phrase from that of Paul (Gal. 3.13), where it is a crucial step in the argument for the believers' freedom from the curse of the law.

74. Conzelmann, *Luke*, p. 201. The lack of any connection between the death of Jesus and the forgiveness of sins was earlier recognized by Cadbury, *Making*, pp. 279-80, and Dodd, *Apostolic Preaching*, p. 25, among others.

instance of a past tense has a future component (Rom. 8.24).[75] Those who are in the process of being saved and who have the promise of salvation are 'in Christ' and they have the Spirit as a guarantee (2 Cor. 5.5). It is therefore not surprising that Paul's theology of atonement has been described as salvation by participation: 'as in Adam all die, so in Christ will all be brought to life' (1 Cor. 15.22).[76] To be in Christ entails the believer dying with him through baptism and that in turn means being dead to sin.

> Do you not know that all of us who have been baptized into Christ Jesus were baptized into his death? We were buried therefore with him by baptism into death, so that as Christ was raised from the dead by the glory of the Father, we too might walk in newness of life (Rom. 6.3-4).

Both Whiteley[77] and Sanders[78] have questioned the interpretation of all references to Christ dying 'for us' as a sacrifice for sin. But, even if they are correct, Christian history shows that such an interpretation has been widely held. Rom. 3.23-25 speaks of all who have sinned being justified by God's grace 'through the redemption (ἀπολυτρώσεως) which is in Christ Jesus whom God put forward as an expiation (ἱλαστήριον) by his blood, to be received by faith'. Whiteley and Bultmann[79] cite Rom. 8.3-4, 2 Cor. 5.21 and Gal. 3.13 as texts that have been similarly interpreted. Whiteley describes these as statements of the fact of atonement, as distinct from the *modus operandi* which is participation, 'expressed by means of the religious language of Judaism'.[80] The language may be that of Judaism but it cannot disguise Paul's radical break with the Jewish way of atonement.

There are a number of obvious differences between the ways in which Paul and Luke express their ideas about atonement but there is one passage where Luke seems to echo Pauline thinking.

> ...that through this man [whom God raised up and who saw no corruption] forgiveness of sins is proclaimed to you, and by him every one

---

75. Sanders, *Palestinian Judaism*, p. 449, who also notes that for Paul resurrection is also in the future.
76. Whiteley, *St Paul*, pp. 132-33.
77. Whiteley, *St Paul*, pp. 130-32. However, the death of Christ is vicarious in that if Jesus had not died all would perish eternally.
78. Sanders, *Palestinian Judaism*, p. 464.
79. Bultmann, *Theology*, I, pp. 296-98.
80. Whiteley, *St Paul*, p. 134.

5. *Repentance and Atonement* 165

that believes (πᾶς ὁ πιστεύων) is freed (δικαιοῦται) from everything from which you could not be freed (δικαιωθῆναι) by the law of Moses (Acts 13.38-39).

Here, for the only time in Acts, the characteristic Pauline verb δικαιόω is found, and on the lips of the Lukan Paul. The verb is used not only in connection with forgiveness of sins but also with the limitations of the law. This seems to make the verse particularly valuable in assessing how far Luke understood and agreed with Paul's theology of atonement. The Lukan Paul makes two points, the first of which, that forgiveness is offered to all believers, is closely similar to Peter's statement to Cornelius (πάντα τὸν πιστεύοντα, 10.43). The second point, that the law is powerless as a way to justification, seems genuinely Pauline.[81] At first glance it may seem that the two points are really two ways, Lukan and Pauline, of expressing the same ideas, since Paul too speaks of the believers who have died with Christ as being freed (δεδικαίωται) from sin (Rom. 6.7, cf. ἐλευθερωθέντες, 6.18).[82] But against this possible similarity is the fact that where Luke speaks of *sins* as acts of wickedness, Paul is dealing with breaking the power of *sin* that holds humankind captive. Furthermore, apart from the debatable exception of taking the Lord's name in vain, the later Tannaitic literature mentions no sin for which a Jew could not repent and be forgiven.[83] For Luke himself, it appears probable that the only unforgivable sin is blasphemy against the Holy Spirit (Lk. 12.10) and that is not an issue here.

What then does Luke have in mind when he speaks of what could not be freed under the law of Moses? Luke provides a valuable clue to his meaning in his description of Paul's audience which contains not only men of Israel but also God-fearers and devout proselytes (13.16, 26, 43). Because the law of Moses was God's gift to Israel alone, it was powerless to free Gentiles from their sins and, more fundamentally, it could not set God-fearers free from the need to be circumcised, should they wish to become full members of Israel. It is the removal of the need for circumcision that concerns Luke here and this interpretation is supported by

---

81. Rom. 7.13-20 gives the sense of the law as self-defeating and Bultmann, *Theology*, I, p. 263, has concluded from a number of passages that 'Prior to faith *there is no true fulfilment of the law*'. Sanders, *Palestinian Judaism*, p. 481, disputes Bultmann's conclusion but admits the persuasiveness of the interpretation. One can imagine a first-century reader coming to the same opinion as Bultmann.
82. Sanders, *Palestinian Judaism*, p. 472.
83. Sanders, *Palestinian Judaism*, pp. 157-59.

the position of the Antioch sermon within the framework of the narrative. The sequence begins with the Cornelius story which contains the only other uses of 'God-fearer' in Luke–Acts (10.2, 22). This is followed by Peter's reply to the advocates of circumcision (11.1-18) and the Antioch sermon. The climax of the sequence is the decision of the Jerusalem council (15.19-21). After each of the last three incidents there is a description of the joy at the news that Gentiles are free from the need to be circumcised (11.18; 13.48; 15.30-31). Luke does, therefore, echo genuine Pauline thinking in the verses quoted above and in Rom. 3.30, as our observation of Luke's unique use of δικαιόω is intended to show. It may be significant that in his letter to the Romans, Paul was probably addressing an audience of Jews and Gentiles, just as at Antioch.

Luke and the Letter to the Hebrews

Having seen how Luke changed the direction of his theology of atonement from an earlier form, we must now briefly compare Luke with a near contemporary NT author.[84] A fitting reason for the comparison is that Hebrews was probably addressed to Jewish Christians[85] who, it seems, were tempted to apostatize, perhaps by returning to Judaism. The author's method of dealing with the problem is to show the superiority of Christianity to Judaism. As far as atonement is concerned he argues that there is a new covenant of which Jesus is the mediator and perfect high priest (7.22; 8.6, 13; 9.11-15; 12.24) and there is a new law that replaces the Levitical code because it was incapable of bringing people to perfection (7.11-12; 10.1). There is the new and single sacrifice of Jesus, the heavenly high priest who offers his own blood because of the failure of the old system (chs. 8–10). Now Christians have an altar 'from which those who serve the [old] tabernacle have no right to eat' (13.10). There is no Gentile mission in Hebrews (ἔθνος is absent from the letter)

---

84. Jones, 'Hebrews', examines certain similarities between Hebrews and Luke–Acts but makes no mention of the very great contrasts. He thinks it might be possible to use the theology of Hebrews 'to amplify the rather jejune and nebulous theology of Acts'; Jones is, however, unwilling to impeach Luke as the first of the heretics (p. 143)! The use of Hebrews in the present discussion is simply to note the contrasts.

85. Kümmel, *Introduction*, pp. 398-401, thinks that the readers were mainly Gentile Christians. If so they were well versed in the LXX. Bruce, 'Hebrews', *Peake's Commentary*, p. 1008, favours a Jewish-Christian readership. His comment on Heb. 7.11 ('if perfection had been attainable through the Levitical priesthood...') is that Gentile readers would reply, 'We never thought it was!'

and, although repentance is mentioned, it is not available for those who have once been enlightened.

> For when men have once been enlightened, when they have had a taste of the heavenly gift and a share in the Holy Spirit, when they have experienced the gift of God's word and the spiritual energies of the age to come, and after all this have fallen away, it is impossible to bring them again to repentance; for with their own hands they are crucifying the Son of God and making mock of his death (Heb. 6.4-6, NEB).

On every point Luke stands opposed to the writer of Hebrews, showing just how firmly he held to the old Israel and resisted any tendency to replace it and those of its institutions that still existed. Hebrews, on the other hand, makes clear yet again how a theory of atonement based upon the death of Jesus must assert that Israel and its way of atonement have been superseded.

Conclusions

Luke's lack of an atoning view of the cross continues to pose problems for commentators. Fitzmyer, for example, rightly asks why we should expect Luke to place the same emphasis on the cross as do Mark and Paul and he suggests that Luke should not be censured because his soteriology differs from theirs.[86] Yet, in spite of this, he still attempts to draw out the saving effects of the cross in Luke by pointing to the story of the penitent criminal and the promise of Jesus, 'Today you will be with me in paradise' (23.43).[87] Yet the criminal is not saved by the death of Jesus but because he is penitent, accepting that his punishment is just. The story is a fitting climax to Luke's account of Jesus' ministry by showing that penitence works.

One reason for Luke's profound change of direction from the general development of soteriology may have been his concern to convince Jewish believers that they had made the right choice and that they remained members of Israel. They still kept the law and, if they should offend, repentance continued to be the way back to forgiveness. This conclusion is in broad agreement with Jervell's comment:

---

86. Fitzmyer, *Luke*, p. 22; but on p. 212 he describes the reason for the omission of Mk 10.45 as 'inscrutable'. He is, of course, very well aware of the importance of repentance for Luke (pp. 237-39), and that, along with forgiveness of sins, makes Luke's 'favorite ways of summing up the effects of the Christ event' (p. 459).

87. Fitzmyer, *Luke*, p. 23.

why do Jewish Christians at Jerusalem and in the diaspora keep the law and so demonstrate its permanent validity? The answer is a fairly simple one. Luke knew only one Israel, one people of God, one covenant.[88]

As it stands, Jervell's comment does not go far enough: it may explain the situation prior to the influx of Gentiles, but it does not account for Luke's conservative position at a time when the Gentile mission was well established. Jervell goes on to speak of Gentiles being saved as Gentiles and 'the idea of a people and an associate people'.[89] But that Luke envisaged two classes of believers is extremely improbable, not least because the incoming Gentiles would have been no closer to Israel than were God-fearers before the mission. The reason for Luke's emphasis on the conversion of God-fearers is that they are changed from being associates on the fringe of Israel into full members. The removal of the need for circumcision by the direct action of God's Spirit and acceptance of that removal by Jewish Christians who were zealous for the law would have made no sense or served no purpose unless full membership of Israel was being offered to the Gentiles. The food regulations and the prohibition of idolatry, with their resemblance to the Noachic laws for strangers in the land of Israel,[90] might suggest that Gentile Christians were only associates were it not that the first statement of the conditions (Acts 15.20) follows immediately after the quotation of Amos 9.11-12. This prophesies the rebuilding of Israel and that the Gentiles will seek the Lord. Overall, the evidence favours the view that, in the age of the Spirit, the Gentiles were entering Israel as full members[91] and that even the Jews acknowledged the Way as a party within Israel (Acts 24.5, 14; 28.22). Unless Gentile believers were full members of Israel then, on Luke's understanding, they would have no way of atonement since the only way described in Luke–Acts is by

---

88. Jervell, *The People of God*, p. 141.

89. Jervell, *The People of God*, p. 143. Wilson, *Luke and the Law*, pp. 104-105, challenges Jervell's view and claims that there is no evidence that 'Luke considered Gentile participation to depend upon a successful renewal of the old Israel...[Luke's] view of the law and his view of the church and Israel are developed in different ways'. But Luke did not regard the church as 'the true or renewed Israel', as Wilson believes (p. 104).

90. Lake, 'Apostolic Council', *Beginnings*, V, p. 208; Montefiore, 'The Spirit of Judaism', *Beginnings*, I, p. 44.

91. Van de Sandt, 'Acts 15.6-21', pp. 92-94, agrees that 'if they [Gentiles] want to become part of Israel they are obliged to keep the law, at least as far as Leviticus 17–18 requires'.

repentance, leading to forgiveness by the God of Israel. Had it been otherwise, Luke, like other NT writers, would have had to root his soteriology in the death of Christ. At the close of the previous chapter we saw how Luke's concentration on the God of Israel profoundly influenced his Christology. In this chapter we have seen the extent to which Luke has moved away from the saving effect of Jesus' death and back to the God of Israel.[92] Jesus is certainly the saviour sent by God, but he does not bring a new way through his own death; instead Jesus brings about the extension of the old way. Whatever Luke may say about the morals or the attitudes of some Jews, he nowhere questions or condemns the efficacy of their way of atonement in the ways we find in Paul's letters or Hebrews. Repentance therefore retains its central role as the way back into the covenant and it is still 'the sovereign means of atonement'.

---

92. Evans, *Saint Luke*, p. 53.

Part III

INTRODUCTION

In earlier discussions we have noted ways in which Luke's views differed from Matthew's over Christology and from Paul's theology of atonement. But Luke's differences with Paul and Matthew are much more fundamental than we have so far discussed: at root they are differences about the status of the historic Israel and its relation to the church.

In Chapter 6 I argue that Luke saw some of the material in Paul's letters as capable of fostering anti-Israel attitudes because it is deeply critical of Jewish institutions and customs. It was this perception that lay behind Luke's counterbalance of a predominantly Jewish portrait of Paul. Matthew's Gospel posed a different problem for Luke, and this is discussed in Chapter 7. Not only did Matthew seem to claim too much for the earthly Jesus, he could also be understood as depicting the church as the true Israel. Moreover, Matthew's implied criticism of the law as insufficiently stringent, together with his low opinion of the Pharisees, would have made it difficult for Jews and Christians to co-exist in any sort of harmony.

Among the arguments against Luke's knowledge of Paul's letters and Matthew's Gospel is the assumption that if he had known them he would have paid more respect to their writings; he would have written a 'better' Gospel and described a more 'Pauline' Paul. But why should it be assumed that Luke would agree with either since he could hardly agree with both? The major differences between the Gospels of Luke and Matthew on the one hand, and between Paul's portrait in Acts and what can be learnt from his letters on the other, suggest that they are the deliberate polemical changes made by a theologian who saw grave potential weaknesses in the works of his two renowned predecessors. Why else would he make the effort to write at such length to Theophilus?

Chapter 6

LUKE, PAUL AND ISRAEL

In the previous chapter we discussed some of the differences between the Lukan and Pauline views of atonement and the law. In that discussion it was not necessary to propose that Luke knew Paul's letters since the purpose was simply to compare Luke's view with an earlier understanding of atonement. However, in this chapter I want to develop the discussion further and to show that Luke wished to refute what he understood to be Paul's views of Israel and its institutions. And since Luke's portrait of Paul as the hero of the Christian mission conflicts with some of what is found in the letters, I must now present evidence that Luke was familiar with the letters. The letters provided the source and inspiration of a development in Christian theology to which Luke was opposed, as well as autobiographical information that Luke was able to use in his portrait. When I have presented the evidence for Luke's knowledge of the letters, I will examine his portrait and the reasons that lay behind it.

Luke and the Pauline Corpus

There is general agreement among present-day commentators that Luke did not know Paul's letters and it is not hard to see why this should be so. In spite of Paul's central role in the latter part of Acts Luke never mentions the letters, although he does report the contents of letters written by James (15.23-29) and Claudius Lysias (23.26-30). Nor does Luke show much awareness (some would say understanding) of the principal ideas contained in the letters. Modern critics find it difficult to believe that anyone who was familiar with Paul's theology could have failed to make use of it as Luke appears to have done. Robert Maddox put the general opinion succinctly: that Luke did not know the Pauline letters, and that if he had any personal contact with Paul at all, it was not in such a way that he could get to know his theology in any more than a superficial way.[1] Yet we know that Paul himself was a polemicist and that he was also the target of attacks because of his beliefs and practices. It is therefore by no means impossible that Luke disagreed with some aspects of Paul's theology and that he found it expedient to make changes in Paul's self-portrait. There are well-known discrepancies between some accounts in Acts and in the letters and these have been discussed by Vielhauer,[2] Haenchen[3] and others,[4] but usually from the standpoint that Paul knew best.

The consensus about Luke's ignorance of the letters and their contents has not, however, gone unchallenged. C.L. Mitton has a hint of doubt[5] and the contention has been opposed by Morton Enslin,[6] John Knox,[7] W.O. Walker[8] and Wolfgang Schenk,[9] as well as, in a more limited way, by P.W. Walaskay.[10] Enslin reminds us that the Tübingen school accepted that Luke knew Paul's letters and that the differences between the letters and Acts posed no problem. To the Tübingen critics 'Acts was essentially a romance...history with a purpose', but the defeat of the Tübingen school meant that acceptance of Luke's knowledge of the letters also became a casualty of the conflict and this led to the present-day view.[11] The basis of the present critical consensus is in essence an argument from silence and, like all such arguments, it suffers from the inbuilt weakness that it cannot tell whether or not the silence is deliberate. There are three possible solutions to the problem: (1) that Luke did not know the letters and thus *could* not use them, (2) he knew the letters but *would* not use them (Knox), and (3) that he knew the letters and made a selective use of them while keeping quiet about

1. Maddox, *Purpose*, p. 68.
2. Vielhauer, 'Paulinism', pp. 33-49.
3. Haenchen, *Acts*, pp. 112-16.
4. Goodenough, 'Perspective', pp. 51-59; Bornkamm, 'Missionary Stance', pp. 194-207.
5. Mitton, *Pauline Corpus*, pp. 19-20.
6. Enslin, 'Luke and Paul'. This article is based largely upon Enslin's earlier article of 1938. I have used the later study.
7. Knox, 'Pauline Corpus', pp. 279-87, argues that Luke knew the letters but that he deliberately made little or no use of them.
8. Walker, 'Acts and the Pauline Corpus', pp. 3-23.
9. Schenk, 'Luke as Reader', pp. 127-39.
10. Walaskay, '*And so we Came to Rome*', pp. 50-53.
11. Enslin, 'Luke and Paul', p. 225.

certain points (Enslin). I shall put evidence for the third solution under two broad headings, literary and general probabilities.[12]

Literary Evidence

Notwithstanding a number of supposedly improbable incidents in Luke's portrait of Paul, there are events that are clearly common to both Acts and the letters, even allowing for the differences between the two versions. Examination of incidents common to both writers shows some verbal similarities which suggests that Luke knew Paul's own account of the incident in some cases. We should also bear in mind that disagreements between two accounts of a common incident are not necessarily evidence of Luke's ignorance—they may be the result of deliberate change to suit Luke's different purpose. There is no *a priori* reason to think that Luke would have treated Paul's letters any less creatively than he treated his other sources. No attempt has been made here to correlate Luke's accounts of Paul's journeys with what might be inferred from the letters.

1. *The Call of Saul-Paul*

a. The event took place near Damascus (Acts 9.3, 6-8; 22.6; 26.12), to which Paul returned (Gal. 1.17). In Acts 26.19, Paul speaks of the heavenly vision (τῇ οὐρανίῳ ὀπτασίᾳ), and this is the only use of ὀπτασία in Acts. Paul's own boasting of visions and revelations (2 Cor. 12.1-4) contains his only use of ὀπτασία, and he also gives an account of being caught up to the third heaven (τρίτου οὐρανοῦ). It is doubtful that here, Paul refers to the Damascus experience since 'he heard things that cannot be told, which man may not utter'. Luke may have combined elements of the visions in his account of the Damascus call.

b. Both writers agree that Paul persecuted the church and that he tried to destroy it. In Acts, with the exception of 7.52, διώκω only has the meaning of 'persecute' in the accounts of the call (9.4, 5; 22.4, 7, 8; 26.11, 14, 15), and the verb also occurs in Paul's self-descriptions (Gal. 1.13, 23; 1 Cor. 15.9). Similarly, 'destroy' (πορθέω) occurs only three times in the NT (Acts 9.21; Gal. 1.13, 23). Loisy regarded these verbs as evidence that Luke knew the letters[13] but Wendt considered the use of

---

12. Schenk, 'Luke as Reader', also considers the evidence for use of the letters in the third gospel.

13. Loisy, *Les Actes*, p. 416; also Enslin, 'Luke and Paul', p. 262.

πορθέω to be a coincidence.[14] As we shall see, other verbal agreements considerably weaken the force of the coincidence theory.

c. At his call Paul is told to preach to the Gentiles (Acts 9.15) but, following the second account of the call (22.6-21), the command takes place after the return to Jerusalem and it comes by a vision in the temple. The same purpose of the call is mentioned in Gal. 1.16 (cf. Rom. 11.13) but in Gal. 1.17 he denies visiting Jerusalem.

2. *The Escape from Damascus*[15]
This involved Paul being lowered (χαλάσαντες, Acts 9.25; ἐχαλάσθην, 2 Cor. 11.33) through a wall (διὰ τοῦ τείχους, Acts 9.25; 2 Cor. 11.33).

3. *The Stoning*
This is placed at Lystra by Luke (λιθάσαντες, Acts 14.19) but Paul gives no location (ἐλιθάσθην, 2 Cor. 11.25). This is the only use of λιθάζω in the letters and the verb is also used in Acts 5.26. Elsewhere Luke uses λιθοβολέω, notably at the stoning of Stephen (7.58, 59) and at the attempted stoning of Paul and Barnabas at Iconium (14.5).

4. *Beating with Rods*
At Philippi Paul and Silas were beaten (ῥαβδίζειν, Acts 16.22) and Paul mentions three such incidents (ἐρραβδίσθην, 2 Cor. 11.25). These are the only occurrences of the verb in the NT.

5. *At Miletus*
In his farewell address to the Ephesian elders, Paul reminds his audience of how he had served the Lord in Asia 'with all humility and tears' (ταπεινοφροσύνης καὶ δακρύων, Acts 20.19) and later, how he had admonished everyone with tears (δακρύων νουθετῶν, 20.31). In 2 Cor. 2.4, Paul reminds his readers that he had caused them pain when he had written earlier 'out of much affliction and anguish of heart and tears' (δακρύων), and in 1 Cor. 4.14 he writes 'to admonish (νουθετῶ[ν]) them as beloved children'. ταπεινοφροσύνη occurs here only in Luke–Acts as well as in Phil. 2.3. In Eph. 4.2, Col. 2.18, 23 and 3.12, the word is used for a general Christian virtue, not as a description of the author's behaviour.

---

14. Wendt, *Die Apostelgeschichte*, p. 173.
15. Enslin, 'Luke and Paul', p. 263.

6. Paul the Pharisee

This is agreed by both writers (Acts 23.6; 26.5; Phil. 3.5) and the Lukan Paul refers to his education at the feet of Gamaliel (22.3) which was 'according to the strict manner of the law of our fathers, being zealous for God' (κατὰ ἀκρίβειαν τοῦ πατρῴου νόμου, ζηλωτὴς ὑπάρχων τοῦ θεοῦ, 22.3). This seems to reflect a similar description in Gal. 1.14 where Paul says that he 'advanced in Judaism beyond many of my own age and people, so extremely zealous was I for the traditions of my fathers' (περισσοτέρως ζηλωτὴς ὑπάρχων τῶν πατρικῶν μου παραδόσεων).[16]

7. The Shipwreck

Following the wreck, Paul and the others landed on Malta, wet and cold (ψῦχος, 28.2). Paul's own list of hardships includes three shipwrecks, danger at sea and exposure and cold (ἐν ψύχει, 2 Cor. 11.25-27). Apart from Jn 18.18, these are the only instances of ψῦχος in the NT.

8. Other Agreements

Walaskay has drawn attention to verbal agreements between Philippians and the accounts of Paul's trials in Acts.[17] These include δεσμά (chains, imprisonment, Phil. 1.7, 13, 14, 17; Acts 20.23; 23.29; 26.29, 31). Moreover, it is only in Phil. 1.7 and 16 that Paul uses 'apology' in an unambiguously legal context (cf. Acts 22.1; 25.16).[18] To these we can add the praetorian guard (τῷ πραιτωρίῳ, Acts 23.35, at Caesarea; Phil. 1.13). Walaskay also notes the fact that it is in Philippians that Paul mentions his Pharisaic background. Among Walaskay's conclusions is that 'Luke has skilfully woven thematic threads supplied by Paul into his own tapestry of the apostle's trial'.[19]

We have noted a number of verbal similarities in these eight incidents common to Acts and Paul's letters, some of which involve words rare in the NT. This is perhaps hardly surprising since some of the events, such as lowering people through walls, are not everyday happenings. Nevertheless, had agreement occurred in one case only then Wendt's assessment (above) would be a reasonable one. But when the list extends to eight events and ten words then coincidence becomes a much less

---

16. Enslin, 'Luke and Paul', p. 262.
17. Walaskay, *'And so we came to Rome'*, pp. 51-52.
18. Walaskay, *'And so we came to Rome'*, p. 97.
19. Walaskay, *'And so we came to Rome'*, p. 51.

convincing explanation. The agreements are not like the parallels that exist between Gospels but this would not be expected given the small amount of personal reminiscence in the letters. Nor do the agreements prove that Luke knew Paul's letters. What they do show is that there is evidence of a connection that calls into question Knox's assessment that no such evidence exists.[20]

We have seen that a significant number of the hardships listed in 2 Cor. 11.23-27 correspond to incidents mentioned in Acts. There is, however, one notable exception: Luke makes no mention of Paul's acceptance of the Jewish punishment of the thirty-nine strokes (11.24). Although this is not evidence of a literary nature it is convenient to consider here why Luke should have omitted an account of the punishment. In his short study of the penalty, A.E. Harvey points out that it would only be received by someone who wished to remain in the Jewish community and that for Paul to receive the maximum number of strokes is a measure of the seriousness of the offences.[21] Among possible offences might be blasphemy, profaning the Sabbath and offences involving food and drink and ritual cleanness.[22] There is no evidence in Acts that Paul profaned the Sabbath but Paul's concern for Gentiles may have meant violating food and purity regulations. According to Acts it is preaching about Jesus (9.20-23), advocacy of the Gentile mission (13.46-50; 22.21-22) and the (false) charge that he was against the people, the law and the temple (21.28-31) that arouses Jewish anger against Paul. And that anger is altogether more violent than flogging: on five occasions Jews plot to kill Paul (9.23; [20.3;] 21.31; 23.12-14; 25.3), and at Lystra they stone him and leave him for dead (14.19).

Luke is also keen to show Paul as an enthusiastic Jew, both by his actions and his declarations (e.g. 16.3; 18.18; 20.16). It might therefore seem that Luke would have included the flogging but this might have implied that Paul had broken the law, and this is vehemently denied in Acts. Since adherence to the law is essential for Luke's description of Paul, flogging, although a sign of Jewishness, had to be omitted because it implied that Paul had broken the law.

---

20. Knox, 'Pauline Corpus', p. 284.
21. Harvey, *Constraints*, pp. 82-84.
22. Harvey, *Constraints*, p. 92.

Other Considerations

If we accept a date for the writing of Acts near the end of the first century then we have a time gap of more than a generation between the last of Paul's letters and Acts. Goodspeed proposed that it was the existence of Acts that led to the collection of Paul's letters with Acts being dated between 80–90 CE[23] although use of the letters does not require a formal collection which Luke could have had on his desk.[24] Undoubtedly Luke makes Paul the central character of the last part of Acts and he could not have done this without knowing something of Paul's actual life. It seems extremely improbable that no one thought to tell Luke that Paul had written letters and, once he knew of them, he would surely have been curious about their contents. It is possible that Luke had other sources for his Pauline narrative, but Schenk is correct to say that it is only necessary to postulate a totally unknown tradition when the well known entities are insufficient.[25] Such is not the case here.

Knox has suggested that the reason for Luke's silence about the letters was their use by an unorthodox group of early Marcionites and this in turn requires Knox to date Acts in the second century.[26] On both points Enslin agrees with Knox.[27] Knox thus accepts Luke's knowledge of the letters but stops short of recognizing Luke's use of them.

The following hypothesis goes further than that of Knox without arguing the need for a second-century date. The proposal is that Luke knew at least some of Paul's letters: Galatians, 1 and 2 Corinthians, Philippians and Romans,[28] all of which are churches included in Luke's accounts of Paul's travels. In Galatians 1–2, Philippians and 2 Corinthians 11 Luke found autobiographical material, much of which is without a specific location or time sequence, and this material became part of the frame on which Luke wove his own Pauline tapestry. Luke felt free to make changes and additions to suit his own dramatic and theological purposes, so that in this sense Paul's letters are one source of the things

---

23. Goodspeed, quoted by Knox, p. 280, but no reference given.
24. Enslin, 'Luke and Paul', pp. 256-57.
25. Schenk, 'Luke as Reader', p. 131.
26. Knox, 'Pauline Corpus', pp. 285-86. Also Dunn, *Unity and Diversity*, pp. 288-96.
27. Enslin, 'Luke and Paul', pp. 270-71.
28. Lindemann, *Paulus*, p. 161, proposes Romans, 2 Cor. 10–13 and perhaps Galatians.

that 'have been accomplished among us', that is to say, within the period of the church's early missions.

Paul in Acts

We must now examine the ways in which Luke challenged the Pauline inheritance and the reasons for that challenge. We begin by looking at his portrait of Paul. In this our main concern is with those aspects of the portrait which show Paul's Jewishness and which compare his status with that of Peter. However, Luke shows not only the Jewish side of Paul but also Paul the Roman citizen and this is an element not found in the letters. This Roman aspect of the portrait has recently been examined in its sociological, historical and legal contexts by J.C. Lentz.[29] Lentz's principal conclusion is that Luke presents Paul as a man of wealth and high social standing who, after his conversion, shows the classical virtues of wisdom, self-control, righteousness and bravery.[30] This shows Paul in a way that exemplifies him as 'an ideal man of status and virtue (ἀρετή)'.[31] Lentz also concludes, on the basis of contemporary evidence, that for a Pharisee to be both a citizen of Tarsus *and* a second generation Roman citizen would have been extremely improbable.[32] Such a three-fold claim to social excellence and virtue must therefore have been intended to appeal to an audience of the higher social classes.

The undoubted strength of Lentz's evidence does, however, lead him to a too-exclusive assessment of other elements in the portrait. To present Paul as a fine example of bravery (ἀνδρεία, a word, incidentally, not found in the NT) which would appeal to those of high social rank in the empire does not exclude, as Lentz suggests it does, Luke's use of the portrait to ease relations between Jewish and Gentile Christians.[33] It is not simply as a Christian that Luke presents Paul as a model for high society but as a *Jewish* Christian, and it is inherently improbable that Luke's Jewish-Christian purposes, so clear elsewhere, should just vanish in the last part of Acts. Lentz offers what is unquestionably an important part of Luke's portrait, but it is only a part.

The differences between the pictures of Paul in Acts and the letters have produced a wide range of critical evaluations that have been prin-

29. Lentz, *Luke's Portrait of Paul*.
30. Lentz, *Luke's Portrait of Paul*, pp. 14, 62.
31. Lentz, *Luke's Portrait of Paul*, p. 63.
32. Lentz, *Luke's Portrait of Paul*, pp. 42, 58-61.
33. Lentz, *Luke's Portrait of Paul*, pp. 171-72.

cipally concerned with questions of historical reliability. Although our main interest is not with such questions, there are points that are relevant to our discussion. For this reason it might be helpful to look briefly at how critical opinion is divided. This has been done in a valuable survey by A.J. Mattill, who has identified four major positions.[34]

1. The 'one Paul' view favoured by conservative commentators.
2. The 'lopsided Paul' view of the school of Restrained Criticism. This holds that Luke's account of a particular incident is sometimes to be preferred to that by Paul since both writers present lopsided pictures. For example, Parkes believes that although the letters are to be preferred theologically, they cannot be properly understood without Paul's own view of himself as 'a loyal and observant Jew'.[35]
3. The 'two Paul' interpretation of which Vielhauer and Haenchen are among the leading exponents. According to this view Acts portrays a legendary Paul and the letters present the historical Paul. Because the two accounts cannot be reconciled, the credibility of Acts must therefore be judged by the letters. This is because of 'Luke's tendency to Petrinize or neutralize the real Paul' and that Acts even contains anti-Pauline traditions.
4. The 'three Paul' school identifies the historical missionary of the Acts travel narrative, particularly the 'we' sections, the legendary Paul who advocated a religion free from Judaism, and Paul as he was described by the mid-second century redactor of Acts. It was the theology of the 'Legendary' Paul that was developed in the letters.

Shortly after the publication of Mattill's article, Jervell argued that Acts brings into the light the Jewish aspect of Paul which, in the letters, lies in the shadows.[36] Such passages in the letters include the exhortation to Jewish Christians not to remove the marks of circumcision (1 Cor. 7.18) and the mention of being a Jew to the Jews (1 Cor. 9.19-20). Surprisingly, Paul's submission to the thirty-nine stripes is not quoted by Jervell, yet it is the clearest indication by Paul of his own Jewishness: in E.P. Sanders's phrase, *'Punishment implies inclusion'*.[37] The

---

34. Mattill, 'The Value of Acts', pp. 76-98.
35. Parkes, *Judaism and Christianity*, p. 85.
36. Jervell, *The Unknown Paul*, pp. 70-71.
37. Sanders, *Jewish People*, p. 192 (Sanders' italics).

importance of the evidence in the letters is that, whatever the purpose behind Luke's picture of Paul, it was imperative that it should not be so outrageous as to be unrecognizable or dismissed as contradicting other memories of Paul. Luke had to stay within reach of historical probability if his own theology was to carry conviction.[38]

Vielhauer's study of the Lukan Paul concentrates on the way and the extent to which Luke took over Paul's ideas.[39] This leads him to focus more on Paul's speeches in Acts and on those incidents, such as the circumcision of Timothy, that appear to conflict with the attitudes of the letters. But where Vielhauer stresses the theology of Paul as it is found in Acts, for Maddox, theology is not the most important aspect of the portrait and he therefore concentrates on Paul's historical function in Acts.[40] According to Maddox, Luke had only a superficial knowledge of Paul's thinking and, furthermore, the different historical situations of Paul and Luke meant that Luke did not have to wrestle with the same problems, notably, a theology of the cross. Yet, as we have seen in the last chapter, Luke did not want a theology of the cross and so he avoided using Paul's theology. This does not mean that he did not understand Paul. The question to be asked about both of these critical approaches is whether they misconstrue Luke's method which was to use narrative as a vehicle for expressing his theology. This means that theology and narrative cannot be separated.

Paul and Apostleship

Paul had been dead for at least twenty years when Acts was written and during that time his fame as a missionary and letter writer would have increased. He was a figure of authority who had claimed to be an apostle in each of his letters except Philippians and Philemon and even when he shows doubts about his worthiness he does not deny his apostleship (1 Cor. 15.9). That this role was accepted by others as the sign of Paul's authority is shown in the way that later writers used his name and status to give authority to their own writings (1 Tim. 1.1; 2.7; 2 Tim. 1.1; Titus 1.1).[41] But does Luke agree that Paul had been an

---

38. Bornkamm, 'Missionary Stance', p. 200, sees no reason 'to contest in a wholesale manner' Paul's synagogue missions as depicted by Luke.
39. Vielhauer, 'Paulinism', pp. 33-34.
40. Maddox, *Purpose*, pp. 67-68.
41. Quinn, 'Last Volume', pp. 62-75, suggests that the Pastorals may be Luke's

apostle? Luke has a precise understanding of the meaning of 'apostle' to which he holds with only two apparent exceptions. According to Luke, there were originally twelve apostles and when Judas fell away his place was taken by Matthias who was enrolled with the eleven (Acts 1.17-20, 26). The election took place immediately prior to the gift of the Spirit at Pentecost (2.1-4), presumably so that there were still twelve Spirit-filled judges for the twelve tribes of Israel. There was no need for a similar replacement when James the brother of John was killed by Herod (12.2) since his martyrdom ensured his place in heaven, awaiting the final judgment.

According to Luke, the criteria for being an apostle were that he should have been a follower of Jesus from the time of John's baptism until the ascension and that he must become a witness to the resurrection (1.21-22). Paul fails the first qualification and there is some doubt about his fulfilling the second. Luke believes that Paul becomes a witness to the resurrection in his preaching but he had not been a witness in the same way as Peter and the others (Lk. 24.13-32, 34, 36-49; Acts 1.2-8).[42] Luke seems to require something more 'physical' than visions of the risen Jesus, but Paul's own accounts show no doubts: 'Am I not an apostle? Have I not seen Jesus our Lord?' (1 Cor. 9.1). He also claims that Christ appeared to him in the same way as to Cephas, the twelve, the five hundred, James and all the apostles (1 Cor. 15.5-8) and in each case the verb is the same, ὤφθη. Yet the fact that not all the witnesses were apostles shows that seeing visions does not, by itself, make an apostle even for Paul. Moreover, Paul knew that the appearance to him was as to 'one untimely born, who was not fit to be called an apostle because he had persecuted the church of God' (1 Cor. 15.8-9). But it is in his letter to the Galatians that Paul makes his most vehement assertion of his apostleship as a necessary prelude to his most radical onslaught on Judaistic Christianity. Nicholas Taylor has conjectured that the reason for this was Paul's separation from the church at Antioch, and that therefore he was left without the backing of an established church.[43] This led Paul to assert that his apostleship, like the

---

third volume and, composed in the eighties, were aimed at restoring confidence in Paul's apostleship. There are two objections to this: first, if Luke suppresses all mention of Paul's letters it is unlikely that he used the letter form in Paul's name. Secondly, it is doubtful that Luke aimed to restore confidence in Paul's apostleship.

42. But neither does Luke report Matthias as a witness.
43. Taylor, *Paul*, pp. 138-39, 156-62.

gospel he preached, came directly by divine revelation through Jesus Christ (Gal. 1.1, 11-12, 15-16).

Each of the accounts of Paul's call in Acts broadly supports Paul's claims of divine revelation through Jesus Christ and that he is to go to the Gentiles. But in the first two accounts it is noticeable that Paul hears the voice but does not himself claim to have seen Jesus (9.3-5; 22.6-8).[44] It is in the secondary accounts by people who were not present at the event that an appearance is mentioned, by Ananias (9.17; 22.14) and Barnabas (9.27). It is not until the third account that Paul includes the words of Jesus, 'I have appeared (ὤφθην) to you for this purpose, to appoint you to serve and bear witness (ὑπηρέτην καὶ μάρτυρα) to the things in which you have seen me and to those in which I will appear (ὀφθήσομαί) to you' (26.16). In Lukan terms, Paul is a ὑπηρέτης but not an eyewitness from the beginning (Lk. 1.2; cf. Acts 1.21-22). Paul also recounts a vision in the temple in which he both sees and hears Jesus (22.17-18).

There are two references to Paul's apostleship and in both cases Barnabas is included (14.4, 14). Although the Western text omits οἱ ἀπόστολοι from 14.14, it is doubtful whether 14.4 is carelessness in Luke's handling of his sources.[45] It seems more probable that it is a deliberate ploy by Luke who, by extending the term to Barnabas, acknowledges Paul's claim yet robbing him of equality with the twelve.

Paul and Peter

The strand of Paul's inequality with the twelve must be balanced by the well-known parallels between the accounts of Peter and Paul. Some of the more obvious instances in Acts are listed below.[46]

---

44. Maddox, *Purpose*, pp. 74-75, believes that Luke will not allow any apostle to be like the twelve after the ascension.
45. Haenchen, *Acts*, p. 428 n. 5. Maddox, *Purpose*, pp. 71-72, regards 'apostle' as a slip by which Luke allows the tradition to shine through. Klein, *Die zwölf Apostel*, p. 213, argues that Paul and Barnabas are not described as apostles in Acts 14.4, 14 but that they are on the side of the twelve. This proposal is unnecessary if we accept that Luke presents Paul as an apostle but in the second rank to the twelve. Luke could hardly deny Paul's apostleship without appearing too aggressive, in view of Paul's insistent claims in the letters.
46. Rackham, *Acts*, p. xlviii, provides a list of some twenty possible parallels.

6. *Luke, Paul and Israel*

	Peter	Paul
1. Giving extended sermons to Jews which use OT citations such as Ps. 16.10 as a proof text of the resurrection	2.14-40	13.16-41
2. The healing of lame men	3.1-10	14.8-10
3. Having extraordinary healing powers	5.15	19.11-12
4. They receive miracles in prison	5.19-20	16.25-34
5. They receive visions concerning Gentiles	10.9-16	26.12-18
6. They have victories over magicians	8.18-24	13.6-12
7. When Gentiles regard them as superhuman both declare that they are men	10.25-26	14.11-15

Yet in spite of these and other parallels it is also clear that Peter upstages Paul over some extremely important issues. It is Peter who is the first to go to a Gentile, to preach to him and to be entertained in his house (10.23-48). It is Peter who is the first to be challenged by Christian advocates of circumcision but convinces them that the customary distinctions between clean and unclean have been overruled (11.1-18). The Cornelius episode legitimizes both the conversion of Gentiles as well as table fellowship between Jewish and Gentile believers, since both food in the vision and the Gentiles are described as common and unclean (10.14, 28).[47] When men from Judaea come to Antioch saying that Gentile believers must be circumcised it is Peter who subsequently puts the case that it is not required (15.1-3, 6-11). Paul and Barnabas are present at the Jerusalem meeting but they only report God's signs and wonders among the Gentiles. They thus provide evidence for what has taken place but they put no argument for the setting aside of the circumcision requirement. The letter from James and the Jerusalem church, setting out the requirements for Gentiles, is taken by Paul and others to the Antioch church which receives it joyfully (15.30-31).

Luke's presentation contradicts or, at least, questions several sections of Paul's letters, particularly those that deal with Peter-Cephas.[48] At

---

47. Esler, *Community and Gospel*, p. 94, places the emphasis on unclean foods whereas Jervell, *The People of God*, p. 66, stresses Gentile admission. Fitzmyer, *Theologian*, p. 193, rightly sees that both food and people are included.

48. Ehrman, 'Cephas and Peter', argues that they are not the same person in Paul's letters (p. 474) and that, in Gal. 2.7-8, 'any sensible person would assume that they were different persons' (p. 468) unless the reader knew that Kephas was the Aramaic equivalent of Peter. Strangely, Ehrman does not mention a similar case in

Corinth the Cephas group is one of the factions causing division in the church (1 Cor. 1.12; 3.22) and Paul is obviously rankled that Cephas and the other apostles could be accompanied by a sister as a wife while Paul and Barnabas have to support themselves by working (1 Cor. 9.4-7). Paul takes this as a slur on his apostleship, as being in some way inferior to that of Cephas and the others. In Galatians 2 the differences between Paul and Cephas are sharper still. According to Paul, Peter's mission area was to the circumcised while his own was to the Gentiles (Gal. 2.7-9) and there is also the criticism of Cephas as one of 'the reputed pillars' of the Jerusalem church (οἱ δοκοῦντες στῦλοι, 2.9; cf. Mk 10.42). This is followed by Paul's account of the Antioch incident in which he had opposed Cephas to his face before the whole church (2.11-14).[49] Even Paul's predominant use of the Jewish form 'Cephas' seems intended to draw attention to Peter taking the Jewish side in church controversies. Only twice does Paul mention Cephas in neutral terms (1 Cor. 15.5; Gal. 2.8) and never in words of enthusiasm. He never suggests, as Luke does, that Peter was an ally in disputes over table fellowship or the circumcision of Gentiles. It may be that Paul's accounts are the more accurate but Luke's readers would have been given cause to revise their opinions about the letters and the author. Those commentators who regard Luke as the defender of Paul or apologizing for him should consider the evidence for Luke defending Peter against the attacks of Paul. Among the reasons for this defence was that, for Luke, Peter represents the twelve whose first concern is the restoration of the kingdom to Israel. Just as Acts 1.1 recalls the Gospel's prologue, so also the apostles' question in 1.6 rekindles the hope for Israel's salvation that had been expressed in the birth stories but had faded after Jesus' death (Lk. 24.21). This restoration, which will include the Gentiles (Acts 15.16-18), is a key theme in Acts. Paul's letters, while showing his enthusiasm for the conversion of Gentiles, show little apparent concern for the historical Israel. I shall examine this in more detail later in this chapter.

Acts 15.7, 14 (Peter and Symeon). Riddle, 'Cephas Problem', thinks two people are indicated in Acts 15.7, 14 but Haenchen, *Acts*, p. 447, suggests that Luke may have wanted to show that James spoke Aramaic. Allison, 'Peter and Cephas', rebuts Ehrman's thesis.

49. Among recent commentators on the incident in Gal. 2 are Dunn, *Jesus, Paul and the Law*, pp. 129-82, and Esler, *Community and Gospel*, pp. 86-89. Dunn's article first appeared in 1983 and it is on this that Esler comments. In his book, Dunn replies to Esler's comments.

6. *Luke, Paul and Israel*

The 'We' Sections

The 'we' sections (Acts 16.10-17; 20.5–21.26; 27.1–28.16) provide further evidence for Luke's understanding and portrayal of Paul. The sections have often been examined as to their historical value: was Luke a companion of Paul, are they the unedited remnants of Luke's sources, or are they Luke's own compositions? The most obvious reading, and the one almost certainly made by Luke's readers, is the first: that the author is claiming first-hand knowledge of some of Paul's travels. He was with Paul on sea voyages, at Miletus when Paul gave his final speech to the Ephesian elders, present at the last visit to Jerusalem and, most important of all, with Paul at Rome.

Vernon Robbins has examined the style of the 'we' sections in the context of the literary genre of Hellenistic sea voyages.[50] Among Robbins's conclusions are that the author intends to show himself as writing from Rome but that the use of the first person plural does not mean that the author was actually present.[51] We can, I think, go further and regard the sections as a device intended to show that Luke was in a position to judge accurately what Paul was really like, what he believed and how he behaved. They are designed to place Luke among the 'eyewitnesses of what has been accomplished among us' so far as Paul's missionary practice and preaching are concerned.

The 'we' passages are a particularly good example of Luke's technique of using historical narrative to make theological points yet without overt polemic. In his letters, Paul generally dealt directly with issues facing the churches, but the narrative method, by its very nature, enables controversial points to be made without direct confrontation. We find the method also in Luke's looking back to the time before Paul became a dominant figure in the Church. By doing this he gives a chronological priority to the preaching and strategy of the Jerusalem church, which also implies a theological priority over the letters. The fact, which the letters acknowledge, that Paul was a newcomer, becomes a subtle theological weapon.

---

50. Robbins, 'The We-Passages'. Fitzmyer, *Theologian*, pp. 17-22, has challenged Robbins's thesis and proposes instead a Lukan diary source. The second person plural is also used for land journeys.

51. Robbins, 'We-Passages', pp. 241-42.

Paul's Missions

In Acts, Paul's missions are conducted principally in the synagogues of the diaspora. At Thessalonica (17.1-9), Beroea (17.10-14), Corinth (18.1-17) and Ephesus (18.19; 19.8-10) it is in the synagogues that many Gentiles are converted. Compared with these instances, there are only two occasions where the reader is told what Paul says to solely Gentile audiences. At Lystra, with the crowds excited by the healing of a lame man, Paul exhorts the people to turn from paganism to the living God who gives witness to himself through the goodness of nature (14.15-17). Jesus is not mentioned, either in the healing or the speech to the crowd and there is no report of any conversions. The second case is the Areopagus speech. This is preceded by the brief comment that Paul preached Jesus and the resurrection (17.18) but, in the main speech, there is only an allusion to the risen Jesus as the man appointed by God to judge the world (17.22-31). The success of the sermon is very small (17.34).

In the latter part of Acts, traditionally thought to describe the church's mission to the Gentiles, Luke gives his readers remarkably little help about how to preach to Gentiles compared with the detailed speeches to Jews. The comparison is a sharp reminder of how Luke's concern for the conversion of Gentiles arises from his concern for Israel. E.P. Sanders has argued strongly that Paul went directly to the Gentiles and did not go through Jewish communities.[52] If this were so then it further underlines how far Luke was prepared to go in order to show that success among the Gentiles was at its greatest when it was synagogue-based.

Although Paul takes the centre stage in the latter part of Acts there are some surprising features about the story. The section from 20.2 to his presence in Rome (28.31) occupies more space than the accounts of the missions,[53] and the list of churches *not* founded by Paul makes impressive reading. There are eight of these including Caesarea, Antioch and Rome.[54] There are also sections in the narrative in which towns and areas are named but with no other apparent motive than to show Paul as a traveller. There is the long journey described in 16.6-10 and another

---

52. Sanders, *Jewish People*, pp. 181-84. But Paul's punishment by Jewish authorities implies religious offences within their jurisdiction.
53. Maddox, *Purpose*, p. 66.
54. Maddox, *Purpose*, p. 69.

list at 21.1-8 in which nine places are mentioned, yet in neither account is there any indication that Paul preached at the stopping places. The mission at Philippi occupies 29 verses (16.12-40) yet it results only in the conversion of the families of Lydia and the jailer. Paul begins the mission by going to a place of prayer (προσευχή, 16.13, 16), a word that normally describes a synagogue in Jewish usage, although Luke elsewhere uses συναγωγή. The fact that the place of prayer is used only by women suggests that Paul did not go to a synagogue at Philippi.[55] Is this why Luke records only a small success?

On some journeys, such as those to Lystra, Iconium and Antioch (14.21-22), Galatia and Phrygia (18.23) and, possibly, Macedonia (20.2-3), the main purpose of the visit is to strengthen those who have already been converted. There is no doubt that Luke is deeply interested in the Gentile mission, but as far as Paul was concerned the real success came through his work in the synagogues. This continued to be Paul's strategy, in spite of his statements about turning to the Gentiles (13.46-47; 18.6). In the pertinent comment of Robert Brawley, 'Luke exhibits less interest in the extension of the gospel beyond Israel than do most of his commentators'.[56]

The Purpose of Luke's Portrait

Luke presents Paul as a law-abiding Jew who holds fast to his Jewishness despite the obduracy and opposition of his fellow Jews. The circumcision of Timothy is carried out in order to placate Jews at Lystra (16.1-3) and his payment for the men under a vow is expressly to convince Jewish Christians that he upholds the law (21.20-24). For himself, Paul tries to reach Jerusalem in time for Pentecost (20.16) and undertakes a vow (18.18), both of which are signs of his personal devotions and that his other actions were not merely diplomatic (*contra* 1 Cor. 9.20?). In spite of having been at Antioch at the time when the disciples were first called Christians (11.25-26), Paul continues to declare that he is a Jew, both to Jews (22.3-5; 23.6) and to Romans (24.10-21; 26.2-23).

---

55. Haenchen, *Acts*, p. 494; Lake and Cadbury, *Beginnings*, IV, p. 191; Moulton and Milligan, *Vocabulary*, p. 547; *BAGD*, p. 713; Schürer–Vermes, *History*, II, pp. 425, 439-40, 445. It seems strange, having been in the city for some days (v. 12), that they did not know the location of the synagogue (cf. 'supposed', v. 13). See also Kee, 'Transformation', and a rejoinder by Oster, 'Supposed Anachronism'.

56. Brawley, *Luke–Acts and the Jews*, p. 71.

At Rome he is finally vindicated by his Jewish visitors who have heard no evil reported of him from the Jerusalem Jews (28.21). This Jewish aspect of Paul may not be too distant from the 'real' Paul, and both Vielhauer[57] and Bornkamm[58] recognize that it reflects elements in the letters. Jervell argues even more fully for this highlighting of a Jewishness which is overshadowed in the letters.[59]

What then is the purpose of Luke's picture? According to Maddox, Luke felt no need to defend Paul but instead wished to celebrate a great Christian leader. Paul therefore embodies the continuity of the gospel as well as being an inspiring example to Luke's church whose lives were marked by controversy, chiefly from outside.[60] Paul's witness is characterized by suffering and by 'carrying the name' as a martyr. As part of the evidence for this view Maddox cites the two occasions when Paul, under arrest, retells the story of his call. He also cites the first account of the call when Jesus says, 'This man is my chosen instrument to carry my name before the Gentiles and kings and the sons of Israel; for I will show him how much he must suffer for the sake of my name' (9.15-16).[61] But suffering, which Paul certainly endures, is not in his case martyrdom, dying for the faith. This is significantly absent from Luke's account of Paul and, in Paul's last description of his call, he reports Jesus as promising that he will deliver Paul 'from the people [i.e. the Jews] and the Gentiles—to whom I send you' (26.17). Here Luke is preparing the reader not for Paul's death in Rome but for his unhindered preaching for two whole years in the capital of the Gentile empire (28.30-31).

R.L. Brawley, on the other hand, sees Luke's portrait as an attempt to defend and legitimate Paul and his gospel.[62] He begins his essay by describing it as an 'avowed revisionist attempt to reclaim some of the seminal features of the dormant concepts of *Tendenz* criticism'.[63]

---

57. Vielhauer, 'Paulinism', p. 38, thinks that Paul's attitude in Acts may agree with the letters but he questions whether it is historically accurate.
58. Bornkamm, 'Missionary Stance', pp. 200, 204.
59. Jervell, *The Unknown Paul*, ch. 4.
60. Maddox, *Purpose*, p. 182.
61. Maddox, *Purpose*, pp. 78-79. Burchard, *Der dreizehnt Zeuge*, pp. 100-101.
62. Jervell, *The People of God*, pp. 175-77, believes that Luke is defending Paul to Jewish Christians. But this could only be done if Luke kept quiet about the contents of much of the letters. The need for such a defence would be further evidence that Luke's readers knew something of the contents and did not like what they knew. See also Brawley, *Luke–Acts and the Jews*, p. 83.
63. Brawley, *Luke–Acts and the Jews*, pp. 68-69.

6. *Luke, Paul and Israel*

Among these concepts is that of F.C. Baur, that Acts is an attempt to reconcile the opposing parties of Jewish and Gentile Christians, rather than defending one party against the other. In order to do this Brawley correctly argues against those present-day commentators who see the Gentile mission in Acts as the result of Jewish stubbornness and the rejection of the Jews.[64]

But does Luke defend Paul (Brawley) and does the gospel remain unchanged in its continuity (Maddox)? One of the most obvious features of Acts is that it does not present the same gospel that is found in Paul's letters. The gospel Luke proclaims is his own and it is this that lies at the root of the differences between the Paul of Acts and the Paul of the letters. To defend Paul's gospel and the 'real' Paul, Luke would have had to present them in ways consistent with the letters and this he does not do. Nor is there a continuity of the gospel between the letters and Acts; the only apparent continuity is between the preaching of the Jerusalem church and Paul in Acts. Paul's own theology would have stuck out like a sore thumb; it was therefore suppressed. In Paul's farewell speech at Miletus (20.18-35) he reminds his audience of how he had been opposed by Jews and that he had preached the full gospel to Jews and Gentiles. Within the structure of Acts, this is Luke's final address to Christians and it contains a warning that:

> fierce wolves will come in among you, not sparing the flock; and from among your own selves will arise men speaking perverse things, to draw away the disciples after them (20.29-30).

Various suggestions have been made about the nature of the division implied in the speech, a division that was no doubt a reality when Luke was writing. Haenchen points to the spread of Gnosticism in Asia Minor by the time of the Revelation of John and he sees Luke's remark that Paul had preached the full gospel as an attack on those who held to secret traditions.[65]

Dunn has summarized the reactions to Paul, both by Gnostic heretics and the 'orthodox' fathers in the second century.[66] He shows how Paul's letters were fertile ground for Hellenistic Gnostics such as Marcion and Valentinus, in spite of their sometimes contorted exegesis. But perhaps even more important is Dunn's claim that orthodox writers

---

64. Brawley, *Luke–Acts and the Jews*, pp. 69-78, 83.
65. Haenchen, *Acts*, p. 596.
66. Dunn, *Unity and Diversity*, pp. 288-96.

could only defend Paul by equally contorted interpretations and that, by the time of Irenaeus, it was the Paul of Acts and the pastorals who was held up as orthodox. Dunn also comments that earlier in the second century, the church moved away from its disengagement from Judaism and the OT law, reversing the process so as to 'appropriate its Jewish heritage'.[67] Certainly *1 Clement* and the letters of Ignatius contain nothing of Paul's seeming rejection of the law on the grounds that it was unable to save; the early fathers revered Paul for his life and endurance, not for his radical teaching about the law (e.g. *1 Clem.* 5.5-7; Polycarp, *Phil.* 3.2; 9; 11.3). The later Acts is dated, the nearer Luke stands to this changing attitude to Judaism and the use of Paul as a noble example. Of course, it is always possible that he was in the vanguard of the change.

J. Knox[68] and J.L. Houlden[69] also see a pre-Marcionite group as the cause of Luke's problems but they do not specifically refer to the Miletus speech. Houlden thinks that Luke's overall purpose was to allay the fears of Jewish Christians who felt threatened by the increasing number of Gentiles in the church and who, perhaps, accused the Jews of the death of Jesus. Certainly Luke was concerned with the threat of division between Jewish and Gentile Christians, perhaps similar to the divisions at Corinth and Galatia between Paul and the Cephas groups. Yet, by attributing the warnings to Paul, Luke had a strong and subtle weapon with which to attack those among the disciples of the 'real' Paul who used his teachings to support their attempts to discredit Jewish Christian beliefs and practices.

I suggested earlier that Luke may have intended to defend Peter rather than Paul and that this is why he used the Peter–Paul parallels, putting Petrine speeches into Paul's mouth and *vice versa*. This would give the impression that Peter and Paul were at one, but the strategy could only be successful if Luke kept silent about Paul's criticism of the law. The plan is completed, as far as Peter is concerned, by making his final speech a form of Paul's less controversial expression of the gospel (15.10-11). Luke also makes Paul obedient to the Jerusalem church (15.22, 25; 21.22-26; *contra* Gal. 1.17–2.10) as well as showing that Paul's apostleship was secondary to that of the twelve. In these ways Luke removes the radicalism of Paul's theology and reduces his authority so that he can put forward his own theology. Walker, who

---

67. Dunn, *Unity and Diversity*, p. 295.
68. Knox, 'Pauline Corpus', pp. 285-86.
69. Houlden, 'Luke's Purpose', p. 64.

accepts that Luke had some knowledge of Paul's letters, believes that Luke did not try to discredit Paul but that he intended to rehabilitate him as a spokesman and champion of orthodox Christianity.[70] This he did by presenting Paul in the tradition of authentic Judaism, alongside Peter, James and John.[71] Walker considers the possibility that Luke may have tried to rehabilitate Peter but concludes that this was not Luke's purpose.[72] Yet making Paul part of the authentic tradition could only imply support for Peter in the controversies with Paul. Peter's disappearance after Acts 15 clearly leaves Paul at the centre of the story, but by now Luke has made his point; it was Peter and not Paul who had originated the Gentile mission without the need for circumcision. Thereafter, Paul carries the message to the diaspora and the Gentiles while Peter, it would appear, remains in Jerusalem with the other Christian leaders. The extensively discussed differences between Acts and Galatians 1–2 should be considered as deliberate refashioning of the account by Luke for his own purpose.

To summarize the picture of Paul; Luke defends Paul only in so far as he makes him fit in with, and follow, the line first set out by Peter. Like Peter, Paul is a visionary, miracle-worker and preacher but he is not a true Lukan apostle. Luke's purpose was indeed irenic as the Tübingen school realized and he smooths the abrasive relationship between Paul and Peter to which the letters give ample witness. By doing this Luke aimed to ease the tensions between Jewish and Gentile Christians. This accords with Esler's conclusions that Luke wanted to remove the obstacles to Jewish–Gentile table fellowship,[73] and it is consistent with Brawley's opinion that Luke's portrait has irenic as well as apologetic motives.[74] The present study suggests that any defence of Paul of the type that Brawley indicates is strictly on Luke's terms since a true defence would have required the affirmation of Paul's theology. Paul is, so to speak, accepted on Peter's terms and, contrary to Maddox's claim, he is obedient to the Jerusalem church.[75] On the basis of Luke's portrait

---

70. Walker, 'Acts and the Pauline Corpus', p. 7.
71. Walker, 'Acts and the Pauline Corpus', pp. 14-15.
72. Walker, 'Acts and the Pauline Corpus', p. 16.
73. Esler, *Community and Gospel*, pp. 105-109, notes the continued existence of Jewish Christians in the second century and their insistence on the importance of Peter over Paul.
74. Brawley, *Luke–Acts and the Jews*, p. 83.
75. Maddox, *Purpose*, p. 72.

we can now turn to examine their different views about Israel and what the implications might be. This, as we shall see, lies at the root of Luke's disagreement with Paul.

The Question of Israel

1. *The Law*

a. *Circumcision*. In the previous chapter we discussed the Lukan and Pauline attitudes to the law in the context of atonement. In this section the focus is the law as a characteristic mark of Israel and as an entrance requirement. Some overlap with the earlier discussion is unavoidable, unfortunately.

It is Haenchen's opinion that Luke and Paul had the same overriding problem, 'the mission to the Gentiles without the law'.[76] This assessment is rather misleading since 'without the law' really means without circumcision as far as Luke is concerned, as the Jerusalem council shows. Paul and Luke agree that circumcision is not required for Gentile believers but for Luke, a generation or so later than Paul, it was much less of a problem and he simply accepts the state of affairs. And, as Jervell has commented, the question of circumcision was 'solved *de facto*, not *de jure*'.[77] In Paul's experience, however, the problem had not been solved and, seeing the practice as positively harmful (Gal. 5.2; Phil. 3.2-3), he tried to justify its abrogation *de jure*.

Of all Paul's arguments that Gentile converts become children of Abraham but without the law, the most plausible is that the covenant and its promise preceded the law by four hundred and thirty years (Gal. 3.17-18; Exod. 12.40). This may have convinced some Jews that Gentiles were not under the law but it left unresolved the question of circumcision because Abraham was himself circumcised.[78] Because circumcision is so intimately bound up with the law in terms of membership of Israel, there never could be convincing scriptural support for Gentile believers remaining uncircumcised as long as they were thought to be entering Israel.[79] Paul might have seemed to be on firmer ground

---

76. Haenchen, *Acts*, p. 112.
77. Jervell, *The People of God*, pp. 135-36.
78. Jervell, *The People of God*, p. 137, regards circumcision as the heart of the law.
79. McElleney, 'Conversion, Circumcision and the law', pp. 328-33, discusses the small amount of evidence for the view that proselytes did not always have to be

when he reminded his readers that God's blessing of Abraham preceded circumcision (Rom. 4.9-10) but he avoided mentioning the requirements in Gen. 17.9-14. In view of the Genesis passage there is no way in which Gen. 15.6 could have supported the extension of God's promise to those who remained uncircumcised.[80] Luke, however, makes no attempt at the impossible task of justifying the exemption from Scripture or by attacking the law as a whole.[81] Instead, he relies on Peter's testimony to God's gift of the Holy Spirit (10.47) and the accompanying signs and wonders which God has shown among the Gentiles (15.7-12). Ultimately, both Paul and Luke agree that it is the gift of the Spirit that proves that circumcision is to be set aside for Gentile believers (Acts 10.44-48; [11.7-8]; Gal. 3.14; 4.6, 29; 5.2-6). Jervell points out that we do not know the circumstances in which the Gentiles were first admitted[82] but the agreement between Paul and Luke offers a clue to a possible scenario. Perhaps, following the preaching of the gospel in synagogues, a number of Jews and God-fearers were converted to faith in Jesus as Messiah. Recognizing their new unity of faith, Jewish believers might then have asked why the Gentiles did not now accept circumcision. To which the Gentiles would reply, 'Why should we when both Jews and Gentiles have been baptized and been given the Spirit?' It seems very probable that the admission of the first Gentiles was the result of pneumatic enthusiasm and that the story of Cornelius' baptism contains a valuable strand of historical truth. It was not the direct result of Jesus' command but the fulfilment of the promise of the

---

circumcised. He concludes that first-century Judaism may have been 'much more open on this question' (pp. 332-33). Schiffmann, 'Crossroads', regards the evidence that Hellenistic Jews did not require proselyte circumcision as extremely weak.

80. Sanders, *Jewish People*, pp. 147-48, comments that 'few moderns will be convinced that Paul proves his case against circumcision by quoting Gen. 15.6 and ignoring 17.9-14'. It is also very doubtful whether it would have convinced Jewish Christians of Luke's time.

81. I have used 'admission' rather than 'mission' because it is difficult to resist the assumption that the first Gentiles to be admitted were sympathetic to Judaism and overheard, so to speak, Christians preaching to Jews. The conversion of Cornelius does not directly reflect this situation because Luke needed to show the conversion taking place on God's authority. But it may have been a presupposition ('You know', Acts 10.36) and Jervell, *People of God*, p. 138, seems to regard Cornelius' keeping the law as self-evident. The move to convert outright pagans is hardly touched on in Acts but it is unnecessary to take Jervell's extreme position as in 'The Church of Jews and God Fearers', pp. 11, 14. See J.T. Sanders', 'Jew and Gentile', pp. 449-51.

82. Jervell, *The People of God*, pp. 135-36.

Spirit that led to the acceptance of devout Gentiles.[83]

The circumcision of Timothy (16.1-3) has nothing to do with the issue of Gentile admission since he was born a Jew by virtue of his Jewish mother.[84] According to Luke, the motive for Paul's action is to appease the local Jews who knew that Timothy's father was a Greek, which implies that he was a born Jew but not a member of the covenant. The problem for commentators has been that it was Paul who carried out the ritual. Vielhauer correctly sees the irrelevance of 1 Cor. 9.19-20 (becoming a Jew in order to win Jews) in trying to relate the Lukan Paul to the Paul of the letters. Instead, he regards the act as in conflict with Paul's remark, 'if you receive circumcision, Christ will be of no advantage to you' (Gal. 5.2).[85] If the aim in the Galatians passage was to convince *Gentile* Christians not to be circumcised, then that too is irrelevant. Writing to Roman Christians, some of whom were presumably Jewish, Paul tells them that there is value in being a Jew and in being circumcised if they obey the law (Rom. 2.25; 3.1-2), a view with which Luke would have agreed. But, in 1 Cor. 7.18-19, Paul says that those who were uncircumcised when they were called should remain so because neither circumcision nor uncircumcision matters. From Acts 18.1-11 we know that the Corinthian church contained Jews,[86] so that in

---

83. Dibelius, *Studies*, p. 122. Haenchen, *Acts*, pp. 355-57, reviews the critical analyses of the Cornelius story.

84. According to *m. Qid.* 3.12, the son of a Jewish mother and a Gentile father would be Jewish. Cohen, 'Timothy', pp. 251-68, questions whether this rabbinic law existed in the first century and, if it did, whether it was observed by Jews in Asia Minor. Cohen thus concludes that Timothy was a Gentile and that only if this was so could 16.1-3 be consistent with 21.21. I must confess that I cannot follow Cohen's argument at this point. Timothy's circumcision is Luke's 'proof' that Paul's accusers in 21.21 are mistaken and this can only be so if Timothy was Jewish. For Luke to have described Paul circumcising a Gentile immediately after the decision at Jerusalem would have been inexplicable. It is possible that, although the rabbinic ruling was formulated in the second century, it expressed earlier thinking rather than a sudden *volte face* in the move from patrilineal descent. Luke's details about Timothy's parents are deliberate and purposeful. See also, Trebilco, *Jewish Communities*, pp. 23-24.

85. Vielhauer, 'Paulinism', pp. 40-41.

86. Luke claims to know details of the Corinthian church but he does not claim it as first hand by the use of 'we'. Timothy and Silvanus/Silas (Acts 18.5; 2 Cor. 1.19), the presence of Apollos (Acts 19.1; 1 Cor. 3.4-6, 22) and knowledge that Paul worked for his living (Acts 18.3; 1 Cor. 4.12; 9.3-7) are some of the agreements. It is

6. *Luke, Paul and Israel*

Luke's eyes Jewish Christians should not follow Paul's advice. Timothy, as a born Jew, is circumcised so that he becomes a full covenant member and Luke supports this view later when Paul pays for the men under a vow; he does this specifically to refute the rumour that he teaches Jewish Christians not to circumcise their children (21.17-24). The circumcision of Jewish Christians is not a matter of indifference to Luke; although they have been baptized they remain members of the covenant of Israel and he wants them to have no doubt about this.

b. *Food and Days*. Jewish food regulations and Sabbath observance were commanded in the law. They served to distinguish between insiders and outsiders[87] and they were among the Jewish practices that were most ridiculed by Gentiles.[88]

Paul's only mention of the Sabbath is as the day for setting aside the collection in aid of the Jerusalem church (1 Cor. 16.2). Elsewhere he is either indifferent to 'days' (Rom. 14.5-6) or in despair of those who observe 'days and months and seasons and years' (Gal. 4.10-11). This is in stark contrast to the Paul of Acts (13.14, 42, 44; 16.13; 18.4). Paul rejected the food laws because they constituted a barrier to Jewish–Gentile table fellowship and this had led to his attack on Peter at Antioch (Gal. 2.11-15). Moreover, the food laws had to be rescinded because, as works of the law, they were opposed to faith. In his advice to believers who were invited to eat with unbelievers, Paul went further still. The believer is free to eat whatever is offered unless told that the food has been offered in sacrifices; then the believer is not to eat for the sake of the unbeliever's conscience (1 Cor. 10.27-30). There is the additional proviso that in eating, no offence should be given to Jews, Greeks or the church (10.32).

Luke presents a quite different picture, partly out of concern for Jewish–Gentile table fellowship but, more fundamentally, from concern for the law. In Conzelmann's opinion, Luke describes Gentile freedom from the law as a problem of historical development from the time when the church kept the law. The problem was to give an account of how the church came to abandon 'the link with Judaism, the law and the

---

of course possible that Luke had read 1–2 Corinthians! See Green, 'Matthew, Clement and Luke', p. 25.

87. Esler, *Community and Gospel*, pp. 73-85, 93-109; Dunn, *Jesus, Paul and the Law*, pp. 216-19.

88. Sanders, *Jewish People*, pp. 102-105.

temple'.[89] Such an abandonment would indeed have cut off the church from Judaism, but where is the clear evidence for this in Acts? The Jerusalem Christians still use the temple (21.23-36) and, as we have seen, any adverse criticism in Stephen's speech is restrained and indirect. Jewish Christians are still zealous for the law, not least because of Jesus' answer to the lawyer's question (Lk. 10.25-28). The extent to which Gentiles are under the law, at least as far as identity markers are concerned, is dealt with by the Jerusalem council (15.4-29). The demands of the Christian Pharisees (15.5) are met not by explicit rejection but by a statement of the conditions that govern Jewish–Gentile fellowship.[90] The importance of these conditions is given a characteristic Lukan threefold emphasis (15.20, 29; 21.25). They are:

1. To abstain from pollution of idols (Lev. 19.4).
2. To abstain from fornication. This may refer to forbidden marriages (Lev. 18.16-18) although, in Jer. 3.2, 9 and Hos. 6.10, πορνεία refers to idolatry. Given Luke's abhorrence of idolatry and magical practices this possible meaning cannot be ruled out.
3. To abstain from what is strangled, that is, meat not ritually slaughtered (Lev. 17.10-12).
4. To abstain from blood (Gen. 9.4; Lev. 17.10-16).

B.S. Easton[91] and Esler[92] are among those who regard the regulations as applying to strangers living in the land of Israel but who are not expected to keep the full law. Another possible basis, suggested by J.L. Houlden, is Deuteronomy 12, in which Israel is urged to reject totally all idols and to abstain from blood, but that clean and unclean persons can eat what they will. Significantly, the regulations are given to Israel as it is about to enter the promised land.[93] The requirements to be observed by

---

89. Conzelmann, *Luke*, pp. 146-47, 212. Also Jervell, *The People of God*, p. 134.
90. Esler, *Community and Gospel*, pp. 97-99.
91. Easton, *Early Christianity*, pp. 41-57.
92. Esler, *Community and Gospel*, pp. 98-99, does not point out that the laws apply to Israel as well as strangers.
93. Houlden, 'The Purpose of Luke', p. 60. But the council is not 'the church's coming of age as the fulfiller and heir of Israel', as Houlden suggests. It is even doubtful whether Luke saw the church as a body akin to Israel, let alone as Israel's heir. In Acts, 'church' is predominantly a local gathering, rather like a synagogue.

6. *Luke, Paul and Israel*

Gentiles are to be understood in the context of James's quotation of God's promise in Amos 9:

> I will rebuild the tent of David, which has fallen;
> I will rebuild its ruins, and I will set it up,
> that the rest of men may seek the Lord,
> and all the Gentiles who are called by my name (Acts 15.16-17).

Peter's final speech which precedes the Jerusalem decree shows that the Gentile burden is to be eased but there is no indication, here or elsewhere in Luke–Acts, that Jewish Christians are freed from the law. It is true that 'neither our fathers nor we have been able to bear' the yoke, and that Jews, like Gentiles, 'will be saved through the grace of the Lord Jesus' (15.10-11). This last comment of Peter's hints at Luke's contradiction of Paul's claim, that Peter behaved as if he believed in salvation through the works of the law rather than through faith in Jesus Christ (Gal. 2.15-16). It is perhaps coincidence, but Luke's only use of ζυγός might be intended as an allusion to its only use by Paul in Gal. 5.1. There Paul speaks of the slavery of the law; once again we see Luke implying Peter's similarity to, but priority over, Paul. Although Peter's words seem to express a Gentile Christian view of the yoke of the law as a burden, even upon Jews, it must also be noted that salvation by God's grace was not a belief foreign to devout Jews. In words attributed to R. Joshua b. Karha (c. 140–65 CE), 'Why does the section *Hear, O Israel* precede *And it shall come to pass if ye shall hearken*?—so that a man may first take upon him the yoke of the kingdom of heaven and afterward take upon him the yoke of the commandments' (*m. Ber.* 2.2, cf. 2.5).

A particular understanding of the law is not only related to a theology of atonement but to an underlying view of Israel. The law is that of the God of Israel and to be a member of Israel entails keeping that Law. Paul believed that salvation for Jews and Gentiles depends on faith and that the law does not rest on faith (Rom. 3.21-22; Gal. 3.11-12). He held that Christ is the end of the law (Rom. 10.4), that the law was a custodian until Christ but that 'we are no longer under custodian' (Gal. 3.24-25) and that believers have died to the law by entering the Body of Christ through faith (Rom. 7.4). Given such views, so clearly expressed, a reader might be forgiven for thinking that anyone holding them could not be, nor would want to be, a member of the historical Israel. In Paul's own case this would seem to be confirmed by those passages in the letters where Paul describes his former life in Judaism and then goes on to state or imply that it counts for nothing compared with being in Christ (Rom. 9.1-5; 11.1-2; Phil. 3.4-11).

By contrast, Luke's understanding of the law is essentially pragmatic: it is something to be obeyed both ritually (Lk. 2.22-27, 39; Acts 16.3) and morally (Lk. 10.25-28; Acts 7.53). The Lukan Jesus neither offers a summary of the law nor does he comment on which should be considered to be the first or greatest commandment.[94] When the lawyer asks Jesus what he must do to inherit eternal life he is told to do the law (10.25-28). S.G. Wilson, in his discussion of the Sabbath controversies and the saying on divorce (Lk. 6.1-11; 13.10-17; 14.1-6; 16.18), concludes that it is difficult to maintain that Jesus did not speak against the law.[95] E.P. Sanders, on the other hand, suggests that Jesus' views about the Sabbath were within the range of current Jewish debate and that Luke's accounts show 'more verisimilitude than the Markan'.[96] Jesus' saying on divorce is more rigorous than that of Moses but, as Sanders remarks, there were other groups that took upon themselves more stringent rules than the law required and that to prohibit what Moses permitted is not the same as permitting what Moses prohibited.[97]

2. *The Covenant*

God's covenant with Israel marked out the nation as the people of God. The covenant combined two traditions: the Abraham covenant which was sealed by circumcision (Gen. 17.4-14), and the Sinai tradition which was confirmed on Israel's part by the acceptance of God's law (Exod. 19.5; cf. 2.24; 20.1–24.12).[98] Paul appears to recognize this double tradition: in Gal. 3.15-18 he argues that the law does not annul God's promises made in the covenant with Abraham whose promised offspring is Christ. In Gal. 4.21–5.1 he uses the allegory of the two women: Hagar represents the covenant of slavery under the Sinai covenant, while the free woman represents the covenant of freedom and it is she who is the mother of believers. Then, as now, the children of the free are persecuted by the children of slavery and, as Markus Barth points out, Paul does not mention that God has mercy on Hagar and that he saves Ishmael's life (Gen. 16.10-15; 21.13-21).[99]

94. Jervell, *The People of God*, p. 139, but see Wilson, *Luke and the Law*, p. 15.
95. Wilson, *Luke and the Law*, pp. 31-37, 43-51, 111.
96. Sanders, *Jewish Law*, pp. 20-23.
97. Sanders, *Jesus and Judaism*, pp. 256-57.
98. Von Rad, *Old Testament Theology*, I, pp. 130-32.
99. Barth, *People of God*, p. 45.

6. *Luke, Paul and Israel*

In the Corinthian letters Paul speaks of the new covenant, of which the eucharistic cup is the blood that flows from the death of Jesus (1 Cor. 11.23-26). At 2 Cor. 3.6-18 Paul goes further, contrasting the old with the new covenant of which he is a minister. The new is 'not a written code but in the Spirit' whereas the old is 'the dispensation of death, carved in letters of stone' (3.6, 7). The old code came to Israel through Moses whose face shone with glory but a fading glory that Paul contrasts with the dispensation of the Spirit (3.7-8, 11). And the veil with which Moses had to cover his glory is still present when Jews read the old covenant: it is a veil that can only be lifted through Christ (3.13-16). One difficulty with Paul's analogy is that the idea of Moses' fading glory does not come from the account in Exod. 34.29-35. The *Targum Onkelos* on Deut. 34.7 ('his eye was not dim, nor his natural force abated') should probably be dated in the third century CE,[100] but it specifically denies that the splendour of Moses' glory changed. R.P. Martin rightly suggests that Paul's description springs from his need to support his comparison of the two dispensations.[101]

Luke presents a strongly contrasting attitude in his account of the transfiguration in which Moses (and Elijah) appear in glory with Jesus (Lk. 9.30-31). Commentators stress Luke's difference here from the versions of Mark and Matthew, for which they offer a variety of explanations, but they miss the implied contradiction of the passage in 2 Corinthians 3. Whatever other reasons Luke may have had for making his addition, it is clear that the glory Moses had when he received the law on Sinai is still to be seen on the mountain of the transfiguration. And, what is equally important, this glory does not differ in degree or kind from that of Jesus. It is remarkable for a late first-century Christian to affirm the enduring glory of the old dispensation.

Apart from the textual variant at Lk. 22.20, there is no mention of a new covenant in Luke–Acts. About this verse there has been a shift in critical opinion over the past forty years, moving away from widespread

---

100. Schürer–Vermes, *History*, I, p. 101.
101. Martin, *2 Corinthians*, pp. 57-64, sees the primary antithesis as between Moses and Paul, 'which shades into the contrast Moses/Christ or Moses/Spirit' (p. 61). He also regards the use of Exod. 34 as Paul's polemical response to Jewish or Jewish-Christian apologetic (pp. 62-64). On the other hand, C.J.A. Hickling, 'The Sequence of Thought in II Corinthians, Chapter Three', takes the view that it is 'unnecessary to invoke opponents with a different evaluation of what has taken place on Sinai' (p. 386).

acceptance of the shorter text that ends with the words 'this is my body' (19a).[102] As an example of how far the critical view has swung, M.L. Soards's study of Luke 22 accepts the longer text without any discussion of the issues involved.[103] But recently C.F. Evans has reviewed the question and he has drawn attention to the following points:

1. There is no adequate explanation of why vv. 19b-20 should have been omitted from the longer text.
2. The shorter text was current by the early second century in Europe, Africa and Syria.
3. The omission of the second cup prepares for Luke's description of the early community meal as 'the breaking of bread' (Lk. 24.30-35; Acts 2.42, 46; 20.7, 11; [27.35]).[104]

Evans's last point needs particular emphasis because the use of wine or a cup at Christian gatherings is not mentioned in Acts. The shorter text that omits vv. 19b-20 removes certain ideas that would be inconsistent with Luke's theology elsewhere in his writings. These are: that Jesus' body was given for believers, a new covenant, that Christ's blood was poured out for believers, and that sharing bread and the cup should be continued as an act of remembrance. The one possible exception is in Acts 20.28 where Paul speaks of the church of the Lord (or God, ℵ B) 'which he obtained with his own blood' or 'the blood of his Son'. The precise meaning of the verse is not, however, clear enough for us to assert that the blood of Jesus played a significant part in Luke's theology. Luke's accounts of post-resurrection meals contain no references to the death of Jesus and, at the meal at Emmaus, the emphasis is on Jesus entering his glory and the Christian interpretation of the Scriptures (24.26-27, 32). To sum up, the evidence suggests that the shorter text is original and therefore Luke did not speak of a new covenant. The only covenant in Luke–Acts is the one that God made with Abraham (Lk. 1.72; Acts 3.25; 7.8).

---

102. Higgins, *The Lord's Supper*, pp. 37-44.
103. Soards, *The Passion according to Luke*. Neyrey, *The Passion according to Luke*, p. 17, goes too far when he writes, 'no one can doubt that Luke is reflecting the long and sacred tradition about the eucharist when he records the interpretive words over the bread and wine'.
104. Evans, *Saint Luke*, pp. 786-88. Franklin, *Christ the Lord*, notes the forward-looking character of the meal (pp. 65-66).

Baptism

Luke and Paul agree that baptism is the rite of entry into the church so that their understandings of the rite will tell us something about the way in which they see the church. In particular, their views of baptism may reveal how they see the relation of the church to Israel.

Luke describes two types of baptism, of which John's is a sign of repentance and this has similarities with the first-century *Sibylline Oracles* (4.162-70).[105] Baptism in Acts still retains the aspect of repentance but it is now carried out in the name of Jesus Christ[106] and is connected with the gift of the Spirit (e.g. 2.38; 10.44-48; 18.24–19.7). Paul's doctrine of baptism is that it is the rite of entry into the Body of Christ and it therefore entails being buried with Christ in his death (Rom. 6.3-4; 1 Cor. 12.13). Because the believer has died with Christ he will also be raised with him (Rom. 6.5) and this has vital consequences for his moral life because he must consider himself dead to sin (Rom. 6.10-11). But since the strength of sin is the law (1 Cor. 15.56) then there is a sense in which the law becomes a thing of the past for Jewish and Gentile Christians. This is confirmed by Paul's view of baptism as the negation of past divisions. Jew and Greek, slave and free, male and female, these are no longer valid marks of distinction (Gal. 3.28; cf. 1 Cor. 12.13);[107] what is important is to become an offspring of Abraham, an heir of promise (Gal. 3.27-29).

Luke's treatment of baptism is markedly different from Paul's.[108] Where Paul propounds a doctrine but very rarely mentions actual events (1 Cor. 1.13-17), Luke records the events but offers no overt theology of incorporation into the church. In Acts, ἐκκλησία refers to local groups of believers[109] so that Luke's concept of 'church' has none of the overarching character that the Body of Christ has for Paul. When Paul tries to overcome divisions at Corinth he frequently speaks of 'the church of God' (1 Cor. 1.2; 10.32; 11.22) and, in 12.27-28, he identifies the Body of Christ with the church. And when Paul writes of his role as a persecutor it is of the church of God (1 Cor. 15.9; Gal. 1.13). The

---

105. Collins, 'Sibylline Oracles', *OTP*, I, p. 388 and n. e2.
106. Acts 2.38; 8.12, 13; 10.48; 16.31-33; 19.5.
107. Betz, *Galatians*, pp. 189-201.
108. When Luke uses the noun 'baptism' it almost always refers to that of John. For Christian initiation, he much prefers the verb.
109. Haenchen, *Acts*, pp. 93-94, and Evans, *Saint Luke*, p. 48.

Lukan descriptions of Paul as persecutor never speak of *the church* but of Jesus and his followers (Acts 9.2, 13, 16; 22.8, 19; 26.9-11, 14).

The identification of the church of God with the Body of Christ becomes even more pronounced in the deutero-Pauline letters (Eph. 5.21-32; Col. 1.18, 24). Although Luke uses ἐκκλησία to refer to Christian groups these must be balanced by his use to describe a riotous pagan mob (19.32, 39, 40) and Israel in the wilderness (7.38).

Paul, Israel and the Church

Although Paul occasionally spoke well of Israel's institutions (e.g. Rom. 3.1-2; 9.4-5), he had much more to say about them that was critical and rejecting. However much modern critics might try to place Paul's views in the context of the Judaism of his own time, the fact remains that his views provided valuable ammunition for second-century Gnostics and Marcionites. As we have seen, Clement and Ignatius largely avoided referring to the more radical aspects of Paul's theology so that, within less than a century of his death, many of those elements of his theology which have been regarded as most characteristic were either ignored or misinterpreted. Nor was it only heretical factions that found in the letters such valuable anti-Israel material. As the church became more infused with Gentiles they would have brought with them their aversions to things Jewish such as food laws, Sabbath observance, circumcision and, above all, monotheism.[110] Paul was well aware of the previous life-styles of many of his Gentile converts as ungodly and wicked (Rom. 1.18-32; 1 Cor. 6.9-11; Gal. 4.8). Luke's converts, by contrast, are predominantly pro-Jewish. It is also noticeable in Acts that the Gentiles who attack Jews do not become believers (16.19-23; 18.12-17; 19.33-41).

The present aim is to examine Paul's understanding of Israel so that we can see those aspects with which Luke would have disagreed. As with Paul's attitude to the law, his real intentions about Israel and the Jews remain matters of debate. The helpful review by Markus Barth shows the wide range of critical opinions,[111] so we need not be surprised

---

110. Schürer–Vermes, *History*, III, pp. 131-32. In spite of official Roman protection of Jewish interests there were widespread cases of anti-Jewish feeling in the cities of the diaspora. There were attacks upon, and mockery of, Jewish customs in Hellenistic-Roman literature but the feelings were 'not so much hatred as aversion' (p. 153).

111. Barth, *People of God*, pp. 20-27.

6. *Luke, Paul and Israel*

if Luke was also numbered among those who, in some eyes, have misunderstood Paul's thinking.

The combined effect of Paul's criticisms of Jews and their practices could well lead to the belief that Israel after the flesh had been replaced by the Body of Christ, a group that is neither Jewish nor Gentile but a new, third entity.[112] This leads to two questions: are there any indications that Paul appropriated 'Israel' for the church and, who, in Paul's view, constituted the 'people' of God? At one level the second question is the easier to answer: λαός occurs eleven times in Paul's letters of which six are in Romans 9–11 where he discusses the fate of Israel. All of Paul's uses of λαός are in quotations from the OT[113] and thus refer to historical Israel. There is one possible exception in Rom. 15.11 which is a version of Ps. 116.1 (LXX), where it may mean Jews and Gentiles. But apart from this one doubtful case, Paul and Luke agree that λαός means the people of ethnic Israel.[114]

The first question is much more difficult to answer if; indeed, an unambiguous answer can be found. The question is raised in its most acute form by the phrase 'Israel of God' in Gal. 6.16 and which Davies describes as an 'insinuating ambiguity'.[115] The phrase comes at the conclusion of a letter in which Paul has argued fiercely that it is the Christians who are the children of promise and who are free in Christ from the obligation of circumcision and food regulations. Seen in the light of the two-covenant allegory (4.21-29) it would be understandable if Luke came to the same conclusion about 6.16 as did J.N. Sanders: 'The true Israel is the new creation, upon which are poured the blessings which "Israel according to the flesh" has forfeited'.[116] Both

---

112. Sanders, *Jewish People*, pp. 172-73.
113. λαός: Rom. 9.25 (Hos. 2.25); 9.26 (Hos. 1.10); 10.21 (Isa. 65.2); 11.2 (Ps. 93.14, LXX). Also Rom. 15.10 (Deut. 32.43); 15.11 (Ps. 116.1 LXX); 1 Cor. 10.7 (Exod. 32.6); 14.21 (Isa. 28.11); 2 Cor. 6.16 (Lev. 26.12).
114. *Pace* Barth, *People of God*, p. 40, who speaks of this 'people' being manifest wherever there is a person who truly worships God and where, 'from all over the world', men and women bear witness to God. But see on Rom. 9.23-26 below.
115. Davies, *Jewish and Pauline Studies*, p. 128.
116. Sanders, 'Galatians', *Peake's Commentary*, p. 979. He also notes on Gal. 4.28-31 (pp. 997-98) that those who adhere to the old covenant will not inherit the promises offered to Christians. Paul is even more emphatic: 'Cast out the slave and her son; for the son of the slave shall not inherit with the son of the free woman' (4.30). Paul's affirmation of Israel's salvation in Rom. 11.26 would have been less convincing to those who had also read Galatians.

W.D. Davies[117] and E.P. Sanders[118] agree that Paul stops short of speaking of a new Israel but Betz notes that the expression 'Israel of God' is found only here in the NT and never in Judaism.[119] He suggests that 'of God' implies an Israel not of God and that the two qualifying words would make sense only as a distinction between a true and a false Israel.[120] According to Luz, Gal. 6.16 is the only instance where Israel could mean the church of Jews and Gentiles[121] and this leads Davies to expect that this meaning would find support in Romans 9–11.[122]

Before looking at Romans 9–11 there is one other passage in which Paul may be distinguishing between two Israels, in the phrase 'Israel after the flesh' (1 Cor. 10.18). The phrase seems to be in contrast with an 'Israel after the Spirit', although Paul never uses the expression. But the implied distinction does support Betz's view about the Israel of God[123] and it adds further weight to the possibility that the Israel of God is the church. Paul may indeed stop short of calling Christians the new Israel. Yet he comes within a hairsbreadth of doing so when he speaks of believers as 'the [true] circumcision (ἡμεῖς γάρ ἐσμεν ἡ περιτομή) who worship God in Spirit and glory in Christ Jesus, and who put no confidence in the flesh' (Phil. 3.3). There may be a similar suggestion in Rom. 2.28-29: 'For he is not [a Jew] outwardly nor is circumcision something outward in the flesh. He is [a Jew] who is a Jew in secret and circumcision is a matter of the heart, spiritual not literal.'[124] Although Paul's submission to Jewish punishment shows his acceptance of his Jewishness, he rarely describes himself as a Jew. He prefers to use terms such as 'being of the people of Israel' (Phil. 3.5), 'Israelite' and 'of the seed of Abraham' (Rom. 11.1; 2 Cor. 11.22) and 'Hebrew' (2 Cor. 11.22; Phil. 3.5).[125] Yet, when he speaks of his own kinsmen, whether or not they are believers, he uses the term 'Jew' freely and 'Israelite' is used

---

117. Davies, *Jewish and Pauline Studies*, p. 129.
118. Sanders, *Jewish People*, pp. 174-75, concludes that 'the Israel of God' refers to Christians.
119. Betz, *Galatians*, p. 322.
120. Betz, *Galatians*, p. 323.
121. Luz, *Das Geschichtsverständnis*, p. 269.
122. Davies, *Jewish and Pauline Studies*, p. 343 n. 20.
123. Jervell, *The People of God*, p. 137.
124. Richardson, *Israel*, pp. 138-39, thinks that Paul is speaking of Christians. Also see Sanders, *Jewish People*, pp. 127, 133 n. 26. There is nothing specifically Christian about Paul's thought here, as Deut. 10.16 and Jer. 4.4 show.
125. Davies, *Jewish and Pauline Studies*, pp. 342-43 and n. 16.

both of Jews (Rom. 9.4) and Jewish Christians (2 Cor. 11.22).

In Romans 9–11 Paul deals with a different problem from that in Galatians; his agonized concern for his own family (ἀδελφῶν μου), the Jews—his kinspeople κατὰ σάρκα (9.3). As if to emphasize the corporate aspect of the problem he not only uses 'Israel' but he does so with much greater frequency than in the rest of the letters. We have already noted his similar use of λαός. Whatever difficulties Paul and his fellow Christians might have had with Jewish groups or individuals (e.g. 2 Cor. 11.24-25; 1 Thess. 2.14-15), in Romans 9–11 he tackles the question of the destiny of Israel as an ethnic and religious totality.

The salient points of Paul's discussion are set out below.

1. Not all who are descended from Israel belong to Israel and not all who are children of Abraham are his descendants (9.6-7). God in his mercy has called 'us' from Jews and Gentiles to be the people of God (9.23-25) which is composed of all who have faith (10.4, 9-10).[126]

2. Gentiles have been grafted on like a wild olive shoot to the olive tree to replace branches that have been broken off; they now share in the tree's riches (11.16-24). These Gentiles are supported by the holiness of the root and it is this that gives holiness to the branches. Davies has redrawn attention to the fact that the wild olive is naturally fruitless and only becomes fruitful when grafted on to the cultivated tree.[127] Gentiles can only bear fruit, therefore, when grafted onto the tree whose root is Abraham.

3. Israel pursued righteousness as if it were based upon the law and works, not on faith (9.30-32). This faith comes from hearing Christ preached, but not all have heeded the gospel (10.14-17).

4. As in the past, a remnant of Israel will be saved (9.27; 11.4-6) and it will be chosen by grace. But when the fulness of the Gentiles comes in then all Israel will be saved (11.25).

126. By a judicious reversal of the clauses in Hos. 2.25 (LXX), Paul brings mention of believing Jews and Gentiles closer to 'those who were not my people I will call my people'. Thus λαός, by the manipulation of the OT text, is used for Christian believers and a verse which originally referred to the return of the ten tribes is now applied to include incoming Gentile believers. See Sanday and Headlam, *Romans*, pp. 263-64.

127. Davies, *Jewish and Pauline Studies*, pp. 153-56.

Paul's belief that all Israel will be saved through God's mercy falls within God's purpose to have mercy on all people (11.32). For the present, however, the situation is that some Jews have become believers and some have not (11.25). Thus far the position seems identical to that described in Acts, but the similarity is only on the surface. 'Israel' in Romans 9–11, for all its apparently corporate character, is simply the collective noun for the Jews, with the emphasis on those who have not believed. They will be saved at the end but the remnant of Israel that is being chosen by grace is made up of Jews who in faith have entered the Body of Christ. They are not being saved by being members of Israel because that is Israel κατὰ σάρκα (1 Cor. 10.18), a description repeated at the outset of these three chapters (9.3). They have all the contrary qualities that 'flesh' has for Paul.[128] Paul is concerned for the salvation of Israel as a part of the salvation of all human beings; he is not concerned for the *restoration* of Israel as the people of God and it is significant that ἀποκαθίστημι and ἀποκατάστασις do not occur in the Pauline corpus. Israel is beloved of God as regards election but most Israelites are the enemies of God as regards the gospel and their function has been to be disobedient so that 'you' now receive mercy.[129] It is by this mercy that Israel will receive mercy (11.28-31).

The salvation of Israel will take place when the full number of the Gentiles has come in, but the Gentiles and believing Jews are by faith entering the Body of Christ. This is how the rest of the Jews will finally be saved, as Rom. 11.12 clearly implies. Using the figure of the olive, Paul believes that the natural branches that have been broken off can be grafted back so as to become true descendants of Abraham, provided that they do not persist in their unbelief (11.23-24). That not all who are descended from Israel belong to Israel (9.6) seems to express the thought found in Rom. 2.9 about the nature of the true Jew. Thus, although Romans 9–11 shows Paul's impassioned and genuine anguish for his kinsmen, it could also be his most subtle and extended attempt to take over the inheritance and title of Israel for the church. If this

---

128. Cranford, 'Election and Ethnicity', pp. 27-41, challenges the growing view that Paul does not limit Israel's election as an ethnic group. The remnant ensures the continuation of covenant privileges but the boundaries of the people of Israel and the people of God are not the same.

129. Barth, *People of God*, p. 37, notes that it is Israel's rejection of the gospel (hardening) that leads to the acceptance of the Gentiles.

6. *Luke, Paul and Israel* 209

is so then it would agree with Gal. 3.6-14 and 6.16.[130]

In order to support his thesis Paul needs to show that the historical Israel has always resisted God's word, that the Gentiles are to be included in God's salvation and that God has foreordained a true remnant. Paul does this by using the Scriptures, notably Isaiah, and it is another distinctive mark of Romans 9–11 that it contains more citations from Isaiah than are found elsewhere in the rest of his letters. Among the citations are:

> Though the number of the sons of Israel be as the sand of the sea, only a remnant of them will be saved (9.27; Isa. 10.22).
>
> Behold I am laying in Zion a stone that will make men stumble, a rock that make them fall; he who believes in him will not be put to shame (9.33; Isa. 28.16).
>
> I have been found by those who did not seek me; I have shown myself to those who did not ask for me (10.20; Isa. 65.1).
>
> All day long I have held out my hands to a disobedient and contrary people (10.21; Isa. 65.2).
>
> God gave them a spirit of stupor, eyes that should not see and ears that should not hear, down to this very day (11.8; Isa. 29.10).

I have presented one possible reading of Romans 9–11 and it verges on one for which Paul has been accused of anti-Semitism.[131] The charge has been refuted by W.D. Davies on the grounds that Paul's theology in these chapters is within the bounds of pre-Jamnian Jewish debate.[132] Davies places Paul in the context of the expectation of the imminent end of the age and at a time when it is questionable whether Christianity was a religious movement separate from Judaism.[133] Davies believes that these two determining factors were not recognized when the letters were later read by Gentile Christians after Jamnia, in the period when Christianity and Judaism separated. The Gentiles 'took Paul to be demanding a complete rejection of the ways of Judaism',[134] but Paul

---

130. Davies, *Jewish and Pauline Studies*, p. 128: 'Galatians demands a clean repudiation of the dominant traditional understanding of Israel'.

131. Davies, *Jewish and Pauline Studies*, pp. 123-52, esp. 133-35, gives reasons for rejecting the charge that Paul was anti-Semitic made by Ruether, *Faith and Fratricide*, p. 104.

132. Davies, *Jewish and Pauline Studies*, pp. 135-37.

133. Davies, *Jewish and Pauline Studies*, pp. 133-35.

134. Davies, *Jewish and Pauline Studies*, p. 137.

himself saw signs of this development, and in Romans 9–11 'determined to combat it'.[135]

Davies' argument for seeing Romans 9–11 in the context of a debate within Judaism is very persuasive yet, as Davies recognizes, Paul failed to rectify the developing situation. And it is not difficult to see why he failed: Romans 9–11 came too late.[136] In his other letters Paul had gone too far along the line of attacking, or at least being indifferent to, key areas of Jewish belief and practice. This attitude is present in the earlier chapters of Romans, and even as late at 9.31–10.5 Paul repeats his view that Israel did not pursue righteousness by faith and that Christ is the end or goal of the law. Nor is Paul clear about how the undoubted salvation of Israel will be accomplished. In Isa. 59.20 the prophet speaks of the deliverer who will come 'for the sake of (ἕνεκεν) Zion'. In Paul's version the deliverer will come 'out of (ἐκ, Rom. 11.26-27) Zion' and Davies cautiously concludes that this will be Christ coming from the heavenly Jerusalem.[137]

Our present concern, as in Chapter 5, is with how Paul was understood or misunderstood, rather than with his actual intentions: only so might we be able to see Luke's purpose. The first and obvious difference is that Luke was writing after 70 CE when the separation of Christians from Judaism would have been greater than in Paul's time. Secondly, the expectation of an imminent end had faded considerably and although Luke retains belief in Christ's coming he cannot realistically have seen it as imminent. These two conditions are exactly those in which Paul's letters could be taken to support and even encourage Gentile antagonism towards Judaism. These were the results that Luke was determined to refute in the interest of unity between Jews and Gentiles in the church and, perhaps, between Jews and Christians.

There is, of course, a very considerable measure of agreement between Paul and Luke. They agree that faith in Jesus as Messiah is essential and that now is the age of the Spirit. Because of this Gentiles are coming in, as Isaiah prophesied, but Paul and Luke appear to disagree on what it is that the Gentiles enter. Both can be strongly critical of those Jews who

---

135. Davies, *Jewish and Pauline Studies*, p. 138.
136. Barth, *People of God*, pp. 19-20, suggests a development of Paul's views from 1 Thessalonians to Romans. We should not fasten on 'any particular dictum of the apostle'. But when the dicta are in conflict, how was (or is) the reader to choose?
137. Davies, *Jewish and Pauline Studies*, pp. 140-42; also Sanders, *Jewish People*, p. 194.

refuse to believe or who oppose the gospel, but they recognize that this reaction to God's word has also been prophesied by Isaiah (Acts 28.26-27; Rom. 11.8, cf. 10.21). Even so, both expect God's final salvation of Israel.

As for Paul's actual beliefs about the church and its connection with Israel, as distinct from how they were later perceived, these have been persuasively put by E.P. Sanders.[138] In brief, Sanders concludes that, apart from Gal. 6.16, the title 'Israel' is not applied to the group of Jewish and Gentile believers but that his conception of the group is based upon the idea of the 'true Israel'. It is this Israel that the Gentiles are entering and which will finally contain all Israel.[139] Sanders notes a similarity between Paul and the Qumran covenanters, who thought of themselves as the only truly obedient Jews and yet were unwilling to apply the title to themselves to the exclusion of other Jews.[140] Sanders believes that Paul would have been horrified by the thought that Christians were a 'third entity'.[141]

Luke, like Paul, does not use 'Israel' to include Jewish and Gentile believers but, unlike Paul, he does not speak of a remnant: λεῖμμα (Rom. 11.5) and ὑπόλειμμα (Rom. 9.27) have no place in Luke–Acts. Luke also expects the final restoration of Israel as an eschatological event (Acts 1.6-7; 3.21; cf. Rom. 9.25), but there is a difference in their views of Israel in the interim. Paul does not see Israel having a positive role to play in the present but, for Luke, Israel exists for the purpose of bringing in the Gentiles—that is Israel's glory (Lk. 2.32; Acts 13.47; 15.16-17) and it will fulfil the promises of Amos 9.11-12 and Isa. 49.6. It is the way in which the tent of David is being rebuilt.

It is partly because of Israel's continuing function that Luke *must* portray Paul as a devout Jew who keeps the law and who conducts his missions almost exclusively in synagogues. It is why Paul is represented as obedient to James and why Acts 15 deliberately contradicts Paul's own account in Galatians 2.[142] Without doubt, Paul is the hero of the latter part of Acts, but he is a thoroughly Lukan hero.

---

138. Sanders, *Jewish People*, pp. 171-79.
139. Sanders, *Jewish People*, p. 173.
140. Sanders, *Jewish People*, pp. 175-76.
141. Sanders, *Jewish People*, p. 173.
142. Luke's version may also have been concerned with historical accuracy. See Taylor, *Antioch*, pp. 96-97.

Chapter 7

LUKE, MATTHEW AND ISRAEL

We conclude this survey by comparing Luke's view of Israel with that of a near contemporary, Matthew. This is followed by a discussion of the ending of Acts and Luke's final statement on the church's relation to Israel. In the earlier discussions of Christology and atonement (Chapters 4 and 5) I compared material from the Gospels of Matthew and Luke in order to show how Luke stood aside from the general development of Christian thinking near the end of the first century.[1] There was no need in that discussion to consider whether or not Luke knew Matthew's Gospel, but in this chapter that question cannot be avoided since the position I have come to adopt is that Luke knew and used Matthew's Gospel. I have made no attempt to deal fully with the question of Luke's sources for reasons of space but I must give some measure of explanation and comment.

When I began this work I assumed that material common to Luke and Matthew but not in Mark derived from a saying source 'Q'. But, as the work has developed, I have concluded that the difference and contrasts between the two Gospels are such as to indicate Luke's deliberate contradiction of some parts of Matthew. Luke has pursued his policy on two broad fronts: by changing the order of material he found in Matthew and by refashioning parts of Matthew's narrative. The details of how and why Luke carried out this policy are discussed in what follows.

There is, perhaps, an understandable reluctance on the part of Gospel commentators to regard later writers as being strongly dissatisfied with the work of their predecessors. Differences that do occur are more likely to be ascribed to their different church situations rather than to major conflicts of belief. Tailoring material to the local needs was an important

---

1. Fenton, *Saint Matthew*, p. 11, suggests the last quarter of the first century or early in the second; Filson, *St Matthew*, p. 15, 'the eighties or even the nineties'; Green, *Matthew*, p. 33, between 90–100 CE.

factor but we have no good reason to suppose that it was the only one. Paul's letters give ample evidence of Christian dissent over deeply important issues.

Luke's prologue (1.1-4) may contain a hint of dissatisfaction with the attempts of 'many [who] have taken in hand (ἐπεχείρησαν) to compile a narrative',[2] especially if ἐπιχειρέω has the implication of failure that it has outside the NT.[3] The only other occurrences of the verb in the NT are in Acts 9.29 and 19.13. In the first case, some Hellenists undertake (ἐπεχείρουν) to kill Paul and, in the second case, Jewish exorcists undertake (ἐπεχείρησαν) to use the name of τοῦ κυρίου Ἰησοῦ in an attempt to cast out evil spirits. They then find themselves mastered (κατακυριεύσας, 19.16—a nice pun) by the evil spirit. Both cases therefore end in failure. Some recent commentators acknowledge the possibility of implied criticism in the prologue[4] as did Origen, although he excluded the other evangelists from the 'many'.[5] Conzelmann implicitly recognizes this critical aspect of Luke's purpose when he says, '[Luke] does not merely want to complement but to replace his predecessors. He offers not a contribution to the tradition but *the* tradition.'[6] The interpretation of Lk. 1.1 and of Luke's intention to write an orderly account (καθεξῆς, 1.3) must be made in the light of whether his writings show significant points of disagreement with, even contradiction of, earlier writings. This is not just a case of whether Luke had more reliable sources than his predecessors but whether his differences were sufficiently deep that he had to challenge their view of things, as Conzelmann's words suggest. Clearly, a great deal hinges on Luke's use of καθεξῆς. Goulder argues that in view of the supportive ἀνατάξασθαι, καθεξῆς should be translated as 'in sequence', which is the meaning elsewhere in Luke–Acts. The reason for this, according to

2. Brown, 'The Role of the Prologues', p. 102.
3. Moulton and Milligan, *Vocabulary*, pp. 250-51, give several cases of ἐπιχειρέω in instances of failure but they conclude that the idea of failure lies not in the verb itself but in the context. In Josephus, *Life*, 40.338, the verb describes the attempts of Justus to write history but with little regard for the truth.
4. E.g. Fitzmyer, *Luke*, pp. 291-92; Danker, *Jesus and the new Age*, p. 24. Marshall, *Luke*, p. 40, sees no disparagement. Alexander, *Preface*, pp. 109-110, makes no comment on the instances in Acts. 'Logically speaking it is impossible to escape the derogatory implications when the phrase is used in the third person'. Yet 'Luke might have used it without taking much note of the precise meaning' (p. 110).
5. Origen, *Homily on Luke 1*.
6. Conzelmann, 'Luke's Place', p. 305.

Goulder, is that 'Luke is writing a reconciliation of Mark and Matthew to reassure Theophilus that the apparently dissonant Gospel tradition is trustworthy'.[7] One difficulty with this explanation is that the traditions of Mark and Matthew *are* actually dissonant in places, and if Theophilus had all three Gospels in front of him he would be even more confused than he was before Luke's texts arrived.

Matthew or 'Q'?

The majority of scholars agree that Luke's predecessors for traditions about Jesus were Mark, Matthew and a collection of sayings, Q. These are among the candidates for Luke's 'many' and hence for being set in order. The majority also accept Luke's use of Mark but the choice between Matthew and Q is more open.[8]

If the problem facing source critics was restricted to giving an explanation of the agreements between Luke and Matthew then the solution would appear to be obvious: the later writer used the earlier. Unfortunately for this solution the Q hypothesis has taken on a life of its own. No longer is it just supposed to solve a problem of literary dependence but it seems to offer a further benefit, that of enabling critics to get behind some of the gospel sayings to the words and teaching of the historical Jesus. But the stubborn non-existence of Q, except in the minds of NT critics, is an obvious drawback. To this must be added the disagreements about its provenance, contents, language and whether it was a written or an oral tradition.[9] Kümmel's comment, that agreement between Luke and Matthew 'proves a common source',[10] goes well beyond the proper meaning of 'to prove'. Indeed, concepts of proof or disproof for *any* source theory are quite inappropriate. And even if the existence of a sayings collection were historically certain, *it still would not answer the question of whether Luke knew and used Matthew*. The doubtful need for Q has been succinctly put by E.P. Sanders: 'If...Luke knew Matthew, it is no longer possible to distinguish between 'M' and 'Q' material. 'Q' material is simply material that Luke took from Matthew but is not in Mark'.[11]

---

7. Goulder, *New Paradigm*, pp. 199-200, 203-204.
8. Green, 'Credibility', p. 149, held a similar view but does so no longer.
9. Petrie, '"Q" is only What You Make It'.
10. Kümmel, *Introduction*, pp. 66-67.
11. Sanders, 'Overlap', p. 454.

Those parts of the NT written prior to the Gospels do not point to the existence of a major collection of Jesus' sayings. There are three occasions in 1 Corinthians where Paul cites teachings of the Lord that may be related to sayings of Jesus recorded in the Gospels. These are 1 Cor. 7.10, cf. Mk 10.11; 1 Cor. 9.14, cf. Mt. 10.10 and Lk. 10.7; 1 Cor. 11.23-25, cf. Mt. 26.26-28; Mk 14.22-24 and Lk. 22.17-19. Paul does not describe the injunction to bless persecutors (Rom. 12.14) as coming from the Lord, but it may be related to sayings in Mt. 5.44 and Lk. 6.28. The conclusion is that, prior to the Gospels, there is little clear evidence for the use of sayings attributed to Jesus.

One of the principal objections to Luke's knowledge of Matthew concerns the ordering of the common material.[12] Streeter's oft-quoted opinion, that if Luke used Matthew then he produced the order of a crank,[13] is supported by Kümmel who finds it inconceivable that Luke should have shattered the sermon on the mount.[14] Similar surprise is expressed by Fitzmyer.[15] Attempts to answer these criticisms either try to minimize the extent of the disorder or to show that Matthew's order is still faintly visible in Luke.[16] Goulder, for example, has proposed that Luke used a scroll of Matthew first in the forward direction, then in reverse.[17] Solutions of this type are in danger of conceding too much and they fail to ask the question, did Luke deliberately break up Matthew's formal scheme and are any traces of Matthew's order an oversight on Luke's part? Luke's prologue implies not only dissatisfaction with the 'many' but that a principal reason for his dissatisfaction was concerned with order and sequence. If it is accepted that Luke broadly follows the Markan order,[18] then the only other material of known order and which is differently placed by Luke is the material in common with Matthew.

There are various understandings of what is meant by a difference of order of material shared between the two Gospels and these are discussed by C.M. Tuckett.[19] By change of order I mean (1) the dislocation of

12. See Goulder, *New Paradigm*, and 'Order of a Crank'.
13. Streeter, *The Four Gospels*, p. 183.
14. Kümmel, *Introduction*, p. 64.
15. Fitzmyer, *Luke*, p. 74.
16. Drury, *Tradition*, ch. 6; Farrer, 'Dispensing with Q'.
17. Goulder, 'Order of a Crank', p. 121.
18. Fitzmyer, *Luke*, pp. 71-72, lists seven changes but Kümmel, *Introduction*, p. 58, lists four.
19. Tuckett, 'Arguments from Order', pp. 197-200.

sequential verses, and (2) the presence of other material between sayings or events which are nevertheless preserved in the same order. Examples may be helpful.

	Matthew	Luke
1	5.3, 4, 6, 11, 12	6.20-23
	5.13	14.34
	5.15	8.16
	5.18	16.17
2	10.27-33	12.3-9
		12.10-50 contains material found only in Luke and from Mt. 6.25-33.
	10.34-36	12.51-53

Arguments for Luke's use of a particular source are not susceptible to a knock-down proof that commands acceptance by all. Scholars of undoubted ability and integrity hold theories about Gospel relationships that others of equal ability and integrity regard as unacceptable. I have not, therefore, attempted to show that Luke knew Matthew before arguing that he made changes to Matthew; rather the reverse. The proposal here is that differences in order and content between the two Gospels are such as to imply a deliberate repudiation by Luke of some aspects of Matthew. I have already discussed some differences between the Gospels (Chapters 4 and 5, above); in this chapter I shall discuss differences that reflect the evangelists' views of Israel and the church.

Matthew and Israel

Matthew wrote at a time when the church was moving towards the identification of itself with the 'new' or 'true' Israel.[20] As far as the historical Israel is concerned he makes it quite clear that it contains Jews only and that the disciples, like Jesus himself, are sent to the lost sheep of the house of Israel (10.5-6; 15.24). Yet, as Richardson points out, it is only in the early chapters that Matthew expresses hope for Israel (1.21; 2.6; 4.16)[21] and of these only 1.21 speaks of salvation for Israel. Apart from this single case the vocabulary of restoration and redemption that Luke applies to Israel is absent from Matthew. In 17.10-13, Jesus tells his

---

20. Richardson, *Israel*, p. 188, and references there.
21. Richardson, *Israel*, p. 189, but only 1.21 is Matthew's own comment—the others are OT citations.

disciples that Elijah does come (present) and will restore all things (future). But with this role being given to the Baptist (17.13) Matthew's readers are left in a quandary because John is now dead and has failed to restore things (14.1-12).[22]

Two further examples demonstrate the different attitudes of the evangelists towards Israel. In the stories of the healing of the centurion's servant both evangelists agree that the centurion's faith is greater than that found in Israel (Mt. 8.10; Lk. 7.9). Matthew follows this with a saying about who will dine with the Patriarchs and that the sons of the kingdom will be cast out. Luke, on the other hand, separates the sayings from the story of the centurion, and those who will be thrust out are 'all you workers of iniquity' (13.27-29; cf. Ps. 6.9). Luke thus avoids Matthew's blanket condemnation of Israel and replaces it with what should perhaps be seen as a typically pious Jewish thought, that those who persist in wickedness will have no share in the world to come.

The second example is in the parable of the vineyard. Both evangelists place the telling of the parable in the temple and both versions warn of the destruction of the farmers and that the vineyard will be given to others (Mt. 21.41; Lk. 20.16, cf. Mk 12.9). Matthew alone adds the comment to the chief priests and Pharisees that 'the kingdom of God will be taken away from you and given to a nation producing the fruits of it' (21.43, 45).

Matthew does not specifically identify the church as the true Israel or as being under a new covenant,[23] but he does regard the church as a world-wide body that holds the keys of the kingdom and has the power to bind and loose (16.18-19). In this context ἐκκλησία has taken on the role attributed to the assembly of Israel (*qahal*) in 1 Kings 8 and 2 Chronicles 6.[24] So that even if the identification is not explicit, there is a strong suggestion of the church as the true fulfilment (and, perhaps, the replacement) of Israel.[25]

---

22. The future ἀποκαταστήσει (cf. καταστῆσαι, Sir. 48.10) causes the problem. McNeile, *St Matthew*, p. 253, reads into the text 'but so far from restoring all things', and holds that because John was killed, the way was left open for the Messiah's suffering (cf. F.W. Green, *Saint Matthew*, p. 211); Filson, *St Matthew*, p. 193.

23. Bornkamm, 'End Expectation and the Church', p. 39, sees the struggle with Israel 'as still a struggle within its own walls'.

24. Bornkamm, 'End Expectation and the Church', p. 38.

25. France, *Evangelist and Teacher*, pp. 210-13.

The possibility that Matthew has a theology of 'newness' in his treatment of Israel has been the subject of debate among Matthean scholars. Although this debate is necessary in order to understand Matthew's true intention, our concern is not so much with his intentions as with how the Gospel might have been understood by a first-century reader, especially one grounded in the LXX. It is not uncommon for readers to misunderstand a writer's intentions and then to attack them. The first theory we must examine concerns the structure of the Gospel. It has been argued that Matthew divided his Gospel into five main sections, each containing narrative and an extended discourse, and that these five sections were intended to correspond to the books of the Pentateuch. Among proponents of this view are Bacon,[26] F.W. Green[27] and, of a five-fold division only, J.C. Fenton.[28] The theory has been examined by W.D. Davies who has concluded that 'the pentateuchal approach must remain questionable when taken on its literary merits'.[29] Correct though Davies most probably is, we must take account of the considerable body of opinion that has seen enough evidence for accepting the pentateuchal structure. And once a five-fold structure has been recognized then similar patterns can be taken as supporting evidence. For example, in the birth stories there are five references to the fulfilment of prophecies, the last of which (N.B. 'prophets', 2.23) is not an OT citation although Matthew, presumably from his five-fold plan, gives it the same form as the other four prophecies. There are also five mentions of the title 'Christ' and five different titles for Jesus: Christ, Emmanuel (1.23), king of the Jews (2.2), 'my [God's] son' (2.15) and Nazarene (2.23). To these patterns can be added the five dreams through which Joseph and the Magi are given divine instructions (1.20-21; 2.12, 13, 19-20, 22). A similar five-fold structure exists elsewhere in Jewish literature: for example, Psalms and the original form of *Pirqe Aboth*.[30] It is quite possible that Luke recognized the five-fold structure in Matthew, saw its pentateuchal implications and decided that it must be broken up because a new Pentateuch would imply a new law and a new Israel. It is interesting to note that part of A.M. Farrer's argument for Luke's dependence upon Matthew

26. Bacon, *Studies in Matthew*, pp. 81-82.
27. Green, *Saint Matthew*, pp. 4-6.
28. Fenton, *St Matthew*, pp. 14-17, notes the five collections of sayings but makes no comment on a new Pentateuch.
29. Davies, *Sermon*, p. 25.
30. Schürer–Vermes, *History*, III, p. 215.

Six Major Differences

1. *The Birth Stories*

R.E. Brown has listed eleven points of agreement between the birth cycles in Matthew and Luke,[32] ten of which occur in Mt. 1.18-21. But these agreements are small compared to the great number of differences between the two cycles that indicate a real difference of motive.[33] We have already discussed the differences in the two genealogies and their significance in the evangelist's understanding of Israel. Davies has suggested that Matthew's Gospel contains, in effect, two accounts of Jesus' origin: the historical origin in the genealogy and the supernatural origin by the act of the Holy Spirit.[34] If this is so then we might expect to find a similar double origin in Luke, and so there is but with the order reversed. Luke's genealogy does not show Jesus to be son of God in a divine sense or in a way that is not shared by all other men on the list. Luke places the human genealogy after the baptism and immediately before the temptation stories (4.1-13) in order to bring out the humanity of Jesus in his temptations and ministry. Matthew, by contrast, places the supernatural origin nearer to the ministry and so draws attention to his more obviously messianic view of the ministry, a Matthean characteristic we discussed in Chapter 4.

After Jesus' birth, Matthew tells of the magi following the star to Bethlehem (2.1-12). Davies sees a possible reference here to Moses overcoming the Egyptian sorcerers (Exod. 7–8, but σοφιστάς, 7.11, ἐπαοιδοί, 7.22), hence implying that Jesus is the new Moses.[35] If Luke appreciated the allusion it would have led him to omit the story and replace it with the story of shepherds with its Davidic allusions (Lk. 2.8-

---

31. Farrer, 'Dispensing with Q', pp. 79-82.
32. Brown, *Birth*, pp. 34-35. Green, 'Credibility', pp. 143-45 gives reasons for (a) thinking that Luke knew and used Matthew's birth stories and (b) for Luke's changes.
33. Drury, *Tradition*, pp. 123-25, compares the two cycles of birth stories and concludes that 'Luke's version impresses...more by its contrasts to Matthew than by its resemblances'.
34. Davies, *Sermon*, pp. 71-72.
35. Davies, *Sermon*, pp. 78-80.

20). But the principal motive for the change would be that magi belong to a class inimical to Luke (Acts 8.18-24; 13.6-12; 16.16-18) and, furthermore, the story would introduce Gentiles into his plan far too early.

Even more important for the present discussion is Matthew's account of the stay in Egypt which contains obvious references to Israel and Moses (2.13-15, 19-23). According to Matthew, it was to fulfil the prophecy of Hos. 11.1, 'Out of Egypt have I called my son', a verse that originally applied to Israel. The first Hebrew to visit Egypt was Abram (Gen. 12.10) but it was Joseph who was compelled to go there (Gen. 37). Now a second Joseph is told to go there for his son's safety. The family returns when 'those who sought the child's life are dead' and Davies notes the use of the plural (τεθνήκασιν, 2.20), whereas it was Herod alone who tried to kill Jesus. Davies suggests that this may reflect the same plural when God tells Moses to return to Egypt (Exod. 4.18-19).[36] Herod's slaughter of the children (2.16) is a clear reminder to the reader of Pharaoh's attempt to kill the male Hebrew babies from which Moses escapes (Exod. 1.16, 22; 2.1-10). There are, therefore, very strong and obvious indications in these stories that Matthew was pointing to a new exodus for (a new?) Israel under a new Moses. There is one further point: we know that for Matthew Israel did not include the Samaritans (10.5-6). The Jewish emphasis is present in Matthew's conflated quotation of Mic. 5.1, 3 where he sees Jesus as the ruler of God's people but adds to Micah's verse that Bethlehem is in the land of Judah.

2. *The Sermon on the Mount*

It is in Luke's treatment of the sermon that the questions of order become most acute and obvious. The material that Luke has in common with Matthew 5–7 is found scattered in Luke 6, 11 and 14, a source of amazement to some critics (see nn. 14, 15 above). Luke thus demolishes the first of Matthew's pentateuchal pillars. But, even before Jesus speaks, the reader is aware that something different is intended in each of the sermons to the disciples. In Mt. 5.1-2 Jesus goes up the mountain, sits down and teaches his disciples whereas, according to Lk. 6.12, Jesus had been up the mountain praying with his disciples and appointing the twelve. He then comes down, stands on a level place and addresses a great crowd of people from 'all Judaea, Jerusalem and the sea coasts of Tyre and Sidon' (6.17). The four changes in the setting begin to look

---

36. Davies, *Sermon*, p. 78.

like deliberate and systematic contradictions by Luke. Matthew's sermon is widely supposed to be modelled on the giving of the law on Sinai but, at the same time, Jesus interprets and intensifies its demands.[37] By making the antitheses, 'you have heard said...but I say to you', Jesus restates the commands on killing, adultery, divorce, swearing oaths, vengeance and loving one's neighbour (5.21-22, 27-28, 31-46). These restatements are absent from Luke, for whom the law of Moses is sufficient. Matthew's presentation of Jesus as the new and superior lawgiver can be seen again in Mt. 11.29-30 when Jesus contrasts the easy yoke of his discipleship with the implied yoke of the law.[38] Luke mentions the yoke of the law only once, when, in the circumcision debate, Peter speaks of a yoke 'which neither our fathers nor we have been able to bear' (Acts 15.10), but there is no mention of the yoke being replaced by another. If Matthew's sermon was intended to show Jesus as the new Moses then it is clear that Luke is more moderate in his claims and, at the same time, closer to the account of Moses coming down from the mountain in Exod. 34.29-32. Reading Matthew, one might get the impression of God giving the law rather than Moses receiving it. Luke, by contrast, shows Jesus as a Mosaic figure coming down from the mountain and giving the law to the people of Israel. Luke's description of the size of the crowd and the places from where it came seems intended as a parallel to the Israelites in Exodus 34. Luke shows Jesus *like* Moses but not as a new and superior replacement. The distinction between the two portraits may seem an over-subtle one. But the Lukan Jesus, both in the sermon and elsewhere, is based on the prophet promised by Moses, whom God would raise up to do the things that Moses did. Luke's Mosaic typology is designed with this aim but Matthew's typology, on the other hand, goes further by giving Jesus' interpretation of the law as if it were being brought by a new Moses.[39] The difference in the presentations becomes more obvious when accounts of the transfiguration are compared.

---

37. Fenton, *St Matthew*, pp. 76-78.
38. Filson, *St Matthew*, pp. 143-44; Green, *Saint Matthew*, pp. 179-80, notes a parallel between Mt. 11.28-29 and Sir. 51.23-27 on discipleship. Green, *Matthew*, p. 122, points out that, for the rabbis, the yoke of the kingdom was the Torah.
39. Green, 'Credibility', p. 137: 'Though Luke depicts Jesus as personally obedient to the Mosaic law, he shows little or no interest in Jesus as its definitive interpreter which is what the Sermon on the Mount...is basically concerned with'.

3. *The Transfiguration*

We have already discussed some of the major differences between Luke's account and those of Mark and Matthew. The most important one for the present discussion is that whereas Matthew and Mark depict Jesus alone being transfigured, Luke describes Jesus, Moses and Elijah appearing in glory (9.30-31). Both Mark and Matthew bring out the superiority of Jesus to Moses and Elijah, the latter soon to be identified with the secondary figure of the Baptist (Mt. 17.11-13). And if Jesus is superior then the implication is that his followers are superior to theirs. Luke, by describing Moses and Elijah having the same glory as Jesus, makes a quite remarkable statement for a Christian writer towards the end of the first century.

4. *The Resurrection*

Benedict Green regards the accounts of Jesus' burial as the first item in the resurrection cycles since the burial is presupposed by the discovery of the empty tomb.[40] And here, in spite of their agreements, Luke and Matthew show significant differences (Mt. 27.57-61; Lk. 23.50-54). Matthew describes Joseph of Arimathea as a disciple of Jesus whereas Luke, following Mk 15.43, says that he is a member of the council (βουλευτής) who was looking for the kingdom of God which suggests that he was still an unconverted Jew. Luke goes further: Joseph is good and righteous (δίκαιος, 23.50: cf. Zechariah and Elizabeth, 1.6, and Simeon, 2.25) and has not consented to the council's actions. To underline Joseph's origins, Luke adds that Arimathea is a Jewish city. The overall effect of Luke's account of the burial is to draw out Joseph's continuity with the pious Jews of the birth stories. Matthew's approach is that 'in his view, there is no middle way between identification with the old Israel, and identification with the disciples of Jesus'.[41]

The differences between the evangelists' accounts of the appearances of the risen Jesus are numerous and obvious.[42] The first of these is the location. In Mt. 28.7, the women are told by the angel that Jesus will meet his disciples in Galilee and then, while still in Jerusalem, Jesus

---

40. Green, *Matthew*, p. 225.
41. Green, *Matthew*, p. 225.
42. Goulder, 'Mark xvi, 1–8', pp. 235-40, sees some agreements between Matthew and Luke in their burial stories.

appears to the women to tell the disciples to go to Galilee (28.10).[43] This is the only appearance of the risen Jesus to the women in the synoptic Gospels and it is unnecessary in Luke's account. Matthew's final mention of Galilee is as the site of the mountain where Jesus delivers his mission charge (28.16-20). John Fenton considers that Galilee symbolizes the Gentile world and that it refers back to 'Galilee of the Gentiles' (Mt. 4.15; cf. Isa. 9.1).[44] Luke retains a reference to Galilee but it is the place where Jesus had prophesied his resurrection (24.6; cf. 9.22).

In Luke, the appearances occur in or near Jerusalem; Emmaus, which may seem to be an exception, is defined by its distance from Jerusalem (24.13).[45] R.H. Lightfoot suggests that Luke did not find the same theological importance in Jerusalem as Mark finds in Galilee[46] but the fact is that Luke mentions Jerusalem five times (24.13, 18, 33, 47, 52) and on one occasion refers to it as 'the city' (24.49). It is not the *same* importance but it is an equal one. The references to Jerusalem in Luke 24 serve as a prelude to the early chapters of Acts where it is the starting point of the Christian mission so that the city's importance to Luke can hardly be in doubt. It also shows that, unlike his predecessors, Luke sees the mission as beginning with the Jews (Jerusalem) and not the Gentiles (Galilee). Lightfoot has also drawn attention to *T. Zeb.* 9.7-8, which Lohmeyer saw as a parallel to Mk 16.7 but in which Jerusalem is replaced by Galilee. The passage contains a valuable insight into the importance attached to Jerusalem in the last days.[47]

> And thereafter you will remember the Lord and repent, and he will turn you around because he is merciful and compassionate... And thereafter the Lord himself will arise upon you, the light of righteousness with healing and compassion in his wings. He will liberate every captive of the sons of men from Beliar, and every spirit of error will be trampled down. He will turn all nations to being zealous of him. And you shall see [God in human form], he whom the Lord will choose; Jerusalem is his name.[48]

---

43. Lightfoot, *Locality and Doctrine*, pp. 70-71: 'Galilee is for Matthew as for St Mark, the most truly holy land, the scene of revelation'.

44. Fenton, *St Matthew*, p. 452.

45. Fitzmyer, *Luke*, p. 1562. Evans, *Saint Luke*, p. 896, regards the absence of 'while he was still in Galilee' as a sign that Luke was intent on revising Mark's text which was an obstacle to his use of Jerusalem. It also removed the apocalyptic view of the resurrection in Mark and Matthew.

46. Lightfoot, *Locality and Doctrine*, p. 79 n. 1.

47. Lightfoot, *Locality and Doctrine*, pp. 73-74.

48. Kee, 'Twelve Patriarchs', *OTP*, 1, p. 807.

The ideas of repentance, turning round and the liberation of the captives are far more in tune with Luke's theology than with Mark's, so that Lohmeyer's suggestion becomes quite unnecessary in Luke's case. If either evangelist were influenced by the text it would surely have been Luke.

In both Mt. 28.6 and Lk. 24.7-8, the resurrection is believed to fulfil Jesus' own prophecies but Luke is alone in supporting his view by using the OT: 'the prophets' (24.25), the Scriptures 'beginning with Moses and the prophets' (24.27), the psalms (24.44-45) and 'thus it is written' (24.46). All these have pointed to the death and resurrection of Jesus and it is he who interprets them to the two disciples while they are on the road (ἐν τῷ ὁδῷ, 24.32). This last phrase is probably a Lukan pun, since the Way is one of his terms for the Christian church (e.g. Acts 19.9, 23). It is the Christian Way in which the full meaning of the Scriptures is opened up by the risen Jesus (cf. 24.45). Whereas Luke believes that Israel's Scriptures are fulfilled by the death and resurrection of Jesus, Matthew is silent about this fulfilment in the resurrection stories.

The continuity of the risen Lord with the earthly Jesus is a vital element in Luke's presentation and it is brought out by the stress on the physical nature of the risen Jesus who can be handled and can eat (24.39-43). The continuity is also brought out in other ways such as the appearance of the two men in dazzling clothing at the tomb (24.4). They point back to the transfiguration and forward to the ascension. This is shown not only in the phrase καὶ ἰδοὺ ἄνδρες δύο (Lk. 9.30; 24.4; Acts 1.10) but also by other verbal links: ἐξαστράπτων, 9.29; ἀστραπτούσῃ, 24.4; and ἐσθῆτι, 24.4; cf. ἐσθήσεσι, Acts 1.10. A third way in which the continuity is made is in the recapitulation of the major titles from the ministry. The two men at the tomb speak of Jesus as Son of Man (24.7) while the disciples refer to him as Jesus of Nazareth, prophet (24.19)[49] and Lord (24.34). When the risen Jesus speaks of himself it is as Christ, but now without any qualifying additions (24.26, 46). Thus the disciples on the human level use the terms they had used during the ministry, while the titles that describe the heavenly aspect, Son of Man and Christ, are used by the two figures from heaven or by the risen Jesus. This is further evidence of Luke's two-stage Christology and it is in marked contrast to Matthew's understanding in

---

49. Wanke, *Die Emmauszählung*, p. 64, points out the parallels to the Moses typology in Acts 3.22-23 and 7.35, 37.

which the resurrection reinforces, rather than changes, the Christology of the earthly Jesus.

Luke and Matthew also show significant differences in their descriptions of Jesus' commissioning his disciples. Davies notes three pieces of evidence in Matthew's version that are suggestive of the new Moses theme.[50]

1. The saying 'I am with you always' (28.20) has echoes of 'Emmanuel, which means God with us' (1.23); moreover, if the prologue contained the idea of a new Moses, then the idea might be expected to return at the end of the Gospel.
2. The mountain setting (28.16) recalls the sermon on the mount and the transfiguration, in both of which the new Moses theme has been detected. I would add to this that there may also be an allusion to the mountain scene of Moses' last appearance in Deut. 34.1-4 in which God shows Moses the promised land that Israel will possess. In Matthew, the new Moses will not be taken away but will be with his disciples in the mission to the nations.
3. In Mt. 28.19 Jesus sends his disciples to teach 'all that I have commanded' and Davies concludes that, although there is no explicit mention of Moses in these verses, 'Jesus is surely the new Moses, a greater than the old, who is the source of a new tradition of a new Israel'. Again, Matthew uses the resurrection to reinforce the 'greater than Moses' theme. Luke restricts his Moses typology to the earthly Jesus and although Peter describes Jesus in terms of the Mosaic prophet (Acts 3.22-23), he is, as Haenchen notes,[51] referring to the earthly and not the heavenly Jesus.

By contrast, Luke's account of the commissioning in the Gospel is set in the context of a meal and the disciples are commanded to preach repentance and forgiveness of sins to all nations in the name of Christ, beginning at Jerusalem (24.47). Not only is the Matthean promise of Christ's continuing presence absent but it is contradicted by Jesus' departure from Bethany (24.50) and again by the ascension story in Acts 1.9-11. It is also possible that Jesus' words 'while I was still (ἔτι

---

50. Davies, *Sermon*, pp. 85-86. The description of Jesus as meek (πραΰς, Mt. 11.29; 21.5) reflects the same description of Moses in Num. 12.3.

51. Haenchen, *Acts*, p. 209.

ὤν) with you' (Lk. 24.44) are a deliberate contradiction of Matthew's 'I am with you always, to the close of the age' (Mt. 28.20). As Luke saw it, it is not Christ who will be with the disciples since his place is now in heaven, hence the double account of the ascension. Instead, the apostles are to receive 'the promise of my Father', 'power from on high' (Lk. 24.49) and 'the power of the Holy Spirit (Acts 1.8; cf. Jn 16.5-7) until Jesus comes in the same way as he departed (Acts 1.11).

And, just as Matthew looks back to his prologue from the end of the Gospel, so too does Luke. The first incident is when the two disciples express their hope that Jesus would have been the one to redeem Israel (λυτροῦσθαι τὸν Ἰσραήλ, Lk. 24.21). In the second instance the disciples return to Jerusalem with great joy (χαρά, 24.41, 52) and they are continually in the temple, blessing God (ἐν τῷ ἱερῷ εὐλογοῦντες τὸν θεόν, 24.53). The vocabulary of this final section of the Gospel is strongly and deliberately reminiscent of the birth stories.[52] There can be little doubt that Luke intended to end his Gospel with obvious reminders of the purpose he so clearly stated in the birth stories: the hope of Israel's redemption and the joy which that hope brings to devout Jews.

5. Attitudes to the Pharisees

Luke shows far less antagonism towards Pharisees than does Matthew, although debate on this question continues to divide critics.[53] The Pharisees did not dominate Judaism at the time of Jesus and therefore Sanders finds 'no substantial conflict between Jesus and the Pharisees'.[54] However, after 70 CE they became increasingly influential and this has led Morton Smith to conclude that Luke and Matthew treat the Pharisees in the context of a debate between Christians and Jews in the

---

52. 'Jerusalem', Lk. 2.22, 25, 38, 41, 43, 45; εὐλογέω, 1.42, 64; 2.28; cf. εὐλογητός, 1.68; ἱερόν, 2.27, 37, 46; cf. ναός, 1.9, 21, 22; λύτρωσις, 1.68; 2.38; χαρά, 1.14; 2.10.

53. Ziesler, 'Pharisees', pp. 146-57. His conclusions have been contested by Kingsbury, 'The Pharisees in Luke–Acts', and by Neale, *Sinners*, pp. 105-107, who believes that Luke's treatment is the most negative of the synoptists. Neale argues that it is best to see Luke's views in terms of plot development (p. 108), but by restricting his study to Luke's Gospel he does not take account of Paul, the Pharisaic hero of Acts. Carrol, 'Luke's portrayal of the Pharisees', recognizes the complexity of the problem, and Brawley, *Luke–Acts and the Jews*, pp. 85-86, considers Luke's attitude ambivalent.

54. Sanders, *Jesus and Judaism*, p. 291.

eighties.[55] References to the Pharisees are therefore an important indicator as to how the two evangelists saw relations between Jews and Christians in their own time. This in turn will reflect their understandings of Israel. Matthew has some nineteen more references to Pharisees than Mark and he never has anything good to say about them. Luke, although by no means uncritical of Pharisees, omits eighteen of Matthew's references. The principal differences between the two evangelists are set out below.

1. Some of the Pharisees' criticisms of the Matthean Jesus are attributed to others by Luke. These include the accusation that Jesus is in league with Beelzebul (Mt. 9.34; 12.24; Lk. 11.15) and the request for a sign (Mt. 12.38; Lk. 11.16, 29-32). The question of tribute to Caesar is raised by Pharisees in Mt. 22.15-17 (par. Mk 12.13-14) but by scribes and chief priests in Lk. 20.19-20. In Mt. 19.3, Pharisees ask whether divorce is permissible (par. Mk 10.2) but the question is absent from Luke, although the saying on divorce is apparently given in the presence of Pharisees (Lk. 16.14, 18). In Mt. 21.42-45, the Pharisees and chief priests understand the saying about the stone rejected by the builders to be directed against them but, in Lk. 20.17-19, it is the scribes and chief priests who see themselves as the target. And it is the Pharisees who ask about the great commandment and the son of David (22.34-35) whereas in Mk 12.28-37 and Lk. 10.25-28 and 20.41-44 the question is raised by others or is a direct statement by Jesus.

Nevertheless, Matthew does acknowledge the teaching authority of the scribes and Pharisees who sit on Moses' seat. For this reason the Matthean Jesus tells his hearers to 'practice and observe whatever they tell you' (23.2-3) although it is open to question, in view of 15.1-20, whether πάντα includes the Pharisaic oral tradition. But if Jesus' disciples follow the teaching and not the hypocritical teachers then their righteousness will exceed that of the scribes and Pharisees (5.20).

2. On three occasions Matthew groups together Pharisees and Sadducees (3.7; 16.1-12; 22.34). This historically improbable combination is never found in Luke–Acts where they are regarded not as allies but as opposed to each other (Acts 23.6-9). Nor does Luke connect the Pharisees with Herodians as do Mark (3.6; 12.13) and Matthew (22.16). On the contrary, according to Lk. 13.31, the Pharisees warn Jesus that Herod wants to kill him. This is a contradiction of Matthew's understanding that it is the Pharisees themselves who want to destroy Jesus

55. Smith, *Jesus the Magician*, p. 153.

(12.14; cf. Lk. 6.11, where there is no mention of killing Jesus). By aligning the Pharisees with Herodians and Sadducees Matthew is again able to suggest their disreputable character.

3. Matthew is the only evangelist who gives the Pharisees a role connected with the death of Jesus. They are told to make the tomb safe and to provide a guard (27.62-66) which, it transpires, is prepared to say that Jesus' disciples moved the body (28.11-15). Such deceit is only to be expected from a group that Matthew describes as blind, hypocrites and a brood of vipers. Richardson has suggested that Matthew's antagonism may have had its origin in a dispute between Matthew's community and a Pharisaic synagogue that also claimed to be the true Israel ('their synagogue[s]' 4.23; 9.35; 10.17; 12.9; 13.54).[56] This may explain why Matthew's attack on the tradition of the elders (15.1-20) omits Mark's explanation of Jewish customs (Mk 7.2-4). It should also be noted that Matthew is not against oral development by Jesus but only against Pharisaic and scribal traditions (cf. Mt. 5.21-48; 7.29).

Not only does Luke ease the unremitting enmity of the Pharisees towards Jesus but he sets out his own programme that shows Jesus and the Pharisees on intimate terms. On three occasions Jesus is the invited guest to eat with a Pharisee—although in each case Jesus criticizes aspects of his host's behaviour. We shall discuss these meals more fully below.

Ziesler has argued that Luke shows a more agreeable attitude towards the Pharisees than Mark does,[57] but Luke's softer approach is even more apparent when it is compared to Matthew's. The favourable picture is clearer still in Acts. Gamaliel, as befits Paul's teacher, pleads successfully on behalf of the apostles (5.34-39; 22.3)[58] and there are Pharisees who have become Christians, albeit Christians who favour circumcision for Gentiles. Twice Paul tells his hearers that he is a Pharisee (23.6; 26.5) and it is because the Pharisees on the council believe in the resurrection that they come to Paul's defence against the Sadducees (23.7-9). The conversion of Paul from a Pharisaic persecutor of the church to its most illustrious missionary represents, in its extreme

---

56. Richardson, *Israel*, p. 194.
57. Ziesler, 'Pharisees', pp. 151-52, rejects Luke's dependence on Matthew since it would be an 'astonishingly cavalier' treatment not found in Luke's use of Mark.
58. Kingsbury, 'The Pharisees in Luke–Acts', pp. 1504-1506, regards the portrait of Gamaliel as 'an ironic character' who 'utters the truth about Christianity'. I am blind to the irony in the description of Paul's teacher.

form, Luke's picture of the Pharisees. In the Gospel some are opponents and some at least are friendly towards Jesus but in Acts the opposition is overcome. The turning point in their attitude is, of course, the resurrection of Jesus.[59] Luke's Pharisees may on occasion oppose the earthly Jesus but they cannot oppose the risen Lord.

J.T. Sanders, in his extended study of Luke's portrait of the Pharisees,[60] notes two types, Jewish and Christian, and he argues that it is the Christian group that causes problems for the church. There certainly are two groups but would Luke's readers have recognized that it was the Christian group that was the problem? There are in Acts two main references to Christian Pharisees: those who advocate Gentiles being circumcised and keeping the law (15.5), and Paul's self-descriptions. And it is Paul who, almost immediately after the council, circumcises Timothy. This is not the circumcision of a Gentile demanded by the Pharisees but, by placing the account so close to the Jerusalem debate, Luke gives the impression of being sensitive to the feelings of Christian Pharisees (cf. 21.17-26). On balance, it seems more probable that Luke's readers understood 'Pharisee' in much the same way that they understood other group terms such as 'Jew' and 'Gentile': that some became believers and some did not.

Having said that, there is a sense in which Pharisees are a special class of Jews for Luke, and Esler is wrong to group Pharisees with scribes, lawyers and chief priests as those most resistant to the gospel.[61] No one in the last three classes tries to save the life of Jesus or invites him to a meal in their houses. Esler has rightly recognized Luke's concern with the problem of table fellowship in the church, yet surprisingly he has overlooked the importance of Jesus' meals with Pharisees in his discussion of Jewish–Gentile table fellowship.[62]

---

59. Brawley, *Luke–Acts and the Jews*, ch. 6, esp. pp. 105-106.

60. Sanders, *The Jews in Luke–Acts*, pp. 94-95. In his paper, 'Who is a Jew and Who is a Gentile', he suggests that Paul was no longer considered a Pharisee (p. 437 n. 14). But ἐγὼ Φαρισαῖός εἰμι (23.6) speaks emphatically of his *present* status in Luke's eyes (cf. 26.4-5).

61. Esler, *Community and Gospel*, pp. 119, 243 n. 5.

62. Esler, *Community and Gospel*, pp. 71, 119, 166, 194-95, correctly stresses the importance of the problem of the rich and poor for Luke. But it is surprising that he makes no comment, when dealing with table fellowship, on the Pharisees who invite Jesus for a meal. Luke's threefold pattern shows their importance. Smith (*Jesus the Magician*, p. 153) sees the meals as a counter to Pharisaic exclusion of Gentiles in Luke's Jewish-Christian church.

The first such meal is the setting for Jesus' anointing (Lk. 7.36-50) at Simon's house. Simon's response to the parable of the debtors shows that he understands what forgiveness entails but, as Jesus points out, he does not put it into practice. Jesus allows the intimate contact of the sinful woman, whereas Simon has failed to fulfil his obligations as a generous host.[63] His Pharisaic code inhibits him from having contact not only with sinners but with the one who allows himself such contact.

At the second meal (11.37-52), Jesus again rebukes his host. On this occasion the dispute is over purity practices, Jesus arguing that it is by giving alms of what is inside the cup that the cup is cleansed. Then follow the three 'woes' attacking Pharisaic tithing and piety. A comparison with the woes in Matthew 23 is suggestive because Matthew lumps together scribes and Pharisees whereas Luke keeps them separate (but cf. 11.45). Luke criticizes the Pharisees for keeping the traditions of men but, unlike Matthew, he does not accuse them of neglecting the weightier matters of the law. However, the attack on the lawyers is much more serious (11.45-52): they offer no help to people in observing the law, they consent to their fathers having killed the prophets and, by taking away the key of knowledge, they neither enter themselves nor do they allow others to enter. But enter what? In Mt. 23.13 it is the kingdom of heaven but Luke leaves his version of the saying open so that it does not exclude the lawyers from the kingdom. C.F. Evans is of the opinion that it is the key to the Scriptures that the lawyers have taken away[64] and this would mean that they prevent others from understanding the law's true requirements.

At the third meal with a Pharisee, Jesus first raises the issue of Sabbath observance, since in his view this cannot exclude doing acts of healing (14.1-6). This is followed by his comments on table-fellowship, beginning with an attack on those who seek the places of honour. Jesus rejects this practice with his insistence on the need to invite those who have no apparent honour. These are the poor, the maimed, the lame and the blind, categories that may reflect the influence of Isa. 58.7 in which God requires that people should share their bread with the hungry and bring the homeless poor into their houses. There are two statements of this obligation to invite outcasts (14.13, 21) and they enclose a parable about

---

63. Fitzmyer, *Luke*, p. 691, and Marshall, *Luke*, pp. 311-12, agree that Simon did not act discourteously, but Evans, *Saint Luke*, p. 363, regards the behaviour as 'churlishness'.

64. Evans, *Saint Luke*, p. 509.

making excuses when invited to a banquet. There can be no doubt, in view of 14.15, that the banquet is the one in the kingdom of God (14.15-24).

These three accounts leave us with something of a difficulty: the Pharisees behave in a generous fashion towards Jesus who then repays their hospitality with criticism. The difficulty is more apparent than real. On one side Luke regards Pharisees as prime candidates for conversion because they believe in the resurrection of the dead, although some, even the well-disposed Gamaliel, do not become believers. And alongside any theological reasons for Luke's attitude is the political reality that, at the time when Luke was writing, the Pharisees were the dominant party in Judaism. Any easing of tensions between Jews and Christians or between Jewish and Gentile Christians would be helped by removing much of the extreme criticism and by describing the conciliatory attitude of Gamaliel. The other side of the problem[65] was that Pharisees very probably advocated those aspects of Jewish *halakah* that were causing difficulties in Luke's church. Such problems might include separation from the common meal, self-indulgent piety and a concern for riches rather than the poor (16.14). Whereas Gentiles had no ritual objections to eating with Jews, we know that for observant Jews there were issues of purity raised by eating with Gentiles. By placing these issues in his Gospel, Luke is able to portray Jesus giving guidelines to (Christian) Pharisees. The accounts of meals with Pharisees provide Luke with the ideal setting in which to counteract difficulties arising from Jewish attitudes within his own church. He says, in effect, if the Pharisees with their rigorous views can associate with sinners and the friend of sinners, then those Jewish Christians with less rigorous standards need have no scruples about table fellowship with Gentile believers. It is from the Pharisees that Luke draws the hero of the second half of Acts, one who mixes freely with Gentiles even though he has lived 'according to the strictest sect of our religion' (Acts 26.5). Paul is the role model for all Jewish Christians, for whom the issues that divided them from Gentiles are nothing compared with the unifying belief in the hope of Israel (23.6; 26.6-7).

6. *Synagogues*

Matthew's view of Jewish synagogues is consistent with his view of Pharisees and in two cases they come under a common condemnation

---

65. Sanders, *The Jews in Luke–Acts*, p. 91.

(23.6, 34). The synagogues are places for hypocrites and places where Jesus' disciples will be flogged (6.2, 5; 10.17-18; 23.6). Only once does Matthew describe Jesus healing in a synagogue (Mt. 12.9-14; Mk 3.1-6; Lk. 6.6-11), and he omits the account of healing a man with an unclean spirit at Capernaum (Mk 1.21-28; Lk. 4.31-37). In the accounts of the healing of Jairus' daughter he omits the detail that Jairus was the ruler of a synagogue (Mk 5.22, 36, 38; Lk. 8.41, 49; cf. Mt. 19.18, 23).

Just as Luke shows less antagonism towards the Pharisees so too there is a marked contrast in his treatment of synagogues. Only once does he refer to 'their' synagogues (4.15) and he has no prophecy that Jesus' disciples will be flogged in them. Luke retains all Mark's stories of synagogue healings and adds to these the healing of a servant of a centurion who had built a synagogue (7.5), a detail absent from Matthew's version (8.5-13). Luke also has the story of healing a woman (13.10-17) in which Jesus arouses the indignation of the synagogue's ruler for healing on the Sabbath and this merits Jesus' condemnation of his adversaries as hypocrites. Luke is not, therefore, uncritical of Jewish synagogues but he does not have Matthew's uniformly adverse opinion of them. This more balanced estimate continues in Acts where synagogues are so often the starting point of missions, some of which meet with success. At 13.15 the synagogue rulers invite Paul to give an exhortation and, at 18.8, Crispus the synagogue ruler becomes a believer.

There is, however, a further development in Acts where, on four occasions, Luke refers to synagogues of the Jews (13.5; 14.1; 17.1, 10). This qualification suggests that Luke, like Matthew, was familiar with non-Jewish, that is, Christian, synagogues. The description 'Jewish synagogue' has none of the implied antagonism that Matthew's 'their synagogues' has and the four cases in Acts are places of Christian mission.

Apart from the evangelists, only two other NT writers mention synagogues. At Jas 2.2 the term is used for a Christian assembly and, at Rev. 2.9 and 3.9, there are references to those who call themselves Jews but who are not and who form the synagogue[s] of Satan. It seems as if Matthew and the author of Revelation represent a line of development among Christians that is severely critical of Jewish synagogues whereas Luke and James offer a far more conciliatory approach, acknowledging that Jews and Christians are in some sense members of the same body (see, for example, Jas 1.1).

There is further but less direct evidence of the different viewpoints of Matthew and Luke in their respective uses of the parent verb συνάγω.

Matthew has seven instances in which the verb is used to describe the gathering of Jesus' opponents and these are concentrated around the end of his ministry and death (23.34, 41; 26.3, 57; 27.17, 27, 62; 28.12). Luke has only one such case in the Gospel (22.66) and three more in Acts (4.5, 26, 27). Thereafter, the verb is used almost exclusively for Christian gatherings.

Summary

We can now draw together the differences between Luke and Matthew. In addition to the contrasts we noted in earlier chapters are the six further areas of difference and these combine to give the impression of deliberate contradiction. Fitzmyer and others raised the question of why Luke should have made such changes and, in the belief that no sufficiently good reason existed, dismissed the idea that Luke knew Matthew. But the present study suggests that a very powerful reason did exist: Luke's deep concern for the restoration of Israel and for relations between Jews and Gentiles in the church. As we have seen, Luke has taken great care to express Christian beliefs in ways that would, as far as possible, be within the range of Jewish hopes and expectations. This approach is in marked contrast to that of Matthew which is more abrasive and strident in its attitude to Judaism. Matthew stands firmly in a Jewish-Christian tradition[66] but one that was opposed to Jewish synagogues, Pharisaic teaching as well as the temple and its cult. That these are treated with far greater sympathy by Luke is epitomized in the comments of the evangelists on the incident when the disciples pluck corn on the Sabbath (Mt. 12.1-8; Lk. 6.1-5). Matthew's sayings, that 'something greater than the temple is here' and 'I desire mercy and not sacrifice' are not only absent from Luke's version, they are alien to his whole approach to Jewish institutions even after the destruction of the temple.

The object of this discussion has been to show that Luke's view of Israel was in conflict with views current among some Christians at the end of the first century. One of the clearest statements of the opposing view, that the church could, and perhaps should, be regarded as the new or true Israel is to be found in Matthew's Gospel. The evidence from this limited investigation does not, of course, prove that Luke knew Matthew but it does suggest at least, that we should be wary of

---

66. Dunn, *Unity and Diversity*, p. 248.

arguments of the type advanced by Fitzmyer. Once we agree with Conzelmann that Luke's intention was to replace and not to complement the tradition, the apparent 'crankiness' of Luke's treatment of Matthew becomes a comprehensible strategy. Because of the theology implicit in Matthew's structure, it would have to be demolished and the materials, where they were suitable, repositioned. Some of the material would have to be drastically reshaped before re-use and other items would have to be rejected. One thing would have seemed clear to Luke: Matthew's Gospel and its implications could not be allowed to go unchallenged.

Israel at the Conclusion of Acts

Thus far in this study we have seen abundant evidence, direct and indirect, that Luke had the restoration of Israel as a major element in his theology. Although Gentiles, in the form of the two centurions, have entered the narrative, it is not until Acts 11.20-21 that anything approaching a mission to Gentiles is undertaken. Luke has therefore covered some *seventy per cent* of his work before the Gentile mission begins in earnest and even then preaching to Jews continues to the end of Acts. The closing scene of Acts, which describes Paul's activities in Rome, is particularly important in any attempt to uncover Luke's attitude to Judaism,[67] not least because it presents his last thoughts on whether there is any point in continuing to preach to Jews. An examination of Acts 28.17-31 therefore makes a fitting end to the main part of the present work. The question we must try to answer is, what is Luke's final opinion of the Jews and how does this affect his belief in the restoration of Israel? In other words, does Luke finally reject not only the Jews but also the promises about Israel in the infancy stories with the corollary that Christians should now turn exclusively to the Gentiles?

1. *The Voyage to Rome*[68]

Before discussing the account of Paul in Rome we must first examine what Luke tells us about the main part of the voyage because he has

---

67. Tyson, 'Jewish Rejection', p. 124: 'a narrative event of special prominence'.
68. My realization of the importance of this voyage for understanding the events in Rome and its place in Luke's conception of the Gentile mission had its origin in a paper by Dr Loveday Alexander to the British New Testament Conference, Nottingham, 1994, entitled 'Acts and the Ancient Reader'.

provided valuable clues for understanding the events in Rome. The account is told in the first person plural which, as Robbins has pointed out, is a common feature of ancient accounts of sea voyages and, in itself, gives no guarantee that it is an eyewitness report.[69] The first leg of the journey, from Caesarea to Sidon, introduces the reader to some of Paul's fellow travellers and to the kindly centurion, Julius (27.1-3). The next stage has a hint of troubles to come because 'the winds were against us' (27.4) but, with the transfer to an Alexandrian ship, difficulties quickly multiply. This is shown by 'dangerous' (ἐπισφαλοῦς, 27.9) and the repetition of 'difficulty' (μόλις, 27.7, 8, 16). Eventually, after fourteen nights drifting, the climax is reached with the shipwreck on the coast of Malta. A storm-tossed voyage of a Jew on a ship crewed by Gentiles and which ends with the God of Israel saving the lives of all on board could well remind Jewish-Christian readers of the story of Jonah (27.13-34; Jon. 1.4-15), and Luke brings out the connection between the narratives by his vocabulary and the actions he describes. The gear and tackle have to be cast out (σκεῦος, 27.17; σκευὴν τοῦ πλοίου, 27.19; σκευῶν...πλοίῳ, Jon. 1.5) and the cargo is thrown overboard (ἐκβολὴν ἐποιοῦντο, 27.18; ἐκβολὴν ἐποιήσαντο, Jon. 1.5). In the Jonah story the sailors want Jonah to pray to his god so that they might not perish (μὴ ἀπολώμεθα, 1.6, 14) whereas Paul promises that not a hair of anyone's head will be lost (ἀπολεῖται, 27.34).

This is not Luke's first story with allusions to Jonah. The stilling of the lake storm (Lk. 8.22-25) has an even more obvious relationship with Jonah[70] as well as links to the earlier story of the miraculous draught of fishes (5.1-11) in which Peter is told of his future mission.[71] The size of the catch is doubtless a sign of Peter's successful preaching (Acts 2.41; 4.4) and of his role in the conversion of the Gentile Cornelius (Acts 10). Luke therefore provides a sequence of detailed boat voyages, the last two connected by allusions to Jonah. The importance for Luke of the

69. Robbins, 'We Passages', pp. 215-16. See also, Lake and Cadbury, *Beginnings*, IV, pp. 324-25.
70. Common features include the embarkation (ἐνέβη εἰς πλοῖον, 8.22; πλοῖον...ἐνέβη εἰς αὐτό, Jon. 1.3); the wind and the storm during which the central character, who is instrumental in calming the storm, is asleep. Also, πλεόντων, Lk. 8.23, cf. πλεῦσαι, Jon. 1.3; ἐκινδύνευον, 8.23, cf. ἐκινδύνευεν, Jon. 1.4; κλύδωνι, 8.24, Jon. 1.4, 12, cf. κλύδωνα, Jon. 1.11; ἀπολλύμεθα, 8.24, cf. Jon. 1.6, 14; φοβηθέντες, 8.25, ἐφοβήθησαν...φόβον, Jon. 1.10, cf. 1.16.
71. In both stories Jesus is on the boat (5.3, *contra* Mk 1.16-20) and the specifically Lukan title 'Master' is used (ἐπιστάτα, 5.5; 8.24).

story of Jonah is that the prophet's Jewish exclusiveness was overcome by God and that he preached God's message of repentance with great success to the Ninevites (Lk. 11.29-30) who, like the sailors, turned to the Lord (Jon. 1.16; 3.6-10; 4.11). Earlier in this study I pointed to a number of texts from Isaiah that illustrate the phrase 'the end of the earth' and combine it with the ideas of gathering Israel's diaspora and of the incoming Gentiles. The importance of such texts for Luke is seen in Lk. 2.30-32 and Acts 13.47. In Acts we see not only Jewish antagonism to Gentile believers but also the sluggishness of the apostles themselves in carrying out the commission given to them twice by the risen Jesus. Acts 10.9-16 shows how strongly Peter resisted breaking Jewish food taboos and there was a similar conservatism among some Jewish Christians about circumcision (11.2-3; 15.1). Thus Peter's conversion, like Paul's, has to be told three times. Israel's world mission, prophesied by Isaiah, was seen by Luke as now taking place as the direct consequence of Jesus' commands and the gift of the Spirit. It is in this context that Paul proclaims to Jews that he will turn to the Gentiles (13.46; 18.6; 28.28).

There is one incident in the voyage that is a vital part of Luke's message: the meal on the ship (27.33-36). This has been shown by Esler to continue Luke's concern for legitimating table fellowship between Jewish and Gentile Christians.[72] It is probably going too far to regard the meal as a eucharist (in spite of εὐχαρίστησεν, 27.35), since that would imply the use of wine as well as bread (cf. Lk. 22.17, 19). Luke's own term 'the breaking of bread', is more appropriate because τροφή is the word used in the narrative for 'food' (27.33, 34, 36, 38) and it is only in Paul's thanksgiving that ἄρτος is used. Nowhere in Acts does Luke mention either wine or cup and, unlike Mark and Matthew, he does not restrict the use of εὐχαριστέω to meals. The feeding of the four thousand (Mk 8.1-10; Mt. 15.32-38) takes place in Gentile territory so that the crowd almost certainly contained Jews and Gentiles, yet neither evangelist is shy about using εὐχαριστέω. Luke omits the story, probably because in his scheme Jew–Gentile sharing could take place only after the resurrection and Pentecost. But now, on board ship, Jews, Gentiles and Christians share bread for their 'strength' (σωτηρίας, 27.34). Haenchen's comment that σωτηρία means 'earthly deliverance only'[73] is a falsely pietistic interpretation that ignores the fact that the

---

72. Esler, *Community and Gospel*, pp. 101-104.
73. Haenchen, *Acts*, p. 707 n. 1.

deliverance is the work of the God of Israel.[74]

Esler also draws attention to the eschatological aspect of the story, that Jesus tells his disciples that they will win their lives (τὰς ψυχάς, Lk. 21.19) and Paul promises that none on board will lose their life (ψυχῆς, 27.22).[75] This should be compared with the use of ψυχή in Jon. 1.14; 2.6, 8. It should also be noted that after mention of the times of the Gentiles (Lk. 21.24) 'there will be signs in the sun and moon and stars...the roaring of the sea and the waves' (21.25). Just before the shipwreck 'neither sun nor stars appeared for many a day' (Acts 27.20).

Luke's account of Paul's voyage and the shipwreck reminds the reader of the two stories of Jesus' boat voyages as well as the story of Jonah, a pamphlet against earlier Jewish exclusiveness. The meal on the ship is further emphasis on the need to overcome that attitude. Both Christians and Jews on the 'voyage' might be tempted to abandon all hope of being saved (τοῦ σῴζεσθαι, 27.20) but if *all* stay in the 'boat' *all* will be saved (σωθῆναι, 27.31) because it is God's salvation (28.28).

2. *Are any Roman Jews Converted?*

The final part of the story (28.23-31) tells of great numbers of local Jews coming to Paul who testifies to the kingdom of God, attempting to convince (πείθων, 28.23) them about Jesus from the law of Moses and the prophets. After speaking to his visitors all day some of his hearers are convinced (ἐπείθοντο, 28.24) but some disbelieve. The account ends with Paul's quotation of Isa. 6.9-10 in which both the prophet and Paul accuse their hearers of being blind and deaf, characteristics that are contrasted with the Gentiles' willingness to listen. The first question to answer is, does 'convinced' mean 'converted'? There is an impressive body of scholarly opinion, including Haenchen,[76] Conzelmann[77] and J.T. Sanders,[78] that holds that no Jews are converted. These critics are joined by Jervell in asserting that Luke has finally closed the door on further missions to the Jews. In Jervell's words, the 'judgment by and

---

74. It is the God of Israel who saves all on the ship, just as he saves Jonah and the sailors: cf. διασώσῃ, Jon. 1.6, and Luke's repeated use of the verb, Acts 27.43, 44; 28.1, 4. See also 'deliverance belongs to the Lord' (σωτηρίου τῷ κυρίῳ, Jon. 2.10).
75. Esler, *Community and Gospel*, p. 104.
76. Haenchen, *Acts*, pp. 723-24, 729.
77. Conzelmann, *Acts*, pp. 227-28.
78. Sanders, 'Salvation of the Jews', pp. 106-109: *The Jews in Luke–Acts*, pp. 296-99.

on the Jews has been irrevocably passed'.[79] By preaching to the Jews in Rome, the message has been proclaimed to Jews throughout the world and no further mission to them is required.[80] The arguments against Jervell's view on the judgment of the Jews and in favour of the eschatological judgment of all people, including the twelve tribes, were considered in Chapter 3. If judgment belongs to the future and if Paul has some success in converting Roman Jews then there is no obvious or compelling reason for Luke to imply that the preaching to Jews should come to an end.

Much of the discussion about whether or not some Jews are converted hinges on the force that can be attributed to πείθω in 28.23 and 24 since the verb describes both what Paul sets out to do and how some Jews respond to his words.[81] There are a number of instances in Luke–Acts where πείθω means 'to convert', although the objective of the conversion depends upon the context. At the conclusion of the Lazarus story Jesus says that the rich man's brothers will not be convinced (πεισθήσονται, Lk. 16.31) even if someone should rise from the dead. What the brothers must be convinced about will determine whether they go to Hades or to Abraham's bosom; it is therefore a matter of life or death, eternal joy or eternal torment. In Lk. 20.6 we are told that all the people are convinced (πεπεισμένος) that John was a prophet. The force of the verb here is shown by the fact that all the people (ἅπαντα τὸν λαόν, 3.21) had been baptized as a sign of repentance in response to John's preaching. And in Acts 5.36-37 the verb πείθω describes those who had followed Theudas and Judas the Galilean. In this case there is a strong implication that the level of commitment, even if misguided, would be the same as that expected of Christian disciples.

79. Jervell, *The People of God*, pp. 63-64.
80. Jervell, *The People of God*, pp. 49, 64. So also, Tyson, 'Jewish Rejection', p. 137: 'Two facts seem clear: for Luke the mission to the Jewish people has failed, and it has been terminated'.
81. Sanders, 'Salvation of the Jews', pp. 107-108, argues that conversion is not involved here because Luke's normal word is belief, often connected with an account or a mention of baptism. Haenchen, *Acts*, p. 729, recognizes that there is a tension between ἐπείθοντο in v. 24 and the fact that all the Jews are treated as obdurate in vv. 26-27. See also his essay, 'The Book of Acts as Source Material', p. 278. Bultmann, 'πείθω', *TDNT*, VI, pp. 1-2, takes the meaning in Acts 18.4 and 28.23 to be 'convince'. He further notes that Paul uses the expression 'to seek to win men' (ἀνθρώπους πείθομεν, 2 Cor. 5.11), and that this may be a description of the apostolic calling. In the NT the word is used predominantly by Paul and Luke.

7. *Luke, Matthew and Israel*

In the synagogue at Thessalonica, some Jews and devout Greeks are persuaded (ἐπείσθησαν, 17.4) to follow Paul and Silas as the result of Paul's preaching, and there is a similar instance at Corinth (ἐπειθέν, 18.4). At Ephesus, Demetrius the silversmith complains that throughout all Asia Paul has persuaded (πείσας, 19.26) a considerable number to turn from the worship of Artemis. Sanders argues that the meaning of conversion is not clear in this passage and that the hearers may only have been persuaded not to believe in idols.[82] But it is hard to understand why the Ephesians should give up their religion unless they intended to follow one that they considered to be superior. Conzelmann puts the matter correctly when he writes 'For the Christian reader, the charge against Paul is a testimony to the victorious advance of the mission'.[83] Finally, when the people of Caesarea beg Paul not to go to Jerusalem, he refuses to be persuaded (μὴ πειθομένου, 21.14) because he must do the will of God.

There is good evidence from these examples that Luke's use of πείθω can, on occasions, have the sense of conversion and a corresponding change of belief. In 28.23-24 some Jews were convinced (ἐπείθοντο) by Paul's words but others disbelieved (ἠπίστουν, 28.24). This suggests that ἀπιστέω is the opposite to πείθω and hence that πείθω is used here as a synonym for πιστεύω. Paul had set out to convince the Jews and it would be beyond the readers' belief that Paul had spoken all day about Jesus and the kingdom with no intention to convert his hearers. We must therefore conclude that Paul's aim was to convert Jews and that he met with some success.[84] The reasonable deduction from this is that Luke does not reject the Jews and that further missions to the Jews are not excluded.[85]

3. *Luke and the Roman Jews*

The reader is intended to appreciate the truth and importance of the events in Rome because they are vouchsafed by the author as an eyewitness (28.14-16). By this means he assures us that the two apparent surprises in the narratives are to be accepted with proper seriousness. The first is that Paul was not the first to bring the gospel to

---

82. Sanders, 'Salvation of the Jews', p. 108.
83. Conzelmann, *Acts*, p. 165.
84. Jervell, *The People of God*, p. 63; Franklin, *Christ the Lord*, p. 114. Tyson, 'Jewish Rejection', p. 126, accepts that some Jews are converted.
85. Franklin, *Christ the Lord*, p. 115; Brawley, 'Paul in Acts', pp. 129-34.

Rome (28.15), which means that the story cannot be regarded simply as bringing the gospel to the end of the earth. The second surprise is that there is no hint of the expected trial of Paul. This foiling of the readers' expectations is either an uncharacteristic anti-climax to Luke's narrative skill or it means that we must look for another motive or motives for the story. The only theological reason that Paul offers to his Jewish brethren for his presence is 'because of the hope of Israel' (28.20). We should therefore expect to find evidence of Luke's continuing concern for the restoration of Israel. The possibility that Luke stopped writing at this point because he ran out of sources has to be rejected in view of the historical improbabilities in the account itself.[86] We shall focus on those features of the story relevant to Luke's attitude to the Jews.

1. The Roman Jews regard Christians as a αἵρεσις (28.22) which, in this context, can only mean a Jewish sect. On two previous occasions Christians have been described as a sect, once by the Jew, Tertullus (24.5), and once by Paul when quoting the Jewish view (24.14). Luke also uses the term to describe parties within Judaism, the Sadducees (5.17) and Pharisees who are now Christians (15.5; 26.5). The use of the term by the Roman Jews recognizes that, in spite of the sect being spoken against, Christians are a part of Israel. Haenchen notes the unfavourable nuance of αἵρεσις when used by or attributed to Jews in the last three occurrences in Acts.[87] But Luke is only partly concerned with the adverse tone. The important point for Luke is that the Jews accept the Christians as a sect within Israel and, as Luke makes clear, on the same footing as other Jewish schools of thought. These, such as the Sadducees and Pharisees, did not exclude each other from Israel in spite of major disagreements.

2. Rome is the only place where Jews come to Paul and do so in great numbers. Hitherto, when Paul had gone to the Jews they often opposed him. The significance of this change has not been sufficiently emphasized by commentators.

---

86. Walaskay, 'And So We Came to Rome', pp. 18-21, 76 n. 19, summarises and examines various interpretations of the end of Acts. Also Haenchen, *Acts*, pp. 726-27.

87. Haenchen, *Acts*, p. 653.

3. There is no aggression on the part of the Roman Jews and Luke's final comment, that Paul taught unhindered (ἀκωλύτως, hap. leg. NT) for two years means that he was free not only from Roman interference but, far more significantly, from Jewish antagonism. It has, after all, been the Jews who have previously hindered Paul's work, not the Romans. Luke's comment is in marked contrast to Paul's experiences at Antioch (13.50), Iconium (14.2) and Thessalonica (17.5). And, in spite of all that he has endured at Jewish hands, Paul can still say that he has no charge to bring against 'my nation' (28.19).

Thus far the account of Paul in Rome points to a softening of Jewish attitudes towards Christians and a willingness not only to listen but, in some cases, to believe. This may not be a return to the Jerusalem springtime but it is much more hopeful[88] than the enmity that had been shown by so many diaspora Jews. Given the undoubted gulf between Jews and many Christians towards the end of the first century, Luke recognizes the gulf but, at the same time, that it is neither total nor insurmountable.

The Use of Isaiah 6.9-10

The major part of Paul's reported speech is the quotation of Isa. 6.9-10. This is a passage which all the evangelists use to explain some aspect of the Jewish failure to understand the gospel (Mk 4.12; Mt. 13.13-15; Jn 12.40). The emphasis in Isaiah is on hearing (Acts 28.26, 27) and this is taken up by Paul's comment: 'Know, therefore, (οὖν) that this salvation of God has been sent (aorist) to the Gentiles; they will listen' (ἀκούσονται, 28.28). Peter Richardson holds that because of its finality 'Luke seems to seal Jewish rejection of the gospel'.[89] Certainly the location in the narrative sequence is important and Luke was well aware of the Gentile mission and its success. But Jewish deafness since the time of Isaiah had not resulted in God's rejection of the Jews. Nor does the interpretation of Richardson and those who agree with him, that the final scene seals Jewish rejection, give sufficient weight to Luke's final sentence. This says that not only did Paul preach unhindered but 'with all [public] openness' (μετὰ πάσης παρρησίας, 28.31). This is surely

88. Tannehill, 'Tragic Story', pp. 83-85, still sees signs of hope at the end of Acts and recalls that Jerusalem will see Jesus when 'the times of the Gentiles are fulfilled' (Lk. 21.24).
89. Richardson, *Israel*, p. 10.

intended to remind the reader of the Baptist's opening declaration that 'all flesh shall see God's salvation' (Lk. 3.6)[90] and this must include Jews *and* Gentiles. And if God has not rejected the Jews then why should Luke or his readers? Acts 28.28 does not offer Jewish deafness as the reason for turning to the Gentiles,[91] almost as if οὖν belonged to the second part of the verse. The promise that the Gentiles will hear is a contrast to, not a consequence of, Jewish deafness. The Gentile mission has its origins in the commands of the risen Lord, not in Jewish obduracy (Lk. 24.47; Acts 1.8; 13.47) and it is carried out on God's authority (10.15, 34, 44).

Paul says nothing about the character of the Jews that the Hebrew prophets have not said over the centuries during which such prophetic anti-Judaism was a hallowed tradition in Israel.[92] By using a quotation from Isaiah, Luke is able to make his criticism of Jewish attitudes, not as a Christian divorced from Israel but as a member of a sect of Israel.[93] This is in accord with his presentation of Paul as a faithful Jew, the only religious identity that Paul accepts (21.39; 22.3; 23.6; 26.4-5).

Jews and Gentiles

Paul's statement that God's salvation has been offered to the Gentiles and that they will listen does not mean the end of the Jewish mission.[94] Paul has made similar statements on two previous occasions, at Pisidian Antioch (13.46-47) and Corinth (18.5-6). Both incidents are followed almost immediately by Paul preaching to Jews—with some success in the Iconium synagogue (14.1) and by the conversion of Crispus, the ruler of the synagogue, at Corinth (18.8). Dibelius has proposed that Paul's statements follow a geographical pattern of Jewish rejection: it first occurs in Asia Minor, then in Greece and finally in Rome.[95] This

---

90. Tannehill, 'Tragic Story', p. 82, is among those who recognize the importance of σωτήριον but not the backward reference to 'all' in the Baptist's citation of Isaiah.

91. Brawley, 'Paul in Acts', pp. 132-33, notes that there is no suggestion that Paul uses the citation of Isaiah to support turning to the Gentiles.

92. Hare, 'Rejection of the Jews', pp. 29, 35.

93. Tiede, *Prophecy and History*, pp. 121-22, describes Luke's use of the quotation as a 'classic prophetic refrain', and on p. 54 he makes the crucial point that only 'from within' does prophetic criticism have integrity.

94. Tiede, *Prophecy and History*, p. 123, suggests that Luke is replying to Jewish objections to the inclusion of the Gentiles.

95. Dibelius, *Studies*, pp. 149-50.

pattern does not, however, exist. After leaving Corinth Paul returned to Asia Minor and, on leaving the Ephesus synagogue, expressed the hope that he would return (18.19-21). When he did return he spent two years there and Luke emphasizes that all the residents of Asia Minor heard the word, both Jews and Greeks (19.1, 8-10).

The large number of instances of Jewish opposition in Acts should not be allowed to deflect attention from the cases of Gentile opposition and anger (16.19-24; 19.23-41). Jews are not the only people who object to the gospel and what Luke shows in these cases is that where traditional religious attitudes are under attack the defenders of the old religion try to hit back. Luke does not have an explicit doctrine of a faithful remnant of Israel, yet there is much in Luke's portrayal of the Jews which reflects the prophetic idea that some will hear and some will not. Luke says nothing new here and, we must note, that he says the same of the Gentiles.

In the past decade or so Luke's attitude to the Jews has been increasingly attacked as anti-Jewish, a view forcibly put by J.T. Sanders.[96] Sanders has argued that Luke depicts the Jews as rejecting and killing Jesus and that therefore the gospel is taken to the Gentiles. In Sanders's opinion this is not reliable history and that 'without that [anti-Semitic] lie [that the Jews killed Jesus] we would not have Lukan theology'.[97] Thus the historical fact that all the earlier Christians were Jews is buried under the theological 'fact' that '*the Jews* have rejected Christ'. According to this argument, Luke needs the theme of mutual rejection in order to persuade Gentiles that Christianity had its origins in Judaism, that 'it is in a sense the "true" Judaism', but that in spite of its origins it is a Gentile religion and not Judaism.[98]

As to the historical accuracy of assertions of Jewish rejection of Jesus and Christian preachers, such assertions are present in the passion narratives of all the Gospels. As early as 1 Thess. 2.14-15, Paul writes that Jews killed the Lord Jesus and hindered Christian preaching to the Gentiles. But whereas Paul goes on to say that God's wrath has come upon them at last (2.16), Luke ascribes the death of Jesus to Jewish ignorance (Acts 3.17) and offers the possibility of repentance and forgiveness (2.38). It was God's plan that Jesus should die and, in this plan, the Jews had a part to play (2.23; 3.18). Luke's forgiving attitude

---

96. Sanders, *The Jews in Luke–Acts*, is his most extended argument.
97. Sanders, 'Parable of the Pounds', p. 667.
98. Sanders, 'Parable of the Pounds', p. 668.

towards the Jews about the death of Jesus has rightly been emphasized by J.L. Houlden.[99] He draws attention to Stephen's prayer for the forgiveness of his killers (7.60) and the textually doubtful prayer of Jesus, 'Father, forgive them, for they know not what they do' (Lk. 23.34). Houlden suggests that the strongest argument for the literary authenticity of Lk. 23.34 is the Stephen parallel. There is further evidence of authenticity in one of the earliest attestations of the verse by Marcion. Given Marcion's removal of Jewish material from Luke's Gospel it seems unlikely that he would have left the saying unless he was convinced that it was a genuine word of Jesus. Sanders accepts that Lk. 23.34 is authentic[100] but he seems unwilling to accept the saying, together with Acts 2.23 and 3.17-18, as a serious and genuine description of Luke's views. His comment—'There are no real Jews in Acts 2–3, only puppets on Luke's stage'[101]—is a measure of that unwillingness. Luke's view of the Jews and Israel is far more subtle and favourable than Sanders's comment allows.

The thesis offered by Sanders requires a predominantly Gentile readership since only Gentiles could tolerate the degree of anti-Semitism discerned by Sanders. But, as we have seen, there are convincing reasons for thinking that Luke's readership contained a significant number of Jews.[102] The present study endorses that view, particularly in the way in which Luke has presented vital Christian beliefs.

Acts is still widely regarded as describing the origin, growth and justification of the Gentile mission but, as Maddox has pointed out, the space devoted to Paul's mission is surprisingly small.[103] Many of the Gentile conversions are the result of preaching in synagogues and the reader is given very little detail of the content of sermons to solely Gentile audiences. Peter's speech to the Cornelius household (10.34-43) is not the instrument of conversion—that is brought about by the direct action of God (10.44-45). Moreover, the Jewish orientation of the speech would only have been persuasive for a Gentile who was already close to Judaism and familiar with its hopes. The short speech by the apostles at Lystra hardly constitutes a Christian sermon (14.15-17) and the jailer at

---

99. Houlden, 'The Purpose of Luke', pp. 56-59, contrasts Luke's forgiving attitude to that of the Maccabean martyrs.
100. Sanders, *The Jews in Luke–Acts*, pp. 227, 234.
101. Sanders, *The Jews in Luke–Acts*, p. 237.
102. Esler, *Community and Gospel*, pp. 30-45.
103. Maddox, *Purpose*, pp. 66-67. Also Lentz, *Luke's Portrait of Paul*.

Philippi, overawed by the miracle of the loosened chains, is answered by a brief formula (16.31). Only at the end of Paul's speech at Athens is there a muted expression of the Christian message (17.31). These speeches contain nothing like the detailed expositions given to Jewish audiences[104] and they would be little help to outright pagans so far untouched by Judaism.

The Jewish sermons may have served a double purpose, encouraging former Jews to hold fast to their new faith and providing models of evangelism towards Jews who remained outside the Way. This is why Luke shows that preaching to Jews can be successful[105] while success in preaching to Gentiles is usually reported in general summaries (11.1; 13.48; 14.27). The assumption that Luke was writing for a Gentile church when the Jewish mission was over does not answer the questions raised by the presence of so many examples of how to preach to Jews and so few examples of how to preach to pagans. It may well be that, in Rengstorf's words, Luke wanted 'to help his readers recognize that any feeling in the church against Jewish evangelism is wrong—it is not in accordance with the will of God'.[106]

The account of Paul in Rome has a strongly Jewish character[107] such as we find in the birth stories. All the people taking part are Jews and the reader is reminded that God's salvation is for all, including the Gentiles (28.28; Lk. 2.30-32; 3.6). We noted earlier that the theological reason for Paul's presence in Rome is 'because of the hope of Israel' and, according to Darryl Palmer, 'hope' in Acts is principally concerned with Christian belief in the resurrection.[108] However, this is not strictly the hope of Israel, although the two concepts are intimately connected. In his speech before Agrippa, Paul says that he is on trial for 'hope in the promise made by God to our fathers, to which our twelve tribes hope to attain'; he then asks why it is thought incredible that God raises

104. Acts 2.22-36, 38-40; 3.12-26; 13.16-41.
105. E.g. Acts 2.37, 41; 4.4; 5.14; 13.43.
106. Rengstorf, 'Election of Matthias', p. 189.
107. Palmer, 'Mission to Jews and Gentiles', p. 62, rightly emphasizes this point. I am grateful to Mr Palmer for sending me a copy of his article which arrived when my script was almost completed. We are in close agreement in matters of detail and in our conclusions. Tyson, 'Jewish Rejection', pp. 127-30, accepts Luke's interest in Jewish religious matters but concludes that it 'does not determine the question of Jewish acceptance or rejection' and that 'Jewish rejection occurred despite the fact that the Christian message was harmonious with Jewish religious traditions'.
108. Palmer, 'Mission to Jews and Gentiles', p. 63.

the dead (26.6-8). Similarly, Paul tells the Jews at Antioch that God has fulfilled his promise to the fathers by raising Jesus (13.32-33). But, as Paul goes on to explain, it is the resurrection of the Davidic son, the one who will fulfil God's promise to Israel: 'I will give you the holy and sure blessings of David' (13.33-34, citing Ps. 2.7 and Isa. 55.3).

The hope of Israel is the hope of the disciples for the redemption of Israel (Lk. 24.21) and it was the fact of the resurrection that rekindled that hope. It encouraged the apostles to ask when the kingdom would be restored to Israel, and the implied answer is that it will be Jesus who redeems Israel in the Father's time. The theological purpose of Paul's presence in Rome is to restate what had been revealed to Simeon, including the divisive effect of Jesus (Lk. 2.34-35).

The final scene of Acts does not imply rejection of the Jews or the end of the Jewish mission. On the contrary, there are signs that Luke was looking for a *rapprochement* between Jews and Christians[109] as a part of his plan to ease the tensions between Jewish and Gentile believers. Prior to the final scene Luke describes two groups as brethren: in 28.14-15 they are Christians and in vv. 17, 21 they are Jews. In v. 11, Luke records the seemingly trivial detail that the figurehead of the ship that brought Paul to Italy was the Διόσκουροι, the heavenly twins.[110] The twins, Castor and Pollux, were an Egyptian cult and a good omen for sailors[111] but, given Luke's antipathy to magic and superstition, this seems an improbable motive for reporting this one detail. A more probable motive for its inclusion is in the two groups of brothers, Jewish and Christian. Is it too fanciful to see the two groups as 'heavenly' brothers at the prow of God's mission to the world (cf. Lk. 5.1-10)?[112]

---

109. Houlden, 'The Purpose of Luke', p. 63, suggests that Luke may have been offering an olive branch, a path 'which Jews might tread towards the church'. And although Houlden accepts that Luke's primary audience was Christian, we have seen that Luke's advice on how to preach to Jews would support the idea of a path (Way?).

110. Lentz, *Luke's Portrait of Paul*, p. 166, gives an interpretation in terms of Paul's high status. Squires, *God's Plan*, p. 107, notes that according to Diodorus, the appearance of two stars over the heads of the Dioscori signified that Orpheus was to be rescued by θεῶν προνοίᾳ. Squires makes no connection with Acts 28.11. On the Christian mission, see Palmer, 'Mission to Jews and Gentiles', pp. 72-73.

111. Haenchen, *Acts*, p. 717 n. 2.

112. According to Jervell, *The People of God*, pp. 50-51, 'brothers' means those who belong to the family of Abraham and share in the promises, but that Luke does not typically apply the term to Christians. Yet it is surely of compelling significance that Luke uses the term in the way we have noted at the completion of his double work.

Chapter 8

SUMMARY AND CONCLUSIONS

The objective of this study has been to examine the place of the restoration of Israel in Luke's theology. But before drawing together the various threads of the argument there is one further area which must be briefly mentioned so that Luke's programme can be placed in a probable historical context. This is the question of Jewish attitudes towards Christians around the turn of the first century.

This enquiry too has its share of uncertainties because, apart from the remarks by Josephus,[1] the main body of evidence has to be extracted from the Tannaitic literature and this necessitates an extrapolation to the first century. Such an analysis has been made by Lawrence Schiffman in an attempt to recover Jewish attitudes to the early Christians.[2] He first sets out the conditions for being a Jew by birth[3] and then the four requirements for the acceptance of a convert (proselyte).[4] These are:

1. Acceptance of the whole Torah, both written and oral.[5]
2. The circumcision of males.
3. Immersion: this was probably both initiatory and purificatory.[6]
4. The offering of sacrifice, although this was no longer required after 70 CE.

Having described the conditions for membership, Schiffman then discusses the question of whether anyone can lose his status as a Jew,

---

1. Schürer–Vermes, *History*, I, pp. 428-41, discusses the authenticity of the two passages in *Antiquities* that have been the subject of a vast literature. The conclusion reached is that *Ant.* 20.200 is by Josephus. *Ant.* 18.64 originally contained some statements about Jesus, but 'the present text is only to some extent his own' (p. 440).
2. Schiffman, 'At the Crossroads', pp. 115-56.
3. Schiffman, 'At the Crossroads', pp. 117-22.
4. Schiffman, 'At the Crossroads', pp. 122-39.
5. Schiffman, 'At the Crossroads', p. 125.
6. Schiffman, 'At the Crossroads'. p. 128.

either for his beliefs (heresy) or by his actions (apostasy).[7] *M. Sanh.* 10.1 mentions three classes of Jew who have no portion in the world to come: the one who says that there is no resurrection of the dead, the one who denies that the Torah is from heaven and the *'apiqoros* (Epicurean) who denies God's actions in the world.[8] Exclusion from the world to come does not, however, deprive a Jew of status as a Jew on earth. The apostate (*meshumad*, 'one who has been destroyed'[9]) and the heretic (*min*) will be punished in Gehenna (*t. Sanh.* 12.5), but neither is deprived of present Jewish status. It goes without saying that none of these exclusions applied to Gentiles since they had never had a portion in the world to come.

The *Birkat haminim*, the twelfth of the Eighteen Benedictions, is a further expression of Jewish attitudes. The (earlier) Palestinian recension reads,

> As for the apostates let there be no hope; and may the insolent kingdom be quickly uprooted in our days. And may the Nazarenes (*noṣrim*) and the heretics (*minim*) perish quickly; and may they be erased from the Book of Life; and may they not be inscribed with the righteous. Blessed art thou, Lord, who humbles the insolent.[10]

The Eighteen Benedictions were recited three times on each weekday in the synagogues and the purpose of this blessing was to exclude the *noṣrim* and the *minim* from the synagogues or, at the least, to make them feel very uncomfortable. There is general agreement that the *minim* were deviant Jews[11] and that this would include Jewish Christians. Schiffman translates *noṣrim* as 'Christians', and finds supporting evidence in John's Gospel (9.22; 12.42; 16.2) that Jewish Christians were excluded from synagogues.[12] Kimelman, on the other hand, concludes from both internal and external evidence that although *noṣrim* includes Jewish Christians, it is a later interpolation in the text.[13] He further believes that, even if John is historically reliable, the practice of excluding Jewish Christians from synagogues was not widespread and that John's

---

7. Schiffman, 'At the Crossroads', pp. 139-46.
8. Schiffman, 'At the Crossroads', p. 142.
9. Schiffman, 'At the Crossroads', p. 145.
10. Schürer–Vermes, *History*, II, p. 461.
11. Kimelman, 'Birkat Ha-Minim', pp. 228-31.
12. Schiffman, 'At the Crossroads', p. 151.
13. Schiffman, 'At the Crossroads'. pp. 151-52; Kimelman, 'Birkat Ha-Minim', pp. 234-44.

8. Summary and Conclusions

comments do not constitute evidence for the formation of *Birkat haminim*.[14]

The picture that emerges from these studies suggests that the Tannaim regarded the early Christians as a group of Jews who believed that Jesus was the Messiah and, as long as their preaching was confined to Jews, the Tannaim held to that view. There was, after all, no sin in believing someone to be the Messiah and Christians would have been regarded by most people, including Luke, as another Jewish sect.[15] It was most probably the Christian mission to Gentiles, which did not require converts to be circumcised, that posed the real issue for Jews. Until the destruction of the temple different Jewish sects were tolerated within Judaism; it was afterwards, when there was strong internal pressure for Jewish unity, that the Pharisaic party and its successors became the dominant force in Judaism.[16] Did the affront to Judaism, caused by the admission of Gentiles, lead Luke to moderate his account of the Gentile mission and did he paint a more favourable picture of the Pharisees than Matthew because of their growing importance and power?

The Christian side of the picture, as Luke describes it, is of a Jewish–Gentile community of Christians that is experiencing internal pressures over issues such as table fellowship. He also pictures Jewish Christians as under external pressure from their own race. It is the Jewish Christians, notably Paul and his helpers, who are the targets of Jewish antagonism in Acts. Although estimates of the true extent of opposition vary,[17] Luke's description is rather what might be expected from the studies of Schiffman and Kimelman, with Jewish believers being attacked for their affiliation with the uncircumcised.

That such a picture is not just a figment of Luke's creative imagination is shown from Paul's own letters which speak of his having been in danger from his own countryfolk and his receiving the thirty-nine stripes (2 Cor. 11.24-26), evidence of missionary work in a Jewish *milieu*. He also mentions Judaean Christians suffering at the hands of Jews who 'hinder us from speaking to the Gentiles' (1 Thess. 2.14-16) and from whom he expects further trouble (Rom. 15.31). Finally, we have Paul's own testimonies that he persecuted the church (1 Cor. 15.9; Gal. 1.13, 23; Phil. 3.6). Yet, although in terms of historical probability it was the

---

14. Kimelman, 'Birkat Ha-Minim', pp. 234-35.
15. Schiffman, 'At the Crossroads', p. 147.
16. Schiffman, 'At the Crossroads', pp. 148-49.
17. Kimelman, 'Birkat Ha-Minim', pp. 233, 244.

admission of Gentiles that was the stumbling block for Judaism, Luke describes Paul as a persecutor prior to the conversion of Cornelius. Luke gives no reason for Paul's acts of persecution, but then neither does Paul himself.

The fact that the messianic age had not arrived with all its promised blessings would have left Jewish Christians specially vulnerable to doubt and wondering whether they had made the right decision. And doubtless Jews outside the church would have used any uncertainty to reinforce their arguments against becoming a Christian, particularly after the fall of Jerusalem. The environment of doubt is mirrored in Paul's farewell address to the Ephesian elders at Miletus with his warnings of fierce wolves outside and perverse teaching within (20.29-30). This is a plausible picture of a Jewish–Gentile church near the turn of the century.

Luke's pastoral task in this situation is twofold. He has to convince Jewish Christians that they have made the right decision—that they are still members of Israel and have not forfeited their portion in the world to come. This is one reason why the resurrection and its witnesses receive such emphasis in Acts and it is why some of Paul's journeys are to visit and strengthen existing congregations. The second task is to show Gentile believers that they are now, by God's grace, members of Israel with the same inheritance as the Jews. This carries the implication that Gentiles must realize that there is no 'us and them'. In Acts, the only Gentiles who are anti-Jewish are unbelievers; the converts are predominantly found in synagogues.

Luke's Plan

With his pastoral purpose in mind, Luke has devised the following strategy. The first step is to show that Israel remains the people of God and that he has always planned to restore Israel to its pre-Davidic unity. This restoration is now in the process of being fulfilled and one aspect of this involves overcoming the division between the descendants of the northern and southern kingdoms, Samaritans and Jews.

The second step is to remind his readers that the prophets look forward to the time of the incoming Gentiles. The Gentile mission is therefore Israel's mission and the route to the fulfilment of Israel's destiny. The age of the Spirit has dawned in which all flesh will see God's salvation (Lk. 3.6, citing Isa. 40.5) and all flesh will receive God's Spirit (Acts 2.17, citing Joel 2.28). Jesus and his followers are therefore to be a light

8. *Summary and Conclusions*

to the Gentiles as Isaiah has promised (Lk. 2.32; Acts 13.47). Luke recognizes Jewish reluctance and the sluggishness of the apostles in beginning this mission and that the initiative has to be taken by God in the conversion of Cornelius. It is this that compels Peter and the Jerusalem leadership to recognize that the Gentiles too have been given the Spirit and it is also the reason why the baptism of Cornelius and his household cannot be withheld. Perhaps Paul's statements of turning to the Gentiles contain at least an element of 'if you will not, we will'. As to the mission to Jews, many thousands become believers and remain zealous for the law, and among these are priests, synagogue rulers and Pharisees; it is in general the Jewish leaders and the Sadducees who do not see the light.

The third stage in Luke's plan is to show that the cardinal areas of Christian belief, Christology and atonement, are consonant with Jewish beliefs and expectations. In his earthly role Jesus is cast as the prophet promised by Moses, the expected Elijah who will come before the day of the Lord. As for his messiahship, this will be fully revealed when Jesus comes at the end of the age to judge all people and to restore all things. The death of Jesus is not a new way of atonement but the way to his resurrection and ascension into heaven which are the prerequisites for the fulfilment of the hope of Israel, and his death leads to the opening up of atonement to the Gentiles. In the interim, before the Messiah comes, Jewish Christians keep the law and so too, in a modified way, do Gentile Christians. This is the way to eternal life and for those who sin repentance remains the way to atonement. In his discussion of Luke's obvious interest in Jewish religious traditions, Tyson argues that Luke shows that Jewish rejection occurred despite the fact that the Christian message fitted into those traditions.[18] However, it seems very improbable that Luke presents Christian beliefs in the way he has simply to highlight Jewish rejection. This would imply that they were not his real beliefs and that he was prepared to sacrifice those beliefs and to risk alienating those Christians with more 'developed' understandings.

Thus far the strategy is designed to bring harmony within the Christian community and to strengthen the resolve of Jewish Christians against inner doubt and outside attack. But there were within the wider church those who appeared to advocate a radical break with Judaism and to imply that the church had replaced Israel in God's plan of salvation. On the Matthean wing, what may have been intended to show the

---

18. Tyson, 'Jewish Rejection', p. 130.

underlying motives for keeping the law looks suspiciously like a new law, more rigorous than the Mosaic code. And there are also signs that Jesus is a new and superior Moses. Moreover, the Pharisees, growing in importance in Judaism, are the subject of virulent invective, whereas in Luke's view common ground must be established between the church and the Pharisees if Christians and Israel are to live together after the events of 70 CE. Luke therefore has not only to put his own case but also to challenge the ideas he sees in Matthew. Hence his surgery on Matthew's Gospel.

At the other extreme is the Pauline corpus, which claims apostolic authority for its author and his thesis that the law has the status of a child's guide (παιδαγωγός, Gal. 3.24-25) that has been superseded for those in Christ. There is more to this than dismissing the law as an entrance requirement. It is a way of thinking that could, if taken at face value, lead to immorality, as seems to have happened at Corinth. More fundamentally, the 'ending' of the law threatens a decisive break with Israel and replacement of it with the Body of Christ.

Paul's authority to propound these views has therefore to be modified. Paul has to be presented as a law-abiding Jew whose missionary success comes, almost entirely, through his work in synagogues. It may be that the real Paul went directly to the Gentiles,[19] though this is not immediately obvious from his letters. If this was Paul's actual method then the missionary plan as described by Luke needs an explanation. One reason for Luke's presentation is that Paul's method might imply that Gentile converts do not enter Israel. It is not that Luke objects to the conversion of Gentiles—just the opposite—it is that he wants there to be no mistake that it is *Israel's* mission. There is thus no instance in Acts of Gentile believers preaching to Gentiles or Jews.

The relationship between Peter and Paul as it is depicted in Paul's letters has been radically changed by Luke. It is Peter who is cast in the role of the *avant-garde*, going to the Gentiles, overruling the food taboos and opposing those who insist that Gentile converts must be circumcised. Even before the Jerusalem council in Acts 15, Peter silences his critics from Jerusalem by declaring that his actions are on the direct authority of God (11.1-18). Paul, by contrast, is still regarded with suspicion by the Jerusalem leadership as late as 21.20-26. This picture seems to be a careful replacement for the Paul–Cephas disagreements in the letters, with Paul now seen accepting the advice of the Jerusalem

---

19. Sanders, *Jewish People*, pp. 179-90.

8. *Summary and Conclusions*

leadership in order to placate those who are zealous for the law.

Luke displays a masterly care and subtlety in his theological and pastoral polemic. He rarely allows himself anything approaching the invective in which Paul and Matthew sometimes indulge. This is partly because he avoids open confrontation with his opponents. Instead, he uses the past to attack the problems of the present and this is the great power of the historical approach that is used throughout Luke's work, whether it is in the history of Israel, of Jesus or of the early church. By claiming to have gone over the work of his predecessors and to have presented an orderly account Luke is able, very tactfully, to undermine his adversaries such as the Matthean school. Similarly, the 'we' passages give Luke an almost impregnable position as an eyewitness against those who might claim too much from their knowledge of Paul's teaching.

The question of the nature and role of the historical Israel was potentially one of the most divisive to face the first-century church. It raised not only the practical problems of the relationship of Jewish and Gentile Christians, but also that of the church and the body from which it was born. Paul's letters and Matthew's Gospel are among the Christian writings of the first century that provide ample evidence that such problems existed. Luke's solution is to point to the restoration of the historical Israel, and if this should seem a less radical solution than Paul's, we should reflect that it would have seemed remarkable for its retrogressive position at around the end of the first century.

As to why Luke should have offered this solution we can only speculate. But it is by no means improbable, bearing in mind his knowledge of things Jewish, that Luke had been a God-fearer prior to his conversion. In a short but very important essay, Marilyn Salmon has questioned J.T. Sanders's reading of Luke's view of the Jews.[20] To the question of whether Luke was an insider or an outsider with regard to Judaism she concludes that Luke perceived himself to be a Jew.[21] Some of the evidence that she cites is similar to that used in the present study, but in addition she notes that Luke's use of 'Gentile' shows a Jewish perspective on the world.[22] In the synoptic Gospels, ἔθνος is found either on the lips of Jews (usually Jesus) or in quotations from the OT. But in Acts, in addition to its use by Jews, ἔθνος is found six times in

---

20. Salmon, 'Insider or Outsider?', pp. 76-82.
21. Salmon, 'Insider or Outsider?', p. 79.
22. Salmon, 'Insider or Outsider?', pp. 79-80.

editorial descriptions, a fact that adds support to Salmon's case.[23] It would not have been necessary for Luke to have been ethnically Jewish and it may be going further than the evidence allows to say that he saw himself as a Jew. Instead it may be more accurate to say that he saw himself as a member of Israel, someone who was once a God-fearer but who is now a member of the Way, an insider. Along with the other incoming Gentiles he is now a member of the historical Israel, one of the people of God.

Finally we must try to assess Luke's place in Jewish Christianity at the turn of the century. J.D.G. Dunn begins his survey of Jewish Christianity as it appears in the NT by looking at its characteristics at the beginning and the end of its development. These points are the early Jerusalem church and the Ebionites of the second and third centuries.[24] The Ebionites were regarded as heretical by 'orthodox' (Gentile) Christians and Dunn has identified three characteristics of the sect.

1. A faithful adherence to the law, including circumcision, yet a rejection of the temple and the sacrificial system.
2. The exaltation of James and the denigration of Paul.
3. An adoptionist Christology that denies the divine birth of Jesus, who is seen as the greatest of Israel's prophets.

From his analysis, Dunn concludes that *'heretical Jewish christianity would appear to be not so very different from the faith of the first Jewish believers'*.[25] Our knowledge of the nature of Jerusalem Christianity is, of course, heavily dependent upon information provided by Acts and there is a strong possibility that Luke has tailored some of the material to suit his own requirements. Nevertheless, some of the characteristics of Ebionism that Dunn has noted are clearly discernible in Acts. Luke's two books contain obvious elements of an adoptionist Christology together with an emphasis on Jesus as the eschatological prophet and there is an expectation of adherence to the law. Moreover, in Acts 21.17-26, this is connected with the authority of James over Paul. But there is no conclusive evidence that Luke rejected the temple and its sacrifices and there is much to suggest the opposite. Luke does not share the view of writers such as Matthew and the author of

23. Acts 11.1; 14.2, 5, 27; 15.3, 12.
24. Dunn, *Unity and Diversity*, pp. 236-66.
25. Dunn, *Unity and Diversity*, p. 242 (Dunn's italics).
26. Dunn, *Unity and Diversity*, pp. 246-52.

8. Summary and Conclusions

Hebrews, that Christ has made the Jewish sacrificial system obsolete. And this is all the more remarkable when we reflect that Luke was in the position, after the destruction of the temple, to make such a claim had he so wished. Given the existence of the opportunity, Luke shows a purposeful restraint.

The evidence therefore points to Luke steering a careful course between the extremes of the hard-line expressions of both Jewish and Gentile Christianity, yet veering always towards agreement with Jewish expectations. It is this Israel-directed aspect that is further reflected in Luke's accounts of the conversion of Gentiles. The majority of these Gentiles are not outright pagans but are, at the very least, sympathetic to the worship of the God of Israel.

Among the questions that I asked at the beginning of this study was whether Luke's criticisms of Jews means that he had finally rejected the Jews and, hence, the restoration of Israel. The results of the study suggest that Luke's attitude to the Jews is determined by his belief that God will restore Israel. Once this is seen as a crucial aspect of Luke's design, then his criticisms of Jews fall into place among the exhortations and warnings of the Hebrew prophets whose line has been completed by Jesus. Not only does Luke look for the restoration of Israel but he has provided many clues about the form that Israel will take: it will be a reunited Israel under Jesus Messiah, the new Davidic king.

ADDED NOTE

When this study was almost complete I learnt of the publication of Eric Franklin's *Luke: Interpreter of Paul, Critic of Matthew* (JSNTSup, 92; Sheffield: JSOT Press, 1994). Since I too have argued that Luke knew and criticized Matthew and also that he was well aware of Paul's theology I was faced with a difficult choice. I could either make a brief acknowledgment of Franklin's study or enter into a full and detailed examination of it. This latter course would have necessitated a major revision of my own programme which would, in turn, distort the point of my overall argument. For although I agree that Luke criticized Matthew and interpreted Paul I have arrived at these conclusions by a very different route to the one followed and developed by Franklin. For this reason I decided on the first approach.

Franklin believes that Luke was a God-fearer who was a follower of Paul and who interpreted Paul for a later age. Luke carried out this interpretation because Israel was central to his own story (p. 35) and he therefore needed to soften what could be seen as Paul's attacks on Israel. But Franklin also holds that Luke agrees with Paul that the law has no saving value and that it no longer defines 'the boundaries of the people of God' (p. 61). Luke thus sees Paul as respecting the law as the boundary of Israel but not of the eschatological people of God (pp. 59, 64-65). I have concluded that Luke was much more critical of Paul and his legacy than is allowed for by Franklin.

Franklin provides an extensive discussion of the possible relationship between Luke and Matthew and he concludes that Luke used Matthew with freedom combined with suspicion (pp. 315, 367). There are, as would be expected, areas of overlap between the two studies and among these are discussion of the distribution of the sayings material, Christology and the birth and resurrection stories. However, our respective approaches differ considerably and we therefore come to different assessments of why Luke made his changes.

In Franklin's opinion, Luke and Matthew shared the same church situation and, perhaps, even a single church (p. 382). It was a situation in which the church lived alongside its Jewish neighbours, yet seeking its own self-definition. But the principal reason behind their differences is their different solutions to the delay in the parousia. Matthew speaks of Christ in the church whereas Luke still expects the coming of the heavenly Lord. Thus, although both evangelists are concerned about the relation of the church to Israel, their solutions spring from different eschatological understandings. My own view is that Luke's criticism of Matthew had much more to do with their different understandings of Israel than with the delay of the parousia.

BIBLIOGRAPHY

Abrahams, I., *Studies in Pharisaism and the Gospel* (First Series; Cambridge: Cambridge University Press, 1917).
Ackroyd, P.R., 'Zechariah', in Black (ed.), *Peake's Commentary*, pp. 646-55.
Alexander, L.C.A., *The Preface to Luke's Gospel: Literary Convention and Social Context in Luke 1.1-4 and Acts 1.1* (SNTSMS, 78; Cambridge: Cambridge University Press, 1993).
Allison, D.C., 'Peter and Cephas: One and the Same', *JBL* 111 (1992), pp. 489-95.
Bacon, B.W., *Studies in Matthew* (London: Constable, 1930).
Baltzer, K., 'The Meaning of the Temple in the Lukan Writings', *HTR* 58 (1965), pp. 263-77.
Barth, G., G. Bornkamm and H.J. Held, *Tradition and Interpretation in Matthew* (London: SCM Press, 1963).
Barth, M., *The People of God* (JSNTSup, 5; Sheffield: JSOT Press, 1983).
Benoit, P., 'L'enfance de Jean-Baptiste selon Luc 1', *NTS* 3 (1957), pp. 169-94.
Betz, H.D., *Galatians* (Philadelphia: Fortress Press, 1979).
Black, M. (ed.), *Peake's Commentary on the Bible* (London: Nelson, 1962).
Bornkamm, G., 'The Missionary Stance of Paul in 1 Corinthians and Acts', in Keck and Martin (eds.), *Studies in Luke–Acts*, pp. 194-207.
—'End-Expectation and Church in Matthew', in Barth, Bornkamm and Held, *Tradition and Interpretation*, pp. 15-51.
Bowman, J., *The Samaritan Problem. Studies in the Relationships of Samaritanism, Judaism, and Early Christianity* (Pittsburgh: Pickwick, 1975).
Brawley, R.L., 'Paul in Acts: Lucan Apology and Conciliation', in Talbert (ed.), *New Perspectives*, pp. 129-47.
—*Luke–Acts and the Jews: Conflict, Apology and Conciliation* (SBLMS, 33; Atlanta: Scholars Press, 1987).
Brown, R.E., *The Birth of the Messiah: A Commentary on the Infancy Narratives in Matthew and Luke* (London: Chapman, 1977).
Brown, S., 'The Role of the Prologues in Determining the Purpose of Luke–Acts', in Talbert (ed.), *Perspectives*, pp. 99-111.
Bruce, F.F., 'Hebrews', in Black (ed.), *Peake's Commentary*, pp. 1008-19.
Bull, R.J., 'The Excavation of Tell er-Ras on Mt. Gerizim', *BA* 31 (1968), pp. 58-72.
Bultmann, R., *History of the Synoptic Tradition* (Oxford: Basil Blackwell, 1972).
—*Theology of the New Testament* (2 vols.; London: SCM Press, 1952).
—'πείθω', *TDNT*, VI, pp. 1-12.
Burchard, C., *Die dreizehnte Zeuge: Traditions-und kompositionsgeschichtliche Untersuchungen zu Lukas' Darstellung der Früzeit des Paulus* (FRLANT, 103; Göttingen: Vandenhoeck & Ruprecht, 1970).

—'Joseph and Aseneth', *OTP*, II, pp. 177-247.
Cadbury, H.J., 'The Speeches in Acts', in Foakes Jackson and Lake (eds.), *Beginnings of Christianity*, V, pp. 402-27.
—*The Making of Luke–Acts* (London: SPCK, 1958).
Carrol, J.T., 'Luke's Portrayal of the Pharisees', *CBQ* 50 (1988), pp. 604-21.
Casey, R.P., 'Simon Magus', in Foakes Jackson and Lake (eds.), *Beginnings of Christianity*, V, pp. 151-63.
Cassidy, R.J., and P.J. Scharper (eds.), *Political Issues in Luke–Acts* (Maryknoll, NY: Orbis Books, 1983).
Charlesworth, J.H. (ed.), *The Old Testament Pseudepigrapha* (2 vols.; Garden City, NY: Doubleday, 1986).
—'Prayer of Manasseh', *OTP*, II, pp. 625-37.
Coggins, R.J., *Samaritans and Jews: The Origins of Samaritanism Reconsidered* (Oxford: Basil Blackwell, 1975).
Cohen, S.J.D., 'Was Timothy a Jew (Acts 16.1-3)? Patristic Exegesis, Rabbinic Law and Matrilineal Descent', *JBL* 105 (1986), pp. 251-68.
—'Crossing the Boundary and Becoming a Jew', *HTR* 82 (1989), pp. 13-33.
Collins, J.J., 'Sibylline Oracles', *OTP*, I, pp. 317-472.
Conzelmann, H., *The Theology of St Luke* (London: Faber & Faber, 1960).
—*Acts of the Apostles* (Philadelphia: Fortress Press, 1987).
—'Luke's Place in the Development of Early Christianity', in Keck and Martin (eds.), *Studies in Luke-Acts*, pp. 298-316.
Cranfield, C.E.B., '"The Works of the Law" in the Epistle to the Romans', *JSNT* 43 (1991), pp. 89-101.
Cranford, M., 'Election and Ethnicity: Paul's View of Israel in Rom. 9.1-13', *JSNT* 50 (1993), pp. 27-41.
Creed, J.M., *The Gospel according to St Luke* (London: Macmillan, 1930).
Cullmann, O., *The Early Church* (London: SCM Press, 1956).
Dahl, N.A., 'A People for His Name (Acts 15.14)', *NTS* 4 (1959–60), pp. 319-27.
—'The Story of Abraham in Luke–Acts', Keck and Martin (eds.), *Studies in Luke-Acts*, pp. 139-58.
Danby, H., *The Mishnah* (Translated from the Hebrew with Introduction and Brief Explanatory Notes; Oxford: Oxford University Press, 1933).
Danker, F.W., *Jesus and the New Age: A Commentary on St Luke's Gospel* (Philadelphia: Fortress Press, rev. edn, 1988).
Davies, A.T. (ed.), *AntiSemitism and the Foundations of Christianity* (New York: Paulist Press, 1979).
Davies, J.G., *He Ascended into Heaven* (London: Lutterworth, 1958).
Davies, W.D., *The Setting of the Sermon on the Mount* (Cambridge: Cambridge University Press, 1964).
—*Jewish and Pauline Studies* (London: SPCK, 1984).
Davies, W.D., and L. Finkelstein (eds.), *Cambridge History of Judaism*, II (Cambridge: Cambridge University Press, 1989).
Dexinger, F., 'Limits of Tolerance in Judaism: The Samaritan Example', in Sanders *et al.* (eds.), *Jewish and Christian Self Definition*, pp. 88-114.
Dibelius, M., *Studies in the Acts of the Apostles* (London: SCM Press, 1956).
Dodd, C.H., *According to the Scriptures* (London: Nisbet, 1952).

—*The Apostolic Preaching and its Developments* (London: Hodder & Stoughton, 1963).
Donaldson, T.L., 'Moses Typology and the Sectarian Nature of Early Christian Anti-Judaism: A Study in Acts 7', *JSNT* 12 (1981), pp. 27-52.
Draisma, S. (ed.), *Intertextuality in Biblical Writings* (Kampen: Kok, 1989).
Drury, J., *Tradition and Design in Luke's Gospel* (London: Darton, Longman & Todd, 1976).
Dunn, J.D.G., *Christology in the Making: A New Testament Inquiry into the Origins of the Doctrine of the Incarnation* (London: SCM Press, 1980).
—*Unity and Diversity in the New Testament: An Inquiry into the Character of Earliest Christianity* (London: SCM Press, 1977).
—*Jesus, Paul and the Law* (London: SPCK, 1990).
—'Yet Once More—"The Works of the Law": A Response', *JSNT* 46 (1992), pp. 99-117.
Easton, B.S., *Early Christianity: The Purpose of Luke–Acts and other Papers* (London: SPCK, 1955).
Ehrman, B.D., 'Cephas and Peter', *JBL* 109 (1990), pp. 463-74.
Eichrodt, W., *Theology of the Old Testament* (2 vols.; London: SCM Press, 1967).
Ellis, E.E., *The Gospel of Luke* (NCB; London: Marshall, Morgan & Scott, 1974).
—'"The End of the Earth" (Acts 1.8)', *Bulletin of Biblical Research* 1 (1991), pp. 123-32.
Enslin, M.S., 'Luke and the Samaritans', *HTR* 36 (1943), pp. 274-97.
—'"Luke" and "Paul"', *JAOS* 58 (1938), pp. 81-91.
—'Once Again, Luke and Paul', *ZNW* 61 (1970), pp. 253-71.
Esler, P.F., *Community and Gospel in Luke–Acts* (SNTSMS, 57; Cambridge: Cambridge University Press, 1987).
Evans, C.A., 'Luke's Use of the Elijah/Elisha Narratives and the Ethic of Election', *JBL* 106 (1987), pp. 75-83.
Evans, C.F., 'The Central Section of St Luke's Gospel', in Nineham (ed.), *Studies in the Gospels*, pp. 37-53.
—*Saint Luke* (TPI New Testament Commentary; London: SCM Press, 1990).
Faierstein, M.M., 'Why do the Scribes Say That Elijah Must Come First?', *JBL* 100 (1981), pp. 75-86.
Farrer, A.M., 'On Dispensing with Q', in Nineham (ed.), *Studies in the Gospels*, pp. 55-88.
Farris, S., *The Hymns of Luke's Infancy Narratives: Their Origin, Meaning and Significance* (JSNTSup, 9; Sheffield: JSOT Press, 1985).
Fenton, J.C., *Saint Matthew* (Pelican New Testament Commentary; London: Penguin, 1963).
Fichtner, J., 'πλήσιον', *TDNT*, VI, pp. 312-15.
Filson, F.V., *The Gospel according to St Matthew* (London: A. & C. Black, 2nd edn, 1971).
Fitzmyer, J.A., *The Gospel according to Luke* (2 vols.; AB; New York: Doubleday, 1981, 1985).
—*Luke the Theologian: Aspects of his Teaching* (London: Geoffrey Chapman, 1989).
—'Jewish Christianity in Acts in Light of the Qumran Scrolls', in Keck and Martin (eds.), *Studies in Luke–Acts*, pp. 233-57.

Foakes-Jackson, F.J., *The Acts of the Apostles* (MNTC; London: Hodder & Stoughton, 1931).
—'Stephen's Speech in Acts', *JBL* 49 (1930), pp. 283-86.
Foakes Jackson, F.J., and K. Lake (eds.), *The Beginnings of Christianity, Part I: The Acts of the Apostles* (5 vols.; London: Macmillan, 1920–1933).
France, R.T., *Matthew; Evangelist and Teacher* (Exeter: Paternoster Press, 1989).
Franklin, E., *Christ the Lord: A Study in the Purpose and Theology of Luke–Acts* (London: SPCK, 1975).
—*Luke: Interpreter of Paul, Critic of Matthew* (JSNTSup, 92; Sheffield: JSOT Press, 1994).
Gager, J.G., 'Jews, Gentiles, and Synagogues in the Book of Acts', *HTR* 79 (1986), pp. 91-99.
Gaster, M., *The Samaritans: Their History, Doctrines and Literature* (Schweich Lectures, 1923; London: Oxford University Press, 1925).
Gaster, T.H., 'Samaritans', *IDB*, IV, pp. 190-97.
Gerhardsson, B., *Memory and Manuscript: Oral Tradition and Written Transmission in Rabbinic Judaism and Early Christianity* (ASNTU 22; Lund: Gleerup, 1961).
Gill, D., 'Observations on the Lukan Travel Narrative and some Related Passages', *HTR* 63 (1970), pp. 199-221.
Goodenough, E.R., 'The Perspective of Acts', in Keck and Martin (eds.), *Studies in Luke–Acts*, pp. 51-59.
Goudoever, J. van, 'The Place of Israel in Luke's Gospel', *NovT* 8 (1966), pp. 111-23.
Goulder, M.D., *Type and History in Acts* (London: SPCK, 1964).
—'Mark xvi.1-8 and Parallels', *NTS* 24 (1977–1978), pp. 235-40.
—'The Two Roots of the Christian Myth', in J. Hick (ed.), *The Myth of God Incarnate* (London: SCM Press, 1977), pp. 64-86.
—'The Order of a Crank', in Tuckett (ed.), *Synoptic Studies*, pp. 111-30.
—*Luke—A New Paradigm* (2 vols.; JSNTSup, 20; Sheffield: JSOT Press, 1989).
Green, F.W., *The Gospel according to Saint Matthew* (Oxford: Clarendon Press, 1936).
Green, H.B., *The Gospel according to Matthew* (Oxford: Oxford University Press, 1975).
—'The Credibility of Luke's Transformation of Matthew', in Tuckett (ed.), *Synoptic Studies*, pp. 131-55.
—'Matthew, Clement and Luke: Their Sequence and Relationship', *JTS* NS 40 (1989), pp. 1-25.
Gunkel, H., 'Die Lieder in der Kindheitsgeschichte bei Lukas', in K. Holl *et al.* (eds.), *A. Harnack Festgabe* (Tübingen: Mohr [Paul Siebeck], 1921).
Haenchen, E., *The Acts of the Apostles* (Oxford: Basil Blackwell, 1971).
—'The Book of Acts as Source Material for the History of Early Christianity', in Keck and Martin (eds.), *Studies in Luke–Acts*, pp. 258-78.
Hare, D.R.A., 'The Rejection of the Jews in the Synoptic Gospels', in Davies (ed.), *AntiSemitism*, pp. 27-47.
—'The Lives of the Prophets', *OTP*, II, pp. 379-99.
Harrington, D.J., 'Pseudo-Philo', *OTP*, II, pp. 297-377.
Harvey, A.E., *Jesus and the Constraints of History* (London: Gerald Duckworth, 1982).
Hatch, E., and H.A. Redpath, *A Concordance to the Septuagint and other Greek Versions of the Old Testament* (Graz: Akademische Druck & Verlagsanstalt, 1975).

Hengel, M., *Studies in the Earliest History of Christianity* (London: SCM Press, 1983).
—*Earliest Christianity* (London: SCM Press, 1986).
—*Between Jesus and Paul: Studies in the Earliest History of Christianity* (London: SCM Press, 1983).
Hick, J. (ed.), *The Myth of God Incarnate* (London: SCM Press, 1977).
Hickling, C.J.A., 'The Sequence of Thought in II Corinthians Chapter Three', *NTS* 21 (1975), pp. 380-95.
Higgins, A.J.B., *The Lord's Supper in the New Testament* (SBT, 6; London: SCM Press, 1952).
Hiers, R.H., 'The Problem of the Delay in the Parousia in Luke–Acts', *NTS* 20 (1974–1975), pp. 145-55.
Hill, D., *New Testament Prophecy* (Basingstoke: Marshall, Morgan & Scott, 1979).
Houlden, J.L., 'The Purpose of Luke', *JSNT* 21 (1984), pp. 53-65.
Jeremias, J., *Jerusalem in the Time of Jesus* (London: SCM Press, 1969).
—*The Parables of Jesus* (London: SCM Press, 1972).
Jervell, J., *Luke and the People of God: A New Look at Luke–Acts* (Minneapolis: Augsburg, 1972).
—*The Unknown Paul: Essays on Luke–Acts and Early Christian History* (Minneapolis: Augsburg, 1984).
—'The Church of Jews and Godfearers', in Tyson (ed.), *Luke–Acts and the Jewish People*, pp. 11-20.
Jones, C.P.M., 'The Epistle to the Hebrews and the Lukan Writings', in Nineham (ed.), *Studies in the Gospels*, pp. 113-43.
Jones, D.L., 'The Title *Christos* in Luke–Acts', *CBQ* 32 (1970), pp. 69-76.
—'The Title *Kyrios* in Luke–Acts', in MacRae (ed.), *SBLSP*, II, pp. 85-101.
Jonge, M. de, 'The Use of the Word "Anointed" in the Time of Jesus', *NovT* 8 (1966), pp. 132-48.
—*Testamenta XII Patriarchum* (Pseudepigrapha Veteris Testamenti Graece; Leiden: Brill, 1964).
Keck, L.E., and J.L. Martin (eds.), *Studies in Luke–Acts* (London: SPCK, 1968).
Kee, H.C., 'Testaments of the Twelve Patriarchs', *OTP*, I, pp. 775-828.
—'The Transformation of the Synagogue after 70 CE: Its Import for Early Christianity', *NTS* (1990), pp. 1-24.
Kilgallen, J., *The Stephen Speech: A Literary and Redactional Study of Acts 7.2-53* (AnBib, 67; Rome: Pontifical Biblical Institute, 1976).
Kimelman, R., 'Birkat Ha-Minim and the Lack of Evidence for an Anti-Christian Prayer in Late Antiquity', in Sanders (ed.), *Jewish and Christian Self-Definition*, II, pp. 226-44.
King, N.Q., 'The "Universalism" of the Third Gospel', *TU* 73 (1959), pp. 199-205.
Kingsbury, J.D., 'The Pharisees in Luke–Acts', in van Segbroeck *et al.* (eds.), *The Four Gospels 1992*, pp. 1497-512.
Klassen, W., and G.F. Snyder (eds.), *Current Issues in New Testament Interpretation* (London: SCM Press, 1962).
Klein, G., *Die Zwölf Apostel: Ursprung und Gehalt einer Idee* (FRLANT; Göttingen: Vandenhoeck & Ruprecht, 1961).
Klijn, A.F.J., 'Stephen's Speech—Acts vii 2–53', *NTS* 2 (1957), pp. 25-31.
Knibb, M.A., 'Martyrdom and Ascension of Isaiah', *OTP*, II, pp. 143-76.

Bibliography

Knox, J., 'Acts and the Pauline Corpus', in Keck and Martin (eds.), *Studies in Luke-Acts*, pp. 279-87.
Knox, W.L., *The Sources of the Synoptic Gospels*, II (Cambridge: Cambridge University Press, 1957).
Kraabel, A.T., 'The Disappearance of the God-Fearers', *Numen* 28 (1981), pp. 113-26.
—'Greeks, Jews and Lutherans', *HTR* 79 (1986), pp. 146-57.
—'Synagoga Caeca: Systematic Distortion in Gentile Interpretations of Evidence for Judaism in the Early Christian Period', in Neusner (ed.), *'To See Ourselves as Others See Us'*.
Kremer, J. (ed.), *Les Actes des Apôtres: Traditions, rédaction, théologie* (BETL, 48; Leuven: Leuven University Press, 1979).
Kümmel, W.G., *Introduction to the New Testament* (London: SCM Press, rev. edn, 1975).
La Potterie, I. de, 'L'Onction du Christ: Etude de théologie biblique', *NRT* 80 (1958), pp. 225-52.
Lake, K., *Apostolic Fathers* (2 vols.; LCL; London: Heinemann, 1912).
—'The Apostolic Council of Jerusalem', in Foakes Jackson and Lake (eds.), *Beginnings of Christianity*, V, pp. 195-212.
Lake, K., and H.J. Cadbury, Foakes Jackson and Lake (eds.), *Beginnings of Christianity. IV. The Acts of the Apostles: English Translation and Commentary*.
Lampe, G.W.H., *St Luke and the Church of Jerusalem* (London: Athlone Press, 1969).
Larsson, E., 'Temple-Criticism and the Jewish Heritage: Some Reflections on Acts 6–7', *NTS* 39 (1993), pp. 379-95.
Leaney, A.R.C., *The Gospel according to St Luke* (London: A. & C. Black, 1966).
Lentz, J.C., *Luke's Portrait of Paul* (SNTSMS, 77; Cambridge: Cambridge University Press, 1993).
Lightfoot, R.H., *Locality and Doctrine in the Gospels* (London: Hodder & Stoughton, 1938).
—*St John's Gospel: A Commentary* (ed. C.F. Evans; Oxford: Oxford University Press, 1957).
Lindemann, A., *Paulus im ältesten Christentums* (Tübingen: Mohr [Paul Siebeck], 1979).
Linnemann, E., *Parables of Jesus: Introduction and Exposition* (London: SPCK, 1966).
Lohse, E., 'υἱὸς Δαυίδ', *TDNT*, VIII, pp. 478-88.
Loisy, A., *Les Actes des Apôtres* (Paris: Nourry, 1920).
Luz, U., *Das Geschichtsverständnis bei Paulus* (Munich: Chr. Kaiser Verlag, 1968).
Maccoby, H., *Early Rabbinic Writings: Cambridge Commentaries on the Writings of the Jewish and Christian World 200 BC–200 AD*, III (Cambridge: Cambridge University Press, 1988).
MacDonald, J., *The Theology of the Samaritans* (London: SCM Press, 1964).
MacRae, G.W. (ed.), *SBL 1974 Seminar Papers* (2 vols.; Cambridge, MA: Society of Biblical Literature, 1974).
Maddox, R., *The Purpose of Luke–Acts* (Edinburgh: T. & T. Clark, 1982).
Mănek, J., 'The New Exodus in the Books of Luke', *NovT* 2 (1955), pp. 8-23.
Mann, C.S., 'Hellenists and Hebrews in Acts VI', in Munck, *The Acts of The Apostles*, pp. 301-304.
Manson, T.W., *The Sayings of Jesus* (London: SCM Press, 1949).

Mare, W.H., 'Acts 7: Jewish or Samaritan in Character?', *WTJ* 34 (1971–1972), pp. 1-21.
Marsh, J., *The Gospel of St John* (Pelican Gospel Commentaries; London: Penguin, 1968).
Marshall, I.H., *Luke—Historian and Theologian* (Exeter: Paternoster Press, 1970).
—*The Gospel of Luke: A Commentary on the Greek Text* (Exeter: Paternoster Press, 1978).
Martin, R.P., *2 Corinthians* (WBC, 40; Waco, TX: Word Books, 1986).
Massyngbaerde, Ford, J., 'Reconciliation and Forgiveness in Luke's Gospel', in Cassidy and Scharper (eds.), *Political Issues in Luke–Acts*, pp. 80-98.
Mattill, A.J., 'The Value of Acts as a Source for the Study of Paul', in Talbert (ed.), *Perspectives*, pp. 76-98.
McCown, C.C., 'The Geography of Luke's Central Section', *JBL* 57 (1938), pp. 51-66.
McEleney, N.J., 'Conversion, Circumcision and the Law', *NTS* 20 (1973–1974), pp. 319-41.
McNeile, A.H., *The Gospel according to St Matthew* (London: Macmillan, 1915).
Minear, P.S., 'Luke's Use of the Birth Stories', in Keck and Martin (eds.), *Studies in Luke–Acts*, pp. 111-30.
Mitton, C.L., *The Formation of the Pauline Corpus of Letters* (London: Epworth Press, 1955).
Moessner, D.P., 'Luke 9.1-50: Luke's Preview of the Journey of the Prophet like Moses of Deuteronomy', *JBL* 102 (1983), pp. 575-605.
—'Jesus and the "Wilderness Generation": the Death of the Prophet like Moses according to Luke', in Richards (ed.), *SBL 1982 Seminar Papers*, pp. 319-40.
—'The Ironic Fulfilment of Israel's Glory', in Tyson (ed.), *Luke–Acts and the People of God*, pp. 35-50.
Montefiore, C.G., 'The Spirit of Judaism', in Foakes Jackson and Lake (eds.), *Beginnings of Christianity*, I, pp. 35-81.
Montgomery, J.A., *The Samaritans, the Earliest Jewish Sect: Their History, Theology and Literature* (Philadelphia: Winston, 1907/New York: Ktav, 1968).
Moore, G.F., *Judaism in the First Centuries of the Christian Era: The Age of the Tannaim* (3 vols.; Cambridge, MA: Harvard University Press, 1927–1930).
Moule, C.F.D., 'Once More, Who were the Hellenists?', *ExpTim* 70 (1958–1959), pp. 100-102.
—'The Christology of Acts', in Keck and Martin (eds.), *Studies in Luke–Acts*, pp. 159-85.
—*The Origin of Christology* (Cambridge: Cambridge University Press, 1977).
Moulton, W.F., and A.S. Geden, *A Concordance to the Greek Testament* (ed. H.K. Moulton; Edinburgh: T. & T. Clark, 5th rev. edn, 1978).
Moulton, J.H., and G. Milligan, *The Vocabulary of the Greek Testament Illustrated from the Papyri and other Non-Literary Sources*, Parts i-viii (London: Hodder & Stoughton, 1914–1929).
Mowinkel, S., *He That Cometh* (Oxford: Basil Blackwell, 1956).
Mueller, J.R., and S.E. Robinson, 'Apocryphon of Ezekiel', *OTP*, I, pp. 487-96.
Munck, J., *The Acts of the Apostles* (AB; New York: Doubleday, 1967).
Neale, D.A., *None but the Sinners: Religious Categories in the Gospel of Luke* (JSNTSup, 58; Sheffield: JSOT Press, 1991).

Neusner, J., and E. Frerichs (eds.), *'To See Ourselves as Others See Us': Christians, Jews, 'Others' in Late Antiquity* (Chico, CA: Scholars Press, 1984).

Neyrey, J., *The Passion according to Luke: A Redaction Study of Luke's Soteriology* (New York: Paulist Press, 1985).

Nineham, D.E., *Saint Mark* (Pelican New Testament Commentaries; London: Penguin, 1963).

Nineham, D.E. (ed.), *Studies in the Gospels: Essays in Memory of R.H. Lightfoot* (Oxford: Basil Blackwell, 1957).

Nock, A.D., *Conversion* (Oxford: The Clarendon Press, 1933).

Oliver, H.H., 'The Lucan Birth Stories and the Purpose of Luke–Acts', *NTS* 10 (1963–1964), pp. 202-206.

Oster, R.E., 'Supposed Anachronism in Luke–Acts' Use of ΣΥΝΑΓΩΓΗ: A Rejoinder to H.C. Kee', *NTS* 39 (1993), pp. 178-208.

Palmer, D.W., 'Mission to Jews and Gentiles in the Last Episode of Acts', *RTR* 52 (1993), pp. 62-73.

Parkes, J., *Judaism and Christianity* (Chicago: Chicago University Press, 1948).

Petrie, S., '"Q" is Only What You Make It', *NovT* 3 (1959), pp. 28-33.

Plummer, A., *The Gospel according to St Luke* (ICC; Edinburgh: T. & T. Clark, 1896).

Plumtre, E.H., 'The Samaritan Element in the Gospels and Acts', *Expositor* 7 (1878), pp. 22-40.

Pummer, R., 'The Samaritan Pentateuch and the New Testament', *NTS* 22 (1976), pp. 441-43.

Purvis, J.D., 'The Samaritans', in Davies (ed.), *Cambridge History of Judaism*, pp. 519-63.

Quell, G., 'πατήρ', *TDNT*, V, pp. 959-74.

Quinn, J.D., 'The Last Volume of Luke: The Relation of Luke–Acts to the Pastoral Epistles', in Talbert (ed.), *Perspectives*, pp. 62-75.

Rackham, R.B., *The Acts of the Apostles* (Westminster Commentaries; London: Methuen, 1901).

Rad, G. von, *Old Testament Theology* (2 vols.; London: SCM Press, 1975).

Ravens, D.A.S., 'Luke and Atonement', *ExpTim* 97 (1986), pp. 291-94.

—'The Setting of Luke's Account of the Anointing', *NTS* 36 (1988), pp. 282-92.

—'Luke 9.7-62 and the Prophetic Role of Jesus', *NTS* 36 (1990), pp. 119-29.

—'Zacchaeus: The Final Part of a Lucan Triptych?', *JSNT* 41 (1991), pp. 19-32.

Reicke, B., 'Instruction and Discussion in the Travel Narrative', *SE*, I (1959), pp. 106-16.

Rengstorf, K.H., 'The Election of Matthias, Acts 1.15ff.', in Klassen (ed.), *Current Issues in New Testament Interpretation*, pp. 178-92.

Richard, E., 'Acts 7: An Investigation of the Samaritan Evidence', *CBQ* 39 (1977), pp. 190-208.

Richards, K.H. (ed.), *SBL 1982 Seminar Papers* (Chicago: Scholars Press, 1982).

Richardson, P., *Israel in the Apostolic Church* (SNTSMS, 10; Cambridge: Cambridge University Press, 1969).

Riddle, D.W., 'The Cephas Problem and a Possible Solution', *JBL* 59 (1940), pp. 169-80.

Ringgren, H., 'Luke's Use of the Old Testament, *HTR* 79 (1986), pp. 227-35.

—*Israelite Religion* (London: SPCK, 1969).

Robbins, V.K., 'By Land and Sea: The We-Passages and Ancient Sea Voyages', in Talbert (ed.), *Perspectives*, pp. 215-42.

Robertson, R.G., 'Ezekiel the Tragedian', *OTP*, II, pp. 803-19.

Robinson, J.A.T., 'Elijah, John and Jesus', *NTS* 4 (1958), pp. 263-82.

—'The Destination and Purpose of St John's Gospel', *NTS* 6 (1960), pp. 117-31.

—'The Most Primitive Christology of All?', *JTS* NS 7 (1956), pp. 177-89. These articles appear in *Twelve New Testament Studies* (SBT, 34; London: SCM Press, 1962).

Robinson, W.C., 'The Theological Context for Interpreting Luke's Travel Narrative (9.51ff.)', *JBL* 79 (1960), pp. 20-31.

Reuther, R., *Faith and Fratricide: The Theological Roots of Anti-Semitism* (New York: Seabury, 1974).

Sabbe, M., 'The Son of Man Saying in Acts 7, 56', in Kremer (ed.), *Actes des Apôtres*, pp. 241-79.

Sahlin, H., *Der Messias und das Gottesvolk: Studien zur protolukanischen Theologie* (Uppsala: Almqvist & Wiksells, 1945).

Salmon, M., 'Insider or Outsider? Luke's Relationship with Judaism', in Tyson (ed.), *Luke–Acts and the People of God*, pp. 76-82.

Sanday, W., and A.C. Headlam, *The Epistle to the Romans* (ICC; Edinburgh: T. & T. Clark, 1902).

Sanders, E.P., *Paul and Palestinian Judaism* (London: SCM Press, 1977).

—*Jesus and Judaism* (London: SCM Press, 1985).

—*Paul, the Law and the Jewish People* (London: SCM Press, 1985).

—*Jewish Law from Jesus to the Mishnah* (London: SCM Press, 1990).

—'The Overlap of Mark and Q and the Synoptic Problem', *NTS* 19 (1972–1973), pp. 453-65.

Sanders, E.P., A.T. Baumgarten and A. Mendelson (eds.), *Jewish and Christian Self-Definition*, II (London: SCM Press, 1981).

Sanders, J.N., 'Galatians', in Black (ed.), *Peake's Commentary*, pp. 973-79.

Sanders, J.T., 'The Parable of the Pounds and Lucan Anti-Semitism', *TS* 42 (1981), pp. 660-68.

—'The Salvation of the Jews in Luke–Acts', in Talbert (ed.), *New Perspectives*, pp. 105-28.

—*The Jews in Luke–Acts* (London: SCM Press, 1987).

—'Who is a Jew and who is a Gentile in the Book of Acts?', *NTS* 37 (1991), pp. 434-55.

Sandmel, S., *Judaism and Christian Beginnings* (New York: Oxford University Press, 1978).

Scharlemann, M.H., *Stephen: A Singular Saint* (AnBib, 34; Rome: Pontifical Biblical Institute Press, 1968).

Scheele, P.W., and G. Schneider (eds.), *Christus Zeugnis in der Kirche* (Essen: Fredebuel and Koenen, 1970).

Schenk, W., 'Luke as Reader of Paul: Observations on his Reception', in Draisma (ed.), *Intertextuality in Biblical Writings*, pp. 127-39.

Schiffman, L.H., 'At the Crossroads: Tannaitic Perspectives on the Jewish–Christian Schism', in Sanders *et al.* (eds.), *Jewish and Christian Self-Definition*, pp. 115-56.

Schmidt, D., 'Luke's "Innocent" Jesus: A Scriptural Apologetic', in Cassidy and Sharper (eds.), *Political Issues in Luke–Acts*, pp. 111-21.

Schneider, G., 'Die Zwölf Apostel als "Zeugen": Wesen, Ursprung und Funktion einer Lukanische Konzeption', in P.W. Scheele and G. Schneider (eds.), *Christus Zeugnis in der Kirche*, pp. 39-65.
—*Das Evangelium nach Lukas* (2 vols.; Gütersloh: Mohn; Würzburg: Echter, 1977).
Schürer, E., *The History of the Jewish People in the Age of Jesus Christ (175 BC–AD 135)* (ed. G. Vermes, F. Millar, M. Black; 4 vols.; Edinburgh: T. & T. Clark, rev. edn, 1973-1987).
Scobie, C.H.H., 'The Origins and Development of Samaritan Christianity', *NTS* 19 (1972-1973), pp. 390-414.
Segbroeck, F. van, C.M. Tuckett, G. Van Belle and J. Verheyden (eds.), *The Four Gospels 1992: Festschrift Frans Neirynck*, II (Leuven: Leuven University Press, 1992).
Selling, G., 'Lukas als Gleichniszähler: Die Erzählung vom barmherzigen Samariter (Lk. 10.25-37)', *ZNW* 66 (1975), pp. 19-60.
Siker, J.S., 'First to the Gentiles: A Literary Analysis of Luke 4.16-30', *JBL* 111 (1992), pp. 73-90.
Simon, M., *St Stephen and the Hellenists in the Primitive Church* (London: Longmans Green & Co., 1958).
Smith, M., *Jesus the Magician* (London: Gollancz, 1978).
Soards, M.L., *The Passion according to Luke: The Special Material of Luke 22* (JSNTSup, 14; Sheffield: JSOT Press, 1987).
Sparks, H.F.D., 'The Semitisms of St Luke's Gospel', *JTS* 44 (1943), pp. 129-38.
Spiro, A., Stephen's Samaritan Background', in Munck, *Acts of the Apostles*, pp. 285-300.
Squires, J.J., *The Plan of God in Luke–Acts* (SNTSMS, 76; Cambridge: Cambridge University Press, 1993).
Stählin, G., *Die Apostelgeschichte* (NTD, 5; Göttingen: Vandenhoeck & Ruprecht, 1962).
Stendahl, K., 'The Apostle Paul and the Introspective Conscience of the West', *HTR* 56 (1963), pp. 199-215.
Streeter, B.H., *The Four Gospels: A Study in Origins* (London: Macmillan, 1924).
Talbert, C.H., *Reading Luke: A Literary and Theological Commentary on the Third Gospel* (New York: Crossroad, 1986).
Talbert, C.H. (ed.), *Perspectives on Luke–Acts* (Edinburgh: T. & T. Clark, 1978).
—*Luke–Acts: New Perspectives from the Society of Biblical Literature* (New York: Crossroad, 1984).
Tannehill, R.C., 'Israel in Luke–Acts: A Tragic Story', *JBL* 104 (1985), pp. 69-85.
—*The Narrative Unity of Luke–Acts: A Literary Interpretation*. I. *The Gospel according to Luke* (Philadelphia: Fortress Press, 1986).
Taylor, N., *Paul, Antioch and Jerusalem: A Study in Relationships and Authority in Earliest Christianity* (JSNTSup, 66; Sheffield: JSOT Press, 1989).
Thielman, F., 'The Coherence of Paul's View of the Law. The Evidence of First Corinthians', *NTS* 38 (1992), pp. 235-53.
Throckmorton, B.H., 'Σώζειν, σωτηρία in Luke–Acts', *SE* VI (1973), pp. 515-26.
Tiede, D.L., *Prophecy and History in Luke–Acts* (Philadelphia: Fortress Press, 1980).
—'The Exaltation of Jesus and the Restoration of Israel in Acts 1', *HTR* 79 (1986), pp. 278-86.

—'Glory to thy People Israel', in Tyson (ed.), *Luke–Acts and the Jewish People*, pp. 21-34.
Trebilco, P., *Jewish Communities in Asia Minor* (SNTSMS, 69; Cambridge: Cambridge University Press, 1991).
Trocmé, E., *Le livre des Actes et l'histoire* (Paris: Presses Universitaires de France, 1957).
Tuckett, C.M., 'Arguments from Order: Definition and Evaluation', in Tuckett (ed.), *Synoptic Studies*, pp. 197-219.
Tuckett, C.M. (ed.), *Synoptic Studies: The Ampleforth Conferences of 1982 and 1983* (JSNTSup, 7; Sheffield: JSOT Press, 1984).
Tyson, J.B. (ed.), *Luke–Acts and the Jewish People: Eight Critical Studies* (Minneapolis: Augsburg, 1989).
—'The Problem of Jewish Rejection in Acts', in Tyson (ed.), *Luke–Acts and the Jewish People*, pp. 124-37.
Van de Sandt, H., 'An Explanation of Acts 15.16-21 in the Light of Deuteronomy 4.29-35 (LXX)', *JSNT* 46 (1992), pp. 73-97.
Vermes, G., *Jesus the Jew: A Historian's Reading of the Gospels* (London: Collins–Fontana, 1976).
—*Jesus and the World of Judaism* (London: SCM Press, 1983).
—*The Dead Sea Scrolls in English* (London: Penguin, 3rd edn, 1987).
Vielhauer, P., 'On the "Paulinism" of Acts', in Keck and Martin (eds.), *Studies in Luke–Acts*, pp. 33-49.
Wainwright, A.W., 'Luke and the Restoration of the Kingdom to Israel', *ExpTim* 89 (1977), pp. 76-79.
Walaskay, P.W., *'And So we Came to Rome': The Political Perspective of St Luke* (SNTSMS, 49; Cambridge: Cambridge University Press, 1983).
Walker, W.O., 'Acts and the Pauline Corpus Reconsidered', *JSNT* 24 (1985), pp. 3-23.
Wanke, J., *Die Emmauszählung: Eine redaktionsgeschichtliche Untersuchung zu Lk 24.13-25* (Erfurter theologische Studien, 31; Leipzig: St Benno, 1973).
Wendt, H.H., *Die Apostelgeschichte* (Göttingen: Vandenhoeck & Ruprecht, 9th edn, 1913).
Wenham, J.W., 'Synoptic Independence and the Origin of Luke's Travel Narrative', *NTS* 27 (1980–1981), pp. 507-15.
Whiteley, D.E.H., *The Theology of St Paul* (Oxford: Basil Blackwell, 1972).
Wilcox, M., *The Semitisms of Acts* (Oxford: Oxford University Press, 1965).
—'Luke 2.36-38 "Anna bat Phanuel, of the tribe of Asher, a prophetess…". A Study in Midrash Special to Luke', in van Segbroeck *et al.* (eds.), *The Four Gospels, 1992*, pp. 1571-79.
Wilkens, U., *Die Missionsrede der Apostelgeschichte: Form- und Traditionsgeschichtliche Untersuchungen* (WMANT, 5; Neukirchen–Vluyn: Neukirchener Verlag, 3rd edn, 1974).
Williams, C.S.C., *The Acts of the Apostles* (London: A. & C. Black, 2nd edn, 1964).
Wilson, S.G., *The Gentiles and the Gentile Mission in Luke–Acts* (SNTSMS, 33; Cambridge: Cambridge University Press, 1973).
—*Luke and the Law* (SNTSMS, 50; Cambridge: Cambridge University Press, 1983).
Winter, P., 'Magnificat and Benedictus—Maccabean Psalms?', *BJRL* 37 (1954–1955), pp. 328-57.
—'Lukanische Miszellen', *ZNW* 49 (1958), pp. 65-77.
Wintermute, O.S., 'Jubilees', *OTP*, II, pp. 35-142.

Winton-Thomas, D., 'Micah', in Black (ed.), *Peake's Commentary*, pp. 630-34.
Wright, R.P., 'Psalms of Solomon', *OTP*, II, pp. 639-70.
Zahn, T., *Die Apostelgeschichte des Lukas* (KNT, 5; Leipzig: Erlangen, 1919–1921).
Ziesler, J.A., 'Luke and the Pharisees', *NTS* 25 (1978–1979), pp. 146-57.

INDEXES

INDEX OF REFERENCES

OLD TESTAMENT

Genesis		3.6	88	17.10-16	198
9.4	198	4.18-19	220	17.10-12	198
11.26	87	4.31 (LXX)	38	18.16-18	198
11.32	87	5.4	134	19.4	198
12.4	87	6.24	47	19.18	91
12.6-7	90	7–8	219	21.1-3	83
12.7	60	7.11	219	26.12	205
12.10	220	7.22	219		
15.1-2	27	12.40	194	Numbers	
15.6	195	14.21-23	133	1.51	85
16.10-15	200	19.1 (LXX)	128	3.10	85
17.1	60	19.3	33	12.3	225
17.4-14	200	19.5	200	18.7	85
17.9-14	195	20	88	19.11-13	83
18.1	60	20.1–24.12	200	21.27 (LXX)	32
21.13-21	200	23.20	131, 132	26.46	46
23	89	32.6	205	27.18	26
33.19	89	32.7-14	65	33.38 (LXX)	128
37	220	33.3	65		
46.17	46	33.5	65	Deuteronomy	
48.1-20	75	34	65, 201, 221	2.5 (LXX)	88
49.31-32	89	34.9	65	4.20	84
50.12-13	89	34.29 (LXX)	128	4.42	84
50.24 (LXX)	38	34.29-35	201	5.17 (LXX)	84
		34.29-32	221	6.4	161
Exodus		34.30 (LXX)	128	10.16	206
1.15–2.10	127	34.35 (LXX)	128	12	198
1.16	220	36.25	143	18	129
1.22	220			18.15-18	129
2.1-10	220	Leviticus		18.15	63, 80, 88, 127
2.11	90	14	85		
2.13	91	14.2-57	86	18.15 (LXX)	128
2.24	200	16.30	143	18.18	127
3.1-10	61	17–18	168	21.22	163

32.43	205	17.10-24	132	*Nehemiah*	
34.1-4	225	17.10	124	12.37	37
		17.17-24	124, 127		
Joshua		18.17-40	97	*Psalms*	
24.32	89	18.17	134	2.1-2	116
		19.8	133	2.7	246
Judges		19.16	115	6.9	217
13	31	19.19	130	15.8-11	
13.2	31	19.20	130	(LXX)	150
13.3	31			17.3 (LXX)	37
13.4	31	*2 Kings*		17.18 (LXX)	40
13.5	31	1.8	131	18.15 (LXX)	38
13.7	31	1.10-12	82	22.18	118
13.14	31	2	133	31.1-2 (LXX)	159
13.25	26, 31	2.2	133	69.21	118
16.21	31	2.4	133	77.35 (LXX)	38
		2.6	133	93.14 (LXX)	205
Ruth		2.8	133	104.38 (LXX)	128
1.6 (LXX)	38	2.9-10	133	105.6	104
		2.11	133	105.43	104
1 Samuel		4.18-37	130	106.2 (LXX)	101
2.1-10	31, 36	4.29	131	106.3 (LXX)	101
2.5	31	5	86, 130	106.23-32	
2.7-8	36	5.1	130	(LXX)	101
2.7	31	5.2-3	130	109.1 (LXX)	150
2.10 (LXX)	37	5.3	98	110	38
15.22	64	5.5	130	110.5 (LXX)	38
16.1-13	42	5.8	130	110.9 (LXX)	38
16.11 (LXX)	43	5.10	130	113.1 (LXX)	128
16.13	26, 115	5.14-15	130	116.1 (LXX)	205
		5.14	130	129.7	38
2 Samuel		17	74	131 (LXX)	66
7.1-2	66	17.24	74	131.5 (LXX)	66
7.6-7	66	17.27-28	74	131.17 (LXX)	37
7.12-16	33, 66	17.29	74		
7.24-29	66	21.1-16	142	*Isaiah*	
22.3 (LXX)	37	21.13	142	2.19-21	135
				3.5	84
1 Kings		*1 Chronicles*		5.1-7	146
1.48	38	4.4	47	6.9-10	49, 237
1.49-53	37	7.30	46	6.9	141
6.1 (LXX)	128	8.25	47	6.10	140
6.11-13	66	11.5	47	7.2	37
8	217	11.7	47	7.13	37
12.25	47			8.9	96
17–24	130	*2 Chronicles*		9.1	40
17.1	97	6	217	10.22	209
17.9	97			11.1	40

11.1-3	39	61.1	116, 117	*Daniel*		
11.2	47	61.2-3	115	7	129	
11.10	100	61.11	39	8.16-17	30	
11.11-12	100	62.11-12	96	8.16	30	
11.12-13	101	63.4	38	8.17	30	
13	135	65.1	209	9.3-19	145	
19.2	84	65.2	205, 209	9.21	30	
23	145	65.9	104	9.23	30	
27.9	159	65.15	104	9.26	30	
28.11	205	65.23	104	9.27	30	
28.16	209	66.1-2	66			
29.10	209	66.14	39	*Hosea*		
29.18	126			1.1	42	
35.5-6	126	*Jeremiah*		1.10-11	105	
40.3	42	3.2	198	1.10	205	
40.5	250	3.6	103	2.25	205	
41.8-9	36	3.9	198	2.25 (LXX)	207	
42.9	39	3.11-12	101	4.3	103	
43.7	32	4.4	206	4.15	103	
43.19	39	8	146	6.6	64, 105	
44.4	39	8.6	141	6.10	198	
44.26	39	8.13	146	10.7-8	105	
45.7	32	13.19-20	102	10.8	104	
45.22	96	13.19	101	11.1	220	
46.8	140, 141	15.19	50, 93, 94			
46.13	97	16.14-15	101	*Joel*		
48.20	96	16.15	50, 93	1.1	42	
49.6	96, 97, 211	17.13	143	2	27	
49.18-22	104	21.12	37	2.28-33	150	
49.21	104	23.5	39, 40	2.28	250	
52.7	115	27.19 (LXX)	50, 93			
53	158	31.9 (MT)	45	*Amos*		
53.12	118	31.18-20	102	5.18-20	135	
55.3	246	31.19 (MT)	141	8.9	135	
56	85	33.15 (MT)	40	9	199	
56.3-7	86	38.9 (LXX)	45	9.11-12	168, 211	
56.3	86	38.18-20		9.11	18, 39	
56.6-7	86	(LXX)	102			
56.7	86	50.19 (MT)	50, 93	*Jonah*		
58.6	114			1.3	235	
58.7	230	*Ezekiel*		1.4-15	235	
58.8	39	1.3	42	1.4	235	
58.10	39	7	135	1.5	235	
58.11	39	26–32	135	1.6	235, 237	
59.20	210	29.21	37	1.11	235	
60.1	39	37.15-17	100	1.12	235	
61.1-3	115			1.14	235, 237	
61.1-2	114			1.16	236	

2.6	237	*Malachi*		*Wisdom of Solomon*	
2.8	237	3	32	5.1-5	141
3.5	146	3.1-2	32	5.3	141
3.6-10	236	3.1	32, 131, 132	11.23	142
3.8	146	3.2	32	12.10	142
3.9	146	3.19-24		12.19	142
3.10	146	(LXX)	135		
4.11	236	3.22-23		*Ecclesiasticus*	
		(LXX)	94, 131	17.24-25	141
Micah		3.23-24		27.30–28.5	148
1.1	43	(LXX)	31, 132	35.12-15	104
4.1-4	135	3.23	32, 33, 41	35.17	104
5	43	3.24 (LXX)	134	35.18	104
5.1-3 (LXX)	42, 43	4.5	131	44.16	142
5.1	220			46.14	38
5.3 (LXX)	43, 44, 220	*1 Esdras*		47.20-21	104
6.6-8	64	9.7-15	85	47.22	103, 104
				48	32
Zephaniah		*2 Esdras*		48.10	32, 33, 41,
3.14-20	135	3.2	69		94, 217
		3.8	69	48.15	141
Zechariah		4.3	69	50.25-26	73
3.8	39, 40	5.2	69	51.23-27	221
6.12	39, 40				
9.9	34	*Judith*		*Baruch*	
9.10	34	16.23	46	4.12	104
11.14	73			4.16	104
12.7-12	37				

NEW TESTAMENT

Matthew		2.20	220	5.3	216
1.2-6	69	2.22	218	5.4	216
1.18-21	219	2.23	40, 126, 218	5.6	216
1.20-21	218	3.1	42	5.11	123, 216
1.21	216	3.2	144	5.12	216
1.23	218, 225	3.4	131	5.13	216
2.1-12	219	3.6	144	5.15	216
2.2	99, 218	3.7	227	5.18	216
2.6	43, 216	4.12	144	5.20	227
2.12	218	4.15-16	40	5.21-48	14, 228
2.13-16	127	4.15	223	5.21-22	221
2.13-15	220	4.16	216	5.27-28	221
2.13	218	4.17	141, 144	5.31-46	221
2.15	218	4.23	228	5.42	140
2.16	220	5–7	220	5.44	215
2.19-23	220	5.1–8.1	127	6.2	232
2.19-20	218	5.1-2	220	6.5	232

6.9-13	150	14.1-12	33, 217	23.13	230		
6.25-33	216	14.3-12	125	23.34	232, 233		
7.11-13	33	15.1-20	227, 228	23.37-39	81		
7.21	122	15.6	136	23.41	233		
7.29	228	15.13	123	24.3	123		
8.5-13	130, 232	15.21-28	124	24.4-5	113		
8.10	217	15.24	216	24.5	123		
8.11-12	100	15.31	137	24.15	30		
8.16-17	117	15.32-38	236	25.14-30	121		
9.13	64	16.1-12	227	25.21-30	121		
9.18-19	124	16.13-15	123	26.3	233		
9.23-26	124	16.14	126	26.24	119		
9.34	227	16.16	113	26.26-28	215		
9.35	228	16.17	123	26.28	144		
10.5-15	82	16.18-19	217	26.29	122		
10.5-6	72, 216, 220	16.20	113	26.39	122		
10.10	215	17.3	128	26.57	233		
10.17-18	232	17.10-13	216	26.61	58		
10.17	228	17.10-12	131	26.68	114		
10.27-33	216	17.11-13	222	26.71	126		
10.32	122	17.11-12	131	27.11	99		
10.33	122	17.11	33	27.17	114, 233		
10.34-36	216	17.13	131, 217	27.22	114		
11.2	113	18.10	123	27.27	233		
11.10	131	18.15	148	27.40	58		
11.14	33, 131	18.19	123	27.42	99		
11.16-19	145	18.35	123	27.46-49	131		
11.20-24	145	19.3	227	27.57-61	222		
11.20	141, 145	19.18	232	27.62-66	228		
11.21	141	19.23	232	27.62	233		
11.28-29	221	19.28	123	28.6	224		
11.29-30	221	20.23	123	28.7	222		
11.29	225	20.30-31	114	28.10	223		
12.1-8	233	21.5	34, 225	28.11-15	228		
12.7	64	21.9	81	28.12	233		
12.9-14	232	21.11	126	28.16-20	223		
12.9	228	21.41	217	28.16	225		
12.14	228	21.42-45	227	28.18-20	149		
12.24	227	21.43	217	28.19-20	144		
12.38	227	21.45	217	28.19	72, 225		
12.41	141	22.15-17	227	28.20	225, 226		
12.42	146	22.16	227	36.52	140		
12.50	122	22.32	137				
12.51-53	216	22.34-35	227	*Mark*			
13.13-15	241	22.34	227	1.2	131		
13.15	140	23	230	1.4	42, 141, 144		
13.54	126, 228	23.2-3	227	1.5	42, 144		
13.57	124	23.6	232	1.6	131		

Index of References

1.14-15	144	12.13-14	227	1.26	33
1.15	141, 144	12.13	227	1.28	27, 30
1.16-20	235	12.26	137	1.29-30	30
1.21-28	232	12.28-37	227	1.29	28, 30
1.24	114	12.33	64	1.30	27, 30
1.32-34	117	13.1-4	57	1.32-33	30, 33, 66, 99, 123, 160
1.39	145	13.4	123		
1.40-44	85	13.6	123	1.32	33, 127
2.10	114	13.14-23	57	1.34	27, 28
2.13-17	145	14.21	119	1.35-37	33
3.1-6	232	14.22-24	215	1.35	27, 33, 127
3.6	227	14.57	57	1.36	31
3.35	122, 136	14.58	57	1.38	27, 226
4.12	140, 141, 241	14.61-62	118	1.41	26
		14.61	113	1.42	226
5.22-24	124	15.18	99	1.43	41
5.22	232	15.29	56, 58	1.45	27
5.35-43	124	15.32	34, 99, 113	1.46-50	35
5.36	232	15.34-36	131	1.46	31, 43
5.38	232	15.38	56	1.47	35, 41, 137, 153
6.1	126	15.43	222		
6.4	124	16.7	223	1.48	31
6.7-12	82			1.50-55	35
6.12	141, 144	*Luke*		1.51-55	35
6.14-29	33	1–2	24, 25, 27, 37, 50	1.51-53	36
6.17-29	125			1.54-55	36
6.45–8.26	14	1.1-4	28, 29, 213	1.54	34
7.1-23	14	1.1	213	1.55	70
7.2-4	228	1.2-3	77	1.58	43
7.13	136	1.2	184	1.64	226
7.24-30	124	1.3	213	1.67	26, 27
8.1-10	236	1.6	27, 32, 222	1.68-69	61, 63
8.28	126	1.7	31	1.68	37, 38, 45, 61, 127, 137, 226
8.29	113	1.9	56, 226		
9.4-5	128	1.10	30		
9.11-13	131	1.12	28, 30	1.69	37, 40, 63
9.12-13	33	1.13	30, 31	1.71	40
9.12	33, 131	1.14	226	1.72-75	45
9.13	33	1.15	26, 30, 31	1.72-73	70
10.1	77, 78	1.16-17	31, 41	1.72	38, 202
10.2	227	1.16	30, 140	1.73	37
10.11	215	1.17	31, 32, 132, 140	1.74	37, 40
10.42	186			1.76-77	37
10.45	167	1.18	27, 28	1.76	41, 42, 127
11.10	34	1.19	33	1.77	37, 40, 149
11.12-25	146	1.21	56, 226	1.78	37, 38, 127
11.17	86	1.22	27, 30, 56, 226	1.79	39, 40
12.9	217			1.80	26

2	42, 44	3.5	151	4.43	78, 144, 145
2.2	136	3.6	41, 120,	4.44	145
2.4	42		127, 242,	5.1-11	235
2.6	42		245, 250	5.1-10	246
2.8-20	43, 219, 220	3.7	81	5.1	81, 136
2.10	226	3.8	154	5.3	235
2.11	26, 41-44,	3.10	81, 151	5.5	235
	48, 113, 160	3.12-13	148	5.12-14	85
2.14	44, 127	3.12	151	5.17-26	150
2.15	42	3.14	151	5.20-24	150
2.22-27	200	3.15	117	5.24	150
2.22	226	3.16	26, 151	5.27-32	144
2.25	26, 27, 32,	3.18	33, 41, 144,	5.32	146, 154
	45, 222, 226		151	6	220
2.26	26, 44, 113	3.20	31, 151	6.1-11	200
2.27	45, 226	3.21-22	26	6.1-5	233
2.28	226	3.21	144, 238	6.6-11	232
2.29-32	45	3.23-38	69	6.11	228
2.29	27	3.23-31	160	6.12	220
2.30-32	96, 236, 245	3.27	69	6.17-18	145
2.30	41, 127	4	126	6.17	220
2.32	26, 45, 211,	4.1-13	219	6.20-23	216
	251	4.1	26, 116	6.22	123
2.33	45	4.3-4	78	6.28	215
2.34-35	27, 246	4.14	26, 116	6.35	127
2.34	26	4.15	232	6.46	122
2.36	27	4.16-30	114	7	130
2.37-38	46	4.16	126	7.2-50	134
2.37	27, 226	4.18-19	115, 116	7.2-3	130
2.38	38, 61, 226	4.18	26, 116,	7.2	130
2.39	200		117, 126-	7.3	25, 93, 130
2.40	47		28, 144	7.4	130
2.41	226	4.19	116	7.5	232
2.43	226	4.21	115	7.6	130
2.45	226	4.23	83	7.9	217
2.46	226	4.24	116, 117,	7.10	130
2.47	47		121, 124	7.11-17	13, 124, 132
2.50	47	4.25-26	127	7.11-15	86
2.52	47	4.25	97	7.11	42
3–24	26	4.27	86, 97, 127,	7.12	127
3	151		130	7.13	43
3.2	29, 42, 125,	4.28-30	121, 125	7.16	63, 127, 130
	136	4.28-29	117	7.18	113
3.3-18	150	4.31-37	232	7.19	43, 134
3.3	144, 149,	4.31-36	83	7.20	134
	151, 154,	4.34	116, 126	7.27	131, 132
	155	4.41	117	7.30	130
3.4-6	42, 137	4.42	81	7.36-50	150, 230

Index of References

7.39	150	9.60	144	12.42	43
7.42	141, 159	9.61-62	130	13	146
7.43	141, 159	9.61	130	13.1-9	147
8.1	134	9.62	130	13.1-5	146
8.11	136	10.1–19.45	134	13.3	146, 154
8.16	216	10.1	43, 82	13.4	81, 146, 150
8.21	122, 136	10.4	130	13.5	146, 154
8.22-25	235	10.7	82, 215	13.6-9	81, 120, 146
8.22	78, 235	10.8	82	13.6	146
8.23	235	10.9	83, 144	13.8	146
8.24	235	10.10-12	145	13.10-17	200, 232
8.25	235	10.11	144	13.15	43
8.26-39	93, 125	10.13-15	83, 145	13.16	70
8.26	78	10.13	155	13.22	77
8.27	93	10.17	83, 145	13.24	101
8.28	127	10.21	26	13.27-29	217
8.37	125	10.25-37	91	13.28-29	101
8.41-42	124	10.25-28	80, 198, 200, 227	13.29	78, 101
8.41	232			13.31	125, 227
8.42	127	10.30-37	78, 83	13.33-34	80, 125
8.49-56	124	10.30	83	13.33	48, 119, 125, 134
8.49	232	10.39	43		
9.1-50	129	11	220	13.34	80
9.1-6	82, 134	11.2-4	150	14	220
9.2	144	11.4	146, 150	14.1-6	200, 230
9.7-62	134	11.13	26	14.1	81
9.9	48, 125	11.15	227	14.13	230
9.10-17	145	11.16	227	14.15-24	231
9.18-20	123	11.28	136	14.15	231
9.20	113	11.29-32	227	14.21	230
9.21	113	11.29-30	236	14.34	216
9.22	118, 223	11.32	146, 155	15	156
9.29	224	11.37-52	230	15.2	147
9.30-31	201, 222	11.37-44	81	15.3-10	147
9.30	224	11.39-41	80	15.3-7	149
9.31	128	11.45-52	230	15.4	149
9.34	128	11.45	230	15.6	147, 149
9.38	127	11.452	80	15.7	147, 154
9.45	82	11.47-51	125	15.9	147
9.51–18.14	78, 81	11.49-51	80	15.10	147, 154
9.51-55	81, 132	11.53	81	15.11-32	147
9.51-53	85	12.3-9	216	15.24	149
9.51	77, 82	12.8	122	15.27	103
9.52-53	92	12.9	122	15.30	103
9.52	78, 82	12.10-50	216	15.32	103, 149
9.53	82, 92	12.10	165	16.14	227, 231
9.55	82	12.11-12	59	16.16-17	80
9.59-62	13	12.12	26	16.16	128

16.17	216	20.16	217	23.50-54	222
16.18	200, 227	20.17-19	227	23.50	32, 222
16.19-31	147	20.19-20	227	23.51	26
16.29	128	20.37	137	24	223
16.30	154, 155	20.41-44	227	24.4	224
16.31	80, 128, 148, 238	20.41	117	24.6	223
		21.1	80	24.7-8	224
17.1	148	21.7-8	113	24.7	224
17.3-4	148, 150	21.7	123	24.13-32	183
17.3	154	21.8	123	24.13	223
17.4	140, 154	21.19	237	24.18	223
17.5	43	21.20	30	24.19-20	126
17.6	43	21.24	237, 241	24.19	63, 116, 126, 224
17.11-19	85, 130	21.25	237		
17.11	77, 78	22	202	24.21	38, 93, 104, 186, 226, 246
17.14	85	22.17-19	215		
17.15	85	22.17	236		
17.18	85	22.18	122	24.25-26	118
17.20	81	22.19-20	202	24.25	224
17.22	103	22.19	202, 236	24.26-27	118, 202
17.24-25	118	22.20	201	24.26	119, 224
17.25	80	22.22	119	24.27	128, 224
18.1	104	22.26	233	24.30-35	202
18.3	104	22.29-30	33, 123	24.32	202, 224
18.5	104	22.29	34	24.33	223
18.6	43	22.30	61, 95, 97	24.34	183, 224
18.7	104	22.32	140	24.36-49	183
18.14	104	22.37	118, 158	24.39-43	224
18.31-32	119	22.42	122	24.41	226
18.37	116, 126	22.47	117	24.44-49	149
18.38	126, 160	22.61	43	24.44-46	149, 150
19.1-10	148	22.64	114	24.44-45	224
19.8	43, 149	22.67-68	118	24.44	128, 226
19.9	40, 70, 149	23	26	24.45	224
19.10	147, 149	23.2	43, 117, 134	24.46	118, 119, 224
19.11-27	57, 121	23.3	26, 34		
19.11	34, 121	23.14	140	24.47	152, 155, 156, 223, 225, 242
19.12	34, 160	23.18-25	114		
19.15	34, 121	23.34	118, 244		
19.35	34	23.35	99, 113	24.49	223, 226
19.37-38	34	23.36	118	24.50	225
19.38	45, 127, 160	23.37	26, 34	24.51	48
19.41-44	34	23.38	26, 34	24.52	223, 226
19.42-44	57	23.39	117	24.53	226
19.44	45	23.43	167		
19.45	45	23.44	135	*John*	
19.46	65, 86	23.45	56	1.21	127, 132
20.6	238	23.47	32	1.29	98

1.49	34, 98	1.8	26, 95, 97,	3.12-15	55
1.77	42		226, 242	3.12	118, 152
2.19	52, 58	1.9-11	225	3.13-15	153
2.21	52, 58	1.10	224	3.13	96, 137
4.5	72, 90	1.11	34, 94, 95,	3.14-15	152, 163
4.9	72		133, 226	3.14	32, 118, 141
4.12	98	1.12	133	3.15	118
4.20-26	73	1.17-20	183	3.17-19	70
4.21-24	105	1.21-26	95, 97	3.17-18	244
4.39-42	72	1.21-22	183, 184	3.17	152, 243
4.40	72	1.22	152	3.18-26	118
5.46	127	1.26	183	3.18-20	113
6.14	127	2–3	244	3.18	113, 118,
6.31-35	98, 99	2	27, 151		119, 152,
7.35	98	2.1-4	183		243
8.48	72	2.3	151	3.19-21	50, 94
8.53	98	2.14-40	150, 185	3.19-20	120
9.22	248	2.14-36	150	3.19	140-42,
10.11-16	98	2.17-21	95		152, 155
10.41	131	2.17	27, 120, 250	3.20-21	33, 92, 118
11.48	98	2.18	27	3.20	119, 152
11.50	98	2.22-36	118, 245	3.21	33, 94, 120,
11.51	98	2.22-24	55		211
11.52	98	2.22	126, 152	3.22-25	152
12.13	34, 98	2.23	163, 243.	3.22-23	91, 118,
12.15	34		244		127, 224,
12.20	98	2.28	152		225
12.40	241	2.29-31	160	3.22	63
12.42	248	2.31-33	119	3.24	118
15.1-6	98	2.36	43, 44, 118,	3.25	120, 202
16.2	248		163	3.26	96, 140, 152
16.5-7	226	2.37-40	150	4.1-12	55
18.18	177	2.37	151, 245	4.1-6	53
18.35	98	2.38-40	245	4.1-3	106
		2.38	151, 155,	4.1-2	67
Acts			203, 243	4.4	92, 235, 245
1	133	2.39	137	4.5-12	64
1.1	186	2.40	151	4.5	233
1.2-8	183	2.41	235, 245	4.8	59
1.3	133	2.42	202	4.10	116, 126,
1.4-11	133	2.45-46	53		163
1.4	133	2.46	65, 202	4.12	40
1.5	26, 133	3	42	4.25-26	116
1.6-7	34, 61, 211	3.1-10	185	4.26	116, 233
1.6	50, 93, 94,	3.1	65	4.27	96, 116,
	104, 120,	3.6	116, 126		117, 233
	123, 186	3.11-26	95	4.30	96, 116
1.7	94	3.12-26	245	4.31	26, 28, 136

4.32	53	7.23-29	60, 62	7.60	244
4.34-37	53	7.23	62, 63, 90,	8	18
5.14	245		127	8.1	55
5.15	185	7.25	40, 90, 91	8.4-17	103
5.17	240	7.26	62, 90, 91	8.4-13	92
5.19-20	185	7.27	61, 91	8.4-10	53
5.21	26	7.30-34	61	8.4-8	70, 72, 87
5.26	176	7.30	59, 71, 91	8.5	72, 92
5.27-32	55, 64, 152	7.32	88, 137	8.9-11	72
5.28	67	7.34	61	8.12	92, 203
5.30-31	152	7.35	38, 59, 61,	8.13	203
5.30	67, 137, 163		224	8.14-17	92
5.31	41, 152, 155	7.36	60, 61, 71	8.14	92, 136
5.33-40	67	7.37	63, 88, 90,	8.17	26
5.34-39	228		91, 127, 224	8.18-24	153, 185,
5.36-37	136, 238	7.38	59, 63, 71,		220
5.37	136		204	8.22	153, 155
6–12	51	7.39-43	62	8.25	92
6	54	7.39-41	71	8.26-40	53
6.1	53, 54, 90	7.39	61, 63	8.26	102
6.2	53, 136	7.40	64	8.32-33	158
6.3	51, 127	7.41	64	9.2	204
6.4	53	7.42	71	9.3-5	184
6.5	51, 55, 59	7.43	65	9.3	175
6.7	68, 136	7.44-45	65, 90	9.4-5	122
6.8-14	53	7.44	71	9.4	175
6.8	51, 60	7.45-47	65	9.5	175
6.9	55	7.45-46	65	9.6-8	175
6.10	51, 53, 59	7.45	65	9.10-16	122
6.11	56	7.46	56, 65, 66,	9.13-20	153
6.13-14	55, 56		137	9.13	204
6.13	52, 56	7.47-50	52	9.15-16	190
6.14	56, 57, 126	7.47	56, 58	9.15	176
6.15	50, 51, 59	7.48	56, 64, 127	9.16	204
7	50, 67	7.49	56, 66	9.17	59, 184
7.2-50	50	7.51-53	64	9.20-23	178
7.2-46	51	7.51-52	60, 62	9.21	175
7.2-3	60	7.51	50, 65	9.23	178
7.2	59, 60, 90	7.52	32, 61, 63,	9.25	176
7.4	62, 87		125, 141,	9.27	184
7.5	88		152, 175	9.29	54, 213
7.8	61, 62, 97,	7.53	56, 57, 59,	9.31	92
	202		63, 200	9.35	140
7.9-14	60, 61	7.55-56	119, 123	9.40	140
7.10	60, 61	7.55	59	10–15	15
7.13	90	7.56	122	10	14, 235
7.16	87, 89	7.58	176	10.1-2	153
7.22	63	7.59	176	10.2	15, 166

10.3-6	116	13.22-23	160	15.12	254
10.9-16	185, 236	13.23	41, 153	15.14	127, 186
10.14	185	13.24	152, 154, 155	15.16-18	18, 186
10.15	242			15.16-17	39, 199, 211
10.22	15, 32, 166	13.26	15, 40, 70, 165	15.19-21	166
10.23-48	185			15.19	140
10.25-26	185	13.32-33	246	15.20	168, 198
10.28	26, 185	13.33-34	246	15.22	192
10.34-43	115, 244	13.38-39	165	15.23-29	173
10.34	242	13.42	197	15.25	192
10.35	116	13.43	15, 165, 245	15.29	198
10.36	116, 195	13.44	136, 197	15.30-31	166, 185
10.37	152	13.46-50	178	15.36	127, 140
10.38	116, 117, 126	13.46-47	189, 242	16.1-3	189, 196
		13.46	17, 136, 236	16.3	178, 200
10.39	163	13.47	40, 96, 211, 236, 242, 251	16.6-10	188
10.43	153, 156, 157, 165			16.10-17	187
				16.12-40	189
10.44-48	195, 203	13.48	17, 136, 166, 245	16.13	189, 197
10.44-47	26, 92			16.14	15
10.44-45	244	13.50	15, 241	16.16-24	17
10.44	242	14.1	232, 242	16.16-18	153, 220
10.48	203	14.2	241, 254	16.16	189
11.1-18	166, 185, 252	14.4	184	16.17	40, 41, 127
		14.5	176, 254	16.18	140
11.1	136, 245, 254	14.8-10	185	16.19-24	243
		14.9	41	16.19-23	204
11.2-3	236	14.11-17	137	16.20	26
11.7-8	195	14.11-15	185	16.22	176
11.14	41	14.11	81	16.25-34	185
11.17	154	14.14	184	16.30	41
11.18	153, 155, 166	14.15-17	188, 244	16.31-33	203
		14.15	140	16.31	41, 245
11.20-21	234	14.19	176	17.1-9	188
11.20	54	14.21-22	189	17.1	232
11.21	140	14.27	245, 254	17.2-3	118
11.24	59	15	94, 193, 211, 252	17.3	119
11.25-26	189			17.4	15, 239
12.2	183	15.1-3	185	17.5	241
12.4	151	15.1	236	17.10-14	188
13.5	136, 232	15.3	140, 254	17.10	232
13.6-12	185, 220	15.4-29	198	17.13	136
13.14	197	15.5	198, 229, 240	17.17	15
13.15	128, 232			17.18	188
13.16-41	185, 245	15.6-11	185	17.22-31	137, 188
13.16-25	68	15.7	186	17.22-25	153
13.16	15, 165	15.10-11	192, 199	17.24	56, 64
13.17	137	15.10	221	17.29	153

17.30	155	20.3	178	22.17-18	184	
17.31	245	20.4	120	22.19	204	
17.34	188	20.5–21.26	187	22.21-22	178	
18.1-17	188	20.7	202	23.4-5	229	
18.1-11	196	20.11	202	23.6-9	227	
18.3	196	20.16	178, 189	23.6	177, 189,	
18.4	197, 238, 239	20.18-35	191		228, 229, 231, 242	
		20.19	26, 176			
18.5-6	242	20.21	154, 155	23.7-9	228	
18.6	189, 236	20.23	177	23.12-14	178	
18.7	15	20.28-30	108	23.26-30	173	
18.8	232, 242	20.28	202	23.29	177	
18.11	136	20.29-30	191, 250	23.35	177	
18.12-17	204	20.31	176	24.5	126, 168, 240	
18.14	26	21.1-8	189			
18.18	178, 189	21.8	53	24.10-21	66, 189	
18.19-21	243	21.11	26	24.14	168	
18.19	188	21.14	239	24.18	81	
18.23	189	21.17 26	229, 254	24.24	122	
18.24–19.7	203	21.17-24	197	25.3	178	
18.25	152	21.20-29	65	25.8	156	
18.28	120	21.20-26	252	25.16	177	
18.36	17	21.20-24	189	26.2-23	66, 189	
19.1-7	154	21.20	26, 55	26.4-5	242	
19.1-6	151	21.21	26, 196	26.5	177, 228, 231, 240	
19.1	196, 243	21.22-26	192			
19.3-4	152	21.23-36	198	26.6-8	246	
19.4	155	21.25	198	26.6-7	231	
19.5	203	21.28-31	178	26.7	97	
19.8-10	188, 243	21.30-33	106	26.9-11	204	
19.9	224	21.31	178	26.9	126	
19.11-12	185	21.39	26, 242	26.11	175	
19.13	213	21.40	54	26.12-18	185	
19.16	213	22.1	177	26.12	175	
19.17	43	22.2	54	26.13-18	122	
19.22	120	22.3-21	66	26.14	54, 175, 204	
19.23-41	137, 243	22.3-5	189	26.15	127, 175	
19.23	224	22.3	228, 242	26.16	184	
19.24	56	22.4	175	26.17	190	
19.26	239	22.5	177	26.18-20	155	
19.27	56	22.6-21	176	26.18	140, 154, 156, 157	
19.32	204	22.6-10	122			
19.33-41	204	22.6-8	184	26.19	175	
19.34	137	22.6	175	26.20	140, 154, 157	
19.39	204	22.7	175			
19.40	204	22.8	126, 127, 175, 204	26.22	128	
20.2-3	189			26.23	119, 122	
20.2	188	22.14	32, 137, 184	26.29	177	

Index of References

26.31	177	28.23	128, 237, 238	6.20	160
27.1–28.16	187			6.23	160
27.1-3	235	28.24	237-39	7	162
27.4	235	28.26-27	211, 238	7.4	199
27.7	235	28.26	241	7.6	161
27.8	235	28.27	140, 241	7.7	161
27.9	235	28.28	17, 41, 127, 137, 236, 237, 241, 242, 245	7.12	161
27.13-34	235			7.13-20	165
27.16	235			7.17	160
27.17	235			7.22	161
27.19	235	28.30-31	190	8.3-4	164
27.20	41, 237	28.31	188, 241	8.3	161
27.22	237			8.24	164
27.31	41, 237	Romans		9–11	13, 205-10
27.33-36	236	1.3	160	9.1-5	200
27.33	236	1.18-32	161, 204	9.3	207, 208
27.34	40, 41, 235, 236	2.4	158	9.4-5	204
		2.9	208	9.4	207
27.35	202, 236	2.12	160	9.6-7	207
27.36	236	2.13	161	9.6	208
27.38	236	2.25	196	9.23-26	205
27.43	237	2.28-29	206	9.23-25	207
27.44	237	3	13	9.25	205, 211
28	21	3.1-2	196, 204	9.26	205
28.1	237	3.20	161	9.27	207, 209, 211
28.2	177	3.21-22	199		
28.4	237	3.23-25	164	9.30-32	207
28.11	246	3.28	161	9.31–10.5	210
28.14-16	239	3.29	159	9.31-32	162
28.14-15	246	3.30	166	9.33	209
28.15	240	3.31	161	10.4	161, 199, 207
28.17-31	234	4.7-8	159		
28.17	246	4.9-10	195	10.9-10	207
28.19	241	5.12	160	10.14-17	207
28.20	240	5.21	160	10.20	209
28.21	190, 246	6.3-4	164, 203	10.21	205, 209, 211
28.22	168, 240	6.5	203		
28.23-31	237	6.7	165	11.1-2	200
28.23-24	239	6.18	165	11.1	158, 206

INDEX OF AUTHORS

Abrahams, I. 156
Ackroyd, P.R. 73
Alexander, L.C.A. 213, 234
Allison, D.C. 186

Bacon, B.W. 218
Baltzer, K. 56
Barth, M. 200, 204, 205, 208, 210
Baur, F.C. 20, 192
Benoit, P. 29
Betz, H.D. 203, 206
Bornkamm, G. 174, 182, 190, 217
Bowman, J. 73, 100
Brawley, R.L. 11, 20, 64, 66, 116, 117, 133, 189-91, 193, 226, 229, 239, 242
Brown, R.E. 15, 25, 29-32, 36, 38, 46, 127, 219
Brown, S. 213
Bruce, F.F. 166
Bultmann, R. 145, 146, 150, 164, 165, 238
Burchard, C. 142, 190

Cadbury, H.J. 15, 52, 54, 66, 117, 133, 163, 235
Carrol, J.T. 226
Casey, R.P. 153, 155
Charlesworth, J.H. 142
Coggins, R.J. 73, 89, 90
Cohen, S.J.D. 16
Collins, J.J. 203
Conzelmann, H. 11, 17-19, 24-26, 42, 51, 77, 78, 82, 111, 114, 128, 144, 148, 163, 197, 198, 213, 237, 239
Cranfield, C.E.B. 162
Cranford, M. 208

Creed, J.M. 28, 29, 36, 37, 133
Cullmann, O. 19

Dahl, N.A. 60, 153
Danby, H. 143
Danker, F.W. 20, 31, 41, 46, 92, 104, 132, 147, 213
Davies, J.G. 128, 133, 136
Davies, W.D. 143, 205-207, 209, 210, 218-20, 225
Dexinger, F. 74
Dibelius, M. 51, 68, 196, 242
Dodd, C.H. 127, 163
Donaldson, T.L. 62
Drury, J. 45, 80, 113, 215, 219
Dunn, J.D.G. 110, 122, 160-62, 179, 186, 191, 192, 197, 233, 254

Easton, B.S. 198
Ehrman, B.D. 185, 186
Eichrodt, W. 143
Ellis, E.E. 96, 111
Enslin, M.S. 82, 86, 174-77, 179
Esler, P.F. 15, 16, 53-56, 66, 69, 71, 90, 185, 186, 193, 197, 198, 229, 236, 237, 244
Evans, C.A. 129
Evans, C.F. 12, 13, 34, 38, 41, 43, 45, 46, 77, 80, 101, 103, 104, 119, 124, 128, 129, 136, 138, 145, 146, 169, 202, 203, 223, 230

Faierstein, M.M. 132
Farrer, A.M. 215, 219
Farris, S. 29, 35, 38, 39, 41
Fenton, J.C. 81, 146, 212, 221, 223
Fichtner, J. 84

Index of Authors

Filson, F.V. 127, 212, 217, 221
Fitzmyer, J.A. 12, 14, 15, 25, 31, 34, 38, 39, 41, 43, 77, 78, 82, 95, 101, 103, 104, 110, 115, 118, 119, 124, 126, 129, 131, 145, 146, 149, 150, 167, 185, 187, 213, 215, 223, 230, 234
Foakes-Jackson, F.J. 50
France, R.T. 217
Franklin, E. 11, 19, 20, 24, 95, 110, 124, 202, 239, 256

Gager, J.G. 16
Gaster, M. 100
Gaster, T.H. 90
Geden, A.S. 97
Gerhardsson, B. 52
Goodenough, E.R. 174
Goudoever, J. van 102
Goulder, M.D. 73, 80, 151, 213-15, 222
Green, F.W. 217, 218, 221
Green, H.B. 40, 122, 144, 157, 197, 212, 214, 219, 221, 222
Gunkel, H. 35

Haenchen, E. 11, 17, 19, 51, 59, 65, 67, 89, 96, 116, 136, 151-54, 163, 174, 181, 184, 186, 189, 191, 194, 196, 203, 225, 236-38, 240
Hare, D.R.A. 129, 242
Harrington, D.J. 31
Harvey, A.E. 31, 43, 114, 135, 178
Hatch, E. 47
Headlam, A.C. 207
Hengel, M. 54, 55
Hickling, C.J.A. 201
Hiers, R.H. 135
Higgins, A.J.B. 202
Hill, D. 124
Houlden, J.L. 192, 198, 244, 246

Jeremias, J. 47, 75, 102, 121, 147
Jervell, J. 11, 14, 15, 17-19, 25, 72, 83, 85, 93-96, 168, 181, 185, 190, 194, 195, 200, 206, 237-39, 246
Jones, C.P.M. 166
Jones, D.L. 44, 110, 111, 113, 114

Jonge, M. de, 112, 115, 127

Kee, H.C. 189, 223
Kilgallen, J. 52, 67
Kimelman, R. 248, 249
King, N.Q. 101
Kingsbury, J.D. 226, 228
Klein, G. 184
Klijn, A.F.J. 62, 63
Knibb, M.A. 75
Knox, J. 174, 178, 179, 192
Knox, W.L. 28
Kraabel, A.T. 15, 16, 75
Kümmel, W.G. 12, 166, 214, 215

Lake, K. 15, 54, 66, 117, 133, 157, 158, 168, 235
Lampe, G.W.H. 70
Larsson, E. 65
Leany, A.R.C. 110, 114
Lentz, J.C. 180, 244, 246
Lightfoot, R.H. 77, 78, 98, 223
Lindemann, A. 179
Linnemann, E. 102
Lohse, E. 33
Loisy, A. 56, 175
Luz, U. 206

MacDonald, J. 73, 75
Maccoby, H. 143, 149
Maddox, R. 13, 15, 53, 56, 65, 90, 173, 174, 182, 184, 188, 190, 191, 193, 244
Mánek, J. 128
Mann, C.S. 53
Manson, T.W. 132
Mare, W.H. 87
Marsh, J. 98
Marshall, I.H. 31-33, 37, 41, 46, 80, 85, 101, 124, 131, 145, 146, 213, 230
Martin, R.P. 201
Massyngbaerde Ford, J. 92
Mattill, A.J. 181
McCown, C.C. 77
McElleney, N.J. 194
McNeile, A.H. 217
Milligan, G. 12, 71, 189, 213

Minear, P.S. 24
Mitton, C.L. 174
Moessner, D.P. 49, 80, 129
Montefiore, C.G. 71, 168
Montgomery, J.A. 73, 75, 76, 83
Moore, G.F. 15, 141-43, 159
Moule, C.F.D. 54, 110, 111, 120
Moulton, J.H. 12, 71, 189, 213
Moulton, W.F. 97
Mowinkel, S. 118, 136
Mueller, J.R. 142

Neale, D.A. 140, 145, 149, 156, 226
Neyrey, J. 202
Nineham, D.E. 33, 146
Nock, A.D. 13

Oliver, H.H. 24, 41
Oster, R.F. 189

Palmer, D.W. 245, 246
Parkes, J. 181
Petrie, S. 214
Plummer, A. 130
Plumtre, E.H. 87
Potterie, I. de la 117
Pummer, R. 88
Purvis, J.D. 73, 74

Quell, G. 102, 103
Quinn, J.D. 182

Rackham, R.B. 61, 150, 184
Rad, G. von 134, 200
Ravens, D.A.S. 129-31, 133, 134
Redpath, H.A. 47
Reicke, B. 80
Rengstorf, K.H. 97, 245
Reuther, R. 209
Richard, E. 88, 89, 91
Richardson, P. 206, 216, 228, 241
Ringgren, H. 37, 84, 96
Robbins, V.K. 187, 235
Robertson, R.G. 129
Robinson, J.A.T. 41, 98, 99, 120, 131
Robinson, S.E. 142
Robinson, W.C. 78

Sabbe, M. 52, 63
Sahlin, H. 28
Salmon, M. 253
Sanday, W. 207
Sanders, E.P. 58, 71, 83, 95, 139-43,
    146-48, 156, 159-62, 164, 165,
    181, 188, 195, 197, 200, 205,
    206, 210, 211, 214, 226, 252
Sanders, J.N. 205
Sanders, J.T. 11, 15, 19, 49, 67, 68, 82,
    84, 195, 229, 231, 237-39, 243,
    244, 253
Sandmel, S. 143
Sandt, H. van de 168
Scharlemann, M.H. 51, 52, 58, 63, 87
Schenk, W. 174, 175, 179
Schiffman, L.H. 195, 247-49
Schmidt, D. 134
Schneider, G. 41
Schürer, E. 37, 46, 74, 80, 189, 201,
    204, 218, 247, 248
Scobie, C.H.H. 70, 87-89, 91
Selling, G. 84
Siker, J.S. 125
Simon, M. 55, 58, 63, 65
Smith, M. 226, 227, 229
Soards, M.L. 202
Sparkes, H.F.D. 28
Spiro, A. 87, 90
Squires, J.T. 137, 246
Stählin, G. 52
Stendahl, K. 160, 162
Streeter, B.H. 77, 215

Talbert, C.H. 147
Tannehill, R.C. 49, 82, 115, 121, 125,
    241, 242
Taylor, N. 183, 211
Thielman, F. 161
Throckmorton, B.H. 40
Tiede, D. 15, 20, 24, 49, 124, 133, 242
Trebilco, P. 196
Trocmé, E. 51
Tuckett, C.M. 215
Tyson, J.B. 234, 238, 239, 245, 251

Vermes, G. 37, 39, 44, 46, 74, 80, 112, 115, 119, 132, 189, 201, 204, 218, 247, 248
Vielhauer, P. 174, 181, 182, 190, 196

Wainwright, A.W. 94
Walaskay, P.W. 174, 177, 240
Walker, W.O. 174, 193
Wanke, J. 224
Wendt, H.H. 61, 176
Wenham, J.W. 80
Whitely, D.E.H. 160, 161, 164

Wilcox, M. 46, 88
Wilkens, U. 52
Williams, C.S.C. 151
Wilson, S.G. 53, 58, 68, 84, 101, 168, 200
Winter, P. 36, 43
Wintermute, O.S. 75
Winton Thomas, D. 43
Wright, R.P. 44, 112

Zahn, T. 52
Ziesler, J.A. 226, 228

GENERAL THEOLOGICAL SEMINARY
NEW YORK